HTML5 for .NET Developers

HTML5 for .NET Developers

SINGLE PAGE WEB APPS, JAVASCRIPT AND SEMANTIC MARKUP

JIM JACKSON II
IAN GILMAN

MANNING

SHELTER ISLAND

For online information and ordering of this and other Manning books, please visit www.manning.com. The publisher offers discounts on this book when ordered in quantity. For more information, please contact

> Special Sales Department
> Manning Publications Co.
> 20 Baldwin Road
> PO Box 261
> Shelter Island, NY 11964
> Email: orders@manning.com

⊖ Recognizing the importance of preserving what has been written, it is Manning's policy to have the books we publish printed on acid-free paper, and we exert our best efforts to that end. Recognizing also our responsibility to conserve the resources of our planet, Manning books are printed on paper that is at least 15 percent recycled and processed without the use of elemental chlorine.

Manning Publications Co.	Development editor: Renae Gregoire
20 Baldwin Road	Technical proofreader: Roland Civet
PO Box 261	Copyeditor: Andy Carroll
Shelter Island, NY 11964	Proofreader: Melody Dolab
	Typesetter: Dennis Dalinnik
	Illustrator: Gerry Arrington
	Cover designer: Marija Tudor

ISBN: 9781617290435
Printed in the United States of America
1 2 3 4 5 6 7 8 9 10 – MAL – 18 17 16 15 14 13 12

To my lovely bride, Michelle, and my beautiful daughters, Norah and Mary. Thank you for your help, support, patience, and understanding.

—J.J.

To Christina and Caitlyn, my amazing wife-and-daughter team.

—I.G.

brief contents

contents

foreword

HTML5 is taking over the world. Oh no!

.NET is dead! Java is dead!

Everything is dead and HTML5 is the only technology left standing!

Wait, none of the above is true at all. It turns out that HTML5 is a wonderful tool in our toolbox, one that makes our other tools even better. In fact, learning HTML5 is one of the best things a .NET developer can do today. .NET on the server and HTML5 in a new browser on the client are a killer combination.

Jim and Ian have written about HTML5 in a voice that speaks directly to the interests and concerns of the .NET developer. The samples are clear and useful but also coded from the perspective of an ASP.NET programmer who wants to get things done. This is hugely helpful for existing ASP.NET and .NET coders who want to get up to speed on HTML5.

HTML5 is a collection of new tags and bits of markup, but the term "HTML5" is overloaded. It also encapsulates CSS3 and new JavaScript APIs, like GeoLocation and LocalStorage. But HTML5 is more than these new tools—it is more than a specification; it's a new way to think about writing web applications; it's an assumption that your client's browser has capabilities and processing power that we couldn't dream up three years ago.

A few years ago, if you wanted a chart in a browser you'd either use Flash or dynamically generate an image on the server side. Today, you can send the browser all the data a chart needs via JSON and then let the user not only see a chart generated with

HTML5 Canvas, but also interact with or even change the data on the client. A few years ago, your server was the only computer with the wherewithal to sort, query, and manipulate interesting cubes of data. Today, you've got a tiny database and a powerful JIT'ed virtual machine inside your client's web browser.

Fortunately for us all, you can write HTML5 today with ASP.NET; and with the release of ASP.NET 4.5, we see additional support for HTML5. The latest Visual Studio also adds improvements in JavaScript and CSS3 editing. All of HTML5 and its wondrous bits and pieces are ready for you in Web Forms, Web Pages, and MVC. Your ASP.NET applications can generate HTML5 that still works in older browsers thanks to the Modernizr feature detection library. You can use HTML5 and JavaScript on the client to call ASP.NET Web APIs on the server. HTML5 is a technology that makes the .NET developer's life more interesting!

There are many books that talk about HTML5 as if it were an island, disconnected from any server technology. This is not the case with *HTML5 for .NET Developers* by Jim and Ian. If you're a longtime ASP.NET developer looking to bone up on new techniques in web development, or if you're just getting started with ASP.NET and you want to make sure you're attacking new problems in the most modern and progressive way, this is the book for you.

SCOTT HANSELMAN
WEB COMMUNITY ARCHITECT
MICROSOFT

preface

In early 2010, I had just finished up a workflow proof-of-concept project and was poking around other projects at Applied Information Sciences, looking for what was next in my software career. Since I had some Silverlight experience and wanted to expand it further, I requested a role on a project to enhance a magazine viewer originally produced by Vertigo (vertigo.com) for Bondi Digital (BondiDigital.com). I ended up rebuilding the processing software that imported the source images and data into the viewer format. This was fortuitous because it was a project role that would continue while many others rotated in and out over the next two years.

When the processing solution was complete, I got involved in the Silverlight area of the application, and it was about this time that Apple's new toy, the iPad, took off. It seemed to the project stakeholders that an HTML-only version of our viewer would be appropriate, so we got to work. For a traditional ASP.NET and Silverlight developer like me, this was new ground, and it took a number of months and hundreds of dollars in books for me to get my footing with JavaScript and to unlearn all the bits and pieces of ASP.NET that hide the true nature of HTML, CSS, and JavaScript.

With a little knowledge and the help of other AIS employees who were working with Manning Publications on various book ideas, I got Mike Stephens' name and called over to discuss a book proposal on Silverlight and GIS, my hobby and one of my technology passions. We were pretty close to writing up a book contract when a Microsoft employee happened to mention in an interview that they (MS) were "refocusing" Silverlight. This came as a shock to all of the Silverlight developers and client companies who had been investing heavily in the technology for rich client-side web solutions.

Despite some backtracking and spinning the news, this appears to have been a correct move on Microsoft's part. While Silverlight is certainly not dead, it has been eclipsed by HTML5 in terms of industry hype and project work moving forward. For web consultancies, this is not such a huge problem, because ASP.NET MVC is a top-tier platform on which to build rich client-side HTML applications. Windows 8 allows HTML/CSS and JavaScript as first-class development languages for native software! It's not a panacea, but it is a great tool to have in the belt.

While all of this was happening in the industry, I became more involved in the new HTML version of the magazine viewer application. And because the Silverlight/GIS book was clearly not going to fly in the marketplace, Mike at Manning asked what other applications I was working on. I responded that we were building a rich HTML5 client, integrating ASP.NET MVC and deploying it to SQL Azure and Azure Web Roles. "We could do a book about any of those things!" was Mike's response. Of course, I didn't think I was nearly qualified enough to write such an authoritative tome, but Mike convinced me that I was, in fact, in the perfect position to do so. As a seasoned developer who had moved from strict ASP.NET and rich-client C# applications into JavaScript and HTML, I was in a good position to describe the technologies from a common perspective.

During the writing of this book we took a few detours to come to the current format. The initial idea, when I was the sole author, was to build a single application that integrated HTML5 APIs into a reference framework. This turned out to be a dead end. The Microsoft Silk project was working on the same thing, only they had actual members of the jQuery team looking over their shoulders and helping them out. This was not a competitive position for our book, and Manning was not excited about the idea of a single-project book; such books can lead to content that is more focused on the project than on learning the technology. The next iteration led to the current focus of one project per chapter and also to the realization that I was not experienced enough to write what could be termed "reference-level" JavaScript code. The manager on the magazine viewer project was lucky enough to find and contract with Ian Gilman, and his expertise provided immediate improvements to that platform and to our collective expertise in JavaScript. Ian is an expert technician and an excellent communicator, so he was a natural choice for the project and for this book. He also brought in the Git source control expertise. You can see our source repository at www.github.com/axshon/HTML-5-Ellipse-Tours, where Ellipse Tours is the original name of the single project.

The next version of the book was nearly complete in early 2012 when Manning decided that a new development editor would be added to the project. With the help of Renae Gregiore, Ian and I reworked the book to focus more on the use of each HTML5 API, rather than providing deep reference material and then trying to spend the last few pages of each chapter building a project with it. This final format reduced the size of the book by moving the MVC-focused chapter and the JavaScript chapter into appendices.

The format you find within these pages is our collective attempt to find the friendliest, fastest route from .NET developer to HTML5/JavaScript expert. Most of the text, server-side code, and JavaScript code comments you will find here are my words, and most of the JavaScript, HTML, and CSS is Ian's work.

We hope that you find the contents informative and interesting. More importantly, we hope that our book gives you great ideas for fantastic and fun new software products. If you have an interesting project that you'd like to make some noise about, feel free to contact me at jim@axshon.net.

JIM JACKSON

acknowledgments

We would like to thank the many people who helped make our book possible, starting with everyone at Manning, from associate publisher Mike Stephens and our development editor Renae Gregoire, to the production team of Mary Piergies, Troy Mott, Andy Carroll, Melody Dolab, Janet Vail, and Dennis Dalinnik.

Special thanks to Scott Hansleman for happily volunteering to write the foreword. We are deeply grateful for his endorsement of our work. We also acknowledge Roland Civet, our technical proofreader, who reviewed the text and tested the code during development and again shortly before the book went to press.

The following reviewers read our manuscript at various stages of its development and we thank them for their feedback and insights: Adam London, Arsalan Ahmed, Arun Noronha, Asif Jan, Francis Setash, Ian Stirk, Jeffrey Jenkins, Joseph M. Morgan, Leo Waisblatt, Mark Nischalke, Osama Morad, PhD, Paul Stack, Peter O'Hanlon, Philippe Vialatte, Rohit Asthana, Stan Bice, and Wyatt Barnett.

Thanks also to Mark LaPointe, John Blumenauer, Glenn Block, Julie Lerman, Tad VanFleet, Steve Michelotti, Oskar Austegard, Ernesto Delgado, and Pete Brown. Thanks for the pointers, direction, and help from the following Microsoft teams: Web APIs, Project Silk, Internet Explorer, and Interoperability Bridges.

Jim Jackson

Many thanks to Ian Gilman who helped to make this book what it is. His knowledge, work, and tireless attention to detail have resulted in a book that I believe will be truly helpful in bringing more and more .NET developers into the age of HTML5.

Heartfelt thanks to my wife for being so patient, supportive, and encouraging during all the late nights, early mornings, and times when it would have been easier for me to stop than continue. The fact that we got through it together is a testament to your faith in me. You are truly appreciated.

Ian Gilman

For their insights and support, thank you to Kevin Hanes, Ben Vanik, Daniel Gasienica, Aseem Kishore, Oskar Austegard, Gennaro Cannelora, and of course Christina Gilman. Thank you most of all to Jim, for bringing me into this endeavor with his great passion for knowledge; it's been a wild ride!

about this book

This book was written for professional .NET developers primarily focused on C# and ASP.NET. While it's useful for other professionals, the focus has been on developing server-side code in C# and ASP.NET MVC, with as little overhead as possible.

Our target reader is a professional who has been placed in the role of developer on a project that is already on an HTML5 and ASP.NET MVC platform or is being transitioned to this platform. Emphasis is placed on as many stable parts of the HTML5 specification as possible, so that while the developer learns effective use of JavaScript, he or she is also able to learn to use these very powerful APIs.

Please note that while the JavaScript and HTML5 techniques you learn in these pages are useful for Windows 8 development, this book does not claim to be a Windows 8 development reference.

How the book is organized

This book is divided into two parts. The first part, consisting of chapters 1 and 2, will give you a general understanding of what HTML5 is and how it can interact with server components using JavaScript and ASP.NET MVC. Chapter 2 focuses on markup and how semantics play a role in HTML5 web application development.

The second part of the book (chapters 3 to 10) covers the various HTML5 JavaScript APIs that are stable and generally supported across browser platforms. Each implementation is tested against browser versions that were available at the time of writing and against previous versions as much as possible. The APIs covered in each chapter are as follows:

- Chapter 3   Audio and video controls
- Chapter 4   Canvas
- Chapter 5   The History API: Changing the game for MVC sites
- Chapter 6   Geolocation and web mapping
- Chapter 7   Web workers and drag and drop
- Chapter 8   Websockets
- Chapter 9   Local storage and state management
- Chapter 10   Offline web applications

There are three appendixes; they give an overview of JavaScript, explain how to use ASP.NET MVC, and guide you on how to install IIS Express.

How to use this book

Each chapter in the second part of the book (chapters 3 to 10) is organized into three parts. The first is a brief introduction, designed to get you thinking about real-world applications for that chapter's focus. This part may also include background information to help you understand the topic more clearly, as is the case with geolocation. The introduction also includes a browser support table that shows which browser versions are compatible with each HTML5 API.

The second part of the chapter is the actual build. As we build the project, we'll show the code and describe where it should be placed in the application source. As each part of an API is used, it's introduced and defined. A Core API icon placed in the margin shows the section where each API is discussed.

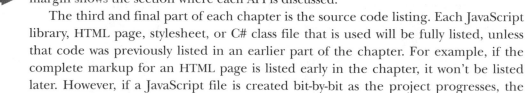

The third and final part of each chapter is the source code listing. Each JavaScript library, HTML page, stylesheet, or C# class file that is used will be fully listed, unless that code was previously listed in an earlier part of the chapter. For example, if the complete markup for an HTML page is listed early in the chapter, it won't be listed later. However, if a JavaScript file is created bit-by-bit as the project progresses, the entire listing will be included in this section.

Working versions of each sample application can be found at www.ellipsetours.com/demos/index.html. The code can also be downloaded from the publisher's website at www.manning.com/HTML5for.NETDevelopers.

Software requirements

The JavaScript portions of this book are completely compatible with any modern desktop or mobile browser. The builds for each chapter require Visual Studio 2010 Service Pack 1 or later. All applications have been tested using Visual Studio 2012 Release Candidate.

Local administrator privileges are required to install Git Bash and node.js, as well as to run these applications.

Each chapter starts off with a browser support table that shows which browser versions are compatible with each HTML5 API.

Code conventions and downloads

All source code in listings or in text is in a fixed-width font like this to separate it from ordinary text. Code annotations accompany many of the listings, highlighting important concepts.

Source code for all working examples in this book is available for download at the publisher's website at www.manning.com/HTML5for.NETDevelopers. Working versions of each sample application can be found at www.ellipsetours.com/demos/index.html.

Author Online

The purchase of *HTML5 for .NET Developers* includes free access to a private web forum run by Manning Publications, where you can make comments about the book, ask technical questions, and receive help from the author and from other users. To access the forum and subscribe to it, point your web browser to www.manning.com/HTML5for.NETDevelopers. This page provides information about how to get on the forum once you're registered, what kind of help is available, and the rules of conduct on the forum.

Manning's commitment to our readers is to provide a venue where a meaningful dialogue between individual readers and between readers and the authors can take place. It's not a commitment to any specific amount of participation on the part of the authors whose contribution to the book's forum remains voluntary (and unpaid). We suggest you try asking the authors some challenging questions, lest their interest stray!

The Author Online forum and the archives of previous discussions will be accessible from the publisher's website as long as the book is in print.

about the cover illustration

The figure on the cover of *HTML5 for .NET Developers* is captioned "An Infantry Offi-cer." The illustration is taken from a 19th-century edition of Sylvain Maréchal's four-volume compendium of regional dress customs and military uniforms published in France. Each illustration is finely drawn and colored by hand. The rich variety of Maréchal's collection reminds us vividly of how culturally apart the world's towns and regions were just 200 years ago. Isolated from each other, people spoke different dia-lects and languages. In the streets or in the countryside, it was easy to identify where they lived and what their trade, profession, military rank, or station in life was just by their dress.

Dress codes have changed since then and the diversity by region, so rich at the time, has faded away. It is now hard to tell apart the inhabitants of different conti-nents, let alone different towns or regions. Perhaps we have traded cultural diversity for a more varied personal life—certainly for a more varied and fast-paced technolog-ical life.

At a time when it is hard to tell one computer book from another, Manning cele-brates the inventiveness and initiative of the computer business with book covers based on the rich diversity of regional life of two centuries ago, brought back to life by Maréchal's pictures.

HTML5 and .NET

This chapter covers

- Understanding the scope of HTML5
- Touring the new features in HTML5
- Assessing where HTML5 fits in software projects
- Learning what an HTML application is
- Getting started with HTML applications in Visual Studio

You're really going to love HTML5. It's like having a box of brand new toys in front of you when you have nothing else to do but play. Forget pushing the envelope; using HTML5 on the client and .NET on the server gives you the ability to create entirely new envelopes for executing applications inside browsers that just a few years ago would have been difficult to build even as desktop applications. The ability to use the skills you already have to build robust and fault-tolerant .NET solutions for any browser anywhere gives you an advantage in the market that we hope to prove throughout this book.

For instance, with HTML5, you can

- Tap the new Geolocation API to locate your users anywhere on the planet

- Build photo editing or animation products with the Canvas API
- Build high-performance user interfaces for using the History and Drag-and-Drop APIs
- Accomplish a tremendous amount of work with just a few lines of JavaScript

What, exactly, is HTML5? In a nutshell, it's one part semantic organization that can add additional meaning to content on the web and one part JavaScript programming interfaces that allow you to do things in a simple web page that weren't possible just a short time ago. The opportunities are limited only by your imagination, and the tools and environments you're currently using to develop software will probably be the same ones that help you build this new class of application. You can see some examples in figure 1.1.

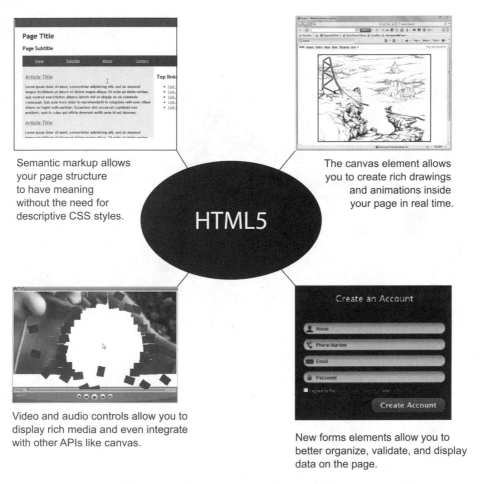

Semantic markup allows your page structure to have meaning without the need for descriptive CSS styles.

The canvas element allows you to create rich drawings and animations inside your page in real time.

Video and audio controls allow you to display rich media and even integrate with other APIs like canvas.

New forms elements allow you to better organize, validate, and display data on the page.

Figure 1.1   From games like Canvas Rider to semantic page layout to audio/video to form presentation, HTML5 has something for everyone in the web design and application space. Rich HTML applications are the new normal for web development.

Fellow developers, now is the time to sit up and take note. The semantic web, which HTML5 taps and which we'll talk more about in the next chapter, is here. Even better, you already have many of the skills you need to build robust applications for this market. The same tools and technologies you use now, like Visual Studio, ASP.NET, and web services, can be effectively integrated into HTML5 applications. You'll need to build on your existing knowledge and expand it into some new areas, but the rewards—such as seamless integration with tablets and phones, ease of deployments and upgrades, and rich client feature sets—are worthwhile.

In this chapter, we'll look at the new toys that HTML5 brings to .NET developers, such as the following:

- New HTML5 elements and microdata, which bring meaning to the markup beyond just the contents of the tags on the page
- New web app form factors that let you add features to your page with little or no additional code
- New JavaScript APIs that not only lead to better performance but also give you the ability to build rich interactive graphics and speed performance in your web apps

We'll also look at JavaScript and why it needs to be a first-class language in your skill set if you intend to take advantage of HTML5, and we'll look at the server-side processes and options for HTML5 available from the .NET framework.

Finally, we'll look at HTML5 applications from end to end, and we'll implement a Hello World example that will give you the minimum JavaScript you need to work through the example applications in this book and will give you a taste of the HTML5 smorgasbord to come.

Without further ado, let's begin with a tour of the new toys that HTML5 adds to your toy box.

1.1 New toys for developers thanks to HTML5

HTML5 is a big topic, and figure 1.2 should give you a better understanding of the various moving parts in a web application that uses HTML5. If it feels like you're looking at the underside of a race car with only a vague idea of how things work, don't worry. We'll provide all the details as we progress through the book. What's important here is the big picture and the basic interactions among the parts.

In this section, we'll give you a high-level but grounded tour of some of the most exciting new features of HTML5, many of which you'll learn how to use in this book. If we won't be covering a particular feature in this book, we'll point you to other good resources on the topic so you can take side trips whenever you need or like. Specifically, we're going to cover the following topics in this section:

- New HTML5 tags and microdata, which help you build search-optimized, semantic pages
- How HTML5 lets you develop across devices and browsers, without having to write multiple programs

- Improvements to JavaScript and the plethora of libraries, extensions, and frameworks that make your development work so much faster and easier
- Identifying and implementing the HTML5 APIs that everyone is talking about by creating user-friendly, graphics-rich, interactive web applications
- Reviewing where Cascading Style Sheets 3 (CSS3) and ASP.NET MVC fit into the picture

For our first stop, we'll turn to HTML5 tags and microdata.

1.1.1 New HTML5 tags and microdata

Imagine that you're a member of a band called Four Parts Water. You're creating a very basic web page just to test out your newly acquired HTML5 knowledge.

You know about HTML tags, which are the little pieces of text inside brackets that you write to render elements on a web page. Each tag starts with an opening < symbol and ends with a closing > symbol. Content is placed next, and then the tag is closed with the </tag> marker. Opening tags may also include attributes to give them further meaning:

```
<div>
    <p>My name is Neil.</p>
    <p>My band is called Four Parts Water.</p>
    <p>I am British.</p>
</div>
```

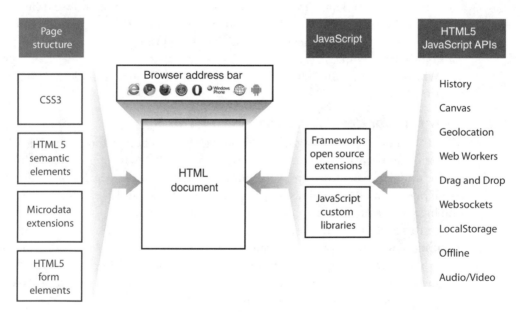

Figure 1.2   The basic organization of a web application built using HTML5. The application is consumed by a web browser that reads an HTML text file and interprets the content, loading other resources like JavaScript files, images, or stylesheets as necessary. The markup is rendered on the page using stylesheets that are linked or placed directly into the markup, and JavaScript code executes at the proper time to change the interface, communicate with the server, or interact with the HTML5 APIs available from the current browser. These APIs can interact directly with the client system, but JavaScript, as a rule, can't.

That's good, but now you want to try adding some microdata. *Microdata* is additional information you can add to your page using special attribute keywords. It can be set, read, and changed via JavaScript, and the values your microdata contains can be nearly anything you like. You can extend tags using microdata to add semantic or other meaningful information that search engines and JavaScript libraries can use to make even more sense of the data on the page. A holistic interpretation of your page data and content will help optimize it for search as well as for accessibility applications like page readers. Microdata extensions can also reduce the amount of code and increase the expressiveness of the markup in nearly any page.

Armed with this knowledge, you write up the code in the following listing (from html5rocks.com), which displays the same basic page with your name and the name of your band, but with extra information meant for web crawlers and search engines.

Listing 1.1 Microdata tags describing content

Itemscope declaration defines boundaries of itemprops for object.

```
<div itemscope>
    <p>My name is <span itemprop='name'>
    Neil</span>.</p>
    <p>My band is called <span itemprop='band'>
    Four Parts Water</span>.</p>
    <p>I am <span itemprop='nationality'>
    British</span>.</p>
</div>
```

Itemprop here is name, standard microdata vocabulary term that's useful for search engines.

Closing tag for element declared with itemscope closes object referenced by microdata.

Band itemprop isn't in standard vocabulary but is allowed nonetheless.

As you can see, the various microdata tags help the engines and crawlers to interpret which pieces of the text are important and what each one means.

1.1.2 HTML5 applications for devices

HTML5 has not only given us .NET developers new ways to make our code make sense on the web; it has also brought us the ability to develop for exciting new devices that used to exist only in the imaginations of sci-fi writers: think iPad, Kindle, and smart phones. Mobile phones have fully featured browsers with display technologies better than most computers available five years ago, and even laptops now have powerful graphics processors. Gaming PCs have graphics support that allows them to seamlessly render complex 3D graphics and animations. HTML5 lets .NET developers enter this new world, where the challenge is to take advantage of the diversity of browser platforms while maintaining functional continuity.

> **NOTE** Currently the web community uses the terms *HTML application* and *HTML5 application* interchangeably. This is because the new functionality that's available as the HTML5 specification comes to market is what is stimulating the new ideas and methods of developing rich internet applications. Here, we'll refer only to "HTML applications," but our examples will be

focused on the parts of HTML5 and JavaScript that make the applications deeper and more useful to users.

How do you develop a single application to work across all the screens listed in figure 1.3? It's certainly possible, but it takes a good understanding of the compromises and features available across the entire range of target browsers. We'll provide you with that knowledge in chapters to come as we teach you how to use HTML5's features in multiple browsers.

1.1.3   Better, faster JavaScript

Another feature that makes HTML applications compelling is the incredible improvement in JavaScript engine performance over the last few years, across all browsers. Gone are the days when JavaScript was only suitable for handling click events or posting forms. Just take a look at figure 1.4 to see how dramatically execution time has improved through various versions.

Add HTML5's native support for JSON data transmission and the array of performance-enhancing coding techniques available, and it gets difficult to say that compiled binary libraries are always faster. While perhaps this is true in many instances, there are plenty of normal operating situations where a JavaScript routine can be just as fast as the same routine compiled in the .NET runtime. This means that plugins like Silverlight and Flash have much less of an advantage in the application market. In some instances, they have no advantage at all.

1.1.4   Libraries, extensions, and frameworks

JavaScript development also benefits from a wide range of open source projects and free tools. While not new toys themselves, these pieces of the application puzzle allow you as the developer to make better, more efficient use of the HTML5-specific toys.

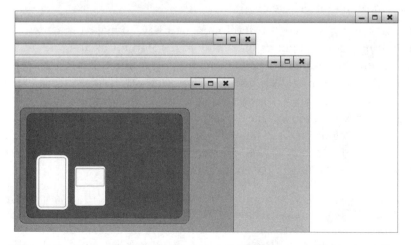

Figure 1.3   The form factor, size, and resolution of browsers available to you is growing all the time.

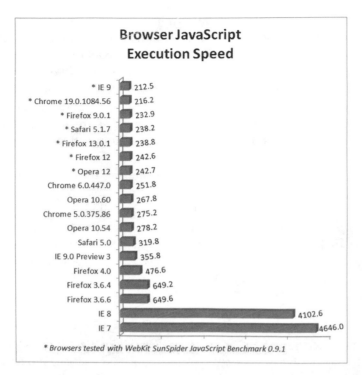

Figure 1.4 **JavaScript engine performance improvements in the past few years (courtesy of webkit.org) have led to impressive speeds all around. In this graph, the time required in milliseconds to perform a large number of very specific JavaScript benchmark tasks is measured.**

Windows 8

The Windows 8 announcement and subsequent release is big news to all .NET developers. It brings a new set of features, better security, and an app store, and it takes the beautiful Windows Store[1] styling from Windows Phone. While this book isn't specifically about building native Windows 8 applications with HTML5, CSS, and JavaScript, the good news is that what you learn here *will* be applicable on this new platform.

The Windows-specific version of JavaScript is called WinJS, and it's JavaScript at heart with the added ability to call native functions and libraries on the host system. The markup and styling from your HTML5 applications should be relatively easy to port into the new Windows 8 environment, making your skills all the more valuable.

In addition, Internet Explorer 10, shipped with Windows 8, is the most compliant, compatible browser ever from Microsoft, and it's incredibly fast. This gives you the option of building your application as an HTML5 web app to use on multiple devices and browsers or as a native Windows 8 application, suitable for deployment to the app store.

In short, this book, while not targeted toward any specific platform, will allow you to use everything you learn to get a major head start on native and browser-based Windows 8 development.

---

[1] See the "Roadmap for Windows Store apps using JavaScript" page in the Windows Dev Center at http://msdn .microsoft.com/en-us/library/windows/apps/hh465037.aspx.

For instance, there are dozens of unit-testing frameworks for JavaScript including QUnit, a free framework for JavaScript and jQuery (github.com/jquery/qunit). You can build complete applications using pattern-based approaches with libraries like Backbone.js (documentcloud.github.com/backbone) or Knockout.js (knockoutjs.com). These frameworks give you a client-side MVC (Model-View-Controller) or MVVM (Model-View-ViewModel) paradigm to build large HTML applications while keeping them maintainable. There are thousands more; just think of any feature you might want for a rich website and search for it. You're almost guaranteed to find something to get you started.

It's hard to say exactly where to start when considering third-party commercial and open source JavaScript libraries. There are components for performing specific tasks, libraries that act as development frameworks, libraries for unit testing, graphics helpers, communications tools, documentation enhancers, and plenty of others. Just take a look at GitHub (http://www.github.com/) and see for yourself. A search for "JavaScript" turns up over 9,000 projects. Now jump over to the jQuery site (www.jquery.com) and take a look at the plugins page. There are almost 500 pages of plugin projects.

Wondering where to start when it comes to libraries? Consider jQuery.

jQuery is the obvious place to start when looking at JavaScript libraries to improve the quality of your applications and speed of your development. It's one of the most popular frameworks for developing HTML applications, used in nearly half of all active websites today.[2] The library, a creation of John Resig, is under constant development and is both fast and easy to use. It also sports a plugin model that allows others to add new features to it.

Microsoft clearly understands that jQuery is an ideal tool for building the next wave of applications, and it has invested a lot of energy into data binding, templating plugins, and pattern-based frameworks like Knockout.js. Using HTML5, a Microsoft developer can now build once and deploy practically anywhere. (Where have we heard that before?) But more important than Microsoft's contribution is the fact that it's an equal partner in the jQuery ecosystem.

Nearly every JavaScript library available today is open for your review and for subsequent inclusion in your website based on the license that accompanies it. In addition to using these libraries outright, you can use them to learn how to do specific tasks or for architectural guidance.

As you work through the examples in this book and become more versed in the JavaScript language, you'll learn to look at these libraries with a critical eye toward

---

[2] See W3Techs "Usage statistics and market share of JQuery for websites" article at http://w3techs.com/technologies/details/js-jquery/all/all.

instancing models, resource allocation, binding to existing elements, and how each library can fit into the overall goals of your application.

1.1.5 New HTML5 JavaScript APIs

There are also various JavaScript objects and APIs that can help your pages interact with the outside world and with the rest of the browser's operating system. There are quite a few such features, but we'll focus our discussion on some of the most stable and useful for building rich web applications.

CANVAS

Canvas is a raster-based drawing mechanism in HTML5. The Canvas JavaScript API has a lot of functionality, and we'll cover it in detail in chapter 4. If you want an early peek though, try using the following code to draw a simple rectangle on a canvas element:

```
var myCanvas = document.getElementById("rectCanvas");
var canvContext = myCanvas.getContext("2d");
canvContext.fillRect(50, 25, 150, 100);
```

The key is to get a reference to the canvas and then grab its context object. The context object is what you use to do all work inside the rendered element.

How can you use it? As a drawing surface, for graphs and charts and for animations ranging from very simple to extremely complex.

HISTORY

The History API in HTML5 is used to add or replace data in the current browser's session history. You can use it to overwrite the current page with something more generic or with a more helpful landing page. You can also use it to add a new item to session history so that on-page navigation events can be accessed using the browser's forward and backward buttons:

```
history.pushState();
history.replaceState();
```

We'll discuss the History API in chapter 5.

How can you use it? To enhance application navigation between views or pages and to remove unwanted steps from the browser history for the current site.

GEOLOCATION

Our favorite API is Geolocation. Using the `geolocation.getCurrentPosition()` function, you can return a latitude and longitude from a device's onboard GPS device. Note that the `geolocation` object is only available to the `navigator` object in JavaScript. `Navigator` isn't, as you might expect, a wrapper just for `geolocation`. It's a global object that contains a number of functional pieces. Check out chapter 6 on geolocation for more on this.

How can you use it? As a tool to let users locate themselves in the world and as the basis for providing meaningful data about points of interest around a user.

WEB WORKERS

A web worker allows your HTML application to use multiple threads. For heavy processing applications or long-running JavaScript tasks, the web worker object can be invaluable. The web worker is declared as a `Worker` object and is passed a JavaScript file:

```
var wrk = new Worker("BackgroundProcess.js");
```

Once instantiated, the background process script and the hosting worker object can listen for messages sent back and forth. The worker object could do this:

```
wrk.postMessage("Hello to the web worker");
```

And inside BackgroundProcess.js, you could do this to send a message back to the host:

```
self.postMessage("Hi from the background process");
```

This is a minimal example without any of the required plumbing code. What's important here is that the values passed back and forth are strings. This leaves open the possibility of sending JSON data objects as well as other more complex arrays of values. We'll cover Web Workers in chapter 7.

How can you use it? To speed application performance by performing processor-intensive calculations in the background, freeing up cycles for graphics rendering and user interaction.

DRAG AND DROP

Drag and drop is a new feature in HTML5 that allows you to programmatically pick up and drop elements on your page relative to the page, to each other, or to the user's desktop. This is done by wiring up events on elements for `drag`, `drop`, `dragover`, and `dragenter`. While a drag operation is occurring, other features of the API can be activated to provide feedback to the user about what is happening. We'll look at drag and drop in chapter 7.

How can you use it? As a means of bringing natural user interactions to web applications reliably and quickly.

WEBSOCKETS

Websockets are a means of breaking away from the request/response paradigm of web page interaction to a bi-directional communication channel. This means that communications can be happening in both directions simultaneously during a session. This is best described with examples, but we need to cover more JavaScript basics first. Look for coverage of Websockets in chapter 8.

How can you use it? For building real-time communication web applications like chat, white boards, or collaborative drawing.

LOCAL STORAGE

The Local Storage HTML5 API provides a solution for storing local data through the use of a key/value style storage specification that's available for reading and writing within a single domain. You can read, insert, update, and delete data very easily and store much more information than would normally be possible in a web application. We'll cover this API in chapter 9.

How can you use it? As the basis for building applications that store user data locally while sending only the data necessary for server functions.

Local Storage doesn't provide any specification for synchronizing with a server database, nor does it provide transactional support. If you need transactional support, you would be better off looking to the IndexedDB HTML5 specification. This API uses a document-database (or NoSQL) style approach, but the specification is incomplete and unstable at this time, so we won't cover it in this book.

OFFLINE ACCESS

The ability of a site to remain available offline is new in HTML5. It's done by specifying a manifest file that describes which files must be downloaded for use offline, which files should only be accessed while online, and which files, when requested, should get a substitute file instead. The manifest file is specified in the top-level <html> element on a page:

```
<html manifest="/cache.manifest">
```

How can you use it? As a means of creating rich games or business applications that function even when an internet connection isn't available.

AUDIO/VIDEO

The Audio and Video tags allow you to play music and video without Flash or Silverlight plugins. Browser vendors have built in their own default players, but you can easily extend or replace them as we'll show in chapter 3. Because support formats vary between browsers, you can create your content in multiple formats and allow the browsers to automatically choose which version to use. This allows for forward and backward compatibility, keeping you current with the ever-changing multimedia format landscape.

A simple audio tag might look something like this:

```
<audio src="/content/music.mp3"></audio>
```

1.1.6 Cascading Style Sheets 3

Cascading Style Sheets (CSS) version 3 technically isn't a part of the HTML5 specification, but the graphics capabilities of media queries and transformations make it a crucial part of any browser-based rich application. Putting your presentation rules into styles allows you to build more manageable and pluggable user interfaces for your clients. Well-engineered cascading styles can also significantly reduce your development time.

We'll cover the core CSS3 concepts necessary for implementing HTML5 applications and understand where CSS3 fits into application design in chapter 2. We'll touch on it again throughout the rest of the book as a means of adding smooth animations and rich styling. While we aren't providing a definitive CSS3 reference in this book, you'll certainly come to realize the benefits of learning CSS more deeply.

The book *Smashing CSS: Professional Techniques for Modern Layout* by Eric Meyer (Smashing Magazine, 2010) is a great addition to any technical library.

1.1.7   *MVC and Razor*

While not directly part of HTML5, MVC (Model-View-Controller) is a software development pattern that allows for the clear separation of concerns between business logic components and user interface display. The Visual Studio templates for Microsoft's latest version of ASP.NET MVC are being constantly updated as free, out-of-band releases directly to the development community. ASP.NET MVC presents a couple of ways to operate in the context of an HTML application.

The first and easiest way is to ensure that all your views are HTML5 compliant. This can be done online at sites like validator.w3.org that allow you to enter a URL and return a listing of valid and invalid markup. This includes the semantic organization of your markup and the use of unobtrusive JavaScript (discussed shortly). You can also build a single HTML page to contain an entire piece of your application and include it in your MVC site. We'll do this in chapter 4, when we cover HTML5 Canvas.

The next method is to use Razor, the view-processing engine that was introduced as part of ASP.NET MVC. Razor facilitates readable inline code within your views, allowing you to write properly formatted HTML with bits of server code interspersed to perform work based on data models that you can build. Using Razor, your markup becomes more terse, easier to read, and faster to code. Using Razor and ASP.NET MVC, you can incorporate all the features of .NET development that you're accustomed to and transition seamlessly into the world of HTML5 application development. Razor is used in our MVC views throughout this book and it's covered in more detail in appendix B on ASP.NET MVC.

1.2   *HTML5 applications end-to-end*

Now that you have a basic understanding of the toys you'll get to learn about and play with in this book, the next thing you need to know is how each piece interacts with the next and where they touch each other in a normal system.

> **NOTE**   At the beginning of each chapter, we'll clearly define which browsers and versions are supported. You should be able to download, install, and test with Google Chrome, Internet Explorer, Firefox, Opera, and Apple Safari. In addition, you can use any mobile browser at your disposal to test site rendering and function.

Figure 1.5 shows a very simplified view of where each part can fit into the overall scheme of an HTML5 application. This is the same diagram you saw in figure 1.2 but with the addition of Microsoft's server-side components. This is by no means the only way these parts can fit together, but it will get you started.

On the server side of an HTML application, MVC controllers will present a view (HTML text sent to the browser), take data from a form POST operation, or send or receive data using Ajax calls. In later chapters, we'll cover all of these communications and how to integrate them in an HTML application.

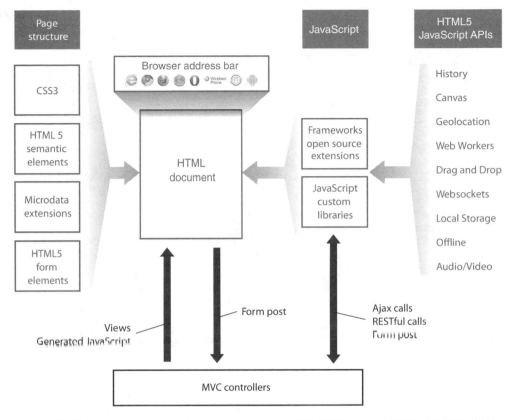

Figure 1.5   Basic client and server interactions between HTML5 features and JavaScript APIs within an application

You might find all these pieces a little overwhelming, so we'll dig a little deeper into each area to help firm up your understanding. We'll start with the page structure.

1.2.1 Page structure and page presentation

Figure 1.6 identifies the *page structure* and where it fits into the scheme of an HTML application.

The structure of a single application page consists of the semantic elements, such as <header>, <footer>, <nav>, <article>, and <section>, as well as any traditional HTML tags, like <div>, <span>, and <a>. Semantic tags, which will be covered in more detail in the next chapter, provide organizational cues and a means of denoting where various parts of the content will exist. Structural elements receive styling using CSS and can have JavaScript behaviors attached at runtime. Elements in the page structure can be delivered from the server at runtime, built from templates on the client, or downloaded on demand.

Note that the styles that a page uses can also determine its structure. A common instance of this is when an element is *floated*. Floated elements (denoted by the CSS

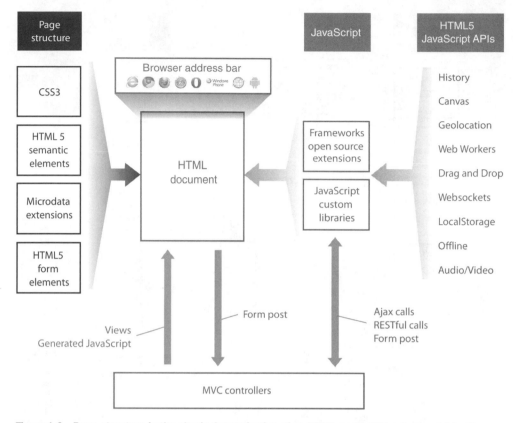

Figure 1.6   Page structure is the physical organization of an HTML page. Which tags exist inside other tags can determine how elements can be moved or accessed using JavaScript.

style `float:left` or `float:right`) don't participate in page flow but will dock themselves to the appropriate side of the window. We'll discuss positioning elements on the page when we look at the Canvas API in chapter 4 and the Geolocation API in chapter 6.

Page presentation is the visual styling that a page structure receives, based on the location of elements in the structure and the stylesheets included on the page. Styles in a stylesheet are the starting point for operations that can occur at runtime. While the page is displayed, changes to the browser layout can trigger media query changes, and interactions by the user can trigger JavaScript functions. We'll cover what media queries are and how they work in chapter 2. For now, the important concept is that by using CSS and JavaScript, you can dramatically change the presentation of the page based on changing conditions in the browser.

1.2.2   Page content

The content of your application can be anything from a map to an editable grid. It can be data from a content management system, pictures uploaded by a user, or news articles. Whatever the content, it's the most important part of your application, and it should be

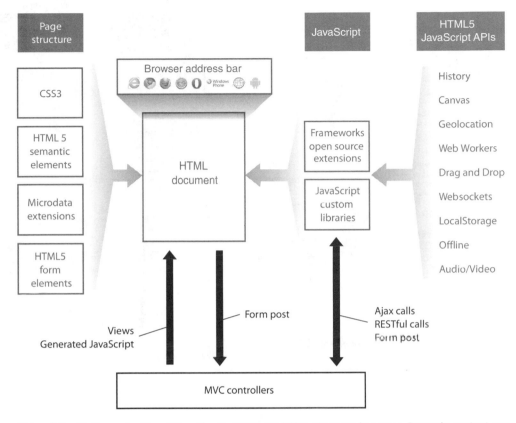

Figure 1.7 Static content is written directly inside the HTML elements in a page. Dynamic content can be delivered to the browser in an MVC application by means of views or via JavaScript and Ajax.

placed in the structure in a way that makes it very obvious what it is and why it's important. Figure 1.7 shows the role that content plays in the HTML application scheme.

Page content can be static, dynamic, or a mix of both depending upon the needs of the application. It can be added by the user while the application executes or be pulled on demand when the application detects updates from some other process.

1.2.3 Application navigation

In HTML5 applications, there are two parts related to navigation: manipulation of the browser URL and posting of values to a server to move to another page. Figure 1.8 highlights the POST operations at the bottom of the diagram and the use of the new HTML5 History API to manage the URL.

Navigation can occur when a user clicks a link to another page or submits a form, or it can be initiated via JavaScript by some other event. In traditional web pages, these operations were abrupt and sometimes jarring, but in a rich HTML application, a user's actions can be considered and handled gracefully. Natural or instinctive interactions are

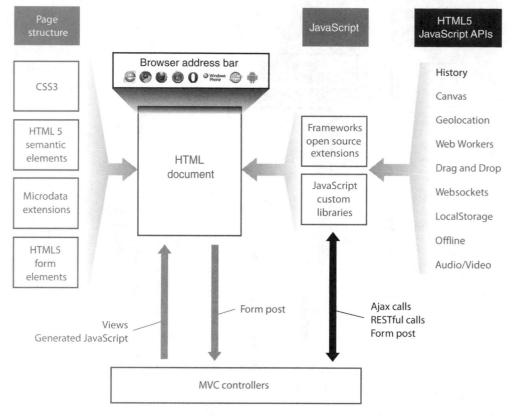

Figure 1.8   Application navigation can happen when a user POSTs a message to the server, when a JavaScript event occurs, or when browser URL changes are intercepted with the HTML5 History API.

an area gaining a lot of traction in the mobile market today because what may seem like small parts of the usability story can have a large effect on user satisfaction. Keeping operations subtle and instinctive is an art form where the ability to draw the eye, the mouse, or the hand to a specific place to perform an operation is critical.

1.2.4   Business logic

The business logic in an HTML application will nearly always be JavaScript on the client; the corresponding server-side implementations can be .NET or any other server technology. As shown in figure 1.9, the custom libraries and frameworks you include in your application will be responsible for changing the user interface, communicating with the server, and integrating HTML5 APIs.

On the communication side, we'll use ASP.NET MVC in this book but you aren't limited to this technology. Any server solution capable of receiving HTTP calls and returning data will work. The decisions you'll have to make will revolve around how, when, and where to validate your business data and which external libraries to use.

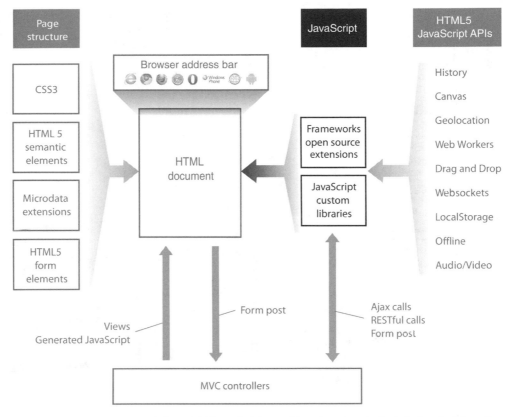

Figure 1.9 **The business logic in an HTML application resides almost exclusively in JavaScript on the client and on the server in .NET libraries.**

1.2.5 Server communications

Communication with the server is accomplished via the initial load of a page, by the posting of a form, or via Ajax calls to web services. A good communication model will keep the traffic frequency low and the content volume to the barest minimum. Figure 1.10 highlights a limitation in ASP.NET MVC whereby all communications will be transmitted through controllers and can be initiated by either a JavaScript Ajax call or through a form POST.

When security is necessary, SSL is available using MVC to keep your data transmissions private, and when security isn't required, it sometimes makes sense to make communications with the server somewhat transparent. Doing this will enable your system to operate in a software-as-a-service (SAAS) model and allow other applications to consume or manipulate your application's data.

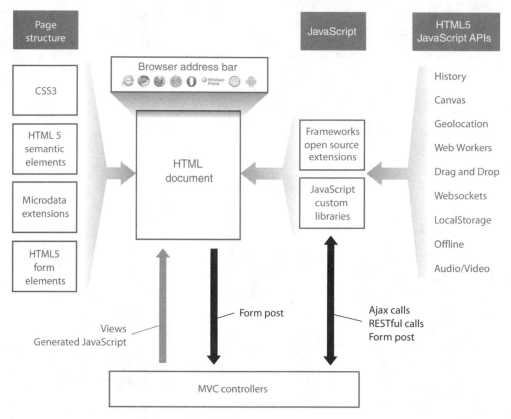

Figure 1.10   Communication with servers is vital to most business applications and can be performed by contacting controller actions using Ajax or by POSTing forms to the server.

1.2.6   The data layer

The data layer is interesting in an HTML application because it can involve both client and server data storage. On the server, you'll store all the normal business data, security, and transactional information. The client is more complex, because you'll often need to store durable state information as well as client data for use offline. Figure 1.11 shows the intersection of JavaScript with the Local Storage API.

Local Storage, as mentioned earlier, isn't the only means of maintaining data on the client, but it currently has the best mix of supported browsers and simplicity in usage. Local Storage has far more support and stability than IndexedDB and is far easier to use than browser cookies, though these other solutions have their place.

Whether or not a page set up to be accessed offline could also be considered part of the data layer is an interesting topic that we'll give some consideration to in chapter 10, but, for now, understand that certain directives placed in your page will allow it to be seamlessly accessed when the browser isn't connected to the internet.

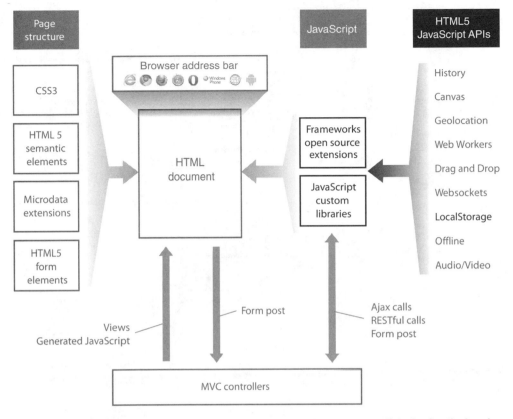

Figure 1.11 **Storage of local data inside an HTML application is best accomplished using the Local Storage API and JavaScript methods to maintain it.**

Now that we've looked at many of the facets of developing applications using HTML5, JavaScript, and .NET, it's time to put it all together by building a Hello World application.

1.3 Hello World in HTML5

Your Hello World application will, in just a few lines of code, display a web page, create a JavaScript object, and get JSON data from an MVC controller to present to the user. Figure 1.12 shows that this application will work in all major browsers. It will also work on iPhone, iPad, Windows Phone, and Android devices with no modifications!

When a user enters a name and a date, the server will add a "verified" tag to the name and validate the date passed in. It will assign a server date to the returned object that will then be displayed in the interface. No additional navigation will be required by the user to perform any of these steps.

This application won't only let you get your hands dirty right away; it will also introduce you to the following features that will be useful immediately and throughout the rest of the book:

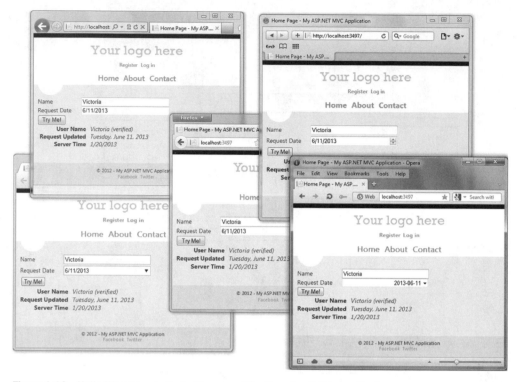

Figure 1.12   Hello World executing with no modifications in all the popular browsers

- Updating or removing Visual Studio NuGet project packages as appropriate
- ASP.NET MVC model binding
- Posting data to a server using Ajax and jQuery
- Using JavaScript to add content to and remove it from the page
- Building and using JavaScript objects
- JavaScript closure and scoping
- The jQuery `ready` handler

In the following sections, you'll create a new template, customize the application, build your JavaScript library, and then build what you need for the server side. Time to get started!

1.3.1   Creating the template

To get started, open Visual Studio normally and start a new project called HelloWorld:

1 Select the Web tab and find the project template called ASP.NET MVC Web Application. The version of the MVC project template will depend on the latest version you have installed in your copy of Visual Studio, but for your purposes

you need at least MVC 3. This can be downloaded for free from the Microsoft site or installed via the Web Platform Installer (http://www.microsoft.com/web/downloads/platform.aspx).

2 Set the project name to HelloWorld, as in figure 1.13, and click OK.
3 Select Internet Application using HTML5 Semantic Markup and the Razor View Engine.
4 Leave the Create Unit Test Project item unchecked.

The template will create a baseline MVC website that you can fire up immediately. You should have folders containing a list of controllers, folders for views, models and scripts, and the web.config file, which is probably familiar to you. In the Scripts folder you'll notice that there are quite a few files that appear to contain version numbers in the filenames. This is a common practice in JavaScript libraries. If you have some familiarity with jQuery, you'll probably also notice, as shown in figure 1.14, that the files are out of date.

The inclusion of NuGet, an open source project started by Phil Haack, in Visual Studio can make updating these files quick and painless. In the Visual Studio menu bar, select Tools > Library Package Manager > Manage NuGet Packages for Solution. In the Manage NuGet Packages window, you can select the Updates tab on the left and see a screen similar to figure 1.15.

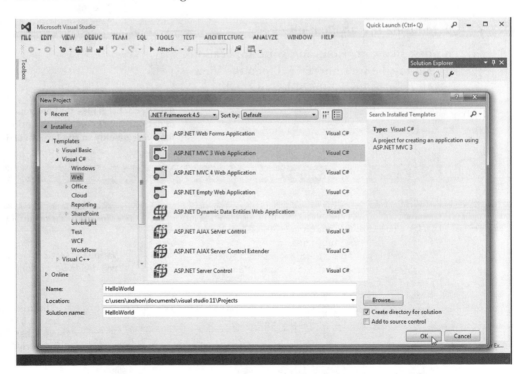

Figure 1.13 Create a new ASP.NET MVC project in Visual Studio using at least MVC 3.

All you need to do is click the Update button next to each package (some are linked, so updates can cascade) until everything is finished. You should now have all the latest JavaScript libraries and project references to continue with the HelloWorld application. These files aren't necessarily linked in the appropriate places, but you'll update those links as you encounter them. In later chapters, we'll only include and update the packages you'll actually be using, but for this exercise we'll keep things a little more simple.

> **TIP** This section covers a number of topics that are specific to the JavaScript language. If you aren't already familiar with the constructs and features of JavaScript, we recommend you read through appendix A on JavaScript at the end of this book.

1.3.2   Customizing the application

The first step to customizing your application is to modify the user interface. Open the Views > Home > Index.cshtml file and add the markup from the next listing.

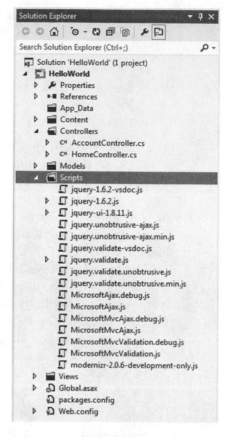

Figure 1.14   The starting MVC project usually contains files that are somewhat out of date. Using NuGet, you can refresh these files very quickly to the latest versions.

Listing 1.2   The Index.cshtml markup

```
@{ ViewBag.Title = "Home Page"; }
<title>@ViewBag.Message</title>
<article id="inputSection">
   <section class="submission">
      <label for="userName">Name</label>
      <input type="text" id="userName" />
   </section>
   <section class="submission">
      <label for="reqDate">Request Date</label>
      <input type="date" id="reqDate" />
   </section>
   <section>
      <button id="makeRequest" type="button">
      Try Me!</button>
```

<article> will be container for area where you'll work.

Various <section> elements will divide up working area.

<button> will be bound to click event handler in JavaScript using its id value.

```
      </section>
      <section id="outputSection">
      </section>
</article>
<script src="/Scripts/HelloWorld.js" type="text/javascript">
</script>
```

◁— **Final <section> will be filled with data returned by server after successful callback.**

The markup will automatically be placed inside the master page of your application by MVC. If you're using version 3 of MVC, the master page file will still contain references to the old files. This is the file you need to open next:

1 Navigate in the Solution Explorer to Views > Shared > _Layout.cshtml. Notice at the top of the page that you have references to various script files. Compare those references to what is in the Scripts folder of the application and update them accordingly.

```
<script src="@Url.Content("~/Scripts/jquery-1.7.2.min.js")" ...
<script src="@Url.Content("~/Scripts/modernizr-2.5.3.js")" ...
```

2 While you're here, find the <h1> tag and change its contents to "Hello World". Run your application now, and you should see something similar to figure 1.16.

3 This is fine but it could use some improvement. Find the Content > Site.css stylesheet and open it up. Scroll to the bottom and add the following styles:

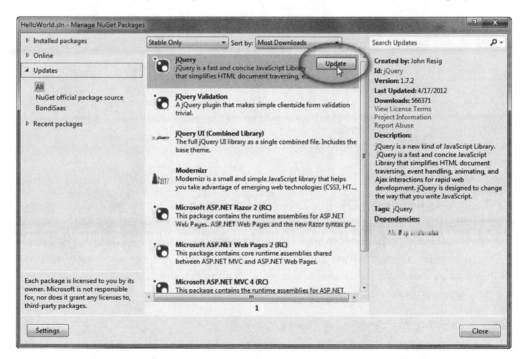

Figure 1.15 Use NuGet to update all the packages that are included by default in the standard MVC solution.

Figure 1.16   The content of the home page has the controls you need for the application, but it still needs additional styling.

```
.submission label {
    display: inline-block;
    width: 100px;
}
.submission input {
    width: 200px;
}
.result label {
    display: inline-block;
    margin-right: 10px;
    width: 115px;
    text-align: right;
    font-weight: bold;
}
.result span {
    font-style: italic;
}
```

These styles will keep things lined up and pretty later on, when you're moving data back and forth between the client and server and dynamically adding and removing HTML elements. The styles all take the same basic selector (the heading for each style that determines which elements will be selected). There are plenty of ways to write styles to get the work done, but we're being very specific with these styles so as not to inadvertently edit other styles in other parts of the page.

1.3.3   *Building the JavaScript library*

You may have noticed in listing 1.2 that we referenced a script file named HelloWorld.js. It's time to create that file. To do this, we'll walk through the following steps:

1   Create the JavaScript file and wire up the jQuery `ready` function.
2   Create the `myApp` object.

3 Create the Ajax request to call the MVC controller.

4 Create the JavaScript function to handle the results from the MVC controller.

5 Create the function that displays results on the page.

Let's get started.

Expand the Scripts folder and add a new JScript file. At the top of this file, add the following bit of JavaScript:

```
$(document).ready(function () {
   myApp.helloWorldWireup();
});
```

This is known as the `ready` handler. It's an event thrown automatically by jQuery when any page that contains the jQuery library reference completes all of its loading and page layout tasks. This isn't necessarily an easy thing to know, so the jQuery team went to great lengths to check multiple sources of information to infer this state of readiness. All you need to do as a developer is wire up the event and you're good to go!

The call to `myApp.helloWorldWireup` doesn't do anything yet, so you'll need to look at that next. The following listing has the declaration for the object, along with a bit of logic to get you started. You'll fill in the stubbed out functions shortly.

Listing 1.3 The myApp object and its functions

```
var myApp = {                                    ◁——  Declare myApp object using var keyword. Object
                                                       is immediately attached to window object.
    helloWorldWireup: function () {          ◁——  First function declaration is
                                                   one you called from ready.
        $("#makeRequest").click(function (event) {
            var nm = $("#userName").val();        Inside click event handler find userName and reqDate
                                                  input boxes and extract values using jQuery.
            var dt = $("#reqDate").val();

            var myData = {                        Create a new temporary object called myData that
                UserName: nm,                     contains the properties you'll send to the server.
                RequestedDate: dt
            };
            // Ajax request will go here          Once you call server
        });                                       processResult function
    },                                            will be called. Stub will be
                                                  filled in shortly.
    processResult: function (returnedData) {  ◁——
    },

    displayResult: function (label, value) {  ◁——  displayResult function allows you
    }                                              to segregate code that changes
}                                                  user interface in your object.
```

Using jQuery selector, find makeRequest button and bind click event handler to it.

Your JavaScript object (`myApp`) will be created as soon as the JavaScript file is loaded and before the `ready` event fires, so you can be sure it exists when you call it. This is the normal flow in an HTML application, regardless of how many JavaScript libraries you're loading.

JavaScript object creation

There are various ways to create an object using JavaScript code. You'll be using a number of them throughout this book, but the simplest is as follows:

```
var myObject = {
    prop: "prop 1",
    prop2: "property 2",
    func1: function() {
        alert('hi there!');
    }
};
```

This tells the JavaScript engine to add a reference in memory to the window object and call it `myObject`. This object will have two properties (`prop` and `prop2`) that are prepopulated with values and a function (`func1`) that, when called, will pop up a message box in the browser. The significant rules for this kind of object are

- Use `var` to declare the object
- Separate the property or function name from the value with a colon
- Separate properties and functions with a comma

Another way to create the same object is as follows:

```
var myObject = {};
myObject.prop = 'prop 1';
myObject["prop2"] = 'property 2';
myObject.func1 = function() {
    alert('hi there!');
};
```

The functionality of this second object is exactly the same as the previous one. The only difference is in the way it's instantiated. The advantage of this method is that each addition of a property or function is independent of the others. This means you can add new properties and functions to your JavaScript objects whenever you like using either the dot notation (`object.property`) or the string notation (`object['property']`).

Two other ways of creating objects are to parse JSON text into objects and to copy one object and/or its properties to another object.

The next step is to fill in the Ajax request. jQuery has a built-in function to do this. It can take a number of different optional properties when executed, but for the purposes of this example, you need only the kind of request to execute (the `type`), the `url` to call, the content type, the `data` to pass, and the function that will be executed when the call succeeds (`success`). Each of these is a property that's assigned in the same manner as the `myApp` object from listing 1.3. Place the code from the next listing in the commented section of the `makeRequest click` event handler.

Listing 1.4 The Ajax request that will call the MVC controller

```
$.ajax({
    type: "GET",
    url: "/Home/GetMessage",
    data: myData,
    contentType: "application/json",
    success: myApp.processResult
});
```

Home/GetMessage URL will be filled in shortly and takes data object created earlier in click handler.

Ensure that request headers pass "json" as correct data type.

When Ajax call returns successfully myApp.processResult will automatically be called with data returned from the server.

When the server is called with the data payload you created earlier, your MVC controller code will update the name, verify that the date passed in is indeed a valid date, and add a new server date property.

With that data in hand from the successful execution of the Ajax call, you can fill in the processResult function. The following listing shows that code.

Listing 1.5 processResult is called automatically when the Ajax call returns successfully

```
processResult: function (returnedData) {
    $("#outputSection section").remove();
    myApp.displayResult(
        "User Name",
        returnedData.UserName);
    myApp.displayResult(
        "Request Updated",
        returnedData.RequestedDate);
    myApp.displayResult(
        "Server Time",
        returnedData.ServerDate);
},
```

Use jQuery to find element with ID of outputSection and clear all contents.

Call displayResult function for each property in data object returned from Ajax call.

Your client-side code is nearly finished. All you need to do is fill in the displayResult function. This function takes a label and a value, concatenates them into a series of HTML elements, and then places them inside the recently cleared out outputSection element. The next listing shows how it works.

Listing 1.6 Adding elements to the page using jQuery and string-based HTML

```
displayResult: function (label, value) {
    var start = "<section class='result'><label>";
    var mid = "</label><span>";
    var end = "</span></section>";
    $("#outputSection")
        .append(start + label + mid + value + end);
}
```

Creating elements using string concatenation is simple and objects created will be styled and laid out automatically.

Using jQuery's append function find outputSection object and insert string contents as HTML elements.

You can run your application now, and all your code will execute. The only problem will be that calls to Home/GetMessage will fail because you haven't implemented that endpoint yet. Next stop, the server!

> **TIP**   During normal operations, most modern web browsers won't report JavaScript errors unless this feature is turned on specifically. An easy way for a developer to see these errors is to open the console, which is a kind of debug engine that most JavaScript engines provide with the browser. The simplest version to use currently is the one found in Google Chrome. When you're in the browser, right-click anywhere on the screen and select Inspect Element. A new window will appear docked to the bottom of the browser or possibly as a completely separate window. Across the top, you'll find the Console button—click it. You should see all the exceptions thrown during the current session.

1.3.4   *Building the server side*

Now that your client side is complete and you have at least a basic understanding of how various pieces of JavaScript are initialized and executed, it's time to build your server implementation. The HTML application you're building in this chapter requires both a client and a server implementation.

Many web applications use the server only as file storage. In these applications, once the resources such as stylesheets, HTML files, and scripts are loaded, the server is never contacted again. Games are a normal example of this kind of application. Your application, however, needs to talk to a server to send information and receive updates. To do that, you need something more than a normal HTML page or MVC controller that returns a view. You need something that takes only data and returns only data. You need JSON.

Your steps here will include

1   Building the model object to contain data on the server.
2   Building the MVC controller method to handle the Ajax request.

JavaScript Object Notation (JSON)

JSON is used for transferring text-based data from one point to another over HTTP and for serialization of JavaScript objects. It can also be used for many other purposes, but its roots are in the web. It's fast, human readable, and broadly supported.

Syntax in JSON is extremely simple. Specific characters are used to wrap text into serialized fields with very little effort and overhead. Data types of field values are implied, not specified, and objects need not conform to a specific schema. Arrays in JSON can contain any kind of object.

Here are the basic rules:

- Curly braces, { }, wrap each object instance, and square brackets, [ ], wrap each array instance.

- Each property in an object has a name and value separated by a colon.
- Each property in an object and each object in an array must be separated from the next by a comma.
- Property names that correspond to keywords must be wrapped in quotes.
- Property values that are strings are always wrapped in quotes.
- Object properties can be other objects or arrays.

Here is a simple JSON object:

```
{"fname":"George", "lname": "Washington"}
```

This code will result in the direct creation of a JavaScript object with two properties, each with a value.

Some projects will require sending large amounts of data to the client, and JSON is perfectly capable of doing this as well. The following JSON code contains an array of two objects, each containing a timeline that can be immediately parsed and used in JavaScript:

```
[{
    "Timeline":"1800s", "StartYear":1800, "EndYear":1899,
    "Events": [
        {"Date":1803, "Event":"Louisiana Purchase"},
        {"Date":1808, "Event":"Napoleon Occupies Spain"},
    ]
},
{
    "Timeline":"1900s", "StartYear":1900, "EndYear":1999,
    "Events": [
        {"Date":1917, "Event":"US Declares War"},
        {"Date":1991, "Event":"Desert Storm"}
    ]
}]
```

JavaScript is used to parse an object from a string using the JSON parser that's either built into most modern browsers or available with the free json2.js library found at http://www.JSON.org/js.html. If your browser doesn't support JSON, just include this script and all the JSON parsing logic will be automatically added. Using this method, you can create an object from a JSON string by calling

```
JSON.parse('string variable');
```

An object can also be turned into a string using the `stringify` method of the same library:

```
var x = JSON.stringify(myObject);
```

Before you can build an endpoint on your server to take a JSON object and turn it into a .NET object, you first need to define the properties for that object. In your solution, add a new class to the Models folder called UserData.cs. This object should contain three properties, so add the code shown here:

```
namespace HelloWorld.Models
{
   public class UserData
   {
      public string UserName { get; set; }
      public string RequestedDate { get; set; }
      public string ServerDate { get; set; }
   }
}
```

This object will hold the user's name, the string version of a request date, and the string version of the current date on the server.

> **NOTE** You could have made these `DateTime` properties, but that would distract from our goal of showing you how to receive, manipulate, and send data from the server. If you want a more detailed investigation of date handling in JavaScript, take a look at appendix A on JavaScript toward the end of this book.

The next step is to build a controller call that can respond to data posted from the client using Ajax. You could create an entirely new controller, but that's unnecessary because you already have the Home controller available. Open that controller by navigating in Solution Explorer to Controllers > HomeController. Note that the MVC convention is to refer to controllers by their name with the suffix of "Controller," so the `AccountController` will be referred to by the URL `/Account` in your browser.

> **NOTE** There is a bit more to controller naming than just the standard naming convention, but that conversation will involve setting up ASP.NET MVC routes. You can find more information about routes as they relate to MVC applications in chapter 5. You can also check out the great books by authors K. Scott Allen, Steven Sanderson, Phil Haack, and Adam Freeman. All contain a wealth of knowledge in this area.

Back in the `HomeController`, you need to add a new method. It will receive a JSON object from the client and automatically transform it into your `UserData` object. It will make some changes to that object and return it, transforming it back into JSON. This action is shown in the following listing.

Listing 1.7 `GetMessage` receives and sends data using client Ajax calls

```
public JsonResult GetMessage(UserData myData)        ◁─┤  Model binding in MVC will automatically
{                                                        convert inbound JSON to UserData object.
   myData.UserName += " (verified)";
   var dt = DateTime.Now.AddYears(-1);
   DateTime.TryParse(myData.RequestedDate, out dt);  ◁─┤  Attempt to parse data to date and leave
   myData.RequestedDate = dt.ToLongDateString();         it as arbitrary value if conversion fails.
   myData.ServerDate = DateTime.Now.ToShortDateString();
   return Json(myData, JsonRequestBehavior.AllowGet); ◁─┐  Method returns JsonResult
}                                                          object so you can generate
                                                           JSON using MVC serializer.
```

Note that in the controller call in listing 1.7 you're taking a `UserData` object as a parameter, but in the client, the object you're passing looks like this:

```
var myData = {
    UserName: nm,
    RequestedDate: dt
};
```

This works because ASP.NET MVC will attempt to transform the input parameters into the appropriate object type using its model-binding mechanism. If you wanted to, you could also have written the controller function signature as follows:

```
public JsonResult GetMessage(string UserName, string RequestedDate) {
```

This would have resulted in the same data being received on the server. The advantages of model binding are that your method signatures are smaller and easier to understand, and your objects are created with constructor methods that perform logic that will be automatically executed when the function is called. These features make MVC controllers and model binding the ideal way to implement Ajax endpoints for an HTML application.

You may be surprised to learn that your first HTML application is complete! Run the solution now and try it out in various browsers. You should see a nearly identical implementation in each. Input a name and a date, and watch the results return from the server after being "verified," as shown in figure 1.17.

As you test your freshly minted application, it's worth taking a look at how various desktop browsers implement the `<input type='date' />` tag (figure 1.18). Opera, for instance, gives you a built-in date picker, whereas Safari has a small up/down implementation that changes the date value one day at a time.

Figure 1.17 After completing the controller call, you should see data from the server displayed and updated automatically.

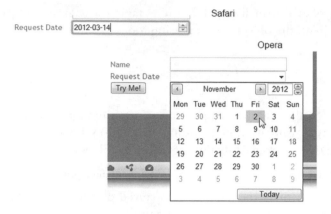

Figure 1.18   The date picker implementations in various browsers highlight the wide range of interpretations in the browser market.

This date field difference highlights both the necessity of testing your HTML applications across a range of expected browsers and the need for feature testing. Feature testing is usually done with a JavaScript library like Modernizr (http://www.modernizr .com/) that will return a Boolean value for a specific feature. If you decide that you absolutely require a feature, and it isn't present in the current browser, you can alert users that they must use a different browser.

Modernizr is the natural choice for this kind of feature detection because it's widely used, well-maintained, and is included by default in all recent versions of ASP.NET MVC. The code is as simple as this:

```
if (Modernizr.touch){
    // .. bind touch events here
}
else {
    alert('touch is not supported');
}
```

1.4   *Summary*

With the level of knowledge you now have about the moving parts and interactions of an HTML5 application built on an MVC foundation, you should be ready to dive into your own applications and start tinkering to see what you can make happen on your own! The architecture is straightforward and the possibilities are endless.

But this chapter is far from the end of the story. In order to build richer, more functional applications that can interact with all the new HTML5 APIs, style properties, and semantic markup we talked about in this chapter, you need to dig deeper, starting with the new semantic elements and CSS features available in HTML5 and CSS3. That's what we'll look at next.

If you're already familiar with the new elements and CSS features, you may want to skip chapter 2 and move straight to the later chapters, where we dive into each of the HTML5 JavaScript APIs to show you how you can use your current .NET skills to build the next generation of applications in the browser.

A markup primer: classic HTML, semantic HTML, and CSS

This chapter covers

- Building and reading semantic markup
- Using block and inline elements appropriately
- Styling elements using Cascading Style Sheets (CSS)

Classic markup is the HTML you're probably familiar with already: `<div>` tags that have `<span>` tags inside them, `<p>` tags that define paragraphs of text, and `<a>` tags that mark links to other content. But classic markup isn't semantic markup, which is a simple concept with far-reaching effects on the World Wide Web.

Think of semantic markup as a structural diagram for your pages. You can get a lot of information about a building from its structural diagrams, and the same is true with the semantic layout of a page. You can't see that a page is laid out semantically just by looking at it, but if you take a look at the source it becomes very clear which items are menus or navigation areas and which areas contain content. This gives search engines and accessibility devices the ability to find the content on your pages and to ignore the parts that are only pointers or helpers toward that content.

In this chapter, we'll look at the various kinds of structural, content, and data-entry tags (classic and semantic) that you'll encounter in HTML5 and then cover the basics of Cascading Style Sheets (CSS)—just enough to get you through this book. If you're familiar with HTML and CSS, you may just want to peruse the headings to see if there's anything new here for you. Otherwise, settle in for a dive into HTML5 that will prepare you for working with its semantic elements and more complex functionality in later chapters.

First, though, let's take a closer look at how semantic HTML markup works.

2.1   *Classic and semantic HTML markup: what's the difference?*

HTML markup is the text the browser uses to render a page. The difference between *classic* markup and *semantic* markup is the meaning of the tags. With classic HTML, for example, a `<div>` tag is a rectangle that renders to the screen and sits with all the other rectangles. The user looks at the content and can tell its meaning from the way it's formatted or the way it's written. A computer, however, can't look at a simple `<div>` tag and see anything meaningful. It's just a brick in the page structure that looks like all the other bricks.

There are popular attributes that you can add to that simple `<div>`, like `<div class='header'>`, that *might* give the tag meaning to a computer, but this isn't guaranteed nor is it written in a specification anywhere. It's just something that has grown organically on the internet over the last decade. Semantic HTML, however, has meaning built right into the tag—guaranteed—with no additional work necessary. This makes `<section>`, for example, readable by a computer as a piece of content that should exist inside another piece of content, whereas `<article>` is content that should be self-contained.

This means that both types of tags (classic and semantic) render to the screen, but only one has intrinsic meaning to computer programs, like a search engine or an aggregator that 'reads' a page.

Organizing your site semantically using HTML5 has the added advantage of making it easier to create sections and areas that are accessible from JavaScript based on data or application conditions. This makes your site easier to understand and build even as it becomes more complex—a remarkable achievement in software development.

As an example, take a look at the following code listing and notice that you can see very quickly exactly where the content should be inside the page. Regardless of how this page looks in a browser, the critical information is easy to find in the code.

Listing 2.1   Sample semantic page structure

```
<!DOCTYPE html>
<html>
<head><title>HTML5 Maps</title></head>
<body>
<header>
  <hgroup>
    <h1>HTML5 Maps</h1>
```

Describes header area for entire page

```
  </hgroup>
</header>
<nav>                                                      Contains navigational
  <ul>                                                     elements
    <li><a href="#">Home</a></li>
  </ul>                                         Describes section
</nav>                                           of data called
<section id="techStart">                        techStart        Identifies
  <article id="whatisGIS">                                         article within
    <section>                                                      section
      Content describing what GIS is and what it does...
    </section>                                              Identifies single
  </article>                                                section or piece
  <article id="samples">                                    of data within
    <section>                                               article
      There are lots of sample maps and articles available here.
    </section>
  </article>
</section>
<footer>
  <a href="...">Terms and Conditions</a>                   Describes page
</footer>                                                   footer
</body>
</html>
```

What is particularly interesting is that when you lay your site out semantically, you gain the ability to select just what you want using JavaScript and style classes with very little effort. For instance, the following code will find all <article> elements on the current page and ensure that they're visible:

```
$("article").show();
```

In a scenario where your page can alternate between a graphic element and text, using semantic markup will allow you to easily discriminate between them to perform logical operations. Let's take a closer look at exactly what makes up an HTML tag.

2.2 Basic structural elements of all HTML tags

HTML, at its core, is all about text that's read by a browser. Browsers read tags and attributes, which in turn are rendered by the browser as elements on the page. Figure 2.1 shows the basic structure of HTML syntax.

Each rendered element on an HTML page is laid out in the browser window in whatever way you, as the developer, tell it. You "tell it" by the way you order and nest elements on the page, with styles and through code. For instance, take a look at this text:

> Go left from the parking lot down Osceola Parkway and turn left on Buena Vista Drive. Turn right on World Drive and continue to your destination.

Now take a look at figure 2.2, which shows the same directions with various bits of markup added.

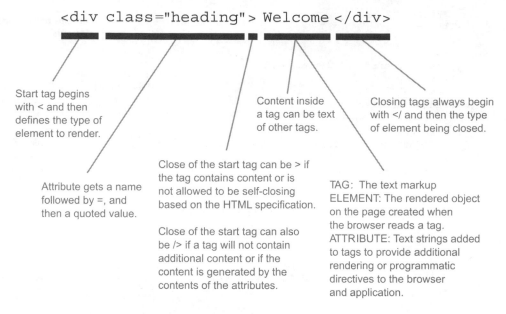

Figure 2.1   **The basic structure of HTML includes tags and attributes rendered as page elements.**

Put yourself in the driver's seat; which set of directions would you prefer? The following listing shows the code we wrapped around the text to generate the directions in figure 2.2, producing an image that allows readers to get more meaningful information, faster.

Listing 2.2   Simple markup to enhance data

```
<div><img src="left.gif"/>
   <span>Left from parking lot</span>
   <span class="rd">Osceola Parkway</span>
</div>
<div><img src="left.gif"/>
   <span>2 miles</span>
   <span class="rd">Buena Vista Drive</span>
</div>
<div><img src="right.gif"/>
   <span>3 miles</span>
   <span class="rd">World Drive</span>
</div>
<div><img src="arrive.gif"/>2.4 miles</div>
```

The code here is "classic" HTML, not the new "semantic" HTML, which comes into play later, when you introduce semantic tags. Throughout the rest of the book, we'll implement both kinds of tags whenever appropriate.

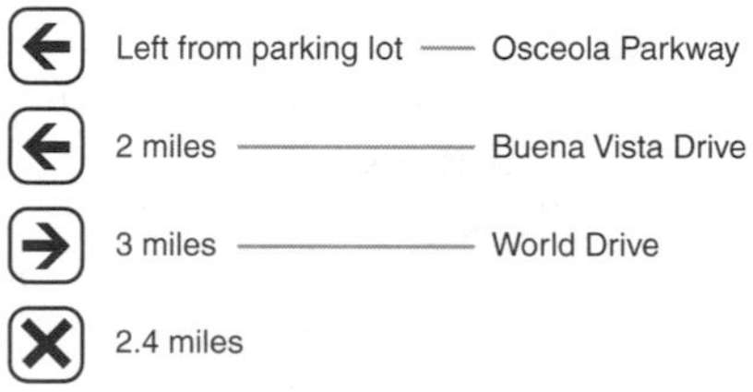

Figure 2.2   **Displaying directions using HTML markup gives the reader more information while maintaining clarity.**

In this section, we'll walk through the various tags and elements that make up the bulk of classic HTML markup:

- Basic tags—These tags focus on the elements that should be present in any page. They're the core bits that make a page a page.
- Block and inline elements—These are the foundational display elements in classic HTML.
- Table elements—These elements are used to render grids of data on the page.
- Form elements—These are the elements used for data input in an HTML page.

First up, the basic tags you need to construct any page.

2.2.1 Working with the basic HTML tags

Nearly everything in HTML is a tag, a directive, or a piece of text. Tag attributes, or text strings added to tags to provide additional rendering or programmatic directives, are either optional or required.

A tag can have one of two formats. First, it can be an opening and closing bracketed element, sometimes with other tags or text content between them:

```
<div>this is my content</div>
```

Here, the <div> tag is just a block that contains the content text. No attributes exist and this will, by default, render as a rectangle on the page.

Here's another example:

```
<a href="http://microsoft.com">MS</a>
```

This tag is an anchor that will render the text "Microsoft" to the screen as a link that will navigate the browser to microsoft.com, because of the href attribute.

Tags can also be self-closing, with the complete content enclosed inside, using attributes:

```
<div style="width:50px; background-color:blue;" />
```

This <div> tag will contain no content but will render a blue rectangle on the screen exactly 50 pixels wide. The style attribute here uses the same syntax as the CSS styles we'll look at later in the chapter.

The close of a tag is signaled with the characters />, although browser vendors are very forgiving and this isn't always necessary. To keep your HTML well-formed, opening tags either need a closing tag associated with them or they must be self-closing. This ensures that your pages will render the same way across all browsers.

A basic page usually has the structure shown in the next listing. This isn't a hard and fast rule, but it definitely makes it easier to find markup in your pages during development.

Listing 2.3 Basic page layout tags

```
<!DOCTYPE html>        ◁┤  DOCTYPE element tells browser what
<html>                        to expect when rendering page.
```

DOCTYPE element tells browser what to expect when rendering page.

Html element wraps all other elements in page.

```
<head>
</head>
<body>
</body>
</html>
```

Head element doesn't render in main browser area but can provide additional touches to page like title and search helper information.

Body element is where content will be rendered.

Now, let's look more closely at the most important tags you'll be using when you work with HTML5.

THE <!DOCTYPE> TAG

This is the only tag we'll discuss that isn't HTML. <!DOCTYPE> is like a "Hello World" nametag for your page. It tells any browser consuming your page how to translate what it finds next. (The <html> tag should always come next and wrap the content of the page.)

The minimal declaration we're using in this book tells the browser to use HTML5 parsing, whereas a more verbose version would include the parsing schema, like this:

```
<!DOCTYPE html PUBLIC "-//W3C//DTD XHTML 1.0 Transitional//EN">
```

THE <HEAD> TAG

The <head> tag goes at the top of the page, right after the doctype that the browser will parse against. The <head> isn't visible but rather contains directives for how to use data on the page, where to go for styling information, and how to display the page in the title bar of the browser.

Deprecated HTML tags

There are a number of deprecated tags in HTML5 that you should not use in new markup. In some cases, the functionality is better achieved with other methods. Other tags were seldom used or were commonly misunderstood, or their use caused usability or accessibility issues.

These tags' functions are replaced with CSS styles: <basefont>, <big>, <center>, <font>, <s>, <strike>, <tt>, and <u>.

These tags have function or accessibility issues: <frame>, <frameset>, and <noframe>.

These tags have been misunderstood or are seldom used: <acronym>, <applet>, <isindex>, and <dir>.

THE <TITLE> TAG

The <title> element nested inside the <head> element of your page sets the text of the page tab in the client browser. It will also be the default title when a user makes your page a favorite or when search engines find your page:

```
<title>Welcome to my page</title>
```

THE <META> TAG

<meta> tags give additional information about the current page. Search engines and plugins use them, and they're editable from code. The <meta> tag consists of a required

content attribute and an optional name value. Additional attributes are http-equiv, used to describe what kind of value is in the content, and scheme, used to help the browser interpret the content data. <meta> tags are also repeatable:

```
<meta name="keywords" content="GPS tracks" />
<meta name="author" content="Jim Jackson II" />
<meta name="author" content="Ian Gilman" />
```

<meta> tags go in the HTML document <head> area.

THE <LINK> TAG

<link> tags create a link between the current page and an external resource. The <link> tag must have the reference value to the external resource, assigned as an href, as well as the kind of relationship the link sets up, called the rel attribute. The <link> tag is most often used to pull in a stylesheet from the site, but it's also possible to assign icon values when adding a link to the desktop:

```
<link href="http://www.ellipsetours.com/css/touch.css" rel="stylesheet" />
<link href="/images/icon.png" rel="shortcut icon" />
```

Links can be either relative, pointing to a location in the same site, or absolute, with the complete URL to the resource listed. <link> tags are located in the head area of the HTML document.

> **WARNING** <link> tags can reference stylesheets from other sites, but most designers consider this bad form unless the page author is also the owner of the other site.

THE <SCRIPT> TAG

A <script> tag places an area of code execution into the HTML page. This can take the form of a link to an external file, using the src attribute, or it can be inline code. Inline code appears between the starting <script> and ending </script> tags, whereas external resource links have only the tag with empty content. The only other attribute that's required in a script tag is the type value, which, in your case will be "text/javascript".

> **TIP** A <script> tag that links to an external source can be closed either with starting and ending script tags <script src=".."></script> or by closing the tag in place <script src=".." />. Both are valid HTML, but only the "complete" version with separate opening and closing tags is valid XHTML. Internet Explorer uses XHTML validation by default, so be safe and use the non-minified tag structure.

Although it's true that script tags can appear anywhere in an HTML page after the opening HTML tag, best practice indicates that scripts should be in one of two places:

- Inside the <head> element (for code that must be available for the screen to initially render)
- Just before the closing </body> tag

Scripts block page rendering while they're loading, and pages render from top to bottom, so putting your scripts at the end of the HTML document makes more sense. Just remember that code here, even if it's self-invoking, won't fire until just before page rendering reaches the closing body tag. You can find more discussion of self-invoking JavaScript in appendix A.

THE <STYLE> TAG

The `<style>` tag embeds a set of styles directly in your page. Embedding styles this way reduces the number of files you have to manage, but doesn't give much benefit beyond that. You can provide additional information in a `title` attribute within the `<style>` tag, but the browser won't use it. The only required attribute is `type`, which, for all the stylesheets in this book will be `text/css`:

```
<style type="text/css">p { background-color: yellow; }</style>
```

THE <BODY> TAG

Once your page finishes processing information in the `<head>` tag of the page, it will start working on the `<body>` element. This is the top-level container for the content on your page. Although you can use styles to place elements outside the viewable area of the `<body>`, the tags for all visible elements will exist inside the `<body>` tag. There are two categories of elements inside the `<body>` tag that display content: block (or block-level) and inline.

2.2.2 Making content flow where you want with block and inline elements

Understanding content flow in HTML is critical, because it determines where tags will be rendered and how surrounding tags will affect any given tag on your page. As mentioned, there are two primary tag layout types: block and inline. Let's take a look at block tags first.

BLOCK ELEMENTS

Block elements are tags that, when rendered, take up a rectangle of space that all other rendered elements in the current container element must either flow before or after. A `<div>`, for instance, will take up all the width available to it on the page, and other content must either come before or after it. Even if the style of the `<div>` is such that it's only one pixel wide, no other content will go next to it unless placed there manually.

A simpler way to think about this is in terms of line breaks. A block element will always try to place itself on a new line in the content and will always try to force the next element on the page onto a new line. You can see this by creating an HTML page with the following markup inside the `<body>` tag:

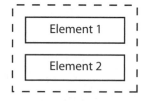

Figure 2.3 Blocking elements render by taking up a full line of width.

```
<p style="width:100px;">Element 1</p>
<p style="width:100px;">Element 2</p>
```

Now, replace the <p> tags with any other element type (<div>, for instance) and see what happens in each case. Paragraph elements are block level so they will present something like figure 2.3.

The tags in table 2.1 will all create block-level elements.

Table 2.1   Block-level HTML elements (HTML5 elements are shown in bold)

<address>	<form>	**<legend>**
<article>	<h1>	<li>
<aside>	<h2>	**<menu>**
<blockquote>	<h3>	**<nav>**
<div>	<h4>	<p>
<fieldset>	<h5>	<table>
<figcaption>	<h6>	<ul>
<figure>	**<header>**	**<section>**
<footer>	**<hgroup>**	

INLINE ELEMENTS

Inline tags render elements that are generally used to style individual pieces of content. They wrap a single piece of content and flow with it based on style properties set in the parent container.

Figure 2.4   Inline elements render on the same line and wrap with the text content on the page.

Elements like <span> are inline and will appear something like figure 2.4 in the browser.

The tags in table 2.2 create inline elements.

Table 2.2   Inline HTML elements (HTML5 elements are shown in bold)

<a>	<input>	**<progress>**
<abbr>	**<keygen>**	<span>
<canvas>	<label>	**<summary>**
<cite>	<link>	<textarea>
<datagrid>	**<mark>**	**<time>**
<datalist>	<map>	**<wbr>**
<details>	**<meter>**	
<em>	**<output>**	

2.2.3 *Dividing data into grids with table elements*

Tables in HTML are a means of dividing data into a grid format. Tables will naturally use a block format, but it isn't uncommon for CSS styles to modify this behavior so that other content flows around them.

A <table> tag will have nested inside it various other tags to produce a grid layout. The nesting of table elements is <table><grouping><row><cell>. Grouping elements are <thead>, <tbody>, and <tfoot>, and they aren't required. Each row definition uses <tr> tags, and individual cells can be either a <thead> to designate a header cell or a <td> to designate a normal cell. The markup in the following listing shows how a typical table could be laid out.

Listing 2.4   A table used to display tabular data

```
<table>
    <thead>                              Table header defines top row or rows.
        <tr>
            <th>Month</th>               Table head cells
            <th>Sandy</th>               should exist inside
            <th>Rocky</th>               header group.
            <th>Total Sales</th>
        </tr>
    </thead>
    <tfoot>                              Table foot should be before
        <tr>                             body group so it's rendered
            <td>Sum</td>                 before table data is complete.
            <td>$1500</td>
            <td>$2000</td>
            <td>$3500</td>               Table cells exist inside table rows but
        </tr>                            can span multiple columns or rows.
    </tfoot>
    <tbody>
        <tr>                             Table body group describes
            <td>January</td>             main content for table.
            <td>$1000</td>
            <td>$900</td>
            <td>$1900</td>
        </tr>
        <tr>
            <td>February</td>
            <td>$500</td>
            <td>$1100</td>
            <td>$1600</td>
        </tr>
    </tbody>
</table>
```

Table rows contain table cells.

When designing a <table> for displaying tabular data, the use of grouping and header tags can help greatly in styling, but when you're using a <table> to lay out your page, you generally won't use these. You're more likely to add attributes to individual cells to allow them to span multiple rows or multiple columns.

TIP In the past, laying out a page using a table was considered bad practice, because tables had to be completely loaded from the server before rendering. Today, with ubiquitous broadband, this isn't such a problem, but some still consider tables heavy-handed for full page layouts, because they're rather rigid and provide no means of separating styling from content. It's best to reserve tables for tabular data, not page layout.

2.2.4 Using HTML form elements

First we should cover the very basics of an HTML form. The action attribute is required and is a pointer to the form's data submission location. This might be the same page or a different page, but wherever it goes, the form data will be included as some kind of encoded value in the URL unless you override the submit action with your own code.

The following HTML will yield a URL submitted to the formRead.html page.

Listing 2.5 A simple form and the resulting URL value when it's posted

Name value of input will determine name in posted URL.

Action attribute can be relative and states where form will post by default.

```
<form action="formRead.html">
    <input type="text" name="first" value="John Q" />
    <input type="text" name="last" value="O'Connor" />
    <input type="submit" />
</form>

http://www.site.com/formRead.html?first=John+Q&last=O%27Connor
```

Resulting URL will be character- and form-encoded by default.

Now let's move on and look at what you can do with HTML5's new input element types.

NEW HTML5 INPUT TYPES FOR FORMS

The new input types in HTML5 have received some good press for two reasons. The first reason is that the types are descriptive of their purpose, so your code can review them semantically. You can tell that an input element of type email should contain an email address, so your code can inject functionality that specifically supports email. The second and closely related reason is that browsers can use these element types to automatically add functionality to your page without your needing to write any code. This saves time and reduces bugs in your forms.

Along with the new input types are various new attributes that apply to the types:

- datetime, date, time, month, week, datetime-local—These <input> types express time-based values. You do this by specifying the type value and allowing the browser to do the work of rendering a selection interface and formatting the text content. If the browser doesn't support this by either validating the text as an appropriate value or providing a select user interface, you'll need to build out that functionality yourself. See the section on jQuery UI in appendix A for more about this.
- number—This <input> type presents a normal text box but validates against a few attribute values. The min and max attributes limit the numbers entered, and the step attribute states the allowed values within those limits. Consider this example:

```
<input id="numPick" type="number" min="0" max="10" step="1" />
```

This will give you a text box whose value must be a whole number from 0 to 10.

There's also a `value` attribute that operates as you would expect, storing the displayed value, and an automatic JavaScript extension that allows you to bump the value up or down arbitrarily or based on the `step` value, using the following syntax:

```
numPick.stepUp();
numPick.stepUp(5);
numPick.stepDown();
numPick.setpDown(10);
```

One other thing to note about `number` is that when the field is selected in some mobile browsers, the virtual keyboard that appears will be numeric instead of alphanumeric. This can be quite helpful in some scenarios.

- `range`—This `<input>` type, in supported browsers, will present a slider control. The attributes are the same as in a `number` input, and the operation is the same except for the interface.

- `search`—This `<input>` type gives you a means to either automatically or manually style a text box with a button next to it so that it's consistent with the look and feel of popular search engines and default browser interfaces. There is nothing behind this in terms of additional software functionality, but it does save some work because it will, in supported browsers, automatically submit just the content of its text box to the server.

- `email`—This is another tag similar to the `number` `<input>` type that gives you additional screen and mobile keyboard enhancements. In an email input box, some mobile devices give a keyboard with "@" and ".com" as extra buttons on the text keyboard. It's subtle but helpful. Currently, there is no support for automatic regex validation of email addresses.

- `url`—Similar to `email`, this `<input>` type might edit the keyboard presentation but does no actual validation of the content of the presented text box. It's a worthwhile addition, though, because having this specific type gives you an easy way to add your own targeted validation.

- `color`—This `<input>` type provides a user interface for selecting a color. The return value is a six-digit hexadecimal color value. There is limited support for the `color` type, but as HTML5 applications increase in the wild, this could become important for online image editing applications as well as for custom interface editors.

2.3   Semantic HTML: The semantic blueprint

Now let's turn our focus to HTML5 semantics. A semantic tag renders an element that describes the kind of content it contains. While a traditional HTML tag, such as a `<div>`, can contain anything, a semantic tag such as `<header>` clearly defines what is inside it.

Organizing elements semantically provides two major values to a page. First, it allows search engines to easily determine what content is worth indexing and what content is just page noise used for styling or navigation. Second, it allows you, as the page developer, to segregate your page in a much more maintainable way. When you come back to a semantic page in a year or two to do some tweaks, it will be easier for you to find your way around if the page has its blueprint built right in. Finally, it makes your content more accessible by allowing screen-reading tools to locate the important content on your page and determine what parts are just navigational noise.

The following listing is an expansion of the original semantic page layout you saw in listing 2.1.

Listing 2.6   Sample semantic page structure

```
<!DOCTYPE html>
<html>
<head>
  <meta name="description" content="..." />
  <meta name="keywords" content="html5,map demos" />
  <title>HTML5 Maps - A resource...</title>
</head>
<body>
<header>                                        ◁──  Describes header area
  <hgroup>                                          for entire page
     <h1>HTML5 Maps</h1>
     <h2>Learn GIS and HTML5 Together</h2>
  </hgroup>
</header>
<nav>                                          ◁──  Contains navigational
  <ul>                                              elements
     <li><a href="#">Home</a></li>
     <li><a href="#">Maps</a></li>                  Identifies
     <li><a href="#">Contact</a></li>              article within
  </ul>                                             section
</nav>                           Describes section
<section id="techStart">      ◁── of data called
  <article id="whatisGIS">         techStart    ◁──
    <header><h2>What is GIS?</h2></header>       ◁──  Specifies
    <section>                                         header for
      Content describing what GIS is and what it does...  article
    </section>                                    ◁──
  </article>                                           Specifies
  <article id="samples">                              single section
    <header><h2>Sample Maps</h2></header>             or piece of
    <section>                                         data with
      There are lots of sample maps and articles available here.   article
      Take a look  <a href="...">here</a> and
      <a href="...">here</a>!
    </section>
  </article>
</section>                                         Creates an aside to
<aside>                                       ◁──  support content but
  <h2>Maps by Vendor</h2>                          that isn't directly
  <ul>                                             related to the content
     <li><a ref="external" href="#">Bing Maps</a></li>
     <li><a ref="external" href="#">Google Maps</a></li>
```

```
    <li><a ref="external" href="#">ESRI Maps</a></li>
  </ul>
</aside>
<footer>
  <a href="...">Terms and Conditions</a>
  <a href="...">Privacy Policy</a>
</footer>
</body>
</html>
```

> Describes page
> footer

We'll cover the semantic HTML5 tags in three categories:

- Content tags, which are wrappers for content
- Application tags, used to present information about how your program is operating
- Media tags, which present rich content

When to use semantic markup

Throughout this book, we'll be building many HTML applications that exist inside a single page. These applications may or may not benefit from the inclusion of semantic markup. To that end, we've tried to build in HTML5-specific tags only when the nature of the content warrants it.

Because semantic markup primarily offers web crawlers, search, and accessibility tools a better understanding of a page, dynamically generated or graphical content doesn't always benefit from the use of semantic markup.

2.3.1 Grouping and dividing page content with content tags

Content tags render elements that contain information a reader or user wants to see. These tags group various kinds of content together and they divide the content that's core to the topic from content that's ancillary or unrelated, such as headers and footers. You can better understand content tags by looking at a page as a document that has headings, subheadings, and various navigational bits.

<SECTION>

`<section>` defines content that should be treated as an independent piece of content within the page. Based on the HTML5 specification, it should not be used as a styling or scripting hook; it should be used to denote a specific piece of content. Bruce Lawson wrote at HTML5doctor.com, "Don't use it unless there is naturally a heading at the start of the section" (http://HTML5doctor.com/the-section-element).

But using the section as a styling mechanism does make sense when looking at the larger semantic scheme. Why would you locate and style elements based on an article but not a section? Feel free to style with sections; just be sure to keep them semantically appropriate.

```
<section>
   <p>Age considers; youth ventures</p>
</section>
```

<HEADER>

Earlier HTML specifications required the use of only one <h1> tag in an HTML page. With the creation of the section and article comes the ability to organize multiple content targets in a page, and the <header> element is the means by which that target can have its own head elements (<h1>, <h2>, and so on):

```
<section>
   <header>
      <h1>Famous Quotes</h1>
      <h2>Victor Hugo on Age</h2>
   </header>
   <p>Forty is the old age of youth; fifty is the youth of old age.</p>
</section>
```

<FOOTER>

The <footer> performs the same function as <header> in a piece of target content, only it goes at the end. It provides a means of segregating the ending of the target content:

```
<section>
   <p>Fortune and love favor the brave.</p>
   <footer>Ovid</footer>
</section>
```

<ARTICLE>

<article> is often confused with <section> because they both perform a page-level segregation of content. They can also both have <header> and <footer> elements. The big difference between an article and a section is their level of independence. Whereas a <section> is part of its parent element or page, the <article> can be an independently distributable piece of content:

```
<article>
   <h1>March scheduled activities</h1>
   <p>Come in like a lion</p>
   <p>Go out like a lamb</p>
</article>
<article>
   <h1>April schedule activities</h1>
   <p>Bloomin' flowers</p>
</article>
```

This leads to additional confusion, because a page can have multiple sections, each with its own articles. Likewise, a page can have multiple articles with various sections inside each article. In the former case, the articles relate to the section but not to each other. In the latter case, the sections are natural dividing points within each article. Semantically speaking, this makes sense:

```
<section>
   <header>
      <h1>Recipes</h1>
   </header>
   <article>
      <h1>30 minute apple pie</h1>
```

```
      <p>...</p>
   </article>
   <article>
      <header>
         <h1>Herb-braised ham with white wine</h1>
      </header>
      <p>...</p>
   </article>
</section>
```

or

```
<article>
   <header>
      <h1>Quotables</h1>
   </header>
   <section>
      <header>
         <h1>Parenting</h1>
      </header>
      <p>Kids are educated by who the parent is, not what he says.</p>
   </section>
   <section>
      <header>
         <h1>Politics</h1>
      </header>
      <p>A fool and his money are soon elected.</p>
   </section>
<article>
```

A good way to think of the difference between an `<article>` and a `<section>` is to consider *section* as a verb and *article* as a noun. A page can be sectioned, but the sections still comprise the page. Alternatively, a page can have articles, but each article ought to be distributable without the page it was originally placed on.

<ASIDE>

An `<aside>` tag exists inside an article or section element and allows for related information to be presented about the subject matter without disrupting the main content flow. It's a content presentation tag, not a layout tag, so avoid using it as the wrapper for sidebar-style `<menu>` structures.

```
<article>
   <p>All war is deception.</p>
   <aside>Sun Tzu: Chinese General and author (Art of War)</aside>
   <p>Strategy without tactics is the slowest route to victory.</p>
   <p>Tactics without strategy is the noise before defeat.</p>
</article>
```

<DETAILS>

The `<details>` element is interesting in that it has an open attribute. By default, this element and attribute are just grouping elements for content, but when activated using JavaScript or via built-in browser capabilities, they provide an additional function controlling whether they're displayed (open) or hidden (no attribute).

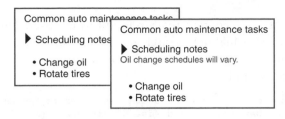

Figure 2.5 The <details> element in both the expanded and contracted modes with <summary> providing a clickable heading (rendered in Chrome)

<SUMMARY>

The <summary> tag is the means of describing a title or heading for a <details> element. It exists inside a <details> element and, in supported browsers, allows you to toggle the open attribute. Unsupported browsers will have to be tested to see exactly how they will render the <summary> tag. Note the rendering of the following code in figure 2.5:

```
<p>Common Auto Maintenance Tasks</p>
<details open="open">
    <summary>Scheduling Notes</summary>
    <em>Oil change schedules will vary.</em>
</details>
<ul>
    <li>Change oil</li>
    <li>Rotate tires</li>
</ul>
```

<FIGURE>

The <figure> tag is used the same way as figures in books, magazines, and technical papers. An image or illustration that provides value to the content is placed within an <article> or <section> to provide additional contextual value:

```
<figure>
    <img src="BlueRidgeMtns.jpg" />
</figure>
```

<FIGCAPTION>

The <figcaption> tag is contained within a <figure> element and provides the caption content for that <figure>. Because a single <figure> element can contain many source images, the <figcaption> can refer to one or more elements inside its parent figure.

```
<figure>
    <img src="skylinedrive.jpg" />
    <figcaption>105 mile road through Shenandoah National Park</figcaption>
</figure>
```

<HGROUP>

The <hgroup> is technically used to group one or more <h1>, <h2>, ... elements and provide only the top level as part of the document outline. This is generally only useful for text-rich websites and CMS systems, so we'll forego any further discussion of it. Note also that <hgroup> may be removed entirely from the HTML5 spec, so use it sparingly, if at all.

<MARK>

<mark> tags surround text in the page content that's relevant to the user. The most common use of the <mark> tag is to highlight search results in a piece of content. <mark> is different from <em> in that it provides a notation of user relevance, not just contextual emphasis by the original author:

```
<p><mark>Wimbledon</mark> is a district in the south west area of London,
    England, located south of Wandsworth, and east of Kingston upon Thames.
    It is situated within Greater London. It is home to the
    <mark>Wimbledon</mark> Tennis Championships and New <mark>Wimbledon
    </mark> Theatre, and contains <mark>Wimbledon</mark> Common.</p>
```

<NAV>

The <nav> tag is a wrapper for the primary navigation elements on your page. <nav> can contain any other element; it's simply a means of grouping the important parts of your page or site navigation in one place. Not every link or menu structure needs to be located in a <nav>, but it's helpful for what you consider the important navigation paths to be contained in a <nav>.

```
<nav>
    <ul>
        <li><a>Home</a></li>
        <li><a>Back</a></li>
        <li><a>Next</a></li>
    </ul>
</nav>
```

PAGE CONSTRUCTION WITH SEMANTIC CONTENT TAGS

Figure 2.6 displays a couple of basic examples of how a page might be structured using semantic tags. Notice that some of the articles can contain sections or the sections can contain articles. This is based on the purpose of the content. Also, you can

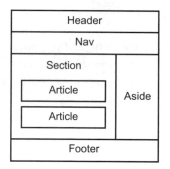

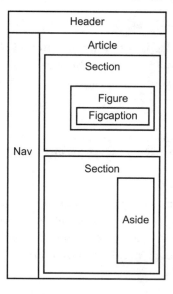

Figure 2.6 When you use semantic tags to structure a page, you can clearly see where content should go and which elements support the primary purpose of the content and which are used to support the site functionality in a more general way.

see that an aside can be placed outside of the section or article data or be nested all the way in, right alongside the content. Any way you slice it, the function of the site and the purpose of the content can be easily ascertained.

2.3.2 Going beyond semantics with application tags

Application tags can present information to the user that is dynamically generated as a result of executing application code. They're also useful in presenting graphical data, as in the case of the <canvas>, or as a data source for other elements, as in the case of the <datalist>.

<CANVAS>

<canvas> is both a tag and a complete drawing API. You can draw pretty much anything you like in a <canvas> as well as style the element itself using normal properties. <canvas> can build images on the fly or allow your users the ability to incorporate existing graphics into their experience. This is a deep topic, and I recommend that if you want to learn more, you check out any of the numerous blogs and books on the subject.

The tag looks simple enough, but it's the entrance point to a significant API. Here is all you need to create a canvas:

```
<canvas />
```

> **SVG and Canvas**
>
> There are two ways of presenting custom imaging content to the user. The first is Scalable Vector Graphics (SVG). SVG uses markup to describe lines and shapes. It's useful for drawing 3D images or very complex illustrations. There has even been some work using SVG to animate drawings. Check out http://www.ro.me for some amazing work in this area.
>
> The second type of drawing uses the <canvas> element, new in HTML5. The canvas element starts out as a blank, stylable rectangle on your page and comes to life by means of JavaScript calls to the canvas's built-in context object.
>
> Both SVG and Canvas are deeply entertaining topics, but only Canvas falls under the HTML5 umbrella. For that reason, we'll spend all of chapter 4 discussing it but we won't be covering SVG.

<COMMAND>

The <command> tag, when placed inside a <menu> element, will define a hook to execute your code. <command> elements can have a type value of checkbox, radio, or command, with the last type providing a normal button-style operation.

```
<menu>
    <command type="command">Save all documents</command>
    <command type="checkbox">Check to include current document</command>
</menu>
```

<DATALIST>

<datalist> is a hidden tag on your page that provides a list of values for another element. When assigning an <input> element to a list attribute, it gets the id that corresponds to the <datalist> to validate its values against. The validation process is your responsibility, although the browser may soon provide you with some help in this regard.

```
<input type="text" name="autos" list="mfg">
<datalist list="mfg">
    <option value="Ford" />
    <option value="Toyota" />
    <option value="Ferrari" />
</datalist>
```

<KEYGEN>

<keygen> is a major step toward client-initiated authentication in HTML. When implemented by the browser, this element will generate a public/private key pair and send the public key to the server with the enclosing form. At the time of this writing, <keygen> is incomplete, but keep it in mind, because when it's finalized, it will be an important part of your security architecture:

```
<keygen name="myformKey" form="newUserInput" />
```

<PROGRESS>

The <progress> tag gives you a quick way to show the percentage of progress of any task. It contains only two required attributes: value and max. The minimum value is 0 and is not editable, which makes this tag not suitable for displaying measurement values or scalar values in a range. The <meter> tag would be more appropriate for those situations:

```
<progress max="120" value="90"></progress>
```

<METER>

The <meter> tag is similar to the <progress> tag in presentation and function, but it has the ability to show an amount in a scale that starts from a non-zero value. Do this by filling in the min and max attributes for the range and the value attribute:

```
<meter min="25" max="75" value="60"></meter>
```

The <progress> and <meter> tags both usually render as a simple status bar.

<TIME>

The <time> tag isn't a means of formatting a time value but rather a means of stating that a piece of content is a date, time, or date/time for purposes of semantic clarity. The <time> tag either contains a date/time value or it can enhance a piece of content that represents a date/time. Build this enhancement with the datetime attribute:

```
<p>The Gettysburg Address, given on <time>November 19, 1863</time> started
    with the words <time datetime="July 1776">Four score and seven years
    ago</time> our fathers brought forth...</p>
```

2.3.3   *Using media tags for audio and video content*

Media tags are covered in chapter 3 and are limited to audio and video content. Elements rendered with media tags can have multiple levels of fallback content so that a single piece of media content is presentable across a variety of browser platforms. These tags render presentation elements that can't necessarily be categorized as either inline or block.

To present audio or video content, you must have that content available via a URL on your server. Cross-domain access of audio and video content is possible, but the owner of the site where the content exists must enable it.

Once you have a valid URL for the content, you just need to add the tag to your page and the user should be able to access it:

```
<audio src="MarineCorpsHymm.mp3" controls autoplay loop />
<video src="DirtyHarry.mp4" controls height="200px" width="400px" />
```

<SOURCE>

A `<source>` tag defines a piece of media content within a media element. It contains a `src` attribute as well as a `type` attribute that corresponds to its media type. (Media types are the correct nomenclature for what are commonly referred to as mime types.)

```
<source src="Chrome.mp3" type="audio/mpeg"></source>
```

<AUDIO>

The `<audio>` tag represents audio content on a page. An `src` attribute can be set or you can place multiple `<source>` elements inside the tag, along with old-school `<object>` tags for injecting plugin players when the browser doesn't support the formats specified in the source elements. Whether the audio content is provided as static or streaming content is dependent on how your server is configured:

```
<audio>
    <source src="CountryBoy.mp3" type="audio/mpeg" />
    <source src="CountryBoy.ogg" type="audio/ogg" />
    <object>Silverlight player here</object>
    Your browser does not support any available audio format.
</audio>
```

Or

```
<audio src="DownOnTheCorner.mp3" type="audio/mpeg" />
```

<VIDEO>

The `<video>` tag performs the same task for video that the `<audio>` tag does for audio content. The same caveats apply regarding video formats and server configuration. The `src` attribute is also present, as is the ability to nest `<source>` and `<object>` elements inside a `<video>` element.

The `<video>` element has some added features, like `loop`, which makes the video automatically restart, and `poster`, which describes the image that should appear before the video starts. `autoplay` is also available:

```
<video controls="controls" autoplay="autoplay" poster="StartImg.jpg">
    <source src="DemolitionMan.mp4" type="video/mp4" />
```

```
        <source src="DemolitionMan.ogg" type="video/ogg" />
        <object></object>
</video>
```

The controls Boolean attribute and the mediagroup attribute of <audio> and <video> are interesting in that they can display to the user a set of controls on the rendered element to allow playback to start, stop, and pause. If the browser is capable, the addition of the controls attribute will show the user a default player. One additional feature of <audio> and <video> is their ability to select from a list of content types and display the one that's most capable, based on the codecs available to the user's browser. You can do this by nesting source elements:

```
<audio controls autoplay>
    <source src="Chrome.mp3" type="audio/mpeg"></source>
    <source src="Chrome.ogg" type="audio/ogg"></source>
</audio>
```

2.4 *Styling HTML5: CSS basics*

You should now have a working knowledge of the new HTML5 elements and know how to use them. Now you need to know how to style these elements when they hit your page. CSS is the proper way to do this.

> **TIP** Although CSS isn't a core HTML or semantic concept, the ability to control how tag structures render on the page is very important. If you already have a basic working knowledge of CSS, feel free to skip this section and move on to chapter 3. This book won't make you a CSS wizard, but we want to make it very clear in this section that the marriage between HTML and CSS is critical in a web application.

By creating a stylesheet file and linking it in the <head> element of your page, your elements will be automatically styled based on your preferences. A stylesheet is nothing more than a text file with a .css extension. Visual Studio has a built-in template for these files, but you can also create them with any text editor.

2.4.1 *Understanding CSS syntax*

A single style consists of a declaration and a body, and a single style statement consists of a name, a colon, and a value. The value can be a string, a space-separated list of values, or an enumerated value, and it terminates with a semicolon. Semicolons separate style statements, and slash-star wrappers mark comments or comment out parts of a style.

Figure 2.7 shows the layout of a basic style.

The body of a style is a list of property/value pairs separated by a colon. Each style property is suffixed with a semicolon, like so:

```
div {
    /* color indicates the text color */
    color: green;
    background-color: red;
}
```

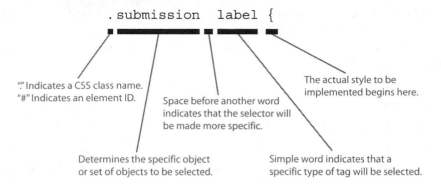

Figure 2.7   The structure of a CSS style declaration

This bit of style will make all `<div>` elements on a page render as red rectangles (`background-color: red`) with green text (`color: green`).

2.4.2   Building selectors, the most critical CSS element

When working with the CSS language, the most important skill you must have is the ability to build a selector. Selectors are blocks of text that begin each style. The layout engine uses them to determine which elements on the page to apply the style to.

Selectors can be very general or very specific, and a selector in your stylesheet may or may not be used at a particular time, depending upon the structure of the page and the specificity of the selector. Not using a style isn't necessarily a bad thing; styles are also applied when the page reflows, so your stylesheet should include styles for any elements you may programmatically add to your page.

Multiple styles can apply to an individual element and, in fact, most elements on your pages will have a number of styles. This is due to the specificity of styles and the fact that elements can be styled based on their tag type, class name, and position on the page. This ability for a style to apply to an element and all contained elements, or for a style to combine with another style or override one of its settings, is the *cascading* effect that makes Cascading Style Sheets so interesting and, at times, frustrating.

THE UNIVERSAL SELECTOR

You may have a universal selector in your stylesheet that says to apply a particular style to everything. This is the format for a universal selector:

```
* { ... }
```

Notice that the style is a little different than the style listed previously for a `<div>` element. The CSS language doesn't consider line feeds or whitespace when processing styles.

TYPE AND DESCENDENT SELECTORS

The next two ways to apply styles to an element are the type and descendent selectors. The type selector uses the name of the element to apply a style, whereas the descendant selector uses multiple names to find an element based on its child relationship to another type of element.

The type selector has two variations. Here's the simple version that selects every instance of a single element type:

```
div { ... }
```

The second version provides a comma-delimited list of element types that performs the same task with multiple different element types:

```
div, section { ... }
```

The descendant selector looks similar to the multi-type selector, but there is no comma between the types. The following will apply its styling to every `<span>` element that exists anywhere inside a `<div>` element on the page:

```
div span { ... }
```

When you want to find a very specific element, you can search for it via a specific `id` or a specific `class` attribute. You use a hash (#) notation before the type to look for the `id` definition, or use a dot (.) to look for a `class` name. This is also possible in conjunction with other selector methods, like element types and child selectors, as shown in the next listing.

Listing 2.7   Various type, descendent, id, and class selector combinations

```
#logo { ... }                                    ◁───  Applies to any element
                                                        with id of logo

.menuSelect { ... }      ◁───  Applies to any element
                               assigned class of menuSelect

div#logoArea { ... }                                  ◁───  Applies to any div
                                                             with id of logoArea
div.userName { ... }              ◁───  Applies to any div assigned
                                        class of userName

div.userName span { ... }              ◁───  Applies to any span inside div
                                             where div has class of userName
div#inputArea a { ... }    ◁───  Applies to any anchor
                                 inside div element where
                                 div has id of inputArea
```

That should give you a good understanding of a large majority of the styles you'll encounter in your work. There is much more to this, and we recommend looking into any book by Eric A. Meyer, one of the foremost CSS professionals in the field today.

2.4.3   Assigning fonts

Fonts assigned in CSS can be a little tricky. Similar to properties like margin and color, fonts can be assigned to a style using a shorthand combined property value or broken out into multiple separate properties.

To use the shorthand, you use the following spaced-delimited properties in order: `style variant weight size family`. A typical font assignment could look like this:

```
p {
    font: italic normal bold 12pt 'Times New Roman',Times,serif;
}
```

The only values required in the combined definition are size and family; the other values will be defaulted if not assigned.

You probably noticed the comma-delimited string at the end of the preceding property definition. The font-family value is based on fonts available on the client's computer, from the most specific to the least specific. So an assignment of

```
font-family: helvetica, arial, sans-serif;
```

will try first to apply the Helvetica font, then the more generic Arial font, and finally the first sans-serif font it can find.

Custom fonts

You can include your own fonts in your page using the @font-face CSS directive. By using this directive, you can reference a font-face kit installed on your hosting server and have it be automatically available to your pages for browsers that support it.

The steps involved in generating a kit for a font aren't difficult, but they can sometimes incur a cost. Check out Google's web fonts (www.google.com/webfonts) or Font Squirrel (www.fontsquirrel.com/fontface/generator) for more information.

2.4.4 Assigning and manipulating colors

Now let's look at how you can assign colors and manipulate them. There are quite a few ways to express a particular color, and you need to understand these ways in order to handle and work with them.

The easiest approach is to use the set of named colors that are recognized by standard CSS. There are a lot of them, and you can get a list from the w3c website at http://www.w3.org/TR/css3-color/#svg-color. This list gives you the name of each available color and displays it along with its hex and RGB values (more on those next).

You can assign any of the available colors to any CSS property that takes a color. This includes text color, background color, and border properties, among many others.

The primary ways of describing a color in CSS with something other than a named value are hexadecimal, RGB, and HSL. There are many ways to find the values that equate to various colors in the interface. The color picker in figure 2.8 is one of many available in various Windows applications.

HEX COLORS

Hex colors are expressed with a hash symbol (#) at the start and then three sets of hexadecimal (base-16) numbers. The three numbers together make up the Red, Green, and Blue components of a color. A single number in a hex color can express up to 256 different values, so a hex color can effectively express over 16 million colors (256 x 256 x 256).

RGB COLORS

The next method of describing a color is to use the direct Red-Green-Blue numeric values from 0 to 255 in a comma-separated format. You then use the rgb(r, g, b) CSS

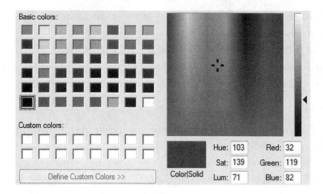

Figure 2.8 **Describing a color with HSL and RGB**

function to assign the color. The values of 0 to 255 express how intense the color is, where 0 has no intensity and is therefore black and 255 has maximum intensity and is therefore white. This means that you can also express an RGB color using percentage values, where each color is assigned an intensity value.

HSL COLORS

The final method of expressing colors is with an HSL value, standing for hue, saturation, and lightness (or luminosity). To understand how HSL works, you must find a color disk that shows all possible colors and has pure red at the top (0 degrees), green at 120 degrees (4 o'clock), and blue at 240 degrees (8 o'clock). Figure 2.9 illustrates this color wheel.

An HSL value specifies first the degrees around the circle and then the saturation (or the intensity) of the color, expressed as a percentage. The final value is the lightness, another percentage where 0 percent is black and 100 percent is white. It might seem a little hard

Figure 2.9 **An HSL color wheel**

to understand, but if you download Paint.NET, a free replacement for Windows Paint, you'll see the color wheel and understand it more clearly.

COLORS WITH ALPHA VALUES

New to the color party lately is the alpha or transparency value in both RGB and HSL colors. These are the RGBA and HSLA CSS functions, and while they appear to have been a part of earlier CSS specifications, they've only recently been broadly supported. The alpha value in the color is expressed as an opacity percentage, where 0 is completely transparent and 1 is completely opaque. Note that setting the opacity CSS property on an HTML element and then assigning it a color with an alpha value makes for a very tricky display, because you have two properties expressing transparency.

2.4.5 *Changing the size of an element with the box model*

Because everything in HTML boils down to a rectangle of stylable content, you can think of it in terms of blocks or boxes. The box model is a way of describing how four different size values in a style can contribute to the size of an element.

Moving from the outside of a rectangular element inward, you'll encounter sized values for margin, border, padding, and content as illustrated in figure 2.10.

When you assign a width value to a piece of content, the actual rendered width of that element on your page will be the value you set, plus left/right padding, plus left/right borders. The final value is the margin, and it doesn't affect the rendered size of your element. The margin is still important to overall layout, though, because it acts as a buffer, "pushing" other content out of the way by the amount assigned in the style.

An experiment is in order here to show exactly what we're talking about. Take a look at the code in the next listing. This code defines a simple style and then adds two <div> tags. The style is set to apply to all <div> elements on the page.

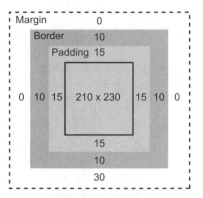

Figure 2.10   The box model of a standard element refers to the accumulated values that affect the rendered size of an element on the page, as well as how it affects other elements around it.

Listing 2.8   A simple box model test creating two divs and a style that applies to both

```
<style type="text/css">
    div {
        height: 50px;
        width: 50px;
        border-width: 10px;
        border-style: solid;
        padding: 5px;
        margin-top: 10px;
        margin-bottom: 20px;
        background-color: #A0A0A0;
        border-color: #000000;
    }
</style>
<div>Box 1</div>
<div>Box 2</div>
```

Height and width of all divs will automatically be set to 50 pixels.

Width of all div borders will be set to 10 pixels.

Padding around content of each div will be 5 pixels.

Top margin of 10 pixels and bottom margin of 20 pixels will be applied to all divs.

This code will render a screen that looks something like figure 2.11.

Now we have to measure each box. If you were to add code to this page to check the height of Box 1 or Box 2, you'd find that each measures exactly 80 pixels. That is to say,

Figure 2.11   How two divs will appear when styled using code from listing 2.8. All measurements in the box model are applied.

```
    50 pixels height
+    5 pixels top padding
+    5 pixels bottom padding
+   10 pixels top border
+   10 pixels bottom border
    ─────
    80 pixels total height
```

NOTE There was a time when the box model in IE was different from all other browsers, which caused no end to headaches, and some hate IE to this day for just that reason. Times have changed, though, and IE now uses the same box model as the others.

If you measure the distance between the edges of each border though, you'll find that you only have 20 pixels of space. How can this be if we have a total top and bottom margin of 30 pixels assigned? The answer lies in the concept of *collapsed margins*, and this is something you'll want to put in the back of your brain for future reference. A collapsed margin is created when two margins intersect. The smallest margin collapses and only the larger one is kept.

You can look up "collapsing margins" on the w3.org website, but here are the rules:

- Margins that intersect will collapse into the largest value among the elements in the group.
- Margins only collapse vertically, never horizontally.
- Margins will collapse only if both elements are block level.
- Margins don't collapse in root-level elements on a page.

That should be all you need to understand how elements are measured on your page and how the various properties that can be applied to elements interact with each other to cause your page to flow.

2.4.6   *Using columns and blocks for layout*

Layout using CSS generally comes down to a question of columns and blocks. How do you create a two- or three-column layout without adding a table to your page and placing all your content inside it? The answer generally lies in the ability of elements to nest inside each other and to float.

A normal `<div>`, you'll recall, is a block-level element and will try to take up the entire width of its container. If you give it a specific width, it will narrow but still not allow elements to either side. With the addition of a CSS property of `float: left` or `float: right` your `<div>` will instantly allow elements to show up beside it. Using this technique, you can stack your block elements side by side.

To get elements to position themselves properly takes some additional work using relative positioning and a good understanding of page flow. We recommend you take a look at a version of the "holy grail" 3-column layout at http://www.alistapart.com/articles/holygrail. This will give you a good understanding of how margins, position, and float properties interact to get CSS to deliver fluid layouts.

Advanced use of CSS to lay out multicolumn pages generally falls into the design realm and isn't really the focus of this chapter or this book. Check out http://www.Smashing-Magazine.com/ and http://www.meyerweb.com/eric/css/ for great design content and helpful tips.

2.4.7 *Changing screen layout based on changing conditions with media queries*

Media queries are often referred to as "@ rules" or "@media rules." Whatever you call them, they're great fun once you understand the concept. They allow you to apply styles to your page based on changing conditions both within the page and outside it, like reorienting a slate device. As the mobile web browser grows in popularity, media queries are gaining in popularity for their simplicity and reliability.

A media query is simply a statement in one of three formats that says "when this condition is met, change these styles." These are the three formats:

- The media attribute of a stylesheet `link` element in a page
- The `@media` statement inside a stylesheet file
- The `@import` statement inside a stylesheet file

Any of these methods is valid and cross-browser compatible. The only difference is in how you decide to break up your presentation styles. Using the `@media` statement inside your stylesheet file will make the stylesheet bigger and harder to manage, but linking to another stylesheet in certain conditions can be difficult to debug.

> **NOTE** All stylesheets are loaded as part of any @ rules assigned within a page, so breaking out your styles into separate stylesheets for different layout options carries a bandwidth cost.

A media query typically starts with a media type (`print` or `screen`) and then applies a property query to that media type. The property value is one of a small number available in the specification. The last value is the DOM property to execute the query against. If you wanted your screen to turn green only when the width was exactly 900 pixels wide, you would write a media query like this:

```
@media screen and (width:900px) {
    body { background-color: green; }
}
```

This is a pretty rigid rule and not a very useful one. Fortunately, there are prefixes available to set a range: `min-` and `max-`. By using these and the two available logical operators, you can start to really play with the layout of your page based on conditions in the browser, without having to write any JavaScript code. This makes your code significantly more maintainable (less code is almost always better), but it can be difficult to unit test, so you may want to keep your rules broader in scope.

The following snippet shows a modified version of the previous rule that will change the screen color when the screen is anywhere from 900 to 2,100 pixels wide:

```
@media screen and (min-width:900px) and (max-width:2100px) {
    body { background-color: green; }
}
```

> This rule adds another parameter and the prefix to specify a value range.

The logical operator not shown is OR, and it's denoted by a comma between the parts of your rule.

Once you have the basic format of a rule down, the format for a linked stylesheet is very simple. The next snippet shows the bit of code you'd use to link another stylesheet when the identical rule from the previous code listing is detected:

```
<link rel="stylesheet"
    media="screen and (min-width:900px) and (max-width:2100px)"
    href="../styles/MediaQueryWide.css" />
```

> Same rule expressed in HTML page rather than stylesheet

You can detect several interface features with media queries, but the ones you'll use most are width, height, device-width, device-height, orientation, aspect-ratio, and device-aspect-ratio. Other detectable features will allow you to get very specific with the color and resolution settings, but these are really beyond the scope of this book.

Quite a few developers find media queries onerous, probably because they have only recently been supported across the entire range of browsers. Changing the entire layout of a screen based on a CSS rule is fine, but detecting that media queries aren't available and then branching your code to handle the environmental change some other way was a massive duplication of effort and a large hole waiting for bugs. Now that media queries are supported across the spectrum of modern browsers, it makes sense to integrate them into your HTML application. This opens up the opportunity for you to divide the presentation even more from the logic of your application.

2.4.8 Adjusting an element's presentation and location with transitions and transformations

Transforms and transitions are generally applied in a method call notation and are the means of adjusting an element's presentation and location. They're available in four major categories: skew, rotate, scale, and translate.

SKEW

When you skew an element, you're changing the relationship between two parallel sides in relation to each other. Think of putting your palms on either cheek and pushing one side of your face up and the other side down. That's a skew, as illustrated in figure 2.12.

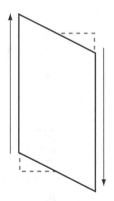

Figure 2.12 Transform skew applied to a rectangular element

ROTATE

Rotating an element using a transform requires you to give a number of degrees within a 360 degree circle around which to rotate the target element. Figure 2.13 shows an element being rotated using a transform.

SCALE

Setting the scale of an element can cause it to grow by applying a percentage value where 1 is 100 percent. Values between 0 and 1 cause the element to shrink, and values greater than 1 will make the element grow. Note that each browser will handle scaling differently and you may encounter pixelation of items if they grow or shrink too much, especially bitmap images. Figure 2.14 illustrates scaling a box up to a larger size.

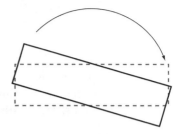

Figure 2.13 Rotate transform applied to a rectangular element

TRANSLATE

A translate transform causes an element to move across the screen a certain distance vertically and horizontally, as illustrated in figure 2.15. Transforms generally don't impact the flow of other elements on the screen, but this isn't guaranteed.

USING CSS3 TRANSFORMS AND TRANSITIONS

As mentioned, the format for calling a transform uses a method call signature:

```
#my_ul li {
    transform: scale(0.75);
}
```

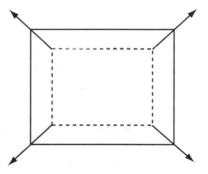

Figure 2.14 Scaling an element to be larger than its specified size

This example shows a scale transform shrinking a list item by 25 percent. The result is immediate on the screen and will incur a reflow of the page.

Regarding the instantaneous effect of a transform, it should be noted that *transitions* are also included alongside many transforms. The transition takes a transform and adds the element of time. Using transitions you can animate elements in your page based on values in your CSS. Like the transforms, you can construct transition style statements in code to make them even more dynamic.

A typical transition, as shown in the following snippet, will cause the hover opacity to take effect in half a second.

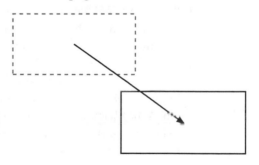

Figure 2.15 Translate transforms cause element locations to change relative to their assigned position.

This gives a nice fade that can be duplicated in jQuery, but using CSS is a little simpler and can be uniformly applied with no code:

```
.myclass {
    transition: opacity .5s ease-in-out;
}
```

Transitions add time element to visual transformation.

```
.myclass:hover {
    opacity: 0.4;
}
```

Transitions take three values: the property to transition, the duration, and the timing function. While a transition can take a number of built-in timing function values for the last parameter value, you can also build your own Bezier functions to apply to your transitions. This leads to some interesting touch-based possibilities.

> **NOTE** One new CSS3 feature that we've intentionally left out is the keyframe animation. This gives you the ability to change the path of an animation beyond a simple A-to-B value. It's currently not widely supported, but when it finally stabilizes, expect it to be the coolest kid on the block.

This leads to the question of which kind of effect to use when animating an element. Do you use a CSS3 implementation or a jQuery one? The answer depends on your scenario. If you're targeting very specific platforms, like the iPad, and you need hardware acceleration, you should consider branching your code to use a WebKit 3D transform/translate combination and then fall back to a more available jQuery animation using JavaScript.

> **WARNING** Some say that you can detect various CSS3 implementations using JavaScript. Although this works much of the time, there are some scenarios where your page won't be pixel-perfect and the browser won't report an error to you. When dealing with advanced CSS3 scenarios, you'll need to visually check all your interfaces for the foreseeable future, because no test frameworks are currently available.

2.4.9 *Changing styles as needed with pseudo-elements and pseudo-classes*

Styles don't have to be static on your page. They can be assigned and removed in code by editing class names, but there's an easier way. CSS defines two ways of editing styles based on detectable conditions: pseudo-classes and pseudo-elements. These are transitory and are applied only while the condition of the selector is met.

A *pseudo-class* for a style is the original style with changes to it based on the named condition. A *pseudo-element* is written in the same way, but it can add new content to the page.

The syntax is the normal selector followed by a colon (:) and then the specific pseudo-class/element name. The most common one that everyone uses is :hover. When assigned to an anchor, anything in the style will be applied to the anchor element when the mouse cursor is inside its boundaries:

```
a:hover { ... }
```

In this case, the style will keep existing properties of the anchor element when the pseudo-class selector doesn't specifically overwrite it.

That was easy, but there are other pseudo-classes/elements that are very handy but seldom used. You should become familiar with them so that you'll recognize them when you see them and can write more effective styles yourself.

The :link, :visited, :active, and :hover pseudo-classes are used primarily for anchors and will apply the styles to anchors that have these properties. The :focus pseudo-class allows you to specify that when a particular element has the focus, it should also get the assigned styles. This is particularly handy in touch-based applications to let the user know where text will be placed. For instance, this pseudo-class can be used to grow the search input box when the user places focus on it.

The next pseudo-classes are used to select ordinal elements within the page. :first-letter and :first-line can give you a great reading experience in your content when used sparingly. They respectively assign styles to the first letter and first line of any element containing text content.

Two important pseudo-elements are :before and :after. They're generally used to place content relative to a selector, which is helpful if you want to allow pages to be edited, such as in a content-management system. By appending the pseudo-element to a selector, you can add additional content to your page to indicate things like the point of insertion of text.

One final pseudo-class that we should discuss is :target. When you use the target pseudo-class, you'll apply the particular style to the href target of the current selector. This means that the href has to be a page-level anchor, one that's prefixed with the hash sign (#) and that refers to an element on the current page. So a link with a :target style of background-color:green assigned would make the target of any link green when the link was clicked.

This is handy, but you should be careful because your entire presentation could change with an on-page navigation event and no traceable code. Check out the presentation by Lea Verou at http://leaverou.me/ft2010 for more great examples of using the :target pseudo-class as well as a lot of other interesting CSS examples.

2.5 Summary

In this chapter we raced through a lot of new and a few old-school features of HTML as an application framework. We reviewed how to lay out a page and how to add semantics to it. We covered some basic styling techniques in CSS and some of the new features in CSS3.

All of this may seem a little overwhelming if you haven't been exposed to these kinds of details before. The normal operation of an ASP.NET website in the past has been to hide much of this from the site's author. Throughout the rest of the book, we'll be investigating the various HTML5 APIs discussed here and including a few tips and tricks for working more fluently with the various CSS and HTML elements that you'll need to know to be productive in building HTML applications.

Now that we've covered the basics of HTML semantic markup and how it integrates with CSS and traditional markup, it's time to get to work on the JavaScript side of the HTML5 equation. To start, we'll look at the audio and video elements in more detail. This will be a good segue, because it involves a lot of markup as well as the building of a simple JavaScript library.

Audio and video controls 3

This chapter covers

- Using audio and video controls with no code
- Integrating JavaScript controls with audio and video
- Simple binding techniques for controlling audio and video
- Understanding audio and video formats

It wasn't so long ago that the only way to play video content was to embed a Quick-Time, Flash, Silverlight, or other custom-installed program inside your HTML page with <object> tags. These elements had very little interactivity with the surrounding page and were, for all intents, islands of media on the page. Audio content was only a little better and, in some cases, worse. When was the last time you visited a page that played a song in the background? From the user's perspective, it's the height of annoyance that you can't do anything with that page other than turn down your computer's volume or navigate away. This chapter will show you how to fix all those problems with HTML5.

HTML5 brings two new tags to the table: <audio> and <video>. Both of these tags implement the same API interface, so while the internal implementations are

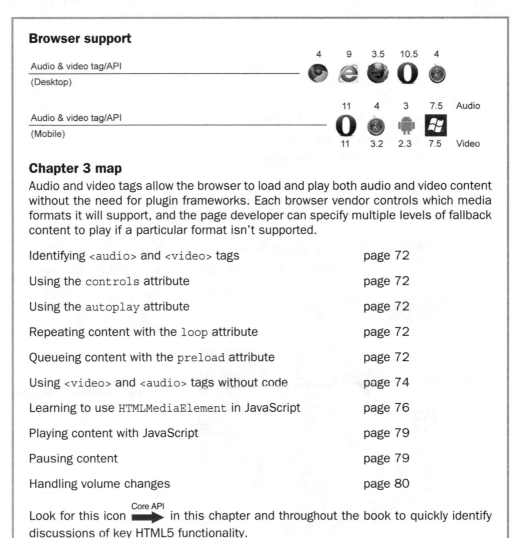

different, the external interfaces are identical. Furthermore, neither tag requires any additional supporting downloads to work in supported browsers. You just add the tag, supply the source content, and your users can see and hear your media. It really is that simple!

You'll also be able to go even farther, as you'll see in this chapter's sample application. This example starts with basic operational features that help you understand how the `<audio>` and `<video>` tags and their JavaScript APIs work, and evolves over the course of the chapter. By the end, it will be able to do the following:

- Download and play audio and video content
- Use HTML objects to control content playback

- Play and pause content using JavaScript
- Change volume and mute media content

When the example is complete, you'll have a working knowledge of the new HTML5 audio and video controls and will be able to start building such content into any existing web application.

As you work through the project, you'll learn how to do several things:

- Use the audio and video tags without JavaScript, as HTML elements
- Control audio and video playback with JavaScript
- Update media types for open source content

Before we get to those topics, let's look at what you'll be building and walk through the steps involved in getting the application started.

3.1 Building a site to play audio and video

Figure 3.1 shows exactly what the site should look like in any compatible browser.

Video: [pause] time: 1.75s

Audio: [pause] time: 111.38s

Volume: [+] [-] [mute] 0.6

Video copyright 2012, Ian Gilman.

Audio by Gennaro's Wax Trio, copyright 2008, BMI, BLZDub Music; used by permission.

Figure 3.1   The sample site will play audio and video content without plugins or extra downloads.

To get started building the application skeleton, perform the following steps:

1 Open Visual Studio and create a new ASP.NET MVC application.
2 Select Internet Application, Razor View Engine, and HTML5 semantic markup.
3 Leave the Create Unit Test check box unchecked.
4 Name the application AudioVideo.
5 When Visual Studio starts, navigate to Tools > Library Package Manager > Manage NuGet Packages for Solution.
6 Select the Installed Packages tab on the left, and then click Manage on the following packages:
   – Entity Framework
   – jQuery UI
   – jQuery Validation
7 When the pop-up window appears, deselect the project and click OK to remove the package from your solution.
8 Select the Updates tab on the left and click the Update button for each package remaining in the center of the window.
9 Open the Razor View file located at \Views\Shared_Layout.cshtml in the solution, and update the script tags at the top to match the newly updated scripts in your solution's Scripts folder.
10 In the menu area, add a new list item:

```
<li>@Html.ActionLink("AV Players", "Players", "Home")</li>
```

This creates a link that points to /Home/Players when the application runs. It won't work yet because that endpoint and its associated view don't exist. That's the next setup step.

11 Navigate to the Controllers folder and open the Home Controller. Add the following snippet of code to create the new endpoint:

```
public ActionResult Players()
{
    return View();
}
```

12 Right-click on the word View, and from the pop-up menu select Add View. This will create a new file called Players.cshtml in the \Views\Home folder of your solution.
13 If you have not done so already, get the audio and video content from the GitHub account and add these four files to your solution's Content folder:
   – gwt.ogg
   – gwt.mp3
   – lego.ogv
   – lego.mp4

The .ogg and .ogv files are open source audio and video formats used for high quality digital media. The format is maintained by the Xiph.org Foundation (http://www.xiph.org/). The .mp3 and .mp4 formats are proprietary but very common.

Finding the audio/video content for the sample application

You can download the audio and video content we use in this chapter from https://github.com/axshon/HTML-5-Ellipse-Tours/tree/master/demos/av/Media.

This GitHub project was originally designed as a monolithic sample application for this book, but we decided that the application-per-chapter paradigm would be more suited to introducing and explaining each HTML5 API in isolation. All the code in this book and some additional content are available in the GitHub repository.

Converting audio and video file formats

There are lots of options for converting your audio and video to Ogg or WebM, but right now the easiest is the free Miro Video Converter (http://www.mirovideoconverter.com/). Once you've installed it, just drag your audio or video file into it and pick a format.

For Ogg video (.ogv), select Theora, an open video format (theora.org). The Theora setting also converts audio files into Ogg audio, but you'll want to change the resulting file extension to .ogg.

Table 3.1 shows the current browser compatibility levels for the .ogg and .ogv formats.

Table 3.1 Open source media format compatibility (.ogg and .ogv)

Browser	Starting version support
Chrome	4
Internet Explorer	Not supported
Firefox	3.5
Opera (desktop)	10.5
Safari (all versions)	Not supported
Opera Mobile	11
Android (all versions)	Not supported
Windows Mobile	Not supported

Now that the application skeleton is in place, we'll look next at the `<audio>` and `<video>` tags and their basic similarities, and at three different ways that you can use the tags in your projects. You'll use one of those ways to build this chapter's sample application.

3.2 *Audio and video tags*

<audio> and <video> tags in HTML5 are similar in that they both implement the
HTMLMediaElement interface. This interface describes all the major functions, properties, and events necessary to play and control multimedia content on the web. You'll
see a few of these events and properties in action later when you build out the
JavaScript side of the player application, but you can get the full story on the W3C site
at http://dev.w3.org/html5/spec/media-elements.html#htmlmediaelement.

The simplest tag that you can implement for rendering audio and video content in
HTML5 plays whatever audio content is in the audio file, as long as it exists in the relative URL specified in the src attribute. It looks like this:

```
<audio src="myaudio.mp3"></audio>
```

The tags become much more powerful when you implement the <source> child tags.
These let you provide multiple formats for your content so it's more likely to be play-
able across different browser platforms. Here's an example:

```
<audio>
    <source src="myaudio.ogg" type="audio/ogg" >
    <source src="myaudio.mp3" type="audio/mp3" >
</audio>
```

The <source> tag is the same for both the <audio> and <video> tags. You just need
to add as many elements as you have available for the specific piece you want the user to
see or hear, and the browser will start from the top and work its way down until it finds
a format that it supports. No checking is done to detect bandwidth, video size, or any
other information about the source media file. If the format is supported, the browser
will use it. End of story.

There is also no concept of "more supported" when it comes to playing source
files. A particular format either is or isn't supported. As you might infer from table 3.1,
there is no format for either audio or video that's universally supported—not even
mp3—so for now you must put on your format-converter hat and translate whatever
you have into formats supported by your target user's browser.

> **NOTE** We decided not to give the full story around which formats are sup-
> ported by which browsers because the format "wars" are still ongoing, with no
> clear winner so far. What is supported on which browser will likely continue
> to change rapidly. Expect to have at least two or three formats for each media
> file you present to your users.

ASSIGNING HTML ATTRIBUTES TO TAGS

Using an audio or video tag as in the previous snippets isn't enough to play your media
content, because you haven't yet assigned the appropriate HTML attributes to the tags to
run the audio content. Audio and video tags can operate in one of three ways:

- Strictly as HTML elements
- Strictly as JavaScript controls
- As a hybrid using both HTML attributes and JavaScript to control playback

In the next few pages, we'll describe the ins and outs of presenting media content using the first method, and then you'll continue building the sample application using the second method.

Because the third (hybrid) method just combines the first two, everything you learn as we proceed should equip you to build out using that method as well. A typical situation where you might use the hybrid method is on a video site that automatically starts playing as soon as content is ready but that allows a user to stop and restart using JavaScript code.

3.2.1   *Using audio and video tags without JavaScript*

Core API

Let's start with the first method: using the tags strictly as HTML elements. You might want to do this when you're building a static site displaying a tutorial or a web page that shows an introductory audio or video clip for a site.

To do this, you can just add the controls attribute to an `<audio>` tag and refresh the page:

```
<audio id="audio" controls>
    <source src="myaudio.ogg" type="audio/ogg" >
    <source src="myaudio.mp3" type="audio/mp3" >
</audio>
```

You should see one of the various audio player formats built into whatever browser you run. The selection of screen shots in figure 3.2 may change over time as browsers are upgraded, but we expect the changes to be minimal.

The other common `<audio>` attributes are listed here; values for each are in the discussion that follows:

```
<audio id="audio"
  controls
  autoplay
  loop
  preload="metadata or none or auto">
```

Let's look at these attributes in a little more detail.

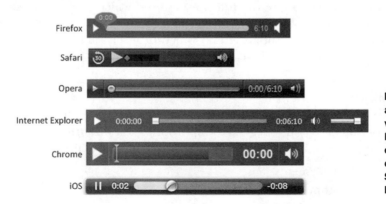

Figure 3.2   **The default audio players for browsers vary in height and width. If layout is a concern, consider creating your own player interface. Section 3.3 shows you how to do that.**

THE CONTROLS ATTRIBUTE

Core API

The controls attribute just needs to be present and doesn't need a value assigned. You may also see it listed as controls="controls", which is the same thing.

The attribute's function, as you saw earlier, is to show the user audio controls. The rendering and function of these are entirely dependent upon what the browser vendor wants to give you. They can be always visible or only visible on hover, depending upon the browser, but this facet of their operation isn't something you as the developer can affect.

THE AUTOPLAY ATTRIBUTE

Core API

The autoplay attribute doesn't need a value set and will start playing the audio content as soon as the element is loaded. This harkens back to the early days of audio content on the internet, when sites would play background music for you while you browsed the site. This is practically never a good idea because it annoys users and uses bandwidth unnecessarily. It does have its place in site design and content presentation, but remember: less is more.

THE LOOP ATTRIBUTE

Core API

The loop attribute will start the audio again after it has completed playing. This can be handy in game development for soundtracks, but again, it can easily be overused. autoplay will continue to play the audio track until the user unloads the page or pauses it. If controls aren't displayed on a track of audio content, and you have loop turned on, you can guarantee that visitors will leave your site as quickly as they can. loop is also an attribute that doesn't need a value set.

THE PRELOAD ATTRIBUTE

Core API

The preload attribute has three possible values: metadata, auto, and none:

- metadata—Requests that the player download enough information about the audio track to show the total length of the track and possibly other information, depending upon the browser vendor's implementation
- none—Tells the browser to download nothing until the user presses the play button
- auto—Attempts to start loading the track as soon as the element is rendered on the page

Keep in mind that these preload settings are *suggestions* for the browser. The browser may choose, for whatever reason, to ignore these settings when downloading audio or video content for the element.

Now that you have a grasp of how a generic HTML5 media tag works, let's spend a moment focusing on the <audio> tag.

3.2.2 *Using the audio tag as an HTML element*

If you worked through the markup in the Players.cshtml page you created in section 3.1, you should have seen the players appear on the page when you ran the application in a browser and, depending upon the attributes you assigned, it may have started playing or been queued up ready to be started by a user.

Forcing audio and video elements to show their controls

There may be times when you land on a page with audio or video controls that has `controls` turned off, and you would like to see them or you want to test your own pages at runtime. If these pages are using the HTML5 tags and jQuery, the easiest way to find the elements and turn controls on is to use the `attr` function:

```
$("#audio").attr("controls", "controls");
$("#video").attr("controls", "controls");
```

This code assumes an audio and video element with IDs of `audio` and `video` respectively, and it will immediately cause the `controls` feature of these elements to be turned on.

The code in the following snippet is a little more detailed and uses the ASP.NET MVC `Url.Content` helper method to build URLs that are relative without parsing HTTP request address strings. Note the order of the `<source>` elements. As mentioned earlier, the browser will always try to play these by starting at the top and working down until it finds a compatible format. It stops there:

```
<audio id="audio">                              ◁── Basic audio tag will give code
                                                    a way to play sounds but
                                                    won't, by default, display.
    <source src="@Url.Content("~/Content/gwt.ogg")"
        type="audio/ogg" >                          Source elements inside media tags
                                                    will attempt to play in order.
    <source src="@Url.Content("~/Content/gwt.mp3")"
        type="audio/mp3" >                          If first source tag is unsupported by
</audio>                                            current browser, next is tried, and so on.
```

Be careful when using the browser default players for `<audio>` content, because they can differ greatly in the amount of space they take up on the page. Take another look at the rendered audio players in figure 3.3 and notice how the Safari player is much narrower and the Internet Explorer player is much wider than Chrome. Any of these could change your page layout if not handled properly.

3.2.3   *Using the video tag as an HTML element*

 Core API

The `<video>` tag in HTML5 is similar to `<audio>` in most of its implementation respects. In fact, anything you can control on an audio track, you can also control on a

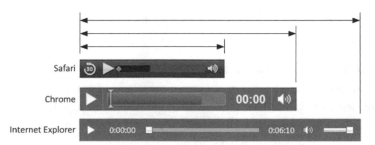

Figure 3.3   The differences between default rendered audio players in various browsers. The Chrome version is the same as the size in most other browsers; Safari and IE fall outside the normal boundaries.

video track. Features, events, and properties are all the same, except that video contains a few more that are inappropriate for audio. With the `<video>` tag, you can assign some additional properties to set the size of the video as well as the image that appears before the video starts to play.

A basic `<video>` tag, like the one in the following snippet, will have source tags nested inside it and use the same format fallback mechanism described earlier. The difference between `<audio>` and `<video>` when rendered is that video will always display unless told not to either in code or by some CSS rule. `<audio>`, on the other hand, won't display if `controls` isn't turned on:

```
<video id="video">
    <source src="@Url.Content("~/Content/lego.ogv")" type="video/ogg" >
    <source src="@Url.Content("~/Content/lego.mp4")" type="video/mp4" >
</video>
```

This code will display the opening frame of the content video but no controls to control the play. One exception to this rule is that some browsers, notably Internet Explorer 9 and above, will allow you to right-click on the video and get a context menu with player controls. These can't be turned on or off, but it's possible in code to override the right-click.

Just like the `<audio>` tag, you can add the `controls`, `autoplay`, `loop`, and `metadata` attributes, and their function is identical. The additional features only available with video are the `height` and `width` attributes, which will constrain the video to a specific rectangle, and the `poster` attribute. `poster` is a URL value that points to a valid image file. The image will be scaled to fit inside the assigned height and width, but the aspect ratio isn't guaranteed to be retained, unlike video content, which will shrink until the correct aspect fits inside the assigned height and width rectangle:

```
<video id="video"
    controls
    autoplay
    loop
    preload="metadata or none or auto"
    poster="@Url.Content("~/Content/VideoPoster.png")">
```

Figure 3.4 shows the default video player controls implemented by the major browsers at the time of this writing. The controls appear inside the boundaries of the video—some push the video content up, some appear over it with a slight transparency effect, but all are rendered at the bottom of the player's rendered area.

Note that the width of the controls will be the same as the width of the player, but the browser vendor can choose any height for the rendered control surfaces. While this is fine for tangential content that isn't necessarily the core purpose of a particular page, the fact is that if you're building the page specifically to present audio or video content, the default players simply won't do. They're visually inconsistent and offer no customization capabilities. Enter the JavaScript APIs.

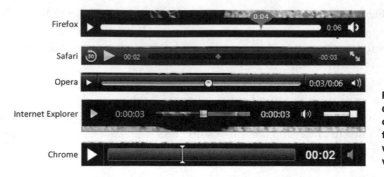

Figure 3.4   The current default video player controls will appear inside the defined height and width properties of the video element.

3.3   *Controlling audio and video playback with JavaScript*

Core API

Using the JavaScript API available for `<audio>` and `<video>` elements, you can control nearly every feature of playback in the client browser. You can also wire up events and properties to any other HTML controls so the presentation is entirely up to the site designer. As mentioned earlier, you can also use the JavaScript APIs to control features of playback while leaving the existing browser-provided controls in place.

Here are some things you can do with these two media elements in code:

- Assign `source` values
- Monitor the state of play
- Get the total duration and current time of the track being played
- Detect and modify the rate of playback
- Assign attributes for loop, autoplay, and controls
- Detect when a track has finished playing
- Turn the volume up or down
- Mute or unmute the volume

As you can see, there are a lot of control features available to you when playing audio and video content, and you're going to use the most common ones in your sample application, such as play/pause, mute/unmute, and volume control. In this section, you'll learn how to use the audio and video APIs as you do the following:

- Build a custom audio and video control surface
- Build the main.js library structure
- Create a JavaScript media player object
- Attach JavaScript to audio and video event models to complete the user's media experience

We'll start with building custom controls.

3.3.1   *Building custom controls for audio and video*

Before you begin, if you've been following along in your solution and fiddling with `<audio>` and `<video>` tag attributes, clear them all out from the Players.cshtml page.

You'll also need to add `id` properties to the tags so that you can easily identify them in code. They should look like this:

```
<audio id="audio">
  <source src="@Url.Content("~/Content/gwt.ogg")" type="audio/ogg" >
  <source src="@Url.Content("~/Content/gwt.mp3")" type="audio/mp3" >
</audio>
<video id="video">
  <source src="@Url.Content("~/Content/lego.ogv")" type="video/ogg" >
  <source src="@Url.Content("~/Content/lego.mp4")" type="video/mp4" >
</video>
```

Next, below the video element add a few standard `<button>`, `<div>`, and `<span>` tags to bind to the control code you'll write shortly. The following listing shows the layout of this markup. These will act as the controlling user interface elements in the final page.

Listing 3.1   Controls for audio and video elements

```
<div id="video-controls">
   Video:
   <button class="play">play</button>        ◁——  Play/pause button
   <span class="time"></span>                       for video content
</div>
<div id="audio-controls">                                   ◁——  Note to show
   Audio:                                                      current time
   <button class="play">play</button>        ◁——  Play/pause button    of video
   <span class="time"></span>                       for audio content
   <div class="secondary-controls">           ◁——  Note to show current
      Volume:                                              time of audio
      <button id="volume-up">+</button>
      <button id="volume-down">-</button>           Volume and mute
      <button id="mute">mute</button>               controls for audio
      <span id="volume"></span>              ◁——  Display for current
   </div>                                              audio volume
</div>
```

Where are all the HTML5 semantic tags?

You may have noticed that in this chapter we're using regular `<div>` and `<span>` tags to organize the structure of our page. We do this in various places throughout the book for a number of reasons.

First, the audio/video content in this chapter is contained in a single page, otherwise known as a single page app (SPA). One of the primary functions of semantic markup is to allow a web crawler, search engine, or accessibility tool to "read" the content of a page, but SPAs generally load content dynamically using JavaScript based on user interaction or other conditions. A web crawler won't execute JavaScript, so it won't be able to load and parse the dynamic content. This makes the semantic tags somewhat useless.

Second, we want to make it abundantly clear throughout the book that while you can use semantic HTML tags right away in all of your web pages and HTML applications, it's optional. The previous (classic HTML) tags are still valid and common throughout the web.

3.3.2   *Building the main.js library structure*

With the controls in place, you can start building the controlling code structures.

Create a new JavaScript library file called main.js in the Scripts folder of your solution and open it. You'll have only three functions in your main.js library, as you can see in the next listing. These will initialize the page, initialize an `audio` or `video` object, and update the volume value on the screen.

Listing 3.2   The basic JavaScript structure of the main.js library

```
$(document).ready(function () {
    Main.init();
});
window.Main = {

    init: function () {
    },

    initMedia: function (name) {
    },

    showVolume: function () {
    }

};
```

Checks for features, creates two objects, and binds volume controls to HTML controls

Takes either "audio" or "video" as parameter and builds player object that's bound to appropriate media element and a few of element's event handlers

Updates volume display on screen

The basic structure here initializes the `Main` object and creates custom objects via `initMedia` to control playback of either audio or video content. Inside the `init` function, you'll test for browser compatibility using Modernizr and then execute the function to create your objects. That code is shown in the following listing.

Listing 3.3   `init` function checks and initializes video and audio elements

```
var self = this;

if (!Modernizr.audio) {
    alert("Audio tag not supported.");
    return;
}

if (!Modernizr.video) {
    alert("Video tag not supported.");
}

this.video = this.initMedia("video");
this.audio = this.initMedia("audio");
```

Checks for audio and video support

Creates audio and video objects and attaches them to Main object

Modernizr checks for audio and video compatibility. Then this code adds two properties to the `Main` object created earlier using `window.Main = {...}`. The properties (`video` and `audio`) are created with the `initMedia` function. Read on to see how and why.

3.3.3 Creating a JavaScript media player object

This `initMedia` function is a great example of how you can reduce the volume of code you write and improve maintainability. In this function, you'll find various elements in the interface, the most important of which is either the rendered `<audio>` or `<video>` element. You then treat that element not as a piece of audio or video content, but as a piece of generic content. You can do this because both tags implement the `HTMLMedia-Element` interface.

To start, look at the next listing very carefully. It's the first part of `initMedia`. There's a lot of locating of elements and assigning of variables going on here.

Listing 3.4 The `initMedia` function assigning properties for a new object

```
var result = {};
result.$media = $("#" + name);
result.media = result.$media[0];

result.$controls = $("#" + name + "-controls");

result.$play = result.$controls.find(".play");
result.$time = result.$controls.find(".time");
```

Find media element with jQuery and pull actual media element from wrapped set.

Find controls `<div>` based on concatenated naming convention.

With controls `<div>` find play button and time `<span>` element.

Core API

Notice that you have `$media`, `$controls`, `$play`, and `$time` all as wrapped sets from jQuery selectors, plus the `media` element that corresponds to either the `<audio>` or `<video>` element based on the input parameter (`name`) value. Why go through all these gyrations? Because a wrapped set will give you all the normal jQuery functionality you need to bind to events, change assigned CSS attributes, and update text values, but it won't give you the ability to call functions on individual API objects. For that, you must have a single object, not a wrapped set.

The next bit of code in the `initMedia` function shows the process of getting a wrapped set and then using the object (not the wrapped set) to execute functions:

```
result.$play.click(function () {
    if (result.media.paused)
        result.media.play();
    else
        result.media.pause();
});
```

Use wrapped set to bind to click event.

You must have single object to check properties like paused or execute functions like play.

Core API

You've just implemented the `click` handler for the `$play` button, so the media (audio or video) will play, but you still have to bind to the various other player events so that you can pause the media and track what's happening while it plays. You can use the `$media` wrapped set for this because you aren't executing specific functions.

Listing 3.5 shows how to bind to the `playing`, `pause`, `ended`, and `timeupdate` events. Again, each time you have to call into a specific function or property of the `HTMLMediaElement` API, either audio or video, you make the call against the `media` local property. This is the last part of the `initMedia` function.

Listing 3.5 Binding events to the media object in the `initMedia` function

```
result.$media
    .bind("playing", function () {
        result.$play.text("pause");
    })
    .bind("pause", function () {
        result.$play.text("play");
    })
    .bind("ended", function () {
        result.media.play();
    })
    .bind("timeupdate", function () {
        var prettyTime =
            Math.round(result.media.currentTime * 100) / 100;
        result.$time.text("time: " + prettyTime + "s");
    });
result.media.play();
return result;
```

Fires when media
element content begins

Fires when
content is paused

Fires when content has finished
playing and before loop restarts

Fires on interval as
media is played

Starts playing
immediately after
binding UI elements
to media events

Returns newly created media object

There's a lot of interplay here with the audio and video elements, the controls on the page, and the `Main` object's various properties. To reiterate, the secret sauce that makes this event binding with jQuery wrapped sets work is the fact that audio and video elements implement the `HTMLMediaElement` interface, making them generally function the same way as each other but with different output to the browser. Figure 3.5 shows the various wrapped sets and properties that you established in your code and how they all play together in the `window.Main` object.

Coming full circle to the object you created in `initMedia`, you first instance an object variable called `result` and then bind a bunch of jQuery wrapped sets and a media object to it. Then you bind the various media events to create a responsive interface. Finally, you start the media content playing and then return the object to the caller, which in this case is the `init` function. It seems complicated, but you're really just setting up the interface and playing the media.

3.3.4 *Completing the media experience by adding volume controls*

Back in the `init` function, you have this code, which should make a lot more sense now:

```
this.video = this.initMedia("video");
this.audio = this.initMedia("audio");
```

 Core API

You're assigning a variable called `video` and one called `audio` to new objects created in the `initMedia` function. These objects take care of everything related to play, pause, loop, and content timer functionality. The only bits left to fill in are those pieces specific to the audio track.

Because the example video track you're using doesn't happen to have audio, your code must diverge from doing work inside the `initMedia` function. If you wanted to

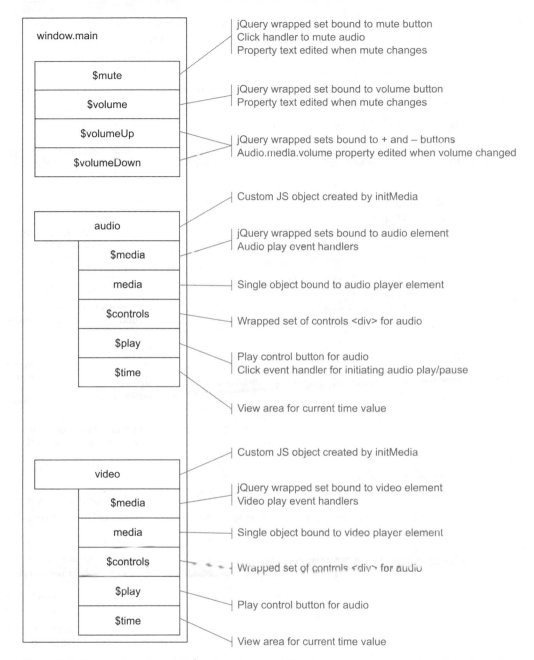

Figure 3.5   Due to the polymorphic[1] nature of `HTMLMediaElement`, you can create both audio and video objects in the same function. Volume control is separated in these objects because it's only being controlled when playing audio content in this example. Therefore, it doesn't need to be part of the polymorphic object.

---

[1] For more on polymorphism and encapsulation, see http://en.wikipedia.org/wiki/Polymorphic_code.

add volume controls to video as well as audio, you could have performed this work inside initMedia, but for this example we'll have you put it inside init so that the volume HTML elements only bind to the audio control. You can, however, still use the audio object you created.

The next listing shows the binding of controls for turning volume up and down and muting the audio, along with a simple binding statement to track the volume-change event. This code fills in the init function of the main object.

Listing 3.6 init function binding UI events to the media object created in initMedia

```
this.$volume = $("#volume");

this.$volumeUp = $("#volume-up")
   .click(function () {
      self.audio.media.muted = false;          Ensure mute is turned off
      self.audio.media.volume += 0.1;          and add 10% to volume.
   });

this.$volumeDown = $("#volume-down")
   .click(function () {
      self.audio.media.muted = false;          Ensure mute is turned off and
      self.audio.media.volume -= 0.1;          subtract 10% from current volume.
   });

this.$mute = $("#mute")
   .click(function () {                              Toggle muted
      self.audio.media.muted = !self.audio.media.muted;    Boolean property.
   });

this.audio.$media
   .bind("volumechange", function () {          Track audio control's volume change
      self.showVolume();                        event to show current volume.
   });

this.showVolume();
```

The final step to getting your application to run is to fill in the showVolume function as shown in the next listing. This will simply round the volume off to the nearest tenth (0.1) value and display it on the page.

Listing 3.7 showVolume function to update volume information on the page

```
var prettyVolume =                                   Round off volume
   Math.round(this.audio.media.volume * 10) / 10;    to nearest tenth
if (this.audio.media.muted) {                     Check muted property
   prettyVolume = 0;                              of audio control
   this.$mute.text("unmute");
}                                       Assign text to $mute
else {                                  element based on
   this.$mute.text("mute");            current mute setting
}
this.$volume.text(prettyVolume);                     Display volume
                                                     on page
```

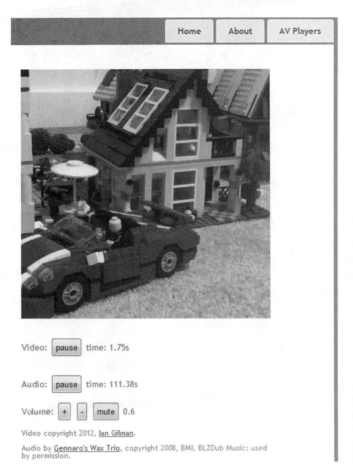

Video: pause time: 1.75s

Audio: pause time: 111.38s

Volume: + - mute 0.6

Video copyright 2012, Ian Gilman.

Audio by Gennaro's Wax Trio, copyright 2008, BMI, BLZDub Music; used by permission.

Figure 3.6　The completed application playing audio and video content, controlled by your own JavaScript and HTML elements

You should be able to run your application in Chrome, Internet Explorer, and Safari and see everything running. Load the Players page, and the music and video should immediately start playing, as shown in figure 3.6.

3.4　Updating media types for open source content

We specifically left out Opera and Firefox in our list of browsers that will work as-is in the Visual Studio solution. These browsers are perfectly compatible with HTML5 <audio> and <video> tags, but when the page is running in your local environment, you may need to make a few tweaks. These tweaks are related to the open source content types, not to any specific server compatibility. Opera and Firefox support the .ogv and .ogg file types by default, so you have to tell the local web server that these are OK to send out.

This section will cover the changes you need to make to the project.

USING IIS EXPRESS

The first thing you need to do is update your solution so that it uses IIS Express. You could push this all the way into an IIS Server instance, but that's really not necessary for your tests and would generally be the job of a network administration person anyway. To update your AudioVideo project, follow these steps:

1   Right-click on your AudioVideo project node in Solution Explorer and select Properties.
2   Click on the Web tab on the left side; you should see a screen similar to figure 3.7.
3   About halfway down the page, in the Servers section of the page, select Use Local IIS Web Server and then check Use IIS Express. You can leave the default Project URL as is. (If you need more information about installing IIS Express, please refer to appendix C.)

ASSIGNING CONTENT TYPES

Now that you have set up the solution to run under IIS Express, you can assign the .ogg and .ogv content types for the local server. Currently, this can only be done using the appcmd executable when running IIS Express. Appcmd is a utility program that can be used for editing a number of configuration values, but updating the available content types is the only change we're after.

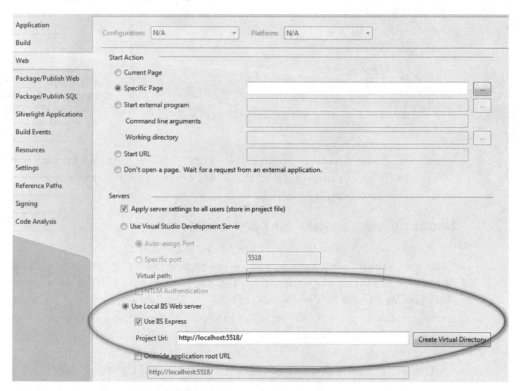

Figure 3.7   Set up the application to run using the local IIS Express instance.

Figure 3.8 The appcmd utility program can add the proper content types to the local IIS Express instance. This setting will then work across all applications that use IIS Express on the local machine.

Follow these steps:

1 Open a command prompt as an administrator.
2 Navigate to either the Program Files or Program Files (x86) folder.
3 Navigate into the IIS Express folder.
4 Run the following command to update the .ogg content type:

```
appcmd set config /section:staticContent
    /+[fileExtension='.ogg',mimeType='audio/ogg']
```

5 Run the following command to update the .ogv content type:

```
appcmd set config /section:staticContent
    /+[fileExtension='.ogv',mimeType='video/ogv']
```

You should see a screen similar to figure 3.8 in the command-line window.

Run your program now using any browser you like, and you should get an identical experience! You're playing audio and video content with no plugins and with very little extraneous code. This is a huge leap forward from what was available just a couple of years ago, and it's only the beginning of what will probably be available in the coming years, as formats and specifications stabilize.

3.5 Summary

Streaming audio and video content may be the core of what you want to accomplish with your website or HTML application, or it may add the final touch of interactivity, interest, and professionalism to your site. Regardless of your reasons for using the <audio> and <video> tags, their current compatibility levels point new applications toward a plugin-free experience, with Flash or Silverlight only being necessary as a fallback until the older browsers die off. The sample application in this chapter gives you a solid foundation to continue building upon. Finding a specific portion of the content using the seek function and monitoring the caching process with various events are some possible directions you could look in for additional studies.

In the next chapter, we'll dig into the basics of drawing on the web using the HTML5 Canvas API. This will be a deeper topic on the JavaScript front, and the project in that chapter should be a really fun way to start learning the correlation between markup and code.

3.6   *Complete code listings*

The following code is provided to let you check your work or build the project from scratch if you haven't been building along.

Listing 3.8   The complete Players.cshtml code

```
@{ ViewBag.Title = "Players"; }
<div id="content">
    <audio id="audio">
        <source src="@Url.Content("~/Content/gwt.ogg")" type="audio/ogg" >
        <source src="@Url.Content("~/Content/gwt.mp3")" type="audio/mp3" >
    </audio>
    <video id="video">
        <source src="@Url.Content("~/Content/lego.ogv")" type="video/ogg" >
        <source src="@Url.Content("~/Content/lego.mp4")" type="video/mp4" >
    </video>
    <div id="video-controls">
        Video:
        <button class="play">play</button>
        <span class="time"></span>
    </div>
    <div id="audio-controls">
        Audio:
        <button class="play">play</button>
        <span class="time"></span>
        <div class="secondary-controls">
            Volume:
            <button id="volume-up">+</button>
            <button id="volume-down">-</button>
            <button id="mute">mute</button>
            <span id="volume"></span>
        </div>
    </div>
    <div id="avfooter">
        <p>Video copyright 2012,
            <a href="http://iangilman.com">Ian Gilman</a>.</p>
        <p>Audio by <a href="http://gwaxtrio.bandcamp.com">
            Gennaro's Wax Trio</a>, copyright 2008, BMI, BLZDub Music;
            used by permission.</p>
    </div>
</div>
<script src="@Url.Content("~/Scripts/main.js")"
    type="text/javascript"></script>
```

Listing 3.9   The complete code listing for main.js

```
$(document).ready(function () {
  Main.init();
});

window.Main = {

  //-----------------
  init: function () {
    var self = this;

    if (!Modernizr.audio) {
      alert("Audio tag not supported.");
      return;
    }

    if (!Modernizr.video) {
      alert("Video tag not supported.");
    }

    this.video = this.initMedia("video");
    this.audio = this.initMedia("audio");

    this.$volume = $("#volume");

    this.$volumeUp = $("#volume-up")
      .click(function () {
        self.audio.media.muted = false;
        self.audio.media.volume += 0.1;
      });

    this.$volumeDown = $("#volume-down")
      .click(function () {
        self.audio.media.muted = false;
        self.audio.media.volume -= 0.1;
      });

    this.$mute = $("#mute")
      .click(function () {
        self.audio.media.muted = !self.audio.media.muted;
      });

    this.audio.$media
      .bind("volumechange", function () {
        self.showVolume();
      });

    this.showVolume();
  },

  //-----------------
  initMedia: function (name) {
    var result = {};
    result.$media = $("#" + name);
    result.media = result.$media[0];
    result.$controls = $("#" + name + "-controls");
    result.$play = result.$controls.find(".play");
    result.$time = result.$controls.find(".time");
```

```
    result.$play.click(function () {
      if (result.media.paused)
        result.media.play();
      else
        result.media.pause();
    });

    result.$media
      .bind("playing", function () {
        result.$play.text("pause");
      })
      .bind("pause", function () {
        result.$play.text("play");
      })
      .bind("ended", function () {
        result.media.play();
      })
      .bind("timeupdate", function () {
        var prettyTime =
          Math.round(result.media.currentTime * 100) / 100;
        result.$time.text("time: " + prettyTime + "s");
      });

    result.media.play();
    return result;
  },

  //-----------------
  showVolume: function () {
    var prettyVolume =
      Math.round(this.audio.media.volume * 10) / 10;
    if (this.audio.media.muted) {
      prettyVolume = 0;
      this.$mute.text("unmute");
    }
    else {
      this.$mute.text("mute");
    }
    this.$volume.text(prettyVolume);
  }
};
```

Listing 3.10   Styles added to site.css to support audio/video formatting

```
/*--- audio/video ----*/

#content {
  width: 100%;
  max-width: 400px;
  margin: 10px auto;
}

#video {
  width: 400px;
  height: 400px;
}
```

```css
#audio {
   display: block;
}

button {
  padding: 5px;
}

#video-controls {
  margin-top: 25px;
}

#audio-controls {
  margin-top: 25px;
}

.secondary-controls {
  margin-top: 10px;
}

#avfooter {
  margin-top: 50px;
  font-size: 12px;
  color: #888;
}

#avfooter a,
#avfooter a:visited {
  color: #555;
}
```

Canvas

This chapter covers

- Building graphics into web applications using HTML Canvas
- Working with text, lines, shapes, and images on Canvas
- Animating elements in Canvas

The Canvas API is new in HTML5, and it provides a means of drawing bitmap-based images inside the browser. Canvas has received a lot of media and developer attention because it is, in fact, a blank canvas upon which anyone can draw practically any visual element. In addition, because the canvas element is an HTML element like any other, it can be addressed in JavaScript as a regular element and participate in page flow and styling. Games are currently the most common use for Canvas, but any kind of image editing or drawing program could also be built using this API.

Ensuring cohesion between your page and a canvas element isn't exactly a stroll down Easy Street though. Drawing on the canvas is only possible using JavaScript, and canvas styling is only available for the entire element, not the pixels you draw onto it, which means that your meticulously designed CSS will have no effect on presentation inside a <canvas> element. In other words, if your site uses Canvas to

Browser support

Chapter 4 map

Canvas is a drawing surface that can be used to create and display bitmap images inside the browser. JavaScript is used to manipulate aspects of the drawing and can also be used to retrieve data about the current image. Forms in a canvas can be described using shapes, lines, pixels, or external image files.

present islands of content rather than as a full-screen presentation tool, you'll have to replicate the styling you created in CSS using JavaScript.

Even with these minor setbacks, though, the speed of graphics manipulation and code execution in modern browsers has opened up new doors to those intrepid souls who have started developing games using the HTML5 Canvas. This is an area that's bound to grow very rapidly.

But Canvas isn't just for games. With Canvas you can also build graphing solutions, edit and compose images, and build powerful visualizations and animations to provide punch and clarity to business data. The sample application you'll build in this chapter—an animated browser screensaver—will consist of a single canvas on the page and a single JavaScript library to do the drawing. As you build it, you'll learn what you need to know to start working with Canvas, such as the following:

- The Canvas drawing context—what it is and how to reference it
- How to draw lines, shapes, and pixels using the Canvas coordinate system
- How to move from one position to another when drawing objects
- How to manipulate images on the client using Canvas
- How to write text on the canvas
- How to animate and add special effects to your creations

When you're done, you'll have an animated browser screensaver, a glimpse of which appears in figure 4.1, that will amaze and thrill your friends!

It will have a number of effects that old-school Windows users will remember from the days of ribbon and spotlight screensavers, but with the new bells and whistles that Canvas enables. You'll also have ample knowledge to start building your own Canvas-based HTML5 applications from scratch.

Figure 4.1   The finished sample Canvas application with animation, image, and text effects

First up, let's lay the foundation for the application and look at the basics you'll need to get any Canvas application up and running in no time.

4.1   *Canvas quick-start*

The fundamental thing that you need to know about working with Canvas in a web page is that it's just what its name implies: a drawing canvas. You can draw whatever you like on it using the various helpers in the API, and you can overwrite bits and pieces as often as necessary. You draw using pixel coordinates and by telling the API what kind of drawing to perform (such as lines, shapes, and gradients). Once a pixel is drawn on the canvas, it's there until you make a change that places another pixel in that same location.

In this section, you'll do the following:

- Create the basic site structure for the sample application
- Learn how to use the `<canvas>` tag
- Assign a size to the canvas
- Create the stylesheet for the sample application
- Learn to set and use the `2d` context object
- Create the core of the sample Canvas application

We'll start by creating the site.

4.1.1 Creating the basic Canvas site structure

To get started, you'll need to create an ASP.NET MVC project in Visual Studio called CanvasTest. You won't be using any MVC functionality in the Canvas project, but you'll be building it in a way that demonstrates how a pure client-side HTML5 application can live inside an MVC website. We're doing it this way to show that Canvas can be a completely independent part of a web application and also to present as much information as possible about this rich API.

Follow these steps to get the project going:

1 Select File > New > Project.
2 In the dialog box, select Web on the left side and then an ASP.NET MVC Web application using whatever version of the ASP.NET MVC template you currently have installed.
3 Name your project CanvasTest.
4 Select Internet Application, Razor View engine, and HTML5 semantic markup.
5 Don't select Create a Unit Test Project, and click OK.

Once inside the new project, open the Home subfolder in the Views project folder and double-click the Index.cshtml view. Replace the entire contents with the simple markup in the next listing.

Listing 4.1 The new Home page in your application will have only scripts and a canvas

```
@{ Layout = null; }
<!DOCTYPE html>
<html>
   <head>
      <title>Canvas Demo</title>
      <link href="@Url.Content("~/Content/main.css")"
         rel="stylesheet" type="text/css" />
      <script src="@Url.Content("~/Scripts/jquery-1.7.2.min.js")"
         type="text/javascript"></script>
      <script src="@Url.Content("~/Scripts/modernizr-2.5.3.js")"
         type="text/javascript"></script>
      <script src="@Url.Content("~/Scripts/main.js")"
         type="text/javascript"></script>
   </head>
   <body>
      <canvas id="main"></canvas>
   </body>
</html>
```

In ASP.NET MVC assigning Layout to null equates to simple page with no master page layout.

Stylesheet will add color, margins, and other styles to elements on current page.

Includes installed versions of jQuery and Modernizr.

Application library you'll be filling in shortly.

Only content presentation element on this page is single canvas you'll style to take up full page.

You'll add the JavaScript file and the stylesheet soon. Right now you need to focus on the `<canvas>` tag itself. This element must consist of opening and closing tags; it can't be self-closing. Therefore, the simplest canvas element on a page must be this:

```
<canvas></canvas>
```

Separate opening and closing tags maintain backward compatibility. If a particular browser doesn't support Canvas, the contents of the `<canvas>` tag will display as the fallback presentation. If Canvas support is available, the contents inside the <canvas> tag won't display.

4.1.2   *Assigning size to the canvas*

The next important point that you need to know about any canvas element is how to assign its size. Because it's a normal HTML element, it's possible to assign height and width style settings. You can also use the defined height and width properties to resize the canvas, like this:

```
var el = document.getElementById("myCanvas");
el.width = 200;
el.height = 250;
```

Note that either method—CSS height and width or direct properties (canvas.height and canvas.width)—will change the size of the canvas, but with completely different results. Figure 4.2 shows the differences between changing height and width on the element versus using CSS styles.

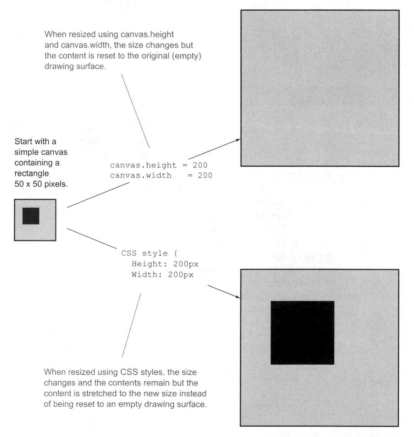

Figure 4.2   Resizing the canvas element on the page can either clear the content or force it to stretch, often blurring or distorting the image. The best way to resize is to use the canvas properties and redraw the image after resizing is completed.

Figure 4.2 also illustrates how important it is to understand where and when your canvas element resizes. If you want your drawing to automatically stretch as the canvas grows, use the CSS height and width settings, but remember that this will also introduce the blurry effect. If you have the image data available to redraw at the new canvas size, assigning the actual height and width properties directly on the canvas will produce better results.

Canvas will participate in the content flow of a page as an inline element, meaning it fills only as much space as it needs without forcing a new line before and after itself. The content that you draw inside the canvas, though, will either scale or be cleared, depending upon the kind of resize you perform.

> **WARNING** The browser won't honor assignment of the direct height and width properties if CSS height or width style properties are applied. The result of that assignment would be a cleared canvas sized to the CSS style specification.

4.1.3 Creating the stylesheet for the sample application

Now it's time to create the stylesheet that you'll be using for the sample application. These styles will be used to ensure that the canvas takes up the full browser display area to enhance the screensaver effect:

1 Create a new stylesheet called main.css in the Content folder of the application.

2 Add the following styles:

```
* {
    margin: 0; padding: 0;
}

html, body {
  position: absolute;
  left: 0; top: 0; right: 0; bottom: 0;
  overflow: hidden; font-family: sans-serif;
}
#main {
    position: absolute; width: 100%; height: 100%;
}
```

These styles will ensure that the <canvas> and <body> elements take up the entire browser space even when resized.

With the structure set up, you can run the application and see a blank page. Inspect the source for that page, and you'll see your canvas element.

The client application for this project is a JavaScript library that will draw and animate all of the content in the finished product. Before you can start to build that application, though, you need to understand the object at the core of the Canvas API, the 2d context.

4.1.4   *Drawing with the 2d context object*

Core API

Before you dive into the code of the Canvas application, you need to understand how to get a JavaScript reference to the drawing API, the actual object that you must use to execute drawing operations with JavaScript. This is a two-step process:

1 Get a reference to the <canvas> element on your page.
2 Find the <canvas> element's context object and create a variable reference to it.

The context object is the actual API that you use to execute drawing functions:

```
var canv = document.getElementById("myCanvas");
var ctx = canv.getContext("2d");
```

Both of these steps will happen together in nearly every piece of code you see because once you reference your <canvas> element, you have very limited options for what you can do. With the exception of setting height or width, you must get a reference to the context object before any drawing operations can begin.

Getting a reference to the context with jQuery is just as simple, as long as you remember that you're working with wrapped sets and not individual elements:

```
var elemCanvas = $("#myCanvas");
var context = elemCanvas[0].getContext("2d");
```

This snippet gets a jQuery wrapped set corresponding to the <canvas> element and then uses the first object in the set to get the drawing API reference, which is the hook used for all the drawing API methods.

The only Canvas functions that aren't available from the context are the previously mentioned height and width property settings. All the rest of the functionality you'll use executes via the context.

What about 3D?

The standard means of operating on an HTML5 canvas element in code is by means of the 2d context object. This would seem to imply that a 3d context also exists, or at least is in the works. In fact, the 2d context was specified for just that reason.

Since its release though, browser vendors have worked toward the adoption of WebGL, a graphics API specifically for 3D development. WebGL currently has narrow (but growing) support, but we won't cover it as part of the HTML5 specification.

4.1.5   *Building the foundation object of the Canvas application*

Armed with an understanding of what the context object is, its purpose, and how to get a reference to it, you're now ready to start working on the sample application.

In your solution, right-click in the Scripts folder and select Add > New Item > jScript (or JavaScript) file. Name the file main.js and open it.

NOTE We'll be using the `document.ready` event handler to contain the code for the Canvas application. Later chapters will use a separate object to handle execution logic, but that's unnecessary here because there's no direct user interaction after the page loads.

The code in the following listing, which resizes the canvas and adds placeholders for later work, goes into the main.js file. If you prefer to read the entire code listing in one shot, it's included at the end of this chapter.

Listing 4.2   A beginning ready handler in the main.js file

```
$(document).ready(function () {
    if (!Modernizr.canvas) {
        alert("This browser does not support the canvas tag.");
        return;
    }
    var $canvas = $("#main");
    var context = $canvas[0].getContext("2d");
    var w;
    var h;
    var maxVelocity = 10;
    var points = [];
    var radians = 0;
    var segments = 3;
    var pointsCount = 15;

    // Image preparation placeholder

    function resize() {
        w = $canvas.width();
        h = $canvas.height();
        $canvas.attr("width", w);
        $canvas.attr("height", h);
        // Resize function body placeholder
    }
    $(window).resize(resize);
    resize();

    // Randomizer placeholder

    function frame() {
        // Frame function body placeholder
    }
    frame();
});
```

Use Modernizr to check for canvas compatibility.

Set up local variables that reference canvas element and 2d context.

Height and width elements are used for drawing on surface.

Velocity, points, and radians are variables used to draw lines and change directions.

Resize function is used to re-initialize local variables when window size changes.

Bind document's resize event to resize function and immediately call it.

Real work of drawing will be done in frame function.

That's all the code you need to get started. The next step is to draw simple elements onto the canvas surface.

4.2   Creating and manipulating shapes, lines, images, and text

The Canvas API gives you the ability to draw simple lines, rectangles, curves, and arcs that can be compiled into any kind of drawing you like. These can be used for anything from

jQuery selectors, wrapped sets, and chaining

You can write selectors in jQuery using CSS syntax. Any object or group of objects you would find and style with a CSS element, class, or ID-selector will also return a set of jQuery objects using the `$(selector)` function. Proper use of selectors is key to the incredible amount of work you can do with just a tiny bit of code using jQuery.

A wrapped set is the object returned by a jQuery selector. Wrapped sets can contain no objects, a single object, or a collection of objects. To determine how many objects a selector has returned, you can check the `length` property of the wrapped set. For example, `$("div").length` will return the total number of `<div>` elements on the current page.

Once you have a wrapped set, you can start to execute functions on it. In jQuery, each function returns the result of the work performed by that function, so if you want to remove all `<div>` elements on your page that have the class name highlighted, you could do this:

```
$("div.highlight").remove();
```

The result returned from the `remove()` function is a wrapped set of the elements just removed from the current page. You could then reinsert those elements in another location on the page using the `appendTo()` function, as follows:

```
$("div.highlight").remove().appendTo("div.hiddenElements");
```

Take care and test thoroughly when editing styles and when removing and inserting elements using jQuery's selector syntax and function chaining. These operations are deceptively simple and extremely powerful.

cartoons to complex business intelligence graphs. You can also paint images and text onto the canvas and manipulate the rendered drawing pixel-by-pixel.

In this section, you'll build up the sample application's logic while doing the following:

- Learn how to draw on a canvas
- Add shapes, lines and images
- Manipulate pixels
- Add text

We'll start with the basics of drawing.

4.2.1 *Understanding the basic drawing process*

Once you have a reference to your canvas `context` object, you're ready to start drawing.

The first thing to note about drawing on the canvas is that you always need at least *x* and *y* coordinates. These numeric values are based on pixels measured from the top left of the canvas, as shown in figure 4.3.

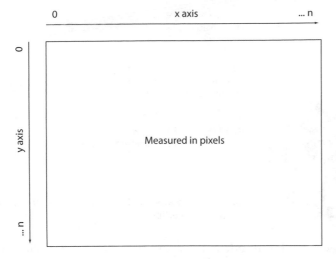

Figure 4.3   Canvas *x* and *y* coordinates are always measured as the number of pixels from the top-left corner.

THE ORDER OF DRAWING OPERATIONS MATTERS

Core API

Keep in mind that when drawing, the order of your drawing operations matters. For instance, consider the following code, which draws a green square on the canvas element. The actual drawing takes place when the `fill` function executes:

```
var canvas = document.getElementById("myCanvas");
var ctx = canvas.getContext("2d");
ctx.rect(20,20,50,50); // rect(startX, startY, width, height)
ctx.fillStyle = "rgb(0, 255, 0)"; // Pure green
ctx.fill();
```

Now look at the following slightly modified example, which creates a black (default color) square on the canvas, because the `fillStyle` property is assigned after the `fill` function executes:

```
var canvas = document.getElementById("myCanvas");
var ctx = canvas.getContext("2d");
ctx.rect(20,20,50,50);
ctx.fill();
ctx.fillStyle = "rgb(0, 255, 0)";
```

As you can see, a slight difference in the sequence produces very different results.

SAVING THE CURRENT STATE OF THE DRAWING CONTEXT

Core API

The next basic drawing operations are the `save` and `restore` functions. These save the current state of the drawing context for properties related to lines, fills, text, and shadows, or restore it back to its previously saved state.

For instance, take a look at figure 4.4, generated by the code in listing 4.3. It shows the progression when you first fill a rectangle with the default color of black and then save the context. Then you change the `fillStyle` to green and create another rectangle. Finally, you restore the context, which returns the `fillcolor` to the default of black and draw a third rectangle.

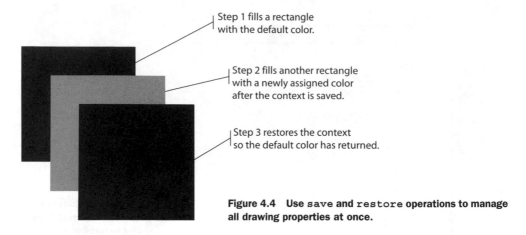

Step 1 fills a rectangle with the default color.

Step 2 fills another rectangle with a newly assigned color after the context is saved.

Step 3 restores the context so the default color has returned.

Figure 4.4   Use `save` and `restore` operations to manage all drawing properties at once.

Although you don't need to put the code in the next listing into your application, you should look at the order of operations carefully.

Listing 4.3   Getting a reference to the drawing context and using it

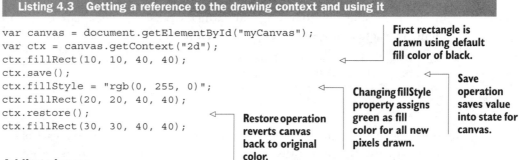

```
var canvas = document.getElementById("myCanvas");
var ctx = canvas.getContext("2d");
ctx.fillRect(10, 10, 40, 40);
ctx.save();
ctx.fillStyle = "rgb(0, 255, 0)";
ctx.fillRect(20, 20, 40, 40);
ctx.restore();
ctx.fillRect(30, 30, 40, 40);
```

First rectangle is drawn using default fill color of black.

Save operation saves value into state for canvas.

Changing fillStyle property assigns green as fill color for all new pixels drawn.

Restore operation reverts canvas back to original color.

4.2.2   *Adding shapes*

With that background knowledge under your belt, you're now ready for more building.

First, you'll draw a rectangle over the entire canvas drawing surface. You've already created a few sample rectangles, so this will be nothing new. The rectangle will be white and 80 percent transparent, which has the effect of causing each previous frame to fade away.

To change how frames fade away, you'll change the opacity from 0.2 to any other value and watch what happens. You could also change the position of the rectangle to create a residual effect around the border of the canvas.

You'll use `context.fillStyle` and `context.fillRect` to draw the shapes.

CONTEXT.FILLSTYLE PROPERTY

Core API   The `fillStyle` property of `context` will set the fill color of all shape elements when they're drawn and, when set, will remain the same until any of the following operations occurs:

- The `<canvas>` element size changes, resulting in the `strokeStyle` returning to the default value.

- The `context.restore` method is called, resulting in the `strokeStyle` returning to the previously saved value, or the default value if no previous value was saved.
- The `strokeStyle` property changes, overwriting the value.

CONTEXT.FILLRECT FUNCTION

The `fillRect` function performs the same function as executing a `rect` function followed by `fill`. The fill operation happens immediately, making this the fastest shortcut method for filling an area with color.

CREATING THE RECTANGLE

To add a rectangle, place the following code just before the `frame` function body placeholder in the JavaScript file. This will create a rectangle that covers the entire drawing area of the canvas, starting at position 0,0. The rectangle will be 80 percent transparent so it will effectively fade everything on the canvas by 20 percent:

```
// ___ clear
context.fillStyle = "rgba(255, 255, 255, 0.8)";
context.fillRect(0, 0, w, h);
```

Note the use of a `fillStyle` that's actually a stringified CSS function. This is perfectly acceptable when using the 2d context as long as the client browser supports the specific function used. If the browser doesn't support the `rgba` function but does support Canvas, the `fillStyle` setting will remain unchanged.

4.2.3 *Adding lines*

Now, set up a `points` array as a local variable in the `ready` handler and add some values to it. This array draws the flying ribbons effect in each frame execution.

A simple loop will get the work done. Replace the randomizer comment with this code:

```
for (var i = 0; i < pointsCount; i++) {
   points.push({
      x: Math.random() * w,
      y: Math.random() * h,
      vx: (Math.random() * maxVelocity * 2) - maxVelocity,
      vy: (Math.random() * maxVelocity * 2) - maxVelocity
   });
}
```

The effect we're after is displayed in figure 4.5: one line with a joint in the middle, randomly bouncing around the screen. Note that the lines won't actually move until you get to the animation section.

`Math.random` is used extensively here to make the line length and direction changes unpredictable and pleasant to watch.

But first you need to draw the lines. To do that, add the code in the next listing to the area above the `frame` function body placeholder.

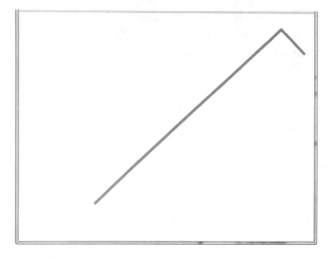

Figure 4.5 By using the `Math.random` **function to generate a list of points, you can generate a bouncing line effect. This same list of points will be used to make other items float around the screen shortly.**

Listing 4.4   Simple line drawing process with the `context` **object**

```
// ___ lines
context.strokeStyle = "#0f0";          ⟵——— Set color of current
context.beginPath();                          context's line.       ⟵—— Begin line-
context.moveTo(points[0].x, points[0].y);                                drawing
for (i = 1; i < segments; i++) {                      ⟵—— Set first position   process.
    context.lineTo(points[i].x, points[i].y);              of context's line.
}                                                                          ⟵—— Create line from
context.stroke();            ⟵——— Draw all lines in context cache.            first position to
                                                                                next position.
```

For just a few lines of code, there's quite a bit going on here. You assign a context property, `strokeStyle`, and then call four different methods to draw the lines on the canvas surface:

```
context.strokeStyle = "#0f0";
```

The `strokeStyle` property uses a CSS-style color string that can also include RGB and RGBA functions. When set, the same rules apply as when setting the `fillStyle` property.

The `beginPath` function will start the line drawing process on the drawing surface:

```
context.beginPath();
```

When you state that you're drawing a path, the `context` will assemble the segments created by calling the path methods into a single line. Each segment is also known as a subpath.

You have a lot of options after you start a path; you can draw straight lines, create simple or complex curves, and join lines together. All are operations that start with a `beginPath` statement. When you call `beginPath`, you're explicitly saying to the context that you want to start a new set of subpaths. You may also want to end a current path by calling either the `endPath` or `stroke` function or by restoring the context to its previous state (see the discussion of `context.restore` in section 4.2.1).

The `moveTo` function sets the current starting position on the drawing surface for the next line:

```
context.moveTo(points[0].x, points[0].y);
```

If you call this function multiple times with no drawing in between calls, only the last call is used. Remember, drawing is a serial (or linear) process.

The `lineTo` function tells the context API to take the last position (either from a previous line or from the last `moveTo` call) and draw a line from it to the new position:

```
context.lineTo(points[a].x, points[a].y);
```

Note that `lineTo` has the same concatenation effect as `arcTo`, `quadraticCurveTo`, and `bezierCurveTo`. The result is a line from the last point to the one passed in the current method.

The `stroke` function is very simple:

```
context.stroke();
```

Whatever is currently in the context's list of subpaths will draw on the surface, and the list of subpaths is cleared. The `stroke` method uses the current context's properties to draw the line.

4.2.4 Adding images

We mentioned that it's possible to work with images in the canvas element. In fact, everything that you draw on the canvas is an image. But can you also import external images like PNGs and JPEGs? Sure! Not only is it possible, it's as simple as getting an image reference and drawing it on your canvas.

Here you'll add two identical images to the canvas but edit the colors on one so that it appears to be a separate image. Figure 4.6 shows what you'll end up with after you work through this section and the next.

Figure 4.6 The images that you'll load are the same, but you'll use the canvas API to edit the colors of one before adding it to the display.

In the sample application, you can include any .png or .jpg file you like—for our purposes, we'll grab a simple smiley face off the internet. Place the image file in the Content folder of the MVC application. Now, in the main.js file, add the code from the following listing in place of the image preparation placeholder text, adjusting the image filename for the image you're using.

Listing 4.5 Adding an image to the DOM and getting a jQuery reference to it

```
var $image = $("<img src='Content/smiley.png'>")
  .hide()
  .appendTo("body");
```

Append it to current document body. This allows you to get image's width and height.

Hide element so it doesn't appear on screen.

Create new element object by passing in HTML string. Store reference in $image variable.

Now that you have an image in your document, you need to draw it onto the drawing surface. Place the code in listing 4.6 above the `frame` function placeholder. This part of your code does much more than just place an image on the canvas, as you can see from the resulting screenshot in figure 4.6. This code will rotate the image and then draw it in the new position.

Listing 4.6   Drawing an image onto a canvas

```
// ____ image
context.save();
context.translate(points[3].x, points[3].y);
context.rotate(radians);
context.drawImage($image[0],
  -($image.width())/2,-($image.height())/2);
context.restore();
```

Restore drawing context so other elements that are drawn appear normally (not rotated).

Save current drawing context to return to it later.

Translate origin point of drawing on drawing surface to center of where you want to place image.

Draw image using center point of image as center point for drawing.

Rotate canvas drawing context (not canvas) specified number of radians.

Using the `drawImage` method, you've added an image to the drawing surface. Once you implement a timer to simulate animation, you'll see the image moving and rotating. You'll also have to take some steps to mitigate the changes that you make to your context as you implement the rotation effect.

TIP If you find that your image isn't drawing on the canvas, the most likely cause is that the image hasn't been completely loaded before calling `draw-Image` on the context object. The easiest solution is to add an anonymous handler function to the `image.onload` event and call `drawImage` in that function. Alternatively, if the image is already part of the DOM, you can wait for the jQuery `ready` event to fire. In our code, we add the image to the DOM by calling the `appendTo` function and then draw it onto the canvas later.

THE CONTEXT.TRANSLATE AND CONTEXT.ROTATE FUNCTIONS

Note that when you drew the image onto the canvas, you assigned coordinate values using the `translate` function and then you used `rotate` to rotate the image using the local `radians` variable:

```
context.translate(points[3].x, points[3].y);
context.rotate(radians);
```

This brings us to an important concept in the drawing surface: The origin point of the canvas is by default at position 0,0, and that's the reference point for the next set of function or property calls on the canvas. Calling the `translate` function with any value other than 0,0 will update the origin position of the drawing surface and anything that uses that setting (like the `rotate` function) will use the new value.

The `rotate` function rotates the drawing surface a specific number of radians, where a single complete circle is `(2 * Math.PI)`. Anything drawn on the surface from the point where `rotate` is called will be tilted at the new angle until the rotation value is changed by either calling `rotate` again or by restoring the context to its previous setting.

THE CONTEXT.SAVE AND CONTEXT.RESTORE FUNCTIONS

We discussed the save and restore operations earlier, but we only hinted at the stacking nature of context properties.

The save operation on the drawing context will take all the current properties and store them in a stack for the current context object. Think of the context.save function as performing a push operation on an array of context settings. The restore function, on the other hand, will pop the last item from the stack of settings and restore the properties as they existed previously. An example will make this clearer.

Figure 4.7 shows the result of creating a square, changing its color incrementally, and saving at each increment. Then, as the code reverses the process and calls restore iteratively, the squares gradually return to the original color.

The code that does it is shown in the next listing.

Figure 4.7 The result of layering multiple layers of fillStyle and then restoring them one at a time

Listing 4.7 Save and restore functions making use of the settings stack

```
var canvas = document.getElementById("myCanvas");
var ctx = canvas.getContext("2d");
var d = 5;       // distance
var c = 0;       // color
for (var i = 0; i < 5; i++) {
    ctx.fillRect(d, d, 40, 40);
    c = (d * 5);
    ctx.fillStyle =
        "rgb(" + c + "," + c + "," + c + ")";
    ctx.save();                                      ◁——⎤ Save current
    d += 10;                                              ⎦ fillStyle property
}
for (var t = 0; t < 5; t++) {
    ctx.restore();                                   ◁——⎤ Restore previous
    ctx.fillRect(d, d, 40, 40);                           ⎦ fillStyle property
    d += 10;
}
```

4.2.5 *Manipulating pixels*

When working with bitmapped images, it's possible to use the Canvas API to manipulate the color of individual pixels in a referenced image.

To do so, the first thing you need to do is add two new variables to the JavaScript file, both at the top of the declaration area:

```
var $imageCanvas = null;
var imageContext = null;
```

The first of these will hold a new canvas element that you create in memory to do the pixel manipulation, and the second a context object for that canvas. You'll modify the pixel colors in the canvas element and then draw that new canvas onto the existing canvas using the same drawImage function you used earlier.

The timing of this is important. Since we're sure that you, like us, would prefer not to load the same image twice, you'll just patch into the load event of the image element and make the variable assignments there. In order to do that, take the full assignment of the image file out of the element creation tag and place it in a jQuery `attr` function. The `attr` function takes a property name and a property value and makes the assignment.

In short, you need to remove the original image assignment from your JavaScript file and replace it with the following code.

Listing 4.8   Manipulating pixels directly using the Canvas API

```
var $image = $("<img>")
.load(function() {
    $imageCanvas = $("<canvas>")
        .width($image.width())
        .height($image.height());

    imageContext = $imageCanvas[0].getContext("2d");
    imageContext.drawImage($image[0], 0, 0);
    try {
        var imageData = imageContext.getImageData(
            0, 0, $imageCanvas.width(),
            $imageCanvas.height());
        for (var i = 0; i < imageData.data.length; i++) {
            if (i % 4 != 3)
                imageData.data[i] = 255 - imageData.data[i];
        }
        imageContext.putImageData(imageData, 0, 0);
    }
    catch(e) {
        $("<div class='error'>Note: Direct manipulation of
            pixels loaded from image files isn't allowed when
            running locally</div>")
        .appendTo("body");
    }
})
.attr("src", "Content/smiley.png")
.hide()
.appendTo("body");
```

Annotations:
- Create new, empty canvas element using size of current image element.
- Get new canvas's context reference and place image on it.
- Check to see if element is in red, green, or blue position for each pixel.
- Get array of image pixels from new context object.
- Walk entire array of image pixel component values.
- Assign pixel and new color in 0 to 255 color range.
- Put image data array back into original canvas, overwriting original pixels.
- If operation fails, assume it's because you're executing locally.
- Assign actual image src value to force load property to execute.

Because you're only loading the image once for the entire application process, this code will execute exactly once, setting up the `$imageContext` variable to be ready for drawing onto the visible canvas. You'll do this after the original image element is drawn, using the next point in your positions array inside the `frame` function:

```
// ___ imageCanvas
if ($imageCanvas) {
    context.drawImage($imageCanvas[0],
        points[6].x - ($imageCanvas.width() / 2),
        points[6].y - ($imageCanvas.height() / 2));
}
```

data[0]	data[1]	data[2]	data[3]	data[4]	data[5]	data[6]	data[7]	data[8]	data[9]	data[10]	data[11]	data[...]
Red (0-255	Green (0-255)	Blue (0-255)	Alpha (0-255)	Red (0-255)	Red (0-255)	Blue (0-255)	Alpha (0-255)	Red (0-255)	Green (0-255)	Blue (0-255)	Alpha (0-255	...

P1	P2	P3	P4	...	...	...	...
...	...	...	...	...	...	...	...
...	...	...	...	...	...	...	...

Figure 4.8 The `ImageData.data` property describes the component colors and transparency of each pixel in the captured area of the drawing surface.

THE CONTEXT.GETIMAGEDATA AND CONTEXT.PUTIMAGEDATA FUNCTIONS

 Core API

In listing 4.8 you called two image data functions on the `context` object that let you find a specific piece of image data and then put it back onto the canvas: `getImageData` and `putImageData`.

The `getImageData` function takes as parameters the starting position and size of the rectangle measured in pixels to retrieve from a canvas drawing context:

```
var imgData = context.getImageData(0, 0, width, height);
```

The returned `data` object contains an array where every group of four values contains the RGBA values for one pixel. Figure 4.8 makes the arrangement of values in the `imgData.data` property clear.

The `putImageData` function uses the `imgData` object from `getImageData` and places it on the drawing surface in the starting position defined in the parameters (after you've edited the pixels, of course):

```
context.putImageData(imgData, 0, 0);
```

By using these two methods, you could do some other interesting things, like offsetting the entire drawing surface by 20 pixels, inverting it, or rotating it. Let your imagination be your guide!

4.2.6 Adding text

We said earlier that you'd be applying text to the canvas. The reality is that you must draw text on the canvas, not write it. The process for doing this isn't as simple or flexible as you might want, but with a little work you can perform basic operations. You can set the font, color, and position of the text, but you won't be able to wrap or edit the text after it's drawn. This means there's a limit to the amount of text you can write on the drawing surface, but it can still be handy.

Figure 4.9 shows an example of how text will appear when rendered onto the screen.

Core API

To draw text, you'll use the context.fillText function, which adds text at the starting point provided. The text immediately draws onto the canvas, honoring the current properties for fill, font, and text alignment. Note that the text is either left-aligned, right-aligned, or centered on the insertion point relative to the current context origin; it's not based on any edge of the actual drawing surface.

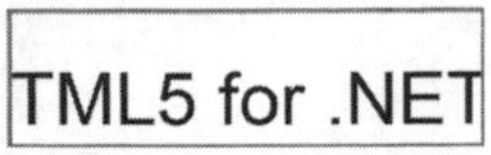

In the sample application, you'll need to start by defining a local variable to contain the text. Then you'll set the fill-Style property to the color you want the text to be and call the fillText function to draw it onto the canvas, starting at the coordinates passed in.

To do this, add the following code snippet in the main.js file, immediately after the code that implements the imageCanvas object:

```
// ___ text
var text = "HTML5 for .NET Developers!";
context.fillStyle = "#00a";
context.fillText(text, points[4].x, points[4].y);
```

> **TML5 for .NET**
>
> **Figure 4.9 You'll use the fillText function to add text to the canvas and float it around the page the same way as you'll do with the rest of the visual elements.**

You've now drawn lines and shapes on the canvas surface and added images and event text. In addition, you've filled shapes with various colors and gone so far as to manipulate individual pixels on the drawing surface. But there are a lot of other features to the HTML5 Canvas API. Things like Bezier curves and gradients are a part of the API, but there are also logical elements that can be added to your applications with JavaScript, like collision detection and simulated gravity. These are helpful for games but also for graphics-intensive simulations and training tools.

The thing they all have in common is that they require animation. That's what we'll look at next.

4.3   Animating and adding special effects to canvas images

In this section, we'll show you how to animate your canvas creations and how to add additional special effects that will bring polish to your presentation. First up, let's animate!

4.3.1   Adding animation

If you run your application right now, you'll see some lines, an image, and a bit of text sitting there on the screen. This is probably not what you've come to expect of the HTML5 <canvas> element, given all the media and community hype. What you're missing is the ability to move things around on the screen. Animation is a key capability in any graphics-based application.

Animation in the HTML5 <canvas> element is simulated, not the real movement of a drawn object from one point on the drawing surface to another point. This is because once you place a pixel on your screen, it's just a pixel, regardless of the method you used to draw it.

This doesn't mean that animation is impossible. On the contrary, once you've established the ground rules for how Canvas animation works, the process is simple and the performance is usually fairly impressive.

The steps involved in animating your canvas are as follows:

1 Clear the canvas of previous pixels by overwriting the surface with a blank rectangle.
2 Draw all elements using saved state variables.
3 Iterate all state variables to their next animated positions.
4 Wait a prescribed duration (frame rate).

You may have been thinking in terms of a 3D object-oriented world, but you should really be thinking in terms of the flip-book animations you drew in the corner of your textbooks in school. Figure 4.10 shows a simple flip-book animation of a circle flying up at an angle, hitting the corner of the screen, and then falling back down to its original position. Repeat this flip series for a continuous animation.

UPDATING VARIABLES AND STARTING ANIMATION

Once you have the variables to redraw your surface and the functions required to perform the drawing operations, you just need the timer and the ability to change your variables so they're ready to draw the next frame. You'll do this now by finishing up the `frame` function.

The following listing gives you everything you need. Remove the `frame` function body placeholder and replace it with this code.

Listing 4.9 Updating variables to perform the timed operations and starting animation

```
// ___ update positions and handle bounce
for (i = 0; i < points.length; i++) {        Get single point
    var p = points[i];                        object from array.
    p.x += p.vx;
    if (p.x < 0) {          If new position is too far    Set new x coordinate
        p.x = 0;            to left, reverse x velocity   based on last location
        p.vx *= -1;         for next iteration.           multiplied by velocity.
    }
    else if (p.x > w) {     If new position is
        p.x = w;            too far to right,
        p.vx *= -1;         reverse x velocity.
    }
                                                          Set new y coordinate
                                                          based on last location
    p.y += p.vy;                                          multiplied by velocity.
    if (p.y < 0) {          If new position is
        p.y = 0;            too far up, reverse
        p.vy *= -1;         y velocity.
    }
    else if (p.y > h) {     If new position is
        p.y = h;            too far down,
        p.vy *= -1;         reverse y velocity.
    }
}
radians += 0.01;            Update rotation radians
                            value for image.

// ___ set up the next frame        Set timer to re-execute frame
setTimeout(frame, 30);             function in 30 milliseconds.
```

Iterate through each point in points array for locations where animated element will be in next iteration.

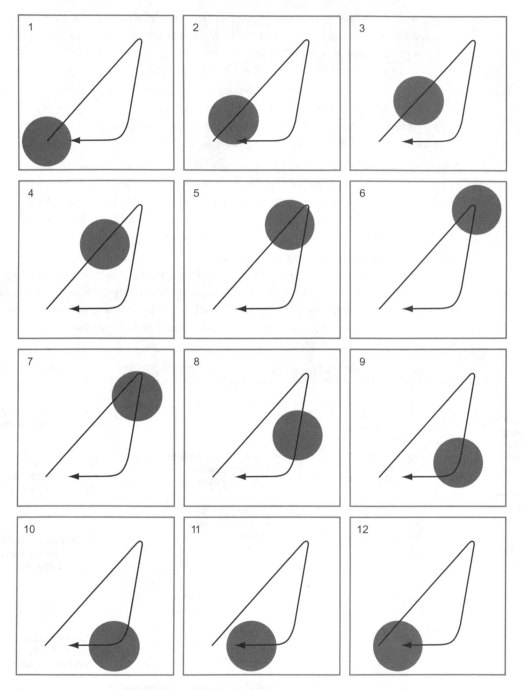

Figure 4.10   A simple flip-book-style animation that moves a circle across the screen and back to its original position using stop-motion animation. This is the essence of animating the HTML5 Canvas; you draw pixels and then draw them again, moved a bit from their previous location, very, very quickly.

Figure 4.11   The canvas element with operational frame timing

Run your application, and you should now see something like figure 4.11.

The screen is animated and each call to the frame function places a 20 percent opaque rectangle over the entire drawing surface, giving a nice fade effect. You should also notice that regardless of the browser you use, the animation effect should perform reasonably quickly. This is because modern browsers are significantly integrated with operating system graphics engines.

This demonstration is relatively straightforward. With a quick search for "HTML5 Canvas animation," you can find other example applications and websites that do amazing things using this flip-book-style of animation.

4.3.2   *Adding special effects with curves and clipping*

There are quite a few other concepts available to you in the Canvas API, such as gradients, blurs, Bezier curves, and advanced cropping mechanisms, but we don't have space to cover every one, so we'll go through just two more before wrapping up—curves and clipping.

Your goal here for the sample application is to give the screen a spotlight look while continuing to animate all the other elements. To do this, you'll create an arc that curves all the way around into a circle and then clip the entire surface to its circumference.

THE CONTEXT.ARC FUNCTION

Core API
The arc function will draw an arc around a center point defined by the first two parameters passed. The third parameter is the arc's radius in pixels from the center point, and the fourth and fifth parameters give the start and end angles in radians. The final parameter is a Boolean that states whether or not the arc should be drawn clockwise (false) or counter-clockwise (true).

This is the code you'll use when you get to the final listing:

```
context.arc(points[5].x, points[5].y, spotlightRadius,
    (Math.PI/180) * 0, Math.PI/180 * 360, false);
```

This code creates a complete circle (360 degree arc) starting at the x and y coordinates passed in. It may make more sense when you look at the named parameters here:

```
arc(x, y, radius, startAngle, endAngle, counterclockwise)
```

Because this function uses radians instead of degrees, you need to use the following formula to determine the start and end angles in a 360 degree circle:

```
(Math.PI/180) * [degrees]
```

The arc function also brings to the fore the fact that any path described on the drawing surface closes automatically if the start and end points are the same or if you call the closePath function on the context. A closed path is either filled or is used as a clipping region.

THE CONTEXT.CLIP FUNCTION

Core API

The clipping feature of the context is a little confusing until you understand how it works and, more importantly, when it's in effect on the drawing surface. Think of the clipping region on your canvas as a cut-out template that you can place anywhere and make any shape that you want. When applied to the context, anything drawn, regardless of where, will appear only if it falls within the boundaries of the region. The boundary can be any path, and anything drawn is clipped while the clip is in effect.

The process is as follows:

1 Describe a closed path (a complete arc, in this case).
2 Call context.clip().
3 Continue drawing (only pixels in the clipping region are painted).
4 Call context.restore() to remove the clipping region.

After calling clip on the context object, the next canvas operations will only draw inside the defined clipping area.

To build the clipping area, you need to add a new variable to the mix to track how big your spotlight effect should be. Place the following code just after you wire up the resize function to the window event and then call it:

```
var spotlightRadius = Math.min(w, h) / 2;
```

Now rework the beginning of the frame function so it looks like the following listing. This code will black out the screen, draw the circle, and then clip the surface to it.

Listing 4.10   Drawing arcs on the drawing surface and clipping the screen to it

```
function frame() {
  context.save();
  // ___ clear
  //context.fillStyle = "rgba(255, 255, 255, 0.2)";       ⟵   Comment out old
  //context.fillRect(0, 0, w, h);                              background fill
  // ___ clear                                                 that created the
  context.fillStyle = "rgba(0, 0, 0, 1)";                      fading effect.
  context.fillRect(0, 0, w, h);                          ⟵   Fill entire screen with
                                                              black rectangle.
  // ___ spotlight
  context.beginPath();
  context.arc(points[5].x, points[5].y,                  ⟵   Create arc path that curves
    spotlightRadius,                                           360 degrees into circle.
    (Math.PI/180) * 0, Math.PI/180 * 360, false);
```

```
context.clip();

context.fillStyle = "rgba(56, 56, 56, 1)";      Fill clipped surface      Clip drawing
context.fillRect(0, 0, w, h);                    with gray fill.           surface to
                                                                            arc's path.
...
```

All code after this listing should stay the same and, as the spotlight is drawn, will automatically clip to the current context's clipping area. To return the screen back to its preclipped drawing area, add a context.restore just before your setTimeout method call at the end of the frame function.

The next time you run your application, you should see something like figure 4.12.

You might notice that even though the canvas element is set to resize, no actual resize events are firing and the canvas takes up only a small portion of the screen. This is because you're missing the stylesheet and a little bit of additional reset code. You'll connect the final dots on this and finish the application shortly.

Figure 4.12 The canvas operating with all features, including the clipping region that creates a spotlight effect

4.3.3 *Managing canvas properties during screen resizing*

The final step to completing the application is to reset various properties when the screen resizes, as shown in the following listing. This code goes in at the end of the resize function in main.js.

> **Listing 4.11 Additional resize code is required to reset various context properties**

```
// resetting the width and height also resets
// these other properties, so we set them again
context.lineWidth = 6;
context.lineCap = "round";
context.lineJoin = "round";
context.font = "100px sans-serif";
context.textAlign = "center";
context.textBaseline = "middle";
```

This step is critical, because when the canvas is resized and is cleared, as described earlier in the chapter, it also resets various other properties. The code in listing 4.11 puts the properties back the way you want them whenever resize is executed.

Running your application again will give you the same experience as before, but with the added benefit of being able to resize your browser window. Congratulations! Your first Canvas application is complete, and you're well on your way to mastering both this specific API and JavaScript development in general.

4.4   *Summary*

In this chapter, you saw what the HTML5 Canvas API is and what it isn't, and you learned some of the basic features that you'll need to know to paint pixels on the drawing surface. As you've seen, Canvas is a great tool for creating games like Canvas Rider, Agent 008 Ball pool, and many others. Lots of developers have built amazing online image editing software and, by the time you read this, there are bound to be plenty of other fantastic examples of Canvas in use.

Canvas might be the most fun toy in the box, but there are other HTML5 toys that can help you build better web applications, like the next API we'll cover, which is History.

4.5   *Complete code listing*

The following listings will help you fill in the blanks for this chapter's sample application, and they'll help you check your work.

Listing 4.12   Styles to support automatic resizing of the canvas element

```
html { width: 100%; height: 100%; }
body { width: 100%; height: 100%; }
#main { position: absolute; width: 100%; height: 100%; }
```

Listing 4.13   Complete JavaScript application code for canvas demonstration

```
$(document).ready(function () {
   if (!Modernizr.canvas) {
      alert("This browser does not support the canvas tag.");
      return;
   }
   var $canvas = $("#main");
   var context = $canvas[0].getContext("2d");
   var $imageCanvas = null;
   var imageContext = null;

   var w;
   var h;
   var maxVelocity = 10;
   var points = [];
   var radians = 0;
   var segments = 3;
   var pointsCount = 7;
   var text = "HTML5 for .NET Developers!";

   var $image = $("<img>")
   .load(function () {
      $imageCanvas = $("<canvas>")
      .width($image.width())
      .height($image.height());

      imageContext = $imageCanvas[0].getContext("2d");
      imageContext.drawImage($image[0], 0, 0);
      try {
         var imageData = imageContext.getImageData(
            0, 0, $imageCanvas.width(), $imageCanvas.height());
```

```
        for (var i = 0; i < imageData.data.length; i++) {
            if (i % 4 != 3) // operate on R, G, B, but not A
                imageData.data[i] = 255 - imageData.data[i]; // invert
        }

        imageContext.putImageData(imageData, 0, 0);
    } catch (e) {
        $("<div class='error'>
            Note: Direct manipulation of pixels
            loaded from image files isn't allowed
            when running locally</div>")
        .appendTo("body");
    }
})
.attr("src", "Content/smiley.png")
.hide()
.appendTo("body");

function resize() {
    // Resize function body placeholder
    w = $canvas.width();
    h = $canvas.height();
    $canvas.attr("width", w);
    $canvas.attr("height", h);
    // resetting the width and height also resets
    // these other properties, so we set them again
    context.lineWidth = 6;
    context.lineCap = "round";
    context.lineJoin = "round";
    context.font = "100px sans-serif";
    context.textAlign = "center";
    context.textBaseline = "middle";
}
$(window).resize(resize);
resize();
var spotlightRadius = Math.min(w, h) / 2;

// Randomizer placeholder
for (var a = 0; a < pointsCount; a++) {
    points.push({
        x: Math.random() * w,
        y: Math.random() * h,
        vx: (Math.random() * maxVelocity * 2) - maxVelocity,
        vy: (Math.random() * maxVelocity * 2) - maxVelocity
    });
}

function frame() {
    context.save();

    // ___ clear
    context.fillStyle = "rgba(0, 0, 0, 1)"; // 100% opaque black
    context.fillRect(0, 0, w, h);

    // ___ spotlight
    context.beginPath();
```

```
context.arc(
   points[5].x,
   points[5].y,
   spotlightRadius,
   (Math.PI/180) * 0,
   Math.PI/180 * 360,
   false);
context.clip();

context.fillStyle = "rgba(56, 56, 56, 1)"; // 100% opaque dark gray
context.fillRect(0, 0, w, h);

// ___ lines
context.strokeStyle = "#0f0";
context.beginPath();
context.moveTo(points[0].x, points[0].y);
for (i = 1; i < segments; i++) {
   context.lineTo(points[i].x, points[i].y);
}
context.stroke();
context.closePath();

// ___ image
context.save();
context.translate(points[3].x, points[3].y);
context.rotate(radians);
context.drawImage(
   $image[0], -($image.width()) / 2,
   -($image.height()) / 2);
context.restore();

// ___ imageCanvas
if ($imageCanvas) {
   context.drawImage($imageCanvas[0],
    points[6].x - ($imageCanvas.width() / 2),
    points[6].y - ($imageCanvas.height() / 2));
}

// ___ text
context.fillStyle = "#00a";
context.fillText(text, points[4].x, points[4].y);

// ___ update positions and handle bounce
for (i = 0; i < points.length; i++) {
   var p = points[i];

   p.x += p.vx;
   if (p.x < 0) {
      p.x = 0;
      p.vx *= -1;
   } else if (p.x > w) {
      p.x = w;
      p.vx *= -1;
   }

   p.y += p.vy;
   if (p.y < 0) {
      p.y = 0;
```

```
            p.vy *= -1;
        } else if (p.y > h) {
            p.y = h;
            p.vy *= -1;
        }
    }

    radians += 0.01;

    context.restore();
    // ___ set up the next frame
    setTimeout(frame, 30);

    }
    frame();
});
```

The History API: changing the game for MVC sites

This chapter covers

- Understanding the basic operation of the History API
- Integrating MVC with the HTML5 History API
- Controlling history in a web application

Suppose you're building a newsreader application for the web and want to incorporate a search feature for things like images, people, and places. You build a responsive HTML5 interface with a popup `<div>` that allows a user to cycle through multiple tabs refining the search. In the background you're using Ajax and jQuery to ping the server for hit counts based on each updated criteria. What do you think will happen when the user cycles through three tabs adding criteria and then, out of force of habit, hits the Back button? Unless you're using the jQuery.address plugin or something similar, the browser will load the previous web page and lose the search. The user will be annoyed.

Not anymore. Thanks to the HTML5 History API, the game has changed. Using the techniques we'll illustrate in this chapter, you'll learn to use ASP.NET MVC's routing and partial view capabilities to build a site suitable for both old and new browsers. The site will work in the "normal" way in older browsers but it'll be more

---

Browser support

	5	10	4	11.5	5					Desktop
History API										
				11.1	4.2	2.2	N/A			Mobile

Chapter 5 map

History is an API that adds the ability for a bit of JavaScript code to control the URLs in a browser's history. This enables you to easily control what happens within an application when users click the forward and back buttons and activate navigation events by clicking links.

history.onpopstate component	page 135
history.pushState component	page 135
history.replaceState component	page 135
Working with browser URLs	page 139

---

responsive and consume less bandwidth in newer browsers, because pages will be accessible in two modes:

- As a standard load from the server without any JavaScript or History integration, perfect for older browsers
- With JavaScript and History to reduce server load and eliminate complete page refreshes

In this chapter, you'll learn how to do these things in your .NET MVC applications as you build a simple restaurant menu website that works both with and without JavaScript and the History API. During the process, you'll create a custom JavaScript library to override the standard HTML anchor click events that the browser uses to navigate to other pages. You'll also use the HTML5 History API to reduce server load and provide a fluid user experience for those users with newer browsers.

These are the major steps along the way:

1 Building the controllers, views, and routing schemes so that they work with the HTML5 History API
2 Building a JavaScript library to control browser history from inside an ASP.NET MVC site
3 Adding finishing touches to the master page and CSS styles to complete the application

Let's begin!

Figure 5.1   With the History API implemented properly, a user could move through each tab of the search dialog box by clicking on the tab and then use the Forward and Back buttons to move between tabs without losing the search state.

5.1 *Building a History-ready MVC site*

The ASP.NET MVC framework has two features ideal for implementing a History-friendly web application:

- A rich routing framework
- Partial views

The rich routing framework will allow your URL to have semantic meaning within the context of your application. For instance, consider the URL in figure 5.1, which shows what a fictitious newsreader application might look like.

Thanks to ASP.NET MVC's routing capabilities, the URL—http://news/search/people in this case—could be a specific MVC application route that's the entry point for all the logic around storing, organizing, and finding information about people. If you're not sure what a *route* is, don't worry; we'll talk more about routes later in this section.

The next feature that makes MVC ideal for working with the HTML5 History API is its ability to present a partial snippet of HTML content, called a *partial view.* Partial views allow your JavaScript code to call a specific URL and get a specific response that feeds asynchronously into various parts of your page. For instance, in the previous newsreader example, a partial view might include an image and a brief search result that the page can display in a pop-up HTML element. Later in this section, you'll build a partial view that will load—on an existing HTML page—an image and text for restaurant menu items.

As a whole, this section will walk you through

- Launching the ASP.NET MVC project in Visual Studio
- Adding controllers and views that can respond to History client events
- Setting up a History-friendly routing scheme
- Creating the application data model

- Loading small bits of content from the server into an existing HTML page on demand

You'll start by creating the project.

5.1.1 *Launching the sample project in Visual Studio*

Before you begin, take a look at figure 5.2, which shows what the finished restaurant menu application will look like.

To get started building this application, follow these steps:

1　Open Visual Studio and start a new ASP.NET MVC project—an internet application that uses the Razor view engine, HTML5 semantic markup, and no unit test project.
2　Name the project MenuHistory, and then look at the resulting project. You should have Account and Home controllers (which you can leave as is) and views to support them.
3　Add an Images folder to the project.

Figure 5.2 The finished History demonstration application will work even in browsers that don't support the History API. In supported browsers, though, the user experience will be enhanced and the server load reduced, because the image and content on the right will load separately without requiring a complete page refresh.

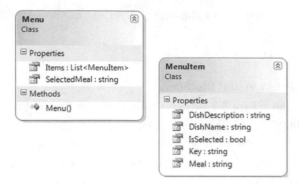

Figure 5.3   The object model that you'll be working with has a simple `MenuItem` object with various properties that are used for display, and a collection of items called the `Menu`.

Throughout this chapter, you'll be dealing with a `MenuItem` object and a `Menu` object that contains a collection of `MenuItem` objects. In the real world, these correspond to a real menu at a restaurant and individual dishes on that menu, grouped by the meal (breakfast, lunch, or dinner). While the exact structure isn't important yet, the object model in figure 5.3 will give you an idea of what it is that you're dealing with.

5.1.2   Adding controllers and views

In this section, you'll create a simple presentation for a list of menu items in an MVC view.

First, you need to add a controller and a view:

1   Right-click the Controllers folder and choose Add > Controller.
2   Name the controller MenuController and use the Empty Controller template.

The `Index` controller action is the default method created for you in an MVC controller, and it will return a `Menu` along with a separate `MenuItem` object that corresponds to the item the user has selected, based on `Meal` and `Dish` parameters. This action will execute when the user clicks on the Menu link at the top of the page.

> **NOTE**   If you have questions about how all of this works, you might pause for a few minutes and take a look at appendix B.

The following listing shows the basic code required in MenuController.cs.

Listing 5.1   Controller action to return a menu and selected item to the view

```
public ActionResult Index(string meal = "", string dish = "")
{
    var menu = new Models.Menu();
    menu.SelectedMeal = meal;
    menu.Items
        .Where(s => s.Meal == meal && s.Key == dish)
        .FirstOrDefault()
        .IsSelected = true;
    return View(menu);
}
```

Menu constructor will create static data needed for system.

Using generic List object allows you to use lambda expressions to filter data.

Object you pass to view will become model for view.

Returned object's isSelected property is set to true.

Method ensures that single object (or null) will be returned.

Figure 5.4 Create a strongly typed view by assigning the model class value. This can be a value populated from the current project's available objects, or you can reference an object from another referenced assembly in the project.

The controller ends with a call to `return View(menu)`. This view doesn't yet exist, so you'll now create it. Right-click inside the body of your `Index` method and select Add View. Set the properties as shown in figure 5.4.

Next, you need to set up some local variables for your new Index.cshtml file. These variables will correspond to, and organize lists of, items for breakfast, lunch, and dinner and will be used to build out the presentation shortly:

1 In the `<h2>` element at the top of the view, place `HTML5 Restaurant Menu` and then open a new bit of code in the Razor view.
2 Use the code in the next listing to set up your variables, add a `using` statement, and change the title of the page.

Listing 5.2 Setting up local variables in a Razor view

```
@model Menu
@using MenuHistory.Models
@{ ViewBag.Title = "Menu"; }
<h2>HTML5 Restaurant Menu</h2>
@{
    var selectedItem = Model.Items
        .Where(s => s.IsSelected == true)
        .FirstOrDefault();
    var selectedDish =
        selectedItem == null ?
        "none" : selectedItem.Key;
```

◁── **Using statement in view acts same as using statement in C# file.**

Find selected item from Menu.Items list if it exists.

Perform null check to get selected dish.

```
List<List<MenuItem>> menuGroups =
    new List<List<MenuItem>>();
menuGroups.Add(
    (from i in Model.Items
    where i.Meal == "Breakfast"
    select i).ToList<MenuItem>()
);
menuGroups.Add(
    (from i in Model.Items
    where i.Meal == "Lunch"
    select i).ToList<MenuItem>()
);
menuGroups.Add(
    (from i in Model.Items
    where i.Meal == "Dinner"
    select i).ToList<MenuItem>()
);
}
```

Create variable to hold 'list of lists' to iterate through each meal with minimal code.

Populate menuGroups variable for each meal in model.

The variables you assigned in listing 5.2 will be available while processing the view on the server. Keep this in mind as you build out your view markup. Even though you're writing markup directly in the view, the C# code will maintain state within the context of the view, and you can use this to build up presentation logic.

The following listing shows how to build the markup that renders links on the page for each item on the menu. This code should come next in your Menu Index.cshtml page.

Listing 5.3   Building markup using Razor

```
<aside class="preview-dish"></aside>
@foreach (var mealList in menuGroups)
{
    var titleClass = Model.SelectedMeal ==
        mealList.First().Meal ? "active" : "";
    <section class="menu @titleClass"
            data-meal="@mealList.First().Meal">
        <h3>@mealList.First().Meal</h3>
        <ul>
            @foreach (var item in mealList)
            {
                var itemClass = selectedDish == item.Key ?
                    "selected" : "";
                <li class="menu-item @itemClass"
                        data-dish="@item.Key">
                    @Html.RouteLink(
                        item.DishName,
                        "Menus",
                        new
                        {
                            meal = item.Meal,
                            dish = item.Key
                        }
                    )</li>
```

Use first item in each group to set up title element for list.

Iterate through dishes in meal list inside unordered HTML element.

Iterate through each list of meal items and, based on first element in list, set up style.

Aside element will be filled and styled later with partial view.

In each iteration, assign data attribute to each section and dish.

Create list item and fill it with route data to build link.

```
      }
    </ul>
  </section>
}
```

So far you've created a simple presentation for a list of menu items in an MVC view. You'll add data soon to make it work, but right now the important point to understand is that the `Menu` view will be generated when the `http://site/Menu` URL is loaded. If the browser supports the History API, the loading of menu item images and extra text will happen by means of dynamically loaded partial views. If History isn't supported, the partial views and the entire page will be loaded when each menu item is clicked.

We'll show you how to use the Modernizr JavaScript object to check for History support shortly, when you build the JavaScript side of the application. Figure 5.5 describes the way this works.

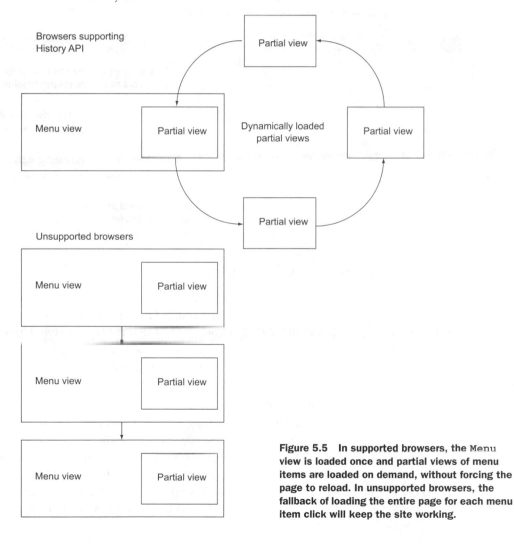

Figure 5.5 In supported browsers, the `Menu` view is loaded once and partial views of menu items are loaded on demand, without forcing the page to reload. In unsupported browsers, the fallback of loading the entire page for each menu item click will keep the site working.

5.1.3   History and MVC routing

If you run the application now, you'll receive an error stating that the route named "Menus" wasn't found. That's because you need to add a route named "Menus" to the application. The routing engine in MVC provides you with a means of directing a particular URL or URL format to a controller and action method, and it automatically parses values from the URL into the parameters you require. This gives you the ability to respond to many different URL formats in an application and map them to application logic easily and quickly.

In your project, follow these steps to add a new route that responds to calls for the extra menu item data:

1 Double-click the Global.asax file.
2 Add the "Menus" route in the following listing right before the default route is registered in the RegisterRoutes method.

Listing 5.4   Building the Menus MVC route

```
routes.MapRoute(                          ⟵ Call new route by name when building
    "Menus",                                routes to ensure proper binding.

    "Menu/{meal}/{dish}",                 ⟵ Use /Menu/Breakfast/
                                            Pancakes pattern.
    new
    {
        controller = "Menu",              ⟵ Specify that Menu controller
                                            and Index action will be used.
        action = "Index",

        meal = UrlParameter.Optional,     ⟵ Specify that meal and dish items are optional so
        dish = UrlParameter.Optional        application shouldn't complain if they don't exist.
    }
);
```

Add new defaults object to route.

The signature for MapRoute you're using here is as follows:

```
MapRoute(string name, string url, object defaults)
```

You use the name parameter (as you did in listing 5.3) to specifically select this route for link building and use the url parameter to provide the pattern. Finally, the defaults object will have property names that are exactly the same (case sensitive) as the parameters in url. This will result in a route being added to your application as soon as it starts.

FOLLOWING ROUTES IN AN ASP.NET MVC APPLICATION

You created the new Menus route by tapping into the default RegisterRoutes() method provided by MVC. This takes a RouteCollection object that's a property of the application's RouteTable. RouteCollection is a list that must contain at least the default route but can contain any number greater than that. Routes added to this collection are evaluated in the order in which they appear—this is a key point to remember, as you'll see shortly. Routing in ASP.NET is really nothing more than an advanced pattern-matching engine for URLs. When receiving an HTTP request, the URL goes through the routing engine, which parses and evaluates it into a set of parameters that are matched to controllers, action methods on those controllers, and additional route values that serve as parameters to the action methods.

Each route in the application's route table can have an optional name but requires at least a URL value. The URL is the pattern and can contain literals, parameters (defined using curly braces), and separator characters. Route names, if used, must be unique within the application.

Routing is probably the most often misunderstood part of MVC. The frustration the route table causes usually stems from adding routes in the wrong order. We said that the order of the routes matters, and here's why. Consider the two routes shown in the next listing.

Listing 5.5   MVC route selection can sometimes give unexpected results

```
MapRoute("Location",            When using URL like http://site/NewYork, default route will be executed
    "{id}",                       because it matches single parameter pattern. This seems correct.
    new { controller = "Maps", action = "GetLocation", id = "" }
);

MapRoute("Default",
    "{controller}/{action}/{id}",
    new { controller = "Home", action = "Index", id = "" }
);
         All other requests ought to go to default route, but because first route has default value for
              id application will always use first route and call Maps controller's GetLocation action.
```

The problem in listing 5.5 is that the Location route isn't specific enough and provides a default value for the location id parameter. You can put all the code breakpoints in the world on the Index action method in the Home controller file and try to figure out why it isn't hit, only to discover after hours of frustrating effort that the Maps controller is executing the GetLocation action with an empty id parameter.

> **TIP**   The big takeaway when it comes to routing is that the routing scheme you use in your application should be specific enough to handle all expected inbound requests, and it should be ordered appropriately to ensure that the correct controller gets each request.

TWO WAYS TO GENERATE INSIDE-THE-VIEW URLS THAT MATCH A SPECIFIC ROUTE

Whereas the first part of the MVC routing system enables you to map incoming requests to specific controllers and actions, the second part lets you generate a URL inside a view that matches a specific route. There are a couple of methods for doing this.

The easiest option is to use the Html.ActionLink() method. This method has a number of overloads, but probably the most common is used to build menus and static links to retrieve views. The default master page in the MVC template uses this method to build the tabs at the top of the page. You'll use it to add a new Menu item to the tab strip. All you need to do is add the following line to the unordered list in the Views\Shared_Layout.cshtml file:

```
<li>@Html.ActionLink("Menu", "Index", "Menu")</li>
```

The method signature here is

```
ActionLink(string linkText, string actionName, string controllerName)
```

so the first incidence of "Menu" will be the text, whereas the last tells MVC to call `Menu-Controller`. The MVC framework will build a link URL that will navigate to the `Menu` controller, `Index` action. This `Html.ActionLink()` method is very helpful, because it will dynamically use the first route in the application's route table that matches the parameters sent in.

The `ActionLink` method is fine for generating simple anchor tags on the server, but you'll be working with the URL on both the client and the server in addition to adding formatted parameters, so the ability to format the URL properly is very important. MVC provides a more specific method for dealing with this kind of situation: the `Html.RouteLink()` method you used back in listing 5.3 will build an `<a>` tag with an `href` attribute using the exact route requested, throwing an exception if parameters aren't supplied or if the route doesn't exist. Here is that bit of code again:

```
@Html.RouteLink(
    item.DishName,
    "Menus",
    new
    {
      meal = item.Meal,
      dish = item.Key
    }
```

This function signature is

```
RouteLink(string linkText, string routeName, object routeValues)
```

`RouteLink` is more rigid than `ActionLink` because it forces the use of a specific route rather than matching based on a regular expression. This is perfect, though, for any situation where a guaranteed URL matching a specific route in the application is required.

> **WARNING**   Although the History API enables you to pick up the URL and edit it using JavaScript, you should always architect your solution in such a way that the page will operate effectively even if the History API isn't available. This may mean that the interface appears exactly the same, or it may require some minor interface differences. Either way, your application shouldn't break just because this API isn't available on the client—a principle known as *graceful degradation*. The sample application you're building in this chapter will do just that.

5.1.4 *Creating the application data model*

You've now completed the view, controller, and routes for the application; it's time to focus on the data model. Data for this sample application could come from any source, be it a database, external web service, or even a text file. In fact, the point of a model in an MVC application is to provide a uniform means of abstracting the data storage mechanisms of your application from the business and flow logic. In your sample application—a restaurant menu—the model will consist of a Menu object that contains a list of menu items.

The first step, then, is to create a Menu class in the Models folder and assign properties as shown in the next listing.

> **Listing 5.6 The Menu and MenuItem model for the History application**

```
namespace MenuHistory.Models
{
   public class Menu
   {
      public string SelectedMeal { get; set; }
      public List<MenuItem> Items { get; set; }
   }

   public class MenuItem
   {
      public string Key { get; set; }
      public string Meal { get; set; }
      public string DishName { get; set; }
      public string DishDescription { get; set; }
      public bool IsSelected { get; set; }
   }
}
```

Using a generic List object to contain your objects makes sense, because it can be operated upon using LINQ expressions to filter and sort, as you did in both the controller and view earlier. The Key property in MenuItem will be the same as the Dish-Name value, except it won't have spaces or special characters. This makes it much friendlier as a routing element in MVC and, by extension, much easier to manipulate using the History API and JavaScript.

In your Menu object, add a constructor with the following contents:

```
public Menu()
{
  Items = new List<MenuItem>();
  Items.Add(new MenuItem()
    {Key="", Meal="", DishName="", DishDescription=""});
}
```

Now using this pattern, fill in the objects with the data. The basic data that you'll use in this sample application is listed in table 5.1, but you can fill in whatever data you like. Just keep in mind that the Key string should correspond to a filename in the

Images folder of the site. If you choose to use the data from table 5.1, you can add your own `DishDescription` text.

Table 5.1 The data for this sample application is simple but provides enough options to show off the History API and MVC routing.

Key	Meal	DishName	DishDescription
Pancakes	Breakfast	Pancakes	...
ScrambledEggs	Breakfast	Scrambled Eggs	...
FrenchToast	Breakfast	French Toast	...
FruitSalad	Lunch	Fruit Salad	...
GrilledCheese	Lunch	Grilled Cheese	...
Hamburger	Lunch	Hamburger	...
Steak	Dinner	Steak	...
ChickenPasta	Dinner	Chicken Pasta	...
Tortilla	Dinner	Black Bean Tortilla	...

You may also choose to just download the images from our GitHub site at this URL: github.com/axshon/HTML-5-Ellipse-Tours/tree/master/demos/history/Menu-History/Images.

Now that the data model is complete, how do you get it to do any work in the application?

5.1.5 *Loading content from the server on demand using partial views*

To get the data model to work, you need to inject your `<aside>` element with a picture and description from the menu object. This is the magic of the History API—the browser doesn't need to refresh the entire page to present users with those new pictures and descriptions each time a link is clicked.

> **NOTE** Remember that the `<aside>` tag's purpose is to provide supporting information for the content that isn't in the critical path.

You'll do this by creating a new view that's a bit more specialized than the page view you've been working on so far. This view won't include the markup to present an entire page. Rather, it will be an HTML island of content that you'll inject into the page, on demand.

To do this, you'll create a controller to support the partial view and a route to direct calls to the new controller. The controller is super-simple to create. Just follow these steps:

1 Right-click on the Controllers folder in your application and select Add > Controller.
2 Name it PreviewController and be sure to use an Empty Controller Template.

The `Index` controller action should be exactly as shown in the following snippet. Note that in order to use the default MVC route, you must name the controller parameter `id`:

```
public PartialViewResult Index(string id)
{
    var menu = new Menu();
    var item = menu.Items.Where(d => d.Key == id).FirstOrDefault();
    return PartialView("Index", item);
}
```

3 Now right-click inside the `Index` method of your PreviewController and select Add View.

4 Make the model a `MenuItem` and check Create as a Partial View. This partial view should look like listing 5.7.

NOTE If you're still not completely familiar with the way ASP.NET MVC works, this section should bring home the fact that each controller in your application can have one or more views. The default name for that view and its associated controller method is `Index`. So the Index method in the PreviewController.cs file corresponds to the Index.cshtml view in the project's Views\Preview folder.

Listing 5.7 The Preview.cshtml partial view displaying image and description

```
@model MenuHistory.Models.MenuItem
<section>
    <figure>
        <img
            src="@Url.Content("~/Images/" + Model.Key + ".jpg")"
            alt="@Html.Raw(Model.DishDescription)" />
        <figcaption>
            @Html.Raw(Model.DishDescription)
        </figcaption>
    </figure>
</section>
```

Url.Content method will generate relative URL for input string provided.

Figure and figcaption tags are used to insert images and annotate them so that image and text are forever linked.

Html.Raw method won't escape or decode parameters and will output exact text passed.

Once you include the sample images (in the Images folder) with names corresponding to the Key values of each dish in the model, you should be able to run the application and enter a URL like this:

```
site/Preview/Index/{dish}
```

Replace the `dish` parameter with any of the dish names in the model, and you'll get something similar to figure 5.6.

It isn't pretty yet, but a few final touches and you'll be ready to start implementing the client-side History architecture. Your goal here is to create ASP.NET MVC views compatible with both modern browsers that support the History API and older browsers that don't. Once you get the pieces in place to make entire page loads work, you

Open-fire grilled to order with no fooling around by our Texas-bred chef

Figure 5.6   The preview partial view will present a `<section>` element with no styling and no wrapping HTML structure. This is a markup island suitable only for insertion into a separate page. When the reader clicks on Steak in the menu, only this image and description will be called from the server and loaded on the page, while the rest of the page remains as is.

can override the partial view behavior and execute it independently of the main page using JavaScript.

You now need to implement the partial view using a `RenderAction` inside the `<aside>` element on the `Menu Index.cshtml` page. The following code shows the action wrapped in a simple null check:

```
<aside class="previewDish">
@{
    if (selectedItem != null)
    {
        Html.RenderAction(
            "Index",
            "Preview",
            new { id = selectedItem.Key }
        );
    }
}
</aside>
```

If you run your application now, you should see something similar to figure 5.7. Everything works, but with only server-side processing. `RenderAction` has pulled in the partial view as a complete HTML island and included it in your page as if it were always there. The client side doesn't know that the content wasn't there the entire time.

At this point, you could call the application complete. For a small application, that might be appropriate, but in the world of HTML5 applications, you're far from done. The problem with the existing application is that each time the user clicks on a menu item, the entire page is refreshed. That's not such a big deal if you have a high-speed connection, but if there's a lot of content on the page, this can be a big deal. What you need is the ability to fill in the partial view of data and change around the styles on the

Figure 5.7 **The final page with a partial view for each menu item and appropriate styling. The site functions but doesn't incorporate the History API, so every menu click will trigger a complete refresh of the page.**

page without refreshing the complete page. This is where the HTML5 History API comes in, and that's where we're headed now.

5.2 Using HTML5 History

Using the History API, you can manipulate the URL of the page without needing to perform a complete refresh. Additionally, because you have MVC views, controllers, and routes controlling the system on the server, your application is completely compatible with any browser, even if JavaScript is disabled or the History API isn't available.

The HTML5 History API allows a visitor to the site to use the back and forward buttons without losing the information needed to present the page. As we explained at the beginning of the chapter, this can be a real asset in a search scenario and it's going to help you serve menu item pictures and descriptions on the same page every time the user clicks a different link. A user with a modern browser will be able to look at each of the breakfast menu items (or any others, for that matter) without the jarring effect of the full page load that will still occur in older browsers.

The History API lets you manipulate the URL and the stack of URLs in the browser's history without performing a complete refresh. In a modern browser, you'd

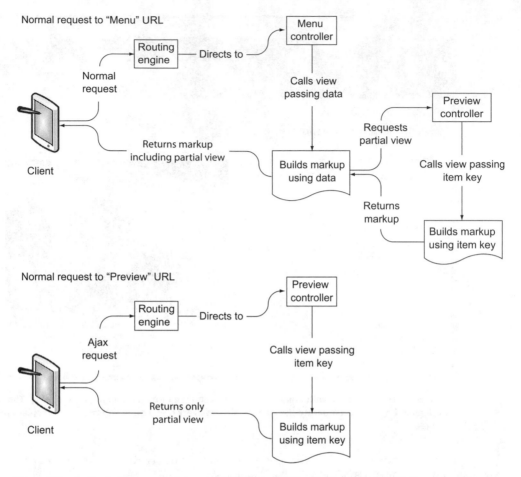

Figure 5.8   A client with a modern browser that supports the History API will initially request the page using the Menu URL, which works through the entire application logic, including the Menu and Preview controllers. This passes the completed HTML page back to the client. After this initial load, all future requests will go directly to the Preview controller and will return just the image and text needed to fill in the preview section of the page.

have traffic as illustrated in figure 5.8, where only the first request gets the entire page and all Ajax requests thereafter only get the partial view.

In this section, you'll learn to use the History API through the effective use of JavaScript and URL formatting. As you move through the section, you'll

- Set up JavaScript to respond to the History events that trigger interface changes
- Use the browser URL to determine what changes need to be made to the interface
- Change the interface based on the previous two steps

First up, the JavaScript.

5.2.1 Adding JavaScript to handle History API navigation events

The first step to using the History API is to attach some JavaScript to the ubiquitous jQuery `ready` handler. This gives you the entry point to the rest of the code, where you attach JavaScript event-handling functions to the history events to trigger the process of loading just a small piece of the page.

Remember, you don't usually want your library to execute until the page is completely loaded. The jQuery team has gone to great effort to figure out when a page is completely loaded and rendered in any browser. That's the reason the `ready` event is the first coded entry point of almost all HTML5 applications.

To begin with the basic plumbing work, follow these steps:

1 Open the _Layout.cshtml file in the Shared folder and remove the jQuery and Modernizr script tags.

2 Replace them with the latest libraries located on the Microsoft CDN.

For your purposes, the script tags at the top of _Layout.cshtml should be edited to read as follows:

```
<script
    src="http://ajax.aspnetcdn.com/ajax/jQuery/jquery-1.7.1.js"
    type="text/javascript"></script>
<script
    src="http://ajax.aspnetcdn.com/ajax/modernizr/
    modernizr-2.0.6-development-only.js" type="text/javascript"></
script>
```

TIP In the preceding snippet, the Modernizr script is set to the development-only version. For your own projects, check out the Modernizr website at modernizr.com to build a custom script that includes only the features you need.

3 Add a new JavaScript file to your application in the Scripts folder and call it main.js.

4 Add the following reference to the JavaScript file just before the closing body element in the _Layout.cshtml page:

```
<script src="@Url.Content("~/Scripts/main.js")" type="text/
    javascript"></script>
```

You'll use the MVC URL helper function to make sure the path is correct when the application is deployed.

5 Finally, open the main.js file and add the `ready` handler in the following listing.

Listing 5.8 Wiring up the jQuery `ready` event

```
$(document).ready(function () {
   if (!Modernizr.history)
      return;                          ◁─┐  If Modernizr doesn't detect HTML5 History API
});                                        support in current browser, do nothing.
```

What is important about this particular ready function is that it will do nothing if the History API isn't detected by Modernizr. A user without this feature in their browser can still click on any menu item and have a full view of the additional content; the browser will just force a complete refresh of the page without the smooth transitions that you'll be building shortly. You're trying to ensure the user experience gracefully degrades when specific capabilities aren't detected, giving the user the best possible experience.

CONNECTING TO THE BROWSER HISTORY EVENT WITH ONPOPSTATE

Core API

Now you need to tie into the history event of the browser. Every browser that supports the History API will have the onpopstate event available for wiring up.

There are two ways to wire this up in a jQuery world; with the base JavaScript event or with the jQuery bind function:

```
onpopstate = function (event) { function body };
```

Or

```
$(window).bind("popstate", function (event) { function body });
```

The onpopstate event fires whenever the user presses the Forward or Back browser buttons, and also, in some browsers, when a page is loaded. The event argument is a standard DOM event with the addition of a state property object. This object contains whatever value was pushed into that particular element in the browser's history stack. The state value can also be null if nothing was assigned to it for the element in question.

In your ready handler, add the following code to the end. This function will execute whenever the onpopstate event fires in the browser window:

```
$(window).bind("popstate", function (event) {
    updateState(history.state);
});
```

We'll get to the updateState function next, but right now you need to understand exactly what this little bit of code does. Whenever the browser's onpopstate event is fired, the state value of the history object for the browser window will be set (by the browser, not by your code) to the value of the data in that item of the history stack. Additionally, the title of the browser window and the document.location will already have been updated when the event fires. Finally, no calls will have been made by the browser to get the resource defined by the new document.location value. Even if there is no caching on the client, no server calls will be made. Figure 5.9 illustrates this process.

MANIPULATING THE HISTORY STACK DIRECTLY USING PUSHSTATE AND REPLACESTATE

Core API

Before the History API existed, the history stack (the browser's URL history) was only changed indirectly by the browser itself when users navigated from page to page. It couldn't be directly changed. But now, with a basic understanding of the History API, you can modify the browser's history for the duration of the current page.

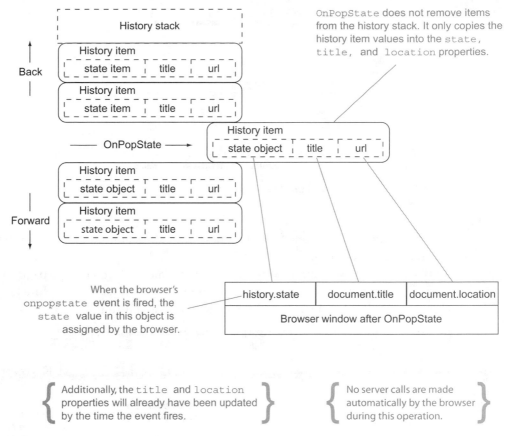

OnPopState does not remove items from the history stack. It only copies the history item values into the state, title, and location properties.

When the browser's onpopstate event is fired, the state value in this object is assigned by the browser.

{ Additionally, the title and location properties will already have been updated by the time the event fires. }

{ No server calls are made automatically by the browser during this operation. }

Figure 5.9 **Understanding** OnPopState **in the History API**

But there are still two missing pieces of logic to explore:

- The links on the menu page are anchor tags that will force the browser to do a complete round trip to the server to get the entire page, defeating the purpose of the History API.
- While you're obtaining values from the history.state property, you aren't assigning that value anywhere because you haven't implemented the update-State function yet.

The history object uses two built-in functions to directly manipulate the history stack: pushState and replaceState. pushState adds a new item to the history stack for the current browser session. Values that are pushed to history won't be available in any other browser or session and can't be enumerated other than to count them using the history.length property. In contrast, replaceState takes the current history entry and replaces the data, title, and URL values without adding or removing anything from the rest of the history stack.

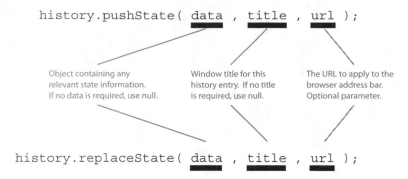

Figure 5.10   `pushState` and `replaceState` **function syntax in the**
`history` **object**

The `pushState` and `replaceState` functions have the same signature, with the syntax
illustrated in figure 5.10.

Back in your application, you won't need to modify the current page in history
after it has completed the load cycle, so you can use the `pushState` function exclusively. In your `ready` function, add the code in the next listing.

Listing 5.9   Using jQuery to override the default behavior of anchors

```
$(".menu-item").click(function (event) {
    event.preventDefault();
    event.stopPropagation();
    var $target = $(this);
    var url = $target.find("a").attr("href");
    var state = stateFromPath(url);
    history.pushState(state, "", url);
    updateState(state);
});
```

stopPropagation keeps event from bubbling beyond event

preventDefault overrides normal click behavior

jQuery selector finds all menu elements

"this" inside click handler will refer to context (the clicked element in this instance)

Gets URL parameter from target object's anchor element

Calls stateFromPath function with URL to build custom state object

Pushes new state object into history

Updates user interface based on new state

While there seems to be a lot going on in this click handler, the fact of the matter is
that you're just overriding default page behavior and adding your own methods in its
place. The History API is acting like a local storage LIFO (last-in-first-out) queue that
stores the URL and data you want without much fuss. The mechanisms you build
around that operation are far more complex than the actual API itself.

At this point, two methods still need to be built out: the `stateFromPath` function
and the `updateState` function. `stateFromPath` parses the current URL to build a
`state` object with the `meal` and `dish` properties that everything else uses. The `update-State` function uses the `state` object to set styles and asynchronously load content to
the page.

In section 5.2.2, you'll build the stateFromPath function because it will give you the opportunity to look more deeply at the page URL and some of its important properties. Afterwards, in section 5.2.3, you'll tackle the updateState function.

5.2.2 Working with the page URL in JavaScript

The location property of the window object in JavaScript is much more than just the URL that appears in the browser's address bar. It is, in fact, a breakout of the major components of the current URL, along with a reload() method that forces the page to re-request everything from the server for the current page. The various properties are all subsets of the entire URL, presented as strings that can be parsed and divided as required, as illustrated in figure 5.11.

By this point, it should be very clear what you're trying to accomplish. In order to build an object that contains the meal and the dish, you take a typical URL used in the application, such as

```
http://www.mysite.com/Menu/Breakfast/Pancakes
```

and divide the pathname into its component parts. The last element in the array is the dish; the element just before it is the meal.

Add the function in the following listing to your main.js file.

Listing 5.10 Dividing the location.pathname to build a JavaScript object

```
function stateFromPath(path) {
    var base = "/Menu/";
    var parts = path.replace(base, "").split("/");    ◁── Remove /Menu/ part of path parameter and split remaining string into array.
    return {
        meal: (parts.length >= 1 ? parts[0] : ""),    Last part of array should be dish and previous part is meal element.
        dish: (parts.length >= 2 ? parts[1] : "")
    };
}
```

This code is by no means ready for prime time. In a production scenario, you'd want to test the entire URL to make sure it's valid according to business rules and that the properties being assigned are in the right order. You should also consider parsing out any querystring values and special characters, and perhaps escaping the outbound text to avoid URL-encoded text.

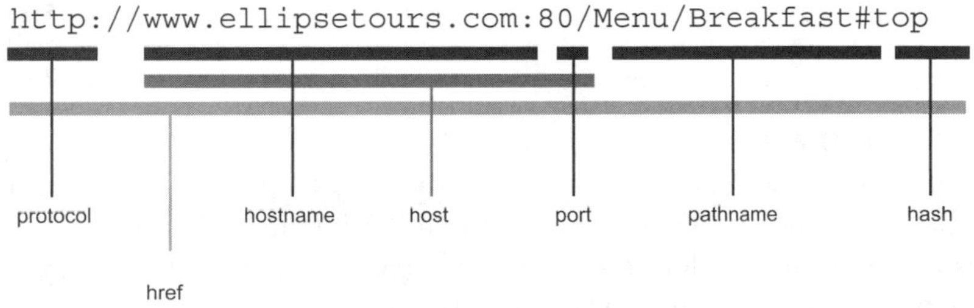

```
http://www.ellipsetours.com:80/Menu/Breakfast#top
```

protocol   hostname   host   port   pathname   hash

href

Figure 5.11 The window.location object properties

> **WARNING** Assigning values using the history.replaceState method will change the current URL of the browser without forcing a server-side hit, but the History API can't edit the protocol, hostname, or host properties of the URL.

5.2.3   *Using History to update the page*

You're almost home! You've tested for the existence of History API support, and you've intercepted the onpopstate event and all menu item click events so that you can call the updateState function. You also worked out a simple mechanism to parse the URL into an object. This is all the background that allows you to change the page based on user interactions without a full page refresh. The updateState function will do just that.

ADDING THE UPDATESTATE FUNCTION

The updateState function goes into your main.js file and makes extensive use of jQuery selectors and Ajax asynchronous server calls to get the preview data. Start with the following code that builds the function signature. The first thing you do inside the function is check to see that the state parameter has been assigned:

```
function updateState(state) {
    if (!state)
        state = stateFromPath(location.pathname);      ◁── If the state value was not
}                                                           passed in, get it from the
                                                            stateFromPath function.
```

The previous snippet ensures that you'll always have a state value, regardless of whether there's a value in history when the onpopstate event fires.

Next, enhance the updateState function to make the edits to the user interface that would be there by default if the MVC view had been called directly with the current URL. Do this by adding and removing CSS classes from elements on the page, appending the code in the next listing to the updateState function.

Listing 5.11   Modifying presentation with jQuery based on the state object

Add active class to selected meal item. →

Locate page element whose data attribute equals selected meal item.

```
var $selectedMenu =
    $(".menu[data-meal='" + state.meal + "']");      ◁──
$(".menu").not($selectedMenu).removeClass("active");   ◁──  Remove active class from
$selectedMenu.addClass("active");                             every other meal item.

var $selectedItem =
    $(".menu-item[data-dish='" + state.dish + "']");    ◁──
$(".menu-item").not($selectedItem).removeClass("selected");   Perform same
$selectedItem.addClass("selected");                           actions against
                                                              dish items.
```

ADDING THE MENU ITEM PREVIEW

The final part of the updateState function is the menu item preview, using the jQuery Ajax $.ajax() function that's provided in the following listing. Note that the URL corresponds to the route you defined for the preview view. The value of data in the callback function should be an HTML island that you can append to the preview container element with no changes.

Listing 5.12 Using Ajax to load an HTML island from the preview partial MVC view

```
var $dishContainer = $(".preview-dish");
var $oldDish = $dishContainer.find("section");

if (!state.dish) {
   $oldDish.fadeOut(function () {
       $oldDish.remove();
   });
   return;
}

var url = "/Preview/Index/" + state.dish;

$.ajax(
   url: url,
   dataType: "html",
   success: function(data) {
      var $newDish = $(data);

      $newDish.find("img").load(function() {

         $newDish.fadeIn(function() {
            $newDish.css("z-index", 0);
         });

         $oldDish.fadeOut(function() {
            $oldDish.remove();
         });
      });

      $newDish
         .css("z-index", 1)
         .hide()
         .appendTo($dishContainer);
   }
});
```

Get reference to preview section and find currently selected dish.

If no selected dish you're at top level, so fade section out.

After fadeout, remove section from DOM.

If no dish is selected there's nothing to fill, so exit.

If dish is selected, compile new URL.

On success, get data as HTML.

Load image from returned data so that everything appears at once.

When image is loaded, fade it into view.

Fade out old image as new one fades in, and remove it when fade is complete.

None of animations will fire until new wrapped set is attached to DOM.

At first, some of the code in listing 5.12 may seem backward, but take a moment to remember the order of operations in jQuery and to consider that CSS styles affecting page flow won't take effect until an element is actually attached to the DOM. To be clear, the order of this code (and the way jQuery executes it) ensures that as one image fades away, the next fades in, but only after the image load is complete. A small amount of careful coding here gives a smooth, subtle, and professional transition to the image previews and, in keeping with your goals, forces a server request for a much smaller data set than is required for a complete page refresh.

5.3   *Two more small steps ...*

The application should work now, but you still need to make some tweaks to the master page and CSS styles to pretty everything up. You need the CSS styling set up so that as sections become active or inactive, you get appropriate "active" and "inactive" effects and a new tab for the menu at the top of the page. It would also be helpful to change the application title that will appear in the header bar of the browser when the page loads.

Hash values and `querystring`s

We've discussed parsing the normal parts of the URL in this chapter, and that's often all you'll need to use the History API in HTML5. But there will be times when additional data is required, both on the client side and on the server. Here are some brief points to remember about `querystring` values that come after the resource name and about hash values, prefixed by a hash (#) symbol, that come at the end of the URL:

- Querystring values have no native JavaScript API to parse them into their component name/value pairs, nor is there a native method in the jQuery library. You can parse these values using regular expressions against the location.href value, but you need to take care and unescape the values before you attempt to present them in your user interface.

- Querystring values are available both on the client and the server.

- Hash values must be escaped and can contain any value or set of values but don't by design have a specification for name/value pairs in the manner of the querystring.

- Hash values are only available on the client. They can't be detected or manipulated on the server other than to be set.

- Hash values are popular for deep-linking content in a way that allows an HTML5 application to see what's requested and take action asynchronously to load additional data. This keeps the user interface responsive even when large amounts of data must be downloaded.

The HTML5 History API also implements the onhashchange event that fires when hash changes take place, but this isn't universally supported, so you should test thoroughly before implementing a solution that relies heavily on this event.

You'll refine the application by making those tweaks now.

CHANGING THE APPLICATION TITLE

To assign the application title, follow these simple steps:

1 Open the Shared/_Layout.cshtml file and find the `<div>` tag with the id of `title`.

2 Change the content of the tag to `"HTML5 Restaurant"` and save the file.

Now the master page will display a better title throughout the application.

CHANGING CSS STYLES

Recall that you're assigning CSS classes to `<section>` tags of either `active` or inactive (empty string) and `<li>` tags of either `selected` or unselected (empty string). An inactive section should still be readable and links-clickable, but the `active` and `selected` elements should stand out so the user knows where they are without having to read the URL. Figure 5.12 shows the look you're after for selected menu items.

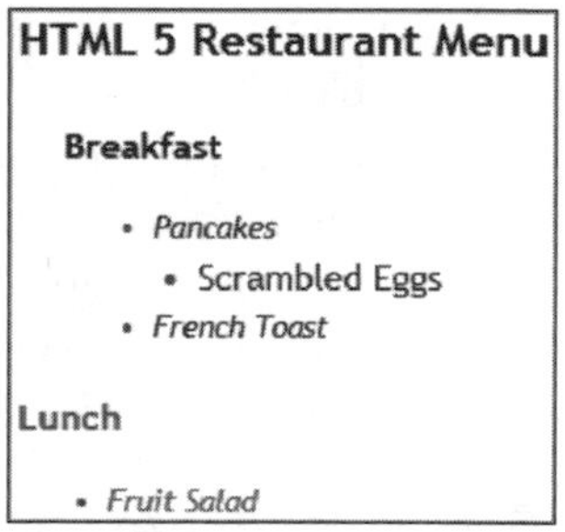

HTML 5 Restaurant Menu

Breakfast

- *Pancakes*
  - Scrambled Eggs
- *French Toast*

Lunch

- *Fruit Salad*

Figure 5.12   The menu application with routes styled based on selected meals and dishes. Selected meals are bold, and selected dishes are inset and changed from italic to normal font.

To tweak your CSS to look like figure 5.12, open the site.css file in the content folder of your MVC application and scroll to the bottom.

NOTE In typical .NET web development, insufficient time is devoted to understanding the critical role that CSS plays in application development and natural user interface design. We're digging into styles here to emphasize this relationship and to drive home the cascading nature of CSS styles.

Listing 5.13 shows the new styles that you'll be creating. With this code, you first override the existing anchor styling so that the menu page can be customized without affecting any other pages. You then build your active and default menu sections with a small inset and color change for active sections. Next, you style your selected and default links and list items to provide a look and feel that gives the user visual cues without a jarring appearance. Place the code from the next listing into your site.css file as described.

Listing 5.13 CSS styles to highlight selected menu items

```
section.menu h3 {
    color: gray;
}

section.menu a:link,
 section.menu a:visited {
    text-decoration: none;
    color: grey;
}

section.menu.active {
    margin-left: 20px;
}

section.menu.active h3 {
    color: black;
    font-weight: bold;
    font-size: larger;
}

section.menu.active a:link,
 section.menu.active a:visited {
    color: black;
}

section.menu li {
    font-style: italic;
}

section.menu li.selected {
    font-style: normal;
    font-size: larger;
    margin-left: 20px;
}
```

Set font color for default section heading.

Override anchor link style for menu sections.

When section is active make title text larger and entire section indented.

Color text of active links black regardless of whether they were previously visited.

When menu list item is selected indent it and remove italic font.

```
.preview-dish {
    position: relative;
    float: right;
    height: 380px;
    width: 480px;
}

.preview-dish section {
    position: absolute;
    width: 100%;
    height: 100%;
    border: 1px solid black;
}
```

Aside element that contains menu photo should be floated to right of screen.

Section element that contains photo will be absolutely positioned inside aside so that it will render in exact same spot every time.

This is good CSS practice for applying a single style to multiple selectors and for overriding existing styles in other parts of the application. Note also that because you're using the `Menu` object's `SelectedMeal` property, you can execute a URL with just the name of the meal (such as /Menu/Dinner) and get a view that highlights an entire section without offsetting a single dish `<li>` element. When these little tricks become second nature to you, you'll find your development speed increasing along with the quality and beauty of your applications.

5.4   *Summary*

In this chapter we looked at how to use partial views and custom routes in ASP.NET MVC to build up a page that's responsive and compatible in any browser. You also learned how to implement the HTML5 History API using asynchronous methods and jQuery animations. These methods could just as easily be used for a photo album website, a newsreader, or a wizard-style questionnaire. Any interaction that represents a progression of steps is a good candidate for History integration.

Using the History API will reduce the number and size of requests to the server as well as provide a richer and more responsive experience for users. The History API may not be the most talked-about API in the HTML5 arsenal, but it deserves attention in any HTML application based on the large benefits in such a small package of features.

In the next chapter, we'll look at one of the most popular of the HTML5 APIs—Geolocation. This technology allows you to develop location-aware websites that can respond to a user's current location in real time.

5.5   *The complete JavaScript library*

The following listing shows you the complete main.js file to provide you with a reference and help you check your work.

Listing 5.14   The complete main.js library

```
// ----------
function stateFromPath(path) {
    var base = "/Menu/";
    var parts = path.replace(base, "").split("/");
    return {
```

```
            meal: (parts.length >= 1 ? parts[0]  : ""),
            dish: (parts.length >= 2 ? parts[1]  : "")
        };
    }
    // ----------
    function updateState(state) {
        if (!state)
            state = stateFromPath(location.pathname);
        // ___ menu
        var $selectedMenu =
            $(".menu[data-meal='" + state.meal + "']");
        $(".menu").not($selectedMenu).removeClass("active");
        $selectedMenu.addClass("active");
        var $selectedItem =
            $(".menu-item[data-dish='" + state.dish + "']");
        $(".menu-item").not($selectedItem).removeClass("selected");
        $selectedItem.addClass("selected");

        // ___ preview
        var $dishContainer = $(".preview-dish");
        var $oldDish = $dishContainer.find("section");
        if (!state.dish) {
            $oldDish.fadeOut(function () {
                $oldDish.remove();
            });
            return;
        }
        var url = "/Preview/Index/" + state.dish;
        $.get(url, function (data) {
            var $newDish = $(data);
            $newDish.find("img").load(function () {
                $newDish.fadeIn(function () {
                    $newDish.css("z-index", 0);
                });
                $oldDish.fadeOut(function () {
                    $oldDish.remove();
                });
            });
            $newDish
              .css("z-index", 1)
              .hide()
              .appendTo($dishContainer);
        });
    }
    // ----------
    $(document).ready(function () {
        if (!Modernizr.history)
            return;
        // ___ history event
        $(window).bind("popstate", function (event) {
            updateState(history.state);
        });
        // ___ clicks
        $(".menu-item").click(function (event) {
            event.preventDefault();
            event.stopPropagation();
```

```
        var $target = $(this);
        var url = $target.find("a").attr("href");
        var state = stateFromPath(url);
        history.pushState(state, "", url);
        updateState(state);
    });
});
```

Geolocation and web mapping

This chapter covers

- Understanding geospatial data and geolocation services
- Building web maps using the HTML5 Geolocation API
- Building and using ASP.NET MVC controllers for JSON data services

The convergence of social media, rich web content, and onboard location services in a mobile device has created a genuine opportunity for developers and businesses that understand the value of "where." When a user asks "where?" what he or she is really asking can be any or all of the following:

- Where am I in relation to where I want to go?
- Where is the person with whom I am communicating, relative to my location?
- How close am I to the product or service I am interested in?
- Is there anything of interest to me nearby?
- When will I arrive, and is there anything that might slow my progress?

Browser support

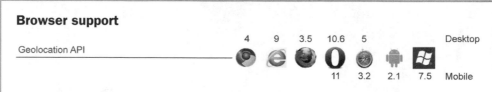

Geolocation API   4   9   3.5   10.6   5   Desktop

                                    11   3.2   2.1   7.5   Mobile

Chapter 6 map

Geolocation is a programming interface that allows JavaScript to read GPS information that the browser gets from the host operating system. Data can be read directly through the interface, or the listeners can be assigned to receive the data whenever the physical location of the device changes.

The following parts of the Geolocation API will be discussed in this book. Section 6.3.1 covers the basics of each object and function in this list, and the rest of the chapter shows how each object and function operates.

The `navigator.geolocation` object

`getCurrentPosition`

`watchPosition`

`clearWatch`

The `position` object

The `coordinates` object

Handling geolocation errors

The position `options` object

The `setAutolocate` function

The question of "where" always boils down to at least two locations: the user's location and the location of the entity the user is interested in. Everything else is just noise and a distraction from this core equation.

Building geolocation into an HTML application—the focus of this chapter—requires you to understand a number of rather abstract concepts, like finding a specific position on the Earth and measuring distances between points across the Earth's surface. In addition, you must understand how those concepts are put into practice using the HTML5 Geolocation API and a third-party mapping API that can display the geospatial data on a web page. We'll show you how to do these things in this chapter, covering the basics you need to work with geographic data. You'll also learn to do the following:

- Use the Geolocation API via JavaScript code to find a user's device
- Work with third-party mapping APIs (the Bing Maps JavaScript API, in particular) that provide a user interface with viewable maps

- Plot data on a map
- Use data from the Geolocation API to change the map
- Enable navigation by combining APIs
- Calculate geospatial data
- Bring server geospatial data into your application

First, we'll spend a little time covering what geospatial data is and what it means in reference to your location on the planet. You need this knowledge to understand how to implement a mapping solution. If you already understand these concepts, feel free to scan the headings or skip directly to the next section, where you'll put that knowledge to use in a real application.

6.1 *"Where am I?": A (brief) geographic location primer*

The practice of finding an exact location for anything on the planet is based on the use of angles to determine where something is on the surface of a sphere. Consider figure 6.1, a rendering of a stress ball, similar to one you might have on your desk

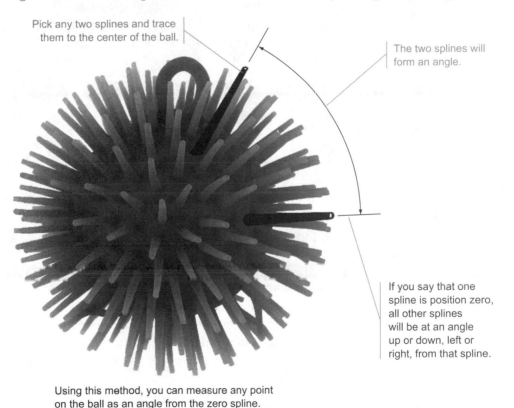

Pick any two splines and trace them to the center of the ball.

The two splines will form an angle.

If you say that one spline is position zero, all other splines will be at an angle up or down, left or right, from that spline.

Using this method, you can measure any point on the ball as an angle from the zero spline.

Figure 6.1 Using a squeeze ball as an example, you can follow any two splines from the surface of the ball to the center and see that an angle is described. The angle can further be divided by how far up or down it goes and how far left or right it goes from a single reference point on the surface.

right now. If you use an arbitrary spline as the zero marker, you can see that any other spline can be identified by its angle up or down, left or right, from the zero spline.

Notice that applying this methodology to locations on Earth, you can divide and subdivide the angles to get as much precision as necessary. You can, theoretically, locate any point on the planet, no matter how microscopic!

Locations based on coordinates versus those relative to a known position

There are two primary ways to determine the location of a user, regardless of the actual mathematical formula used. The first is using a conventional geographic coordinate system based on angles of latitude and longitude. This system allows you to specify two numbers, and it results in a precise location anywhere on the planet.

The second method locates the position of something relative to a known position. Using this method, you can state that from your current position, the thing of interest is at 90 degrees and 20 meters away. You could also state that it's 20 meters away at 3 o'clock. The critical values required are the absolute position of the starting point, the direction the person at the starting location is facing, the distance to the target, and the bearing of the target based on the starting direction.

A common scenario where this second kind of location method is used is in a tactical or military environment. Each team member knows where the other teammates are and can direct actions based on that knowledge. They must act quickly and don't need to remember which way is north or exactly how far something is from each member. Rather, a team leader must be able to tell each member where something is relative to either himself or another team member. This method is generally less accurate because multiple variables are involved and each has a margin of error, but it's quick and useful when precision isn't necessary.

We'll be focusing on the first, more scientific method in this chapter.

This very general explanation is helpful, but it's still not enough to be useful to you in building an application. For that, you also need to know some standard terminology for describing a unique position.

LATITUDE AND LONGITUDE

Latitude is the name for the number of degrees north or south from the equator. Positive numbers will always describe points between the equator and the North Pole whereas negative numbers describe points between the equator and the South Pole. Latitude registers between −90 and 90 degrees, so 90 degrees of latitude would describe a straight line from the center of the Earth to the North Pole. If you want to express these values without using negative numbers, you can say that degrees of latitude are either north or south of the equator.

Longitude is the value in degrees east or west from the prime meridian. The prime meridian runs from the North Pole to the South Pole, straight through Greenwich, England, and down through the western part of Africa. Points to the west of the prime meridian are negative values while points to the east are positive. These values can also be expressed as degrees east or west of the prime meridian. When using just the numbers without the east or west tags, longitude values increment until they reach 180 degrees on the other side of the planet. Near that point, you can have a longitude value of 179.9999 and move slightly and be at –179.9999.

Putting it all together, you can identify any single point on Earth with a pair of numeric values describing angular latitude and longitude values from the corresponding zero lines. Here are a couple of examples:

- The Washington Monument is at 38.8891 degrees latitude, –77.0355 degrees longitude. This is also 38.8891 degrees north and 77.0355 degrees west.
- The Eiffel Tower is at 48.8584 degrees latitude, 2.2944 degrees longitude. This is the same as saying it's 48.8584 degrees north and 2.2944 degrees east.

Figure 6.2 shows exactly how these values flow across the planet from the equator north and south and from the prime meridian east and west.

This seems pretty straightforward, and possibly even lame. "I learned this in elementary school! What does this have to do with the Geolocation API?" you might be thinking. The real value to you as an application developer comes when you have *multiple* geographic coordinates. After all, what developer cares about the latitude and longitude of the Washington Monument or the Eiffel Tower? But taken together, when you have

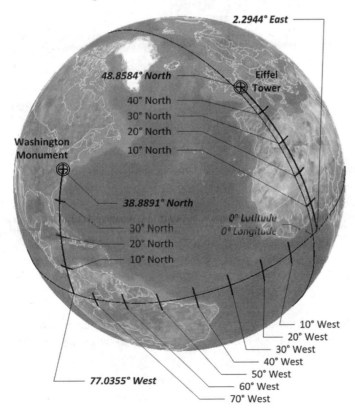

Figure 6.2 Longitude is the number of degrees of angle around the Earth east or west of the prime meridian, and latitude is the number of degrees north or south of the equator.

multiple values and an arbitrary meaning for each point, you can measure the distance between any two points to determine travel information, distribution over an area, and even changes to spatial data over time. Multiple points are where spatial coordinates meet real-world data and become geographic information systems (GISs).

To carry the example one step further, you could use the `computeDistance` JavaScript function you'll write later in this chapter to determine that the distance between the Washington Monument and the Eiffel Tower is 6,162 kilometers, based only on their latitude and longitude coordinates.

Why is position zero in Europe?

Zero degrees of latitude makes sense in that it's the exact center of the spinning planet. But why is zero degrees of longitude set for a random location in western Europe? It was actually established in the mid-1800s based on the fact that England, as the prime super-power of the time, controlled most of the world's shipping. Since navigation at sea needed to be somewhat consistent, most seafarers of the time adopted the British prime meridian for their maps. What this really means is that the prime meridian is both arbitrary and based almost completely on a combination of convenience and politics.

MAKING GEOSPATIAL DATA MEANINGFUL WITH GIS

GIS is the science and practice of adding meaning to one or more geographic points. The study of demographics, weather systems, geology, hydrology, and a myriad of other scientific disciplines center on the question of where an entity of interest is and, frequently, how that entity changes over time. GIS, as an industry, covers the range from spatial data collection, storage, and retrieval to the deep analysis of spatial data as it relates to other data.

The missing link ... altitude

You may have noticed that we included only latitude and longitude in our discussion. Altitude is the third piece of coordinate data, describing the distance straight up from any point on the planet, measured from sea level. We're intentionally avoiding the discussion of altitude here because, while it's important to many types of GIS data collection, many mobile geolocation implementations don't use it. Also, many of the normal web mapping functions, like routing and address location, don't need altitude to function properly.

Now, armed with the nonfunctional geolocation information that you need in order to understand how this chapter's sample application works, let's start building.

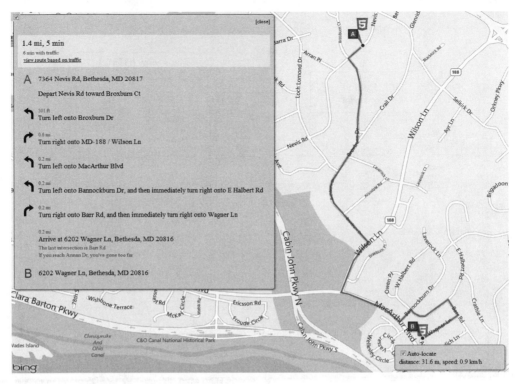

Figure 6.3 The finished geolocation application will allow you to auto-locate yourself on the map and get directions to the point you click on the map.

6.2 Building a geolocation application

The application you'll build in the rest of this chapter uses ASP.NET MVC, JavaScript, and HTML5. There's a screenshot of it in figure 6.3.

To help you build the mapping application, we'll take you through the following steps:

1. Setting up the initial MVC project
2. Creating a new mapping page and adding it to the application menu
3. Getting a free Bing Maps account and displaying basic maps on the page
4. Using the Geolocation and Bing Maps APIs to auto-locate yourself on a map
5. Upgrading the Geolocation API code to follow the user as the device moves around
6. Adding server support for building turn-by-turn directions

When you're finished, you'll have a number of moving parts in your application, all of which are illustrated in figure 6.4.

Let's get started with the basic application setup.

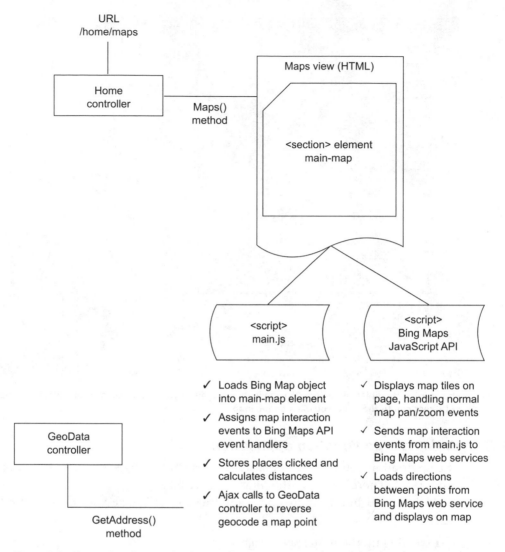

Figure 6.4   The geolocation application you'll create in this chapter will communicate with the server by means of a method on the `HomeController` (/home/maps) and through a JSON-enabled controller call (/GeoData/GetAddress). The Bing Maps JavaScript API will work directly with the `<section>` object assigned as the map to display information, and user interaction will be handled using your own custom JavaScript library.

6.2.1   *Basic application setup*

The initial setup is relatively painless:

1   Open Visual Studio and create a new ASP.NET MVC project called GeoMapping.
2   Update all of the NuGet packages by navigating to Tools > Library Package Manager > Manage NuGet Packages for Solution.

3 Find the Updates tab and go through each list item in the center of the screen and click the Update button.

4 Open the Scripts folder and find the jQuery and Modernizr libraries listed. Note the version numbers of the files.

5 Navigate to the Views > Shared > _Layout.cshtml file, which is the default master page for the application.

6 Find the scripts listed at the top of the page and update the version numbers.

Now you're ready to get on with the real work of creating the mapping web page.

CREATING THE PAGE AND A MAPPING ENDPOINT

Your first substantial step is to create the page that will contain your map and wire it up to the MVC navigation. To do this, you'll create a new stylesheet because the JavaScript map requires absolute positioning; you'll also need to tweak the page to allow for a full browser presentation.

In your new solution, open the `HomeController` and add the following snippet of code inside the class definition:

```
public ActionResult Maps()
{
    return View();
}
```

That's all you need to create the new mapping endpoint. MVC will now recognize the URL `yoursite/Home/Maps`, although nothing will appear there yet.

CREATING THE INTERFACE FOR THE APPLICATION PAGE

Next, you need to create the interface page:

1 Right-click on the `View()` text inside the `Maps` method and select Add View.

2 In the pop-up menu that appears, deselect the check box for Use a Layout or Master Page, and click Add.

A new view called Maps.cshtml will be created. Place the code in the following listing into the new view. This will create the HTML structures you need to display the application.

> **Listing 6.1 The interface for the geolocation application page**

```
@{ Layout = null; }
<!DOCTYPE html>
<html>
<head runat="server">
    <title>Bing Maps and Geolocation</title>
    <link href="@Url.Content("~/Content/Maps.css")"
        rel="stylesheet" type="text/css" />
    <script
        src="@Url.Content("~/Scripts/jquery 1.7.2.min.js")"
        type="text/javascript"></script>
    <script
        src="@Url.Content("~/Scripts/modernizr-2.5.3.js")"
        type="text/javascript"></script>
```

jQuery and Modernizer aren't required for mapping but are helpful for working with DOM and for feature detection respectively.

```
        <script src="http://ecn.dev.virtualearth.net/
            mapcontrol/mapcontrol.ashx?v=7.0"
            type="text/javascript"></script>
</head>
<body>
    <aside class="box-round box-shadow">
        <input id="auto" type="checkbox" />
        <label for="auto">Auto-locate</label>
        <div id="status"></div>
    </aside>
    <section id="main-map">
    </section>
    <section id="itinerary" class="box-round box-shadow">
        <div class="close">[close]</div>
    </section>
    <script src="@Url.Content("~/Scripts/config.js")"
        type="text/javascript"></script>
    <script src="@Url.Content("~/Scripts/main.js")"
        type="text/javascript"></script>
</body>
</html>
```

Mapcontrol script is required and should come from virtualearth.net domain.

We'll use <aside> element to hold controls that test GIS functionality.

One element on page should have unique ID that you can assign to map object.

Itinerary will be displayed or hidden based on current application state.

CREATING THE STYLESHEET

Now you need the stylesheet (maps.css). It goes in the Content folder in your application, but we won't list the entire contents here. It's boring and not relevant to the operation of the application. If you're building the app as you read along, skip to the end of the chapter to grab the code (listing 6.12) and then come back here to continue.

> **TIP**   The styles may seem beside the point in a mapping and GIS chapter, but keep in mind that in the world of HTML5, details count, and users demand a clean, fluid experience in their browsers. Adding rounded corners and drop shadows, and making your application cover every bit of real estate available on a device can make the difference between a good experience and a great one.

ADDING A LINK TO THE MENU BAR

Next, you need to tell MVC to add a new link to the top menu bar, so that when you run your application you'll see the new tab, as in figure 6.5.

To add the Maps menu item, follow these steps:

1   In your application, open the Views\Shared_Layout.cshtml file.

2   Find the menu <ul> element, and at the bottom of its content add a new list item:

```
<li>@Html.ActionLink("Maps", "Maps", "Home")</li>
```

Figure 6.5   The new Maps menu item should appear in the application after you edit the master page.

Unfortunately, when you click on the new Maps menu item, the resulting page doesn't display anything. A view that used a master page would at least have the menus, but because we assigned Layout=null in the view, this particular page doesn't even have that.

The reason is that you still need to get the map API up and running. Remember, you're working with two different APIs in this chapter: the Bing Maps JavaScript API that provides a user interface with viewable maps, and the HTML5 Geolocation API that allows your JavaScript code to find out where the user's device is currently located. Your next step is to build the maps UI.

6.2.2 Using the Bing Maps JavaScript API

The world of web-based mapping and GIS is broad and deep. Here's just a small sample of companies offering mapping or GIS services for web applications:

- Bing Maps—http://www.bingmapsportal.com
- Google Maps—https://developers.google.com/maps/
- Esri—http://www.esri.com/software/arcgis/web-mapping
- OpenStreetMap—http://www.openstreetmap.org
- Yahoo! Maps—http://developer.yahoo.com/maps

Each of these services provides a JavaScript library that you can link to in your site to display and control maps. Each of these libraries also provides a deep set of GIS and display features that can be used in conjunction with the Geolocation API to provide a rich location-based experience. These companies and organizations also provide web services that you can call from your client or server to get additional data or to perform calculations. For instance, there are data sets available for the U.S. census, and rainfall and climate information for the entire planet. Or you might want to do advanced calculations based on something called a *viewshed*. This is the calculated area that's visible to the human eye from any point on the map based on known terrain information.

You'll be using the Bing Maps JavaScript API for a couple of reasons. First, as a Microsoft developer, you'll probably already have an MSDN user ID you can use to sign up for a Bing Maps Developer account. Second, Bing Maps competes directly against Google Maps, which is currently the most popular web mapping service by far. As such, you're more likely to be familiar with Google Maps, so using a different API should help broaden your horizons and help you understand the work involved in changing out services, should the need ever arise.

OPENING A BING MAPS ACCOUNT

The first thing you need to start using Bing Maps is a developer account. Go to http://www.bingmapsportal.com and sign in with your Windows Live ID. From there you can follow the steps to set up the key strings that you'll supply to the Bing Maps API to get maps. This key will be used to track usage and billing for the various services offered by Microsoft.

You mean I have to pay for maps?

Outside of the OpenStreetMaps series of APIs, you'll certainly have to pay for maps deployed to a production website if you're charging for your service. If you don't charge for your application, or if your application will be used for a non-profit organization, you may be able to get your mapping features for free. Additionally, as a developer, you'll get a certain number of API hits for free as part of your developer agreement. Read the terms and conditions carefully before spending too much time developing against a single service, so you aren't boxed into untenable expenses when you go live with your application.

If you're able to put maps on your site for free, you'll often find as part of your agreement that you can use services freely with some restrictions on the kind of maps you can display and the specific services you implement for each vendor.

DISPLAYING A MAP ON THE PAGE

Once you have your license key, you'll need to create a map on your page. By default, the Bing map will be placed inside a `<div>` tag and will immediately take up the entire interface. Use styles to set its absolute position, height, and width to achieve the layout you're looking for.

Note that the Maps.cshtml page references two JavaScript files that don't yet exist:

- /Scripts/config.js
- /Scripts/main.js

Create new JavaScript files in the Scripts folder using these names. Now open the config.js file and add the following code, inserting your Bing Maps key as the value:

```
window.config = {
    mapKey: "your key here"
};
```

This will allow you to change your map key when moving between environments and keep it out of your main codebase, where it doesn't belong. You may also decide to use this `config` object to store other data, or you may prefer to get your key from a remote server.

Now that the structure is in place, let's see how you can make the map display on the page and integrate the Geolocation API. Open the main.js file and add the code in the next listing.

> **Listing 6.2 Initializing the Bing Map on your page using the jQuery `ready()` function**

```
$(document).ready(function () {
    gis.init();                                Call gis object's ready function
});                                            when page has loaded.

window.gis = {
    map: null,
    watchID: null,                             gis contains map
                                               property assigned below.
```

```
$autoCheckbox: null,
$status: null,
$itinerary: null,
startTime: 0,
distance: 0,
previousLocation: null,
places: [],
directionsManager: null,

init: function () {
   var self = this;

   this.$status = $("#status");

   this.$itinerary = $("#itinerary")
      .click(function () {
         self.$itinerary.fadeOut();
      });

   this.map = new Microsoft.Maps.Map(
      $("#main-map")[0],
      { credentials: config.mapKey }
   );

   Microsoft.Maps.Events.addHandler(
      this.map, "click", function (event) {
         self.handleClick(event);
      });

   this.$autoCheckbox =
      $("#auto").change(function () {
         self.setAutoLocate(
            self.$autoCheckbox[0].checked);
      });

   if (Modernizr.geolocation)
      this.setAutoLocate(true);
}};
```

Assign local properties that will contain interface elements to avoid requerying DOM during execution.

Map object is created and assigned to local variable using UI <div> element and configured map key.

Using Modernizr check for HTML5 Geolocation API and assign auto-locate check box event handler.

If you run your application now (and if you filled in your Bing Maps key), you should be able to click on the Maps tab and see a map similar to the one in figure 6.6.

Try it out! You can zoom in and out to anywhere on the planet and switch between road and aerial views. Spend some time getting a feel for how the map pans and zooms with mouse clicks, scroll wheel operations, and the map controls in the top-left corner. Once you feel confident about the user's experience, continue on in the next section to start adding functionality to your map. We'll start by showing you how to integrate the HTML5 Geolocation API with the user interface elements and the mapping API features.

6.3   *Using the Geolocation API*

The HTML5 Geolocation API is a great entry point into the world of spatially integrated web applications. The API itself doesn't provide any mapping support or GIS capabilities. It will return a location and a time stamp and, depending upon the browser, perform very basic calculations to tell you the direction and speed of the device, but

Figure 6.6   The working Bing Maps JavaScript API

nothing beyond that. In order to use it effectively, you have to add logic around the API to display maps and determine geospatial relationships between the device and the world around it.

To get a better understanding of how this puzzle fits together, in this section you'll

- Interact with device location services
- Plot a point on a map
- Integrate geolocation and a map
- Navigate a map using geolocation

First, let's go over the basic operating principals of the Geolocation API and then use the Bing mapping service to exercise some basic geospatial functions.

6.3.1 API functions for interacting with device location services

Core API

The `geolocation` object is available as an object property attached to the `window` `.navigator` object. You can detect its availability with a simple truthy statement in JavaScript:

```
if (window.navigator.geolocation) {
    ... do work ...
}
```

The `window.navigator` object has three methods for interacting with device location services:

- `getCurrentPosition`—This will return a `Position` object based on the last known or cached location. It takes function callbacks for success and errors and an `options` object.
- `watchPosition`—This sets up an iterative watch operation that pings the location services of the device and returns a `Position` on each iteration. This function will return a number that uniquely identifies the watch operation. (Note that the specification states this value is a "token," but in reality it's a numeric value that will increment as you add new position watches.) It takes the same success and error callback functions as well as the `options` object.
- `clearWatch`—This ends a `watchPosition` loop based on the unique ID specified in the input parameter.

THE POSITION OBJECT

Core API

The `Position` object is returned by both the `getCurrentPosition` and `watchPosition` callback functions, and it has only two properties:

- `coords` object property—This property corresponds to a single coordinate object.
- `timestamp` property—This is a numeric value that can be converted quickly into a JavaScript date object by passing it in as a parameter to `Date()`.

> **TIP** Some browsers support additional features on the `Position` object, but these aren't part of the version 1 HTML5 Geolocation specification and shouldn't be counted on for across-the-board availability. For instance, recent versions of Firefox for Windows will return an Address object property attached to `Position` that could potentially save your application from needing to use a paid geolocation service to get an accurate address for a position.

THE COORDINATES OBJECT

Core API

Coordinates are the meat of the `Position` object, and they contain a set of properties corresponding to the found location:

- `latitude`—The decimal value of the current latitude.
- `longitude`—The decimal value of the current longitude.
- `accuracy`—The number of meters (radius) that the latitude and longitude coordinates are considered accurate to.

- altitude—The height above sea level in meters.
- altitudeAccuracy—The number of meters the altitude value is considered accurate to.
- heading—The direction of travel in degrees, based on 0 degrees as true north. A degree heading from the coordinate object can be read directly onto a compass.
- speed: Speed at which the device is traveling, in meters per second.

Among the properties of the coords object, only latitude and longitude are guaranteed to be populated. Accuracy and altitude information can be either null or NaN (not a number) but will never be undefined.

THE ERROR HANDLER CALLBACK AND ERROR OBJECT

Core API

The error handler callback is an optional parameter for both getCurrentLocation and watchPosition. When fired, it will return an error object that contains a numeric code value and a message. Although the error code is numeric, it can be called based on constants defined in the error object itself:

```
errHandler(err) {
    switch (err.code) {
        case err.TIMEOUT:
            // Could not acquire position
            break;
        case err.POSITION_DENIED:
            // User did not allow geolocation usage
            break;
        case err.POSITION_UNAVAILABLE:
            // Browser could not access location based services
            break;
    }
}
```

THE POSITION OPTIONS OBJECT

Core API

The options object is also optional on both the getCurrentLocation and watch-Location function calls. When supplied, it can have any or all of the following properties:

- enableHighAccuracy—A Boolean value of true indicates that the application would like the most accurate results possible. This may delay the results until more satellites are found, or it may reduce battery life by tracking more GPS locators more frequently. The actual implementation of high accuracy varies by platform. The default value is false.
- timeout—An integer value (milliseconds) indicating how long to wait after calling getCurrentPosition before the error handler is invoked with the TIMEOUT error. The default value is zero.
- maximumAge—The number of milliseconds during which it's acceptable to return a cached position object. If set to a non-zero value, the API can return a previously cached position without re-executing its hardware-based GPS location operations. If not supplied to getCurrentPosition, the default

value is zero. If not supplied to `watchPosition`, the value returned can be the most recent position returned or the first position returned when executing the loop.

Overall, the operational set for the Geolocation API is simple and straightforward, but the ability to build location into an existing application gives you some great consumer and corporate possibilities. As mentioned earlier, though, you can't do much when all you have is a location and no reference to other points of interest around you. To resolve that, we'll now look to the Bing Maps Ajax Control that can be easily integrated with geolocation to provide mapping and GIS capabilities to your HTML application.

6.3.2 Plotting a point on a map

Any single point on the map will correspond to a position on the Earth that, as we discussed earlier, has latitude and longitude coordinates. The Bing Maps Ajax Control can find this point by referencing the *x* and *y* coordinates of a `click` event.

Earlier, when you started working on the main.js file, you placed the following bit of code in the `init` function:

```
Microsoft.Maps.Events.addHandler(this.map, "click", function (event) {
    self.handleClick(event);
});
```

That code wires up the map's `click` event to the `Events` object, which is a property of the `Microsoft.Maps` object and has the `addHandler` function listed along with a few others. You can remove a handler with `removeHandler` and check to see if a specific handler is attached using `hasHandler`. The `addThrottledHandler` function gives you the ability to add a handler that will reduce event noise on the map by firing the target event at a minimum interval, based on the `throttleInterval` parameter passed in. This is perfect for tracking mouse movement without causing undue load on the browser's UI thread.

The preceding event wire-up code calls the `handleClick` function of the gis object, which you haven't yet created, so that's the next step. Add the code from the following listing to main.js just after the init function's closing brace.

Listing 6.3 The click event handler will find the coordinates for any point on the screen

```
handleClick: function (event) {
    var self = this;

    if (event.targetType != "map")           ◁─── Check to see that
        return;                                     map was actually
                                                    clicked.
    if (this.places.length >= 2)
        this.clearPlaces();

    var point = new Microsoft.Maps.Point(     With event find x and y
        event.getX(), event.getY());          coordinates that were clicked.
```

```
    var loc = event.target.tryPixelToLocation(point);
    var pin = new Microsoft.Maps.Pushpin(loc, {
        icon: "/Content/html5.png",
        width: 32,
        height: 32
    });

    var place = {
        pin: pin,
        address: null
    };

    this.map.entities.push(pin);
    this.places.push(place);

    // Ajax call to server will go here
},
```

Convert x,y coordinates to map location object.

Add pushpin to map at new location.

Places property will contain references to clicked locations for routing feature.

Add new pushpin to map so it can be viewed.

Note that the map object is referenced in two ways:

- self.map in the JavaScript library
- target property in the click event handler

The getX and getY functions both return the *x* and *y* values in pixels identifying where the user clicked. You have to use the tryPixelToLocation function to turn this into a map point with latitude and longitude. tryPixelToLocation returns null if it can't find a geographic location from an x,y combination.

CREATING PUSHPINS

A Pushpin must have in its constructor two arguments: a location object and an options object. options can be null, but the parameter itself is required.

The default Pushpin object is defined in the Bing Maps Ajax Control and isn't editable, but you can create your own. The following code shows how to create a new Pushpin with an image as its display object:

```
var pin = new Microsoft.Maps.Pushpin(loc, {
    icon: "Images/html5.png",
    width: 32,
    height: 32
});
```

You can search MSDN for the PushpinOptions object to see a complete list of the properties available for this object.

ADDING AN ARRAY OF OBJECTS OVER THE MAP

The entities property of the map object is an array of objects that will appear on the map. These objects, such as the official HTML5 logo, may be in the visible area or located somewhere off-screen.

For instance, if you draw a route, the map control will track all the points and lines on that route but only display what's in the current viewable map. You don't have to worry about showing or hiding elements as they enter or exit the viewable map area. If they're not in the current viewable map area, they will appear as the user pans and zooms around on the map. Consider the entities property to be

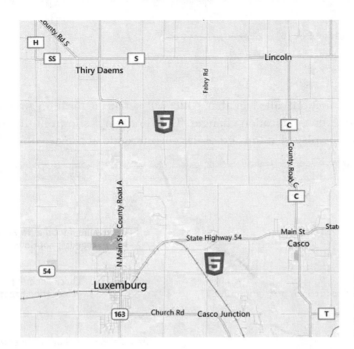

Figure 6.7 The map will place an HTML5 logo in every position clicked on the map when the auto-locate check box is checked on the page.

something like a transparency over the map. It doesn't affect the imagery, but it can be used to enhance it.

NOTE The official logo for HTML5 can be loaded from http://www.w3.org/html/logo/—your purposes are best served with a 32x32 pixel version. You can download this file and place it in the content folder of your application, or choose your own.

TRY IT OUT!

Run your application now. You should see the map and be able to click on any point. When you do, the HTML5 logo will appear where you clicked. Click again and a second point will be added to the map. Once two points have been added to the map, the third click will remove the first two points and add the third. Your page should end up looking something like figure 6.7.

6.3.3 Integrating geolocation and a map

Earlier in this chapter we walked through the parts of the Geolocation API that you'll be using. It's time to put these pieces of the API together to locate the user in the world.

First, take a look at the init function. You used this code earlier to wire up the auto-locate check box's change event:

```
this.$autoCheckbox =
    $("#auto").change(function () {
```

```
        self.setAutoLocate(
            self.$autoCheckbox[0].checked);
    });

if (Modernizr.geolocation)
    this.setAutoLocate(true);
```

Core API

The `setAutoLocate` function called in that code will set up a location watch and update the map whenever the location changes. The function is shown in the following listing and should be placed at the end of the current code in the `gis` object.

> **Listing 6.4 `setAutoLocate` will handle errors and watch the current position**

```
setAutoLocate: function (value) {
    var self = this;

    if (this.auto == value)                                    Determine if local auto variable
        return;                                                has changed; if not do nothing.

    if (value && !Modernizr.geolocation) {
        this.$status                                           Check again for
            .text("geolocation not supported");                geolocation capability.
        return;
    }

    this.auto = value;                                         At startup check box is in indeterminate
    this.$autoCheckbox[0].checked = this.auto;                 state so assign it definite value.

    if (this.auto) {
        this.$status.text("locating...");                      Call Geolocation's watchPosition
        this.watchID = navigator.geolocation                   function if auto is true and get
            .watchPosition(function(position) {                numeric ID value for watch.
                self.updateForPosition(position);                        Update map
            },                                                           position when
            function(error) {                                            watch value
                if (error.code == error.PERMISSION_DENIED)               changes.
                    self.$status.text("Please enable geolocation!");
                else if (error.code == error.POSITION_UNAVAILABLE)      Handle errors
                    self.$status.text("Unable to get location.");       with anonymous
                else if (error.code == error.TIMEOUT)                   function using
                    self.$status.text("Timeout error");                 error.code
                else                                                    value.
                    self.$status.text("Unknown error");

                self.setAutoLocate(false);                     If error occurs turn
            },                                                 off auto-location.
            {
                enableHighAccuracy: true,                      Assign options to allow for
                maximumAge: 30000                              best accuracy of data.
            }
        );
    }
    else {                                                     If auto is false call
        navigator.geolocation.clearWatch(this.watchID);        clearWatch and set
        this.watchID = null;                                   watchID value to turn
    }                                                          off location tracking.
},
```

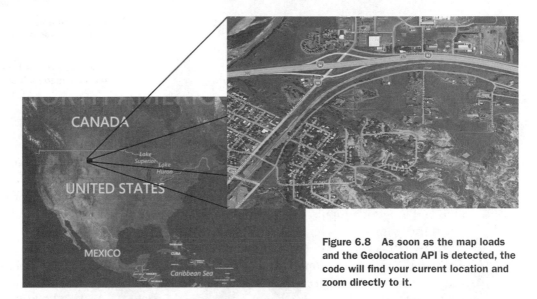

Figure 6.8 As soon as the map loads and the Geolocation API is detected, the code will find your current location and zoom directly to it.

CONSIDERING TIMING AND DEVICE BATTERY LIFE

You're still missing the updateForPosition function, but before we get to that, let's discuss the nature of watchPosition in terms of timing and possible device battery life.

GPS locators are generally radio devices that often maintain a constant fix on multiple satellites. As such, they can take up a lot of power on a mobile device. While you can't tell watchPosition how often to return a new location, you can give it plenty of wiggle room in caching a position using the maximumAge option. You could also decide to call getCurrentPosition inside a setInterval loop, but at that point you're still counting on the internal implementation of the device to maintain satellite tracking.

The current crop of devices on the market aren't really suited for long-term GPS tracking, but as geolocation becomes more a part of the mobile space, expect things to change and the power consumption and accuracy of these devices to improve.

6.3.4 Navigating the map using geolocation data

The next step in tracking the user on the map is to actually perform work with the data returned from the Geolocation API. The effect you're looking for is displayed in figure 6.8, where, when geolocation is detected, the screen will update the current view and zoom level with the new position. When the map loads to the full-world view, it will immediately zoom to your current location.

The function to make this happen is updateForPosition. Review the following listing and add it to your gis object.

Listing 6.5 updateForPosition applies the current position to the map object

```
updateForPosition: function (position) {
    var loc = new Microsoft.Maps.Location(
        position.coords.latitude,
        position.coords.longitude);
```

Geolocation position object has latitude and longitude necessary to build map location.

```
var a = Math.min(25000,
   position.coords.accuracy) / 5000;
var zoom = 16 - Math.round(a);
this.map.setView({
   zoom: zoom,
   center: loc
});

// watched route drawing goes here
},
```

Round current level of accuracy to assign valid zoom level.

After creating location use it to center map on location.

Notice that the position object returned by the Geolocation API isn't the same as the location object you used for locating things on the map. Using the Bing Maps API, you can build a location object from either the pixel location on the map or from latitude and longitude inputs. Everything comes back around to the latitude and longitude though.

The setView function can take a number of properties in the ViewOptions object parameter. The center property takes a single location, and the bounds property can take a LocationRect object that describes a rectangle using the top-left location and height and width values in degrees. Heading can be used to describe which direction appears at the top of the map, and the zoom level can be set from 1 (whole Earth) to a max value that can be different for each location but is generally between 12 and 20.

Here are a few examples:

```
this.map.setView({
   zoom: 14,
   center: loc,
});
```

Or

```
this.map.SetView({
   zoom: 14,
   center: loc,
   heading: 45
});
```

Or

```
this.map.SetView({
   locationrect: rect
});
```

PERFORMING GEOSPATIAL CALCULATIONS WITH COORDINATES

Locating yourself on a map is pretty important, but what happens when you want to show more data on the map, like a line to show where you've traveled? The coordinates object contains heading and speed values, but it's worthwhile to add some of your own calculations.

Go back into the updateForPosition function and add the code in listing 6.6 to do some basic work with the positions. Then draw a Polyline on the map. This will result in your application displaying the current total distance traveled and the speed at which the user is traveling. This code should go in at the end of the updateFor-Position function in main.js.

Listing 6.6 Drawing lines between locations and calculating various travel properties

```
if (this.previousLocation) {
    var distance =
        this.computeDistance(this.previousLocation, loc);
    if (distance > position.coords.accuracy / 2) {
        var line = new Microsoft.Maps.Polyline(
            [this.previousLocation, loc], null);
        this.map.entities.push(line);

        this.distance += distance;
        this.previousLocation = loc;
    }
    var millisecondsPerHour = 1000 * 60 * 60;
    var hours =
        ($.now() - this.startTime) / millisecondsPerHour;
    var kilometerDistance = this.distance / 1000;
    var speed = kilometerDistance / hours;
    this.$status.html("distance: "
        + (Math.round(this.distance * 10) / 10)
        + " m, speed: "
        + (Math.round(speed * 10) / 10)
        + " km/h");
}
else {
    this.previousLocation = loc;
    this.startTime = $.now();
    this.$status.text("located");
}
```

Get distance using haversine-based function and last and current locations.

If distance in meters traveled is less than current level of accuracy don't continue because you may not have actually traveled.

Create Polyline object to display line between last and current positions.

Total up distance traveled.

Replace last position with current position to get ready for next watchPosition event.

Using total distance and time calculate and display average speed.

How many lines can you add to a map?

Polyline is a common object in mapping applications because it can represent either a straight line between two points or an array of line segments along a route. Most mapping services, like the Bing Maps Ajax Control, are highly optimized to allow for many lines to be drawn on the surface without incurring too much processing overhead. You should be careful about the amount of data you're trying to display, but the real threshold is actually quite high.

Once the page is loaded and is following the user, the user should see something like figure 6.9.

USING THE HAVERSINE FORMULA TO CALCULATE DISTANCES

You probably noticed the reference to the haversine formula. If you've done any geospatial work at all, you'll recognize this function. We won't be getting into the details of how this formula does its work, but there are a couple of things that you should be aware of when working with it.

First is the `kilometerConversion` variable. This corresponds to the average radius of the Earth in kilometers. The value has about a three meter variance on the planet, because the Earth isn't exactly round, but bulges a bit in the center.

The second thing you need to be aware of about the haversine formula is that it doesn't measure the distance across the surface of the Earth. What it actually does is determine the angle differential between point A and point B and calculate the distance across that arc at the distance of the radius provided. An example may help explain this better.

Imagine you're holding a grapefruit in your hand, and you're pushing two chopsticks into it so that their tips touch at the exact center of the sphere. The point where each chopstick enters the surface of the grapefruit can be located by degrees of longitude around the circumference, starting from a known position (the prime meridian) and degrees of latitude between the exact top and bottom points. With those values, you can calculate the angle between the two chopsticks. All you need now is the distance from the center to the surface where the chopsticks enter the grapefruit, and you can use the haversine formula to tell you the distance between each hole. This formula is used to find the "great-circle" distance: the distance along an arc between two points described by latitude and longitude coordinates.

Figure 6.9 Following the position of the current user, the application will track and note any change of position in real time. Accuracy will depend on the location and device used, but as you can see, a run-of-the-mill iPhone is accurate enough to tell you which side of the street you're on.

For more details on the haversine formula …

The haversine formula has an implementation in every programming language because it makes geographic distance calculations easy and fast. While the trigonometry involved is well beyond the scope of this book, you can find many resources that detail its function. One of the best is the Wikipedia page at en.wikipedia.org/wiki/Haversine_formula.

The following listing shows a JavaScript implementation of the haversine formula for your sample application; place it in the `gis` object in your solution.

Listing 6.7 The haversine formula for JavaScript

```
computeDistance: function (locationA, locationB) {
    var latA = locationA.latitude;
    var lonA = locationA.longitude;
```

```
var latB = locationB.latitude;
var lonB = locationB.longitude;
var kilometerConversion = 6371;

var dLat = (latB - latA) * Math.PI / 180;
var dLon = (lonB - lonA) * Math.PI / 180;
var a = Math.sin(dLat / 2) * Math.sin(dLat / 2) +
    Math.cos(latA * Math.PI / 180) *
    Math.cos(latB * Math.PI / 180) *
    Math.sin(dLon / 2) * Math.sin(dLon / 2);
var c = 2 * Math.atan2(Math.sqrt(a), Math.sqrt(1 - a));
var meters = c * kilometerConversion * 1000;

return meters;
}
```

You could stop here and have a pretty good web mapping solution. You're able to locate the user and follow them as the device moves around. You also have a beautiful map with a lot of built-in functionality. But in the world of .NET development, you have a bunch of additional options available on the server that allow you to build even more features. Your next step is to add server support for routing.

6.4 Building a service to find address information

The server side of your application will be an MVC controller endpoint that returns an address based on latitude and longitude coordinates. This is referred to as reverse geocoding, and it's available as a service from many providers.

The Bing Maps REST Services platform is one such provider. This service is an integrated part of the Bing platform, so your existing developer map key will also work for this service. You'll be using a JSON-enabled MVC controller to receive the coordinates and send back the address.

> **NOTE** You could just call the Bing REST service from the client, but we decided that adding the server component was important because applications frequently need to curate data that's sent to the client by adding and removing various parts. This example can be easily extended to provide application-specific geospatial data (or any kind of data) to the client via JSON controller actions.

First, you'll build a controller to handle geospatial data, and then you'll learn to display routes between coordinates.

6.4.1 Modeling a point on the Earth in .NET

You need to add two new objects and a controller to the application to support the new functionality. Follow these steps to build the objects:

1 In Visual Studio, find the Models folder, right-click and select Add > Class.
2 Name the new file GeoObjects. This file will contain two classes, `GeoPoint` and `GeoAddress`, which correspond to the input coordinates and the output address.
3 Add the code from the following listing to activate the properties for these two objects.

Listing 6.8   The `GeoPoint` and `GeoAddress` objects are used for reverse geocoding

```
public class GeoPoint
{
    public double Latitude { get; set; }
    public double Longitude { get; set; }
}

public class GeoAddress
{
    public string AddressLine { get; set; }
    public string AdminDistrict { get; set; }
    public string AdminDistrict2 { get; set; }
    public string CountryRegion { get; set; }
    public string FormattedAddress { get; set; }
    public string Locality { get; set; }
    public string PostalCode { get; set; }
}
```

BUILDING THE AJAX ENDPOINT

Next, you need to build the server endpoint that your client application will use as an Ajax endpoint. Remember, you have a comment placeholder in the main.js file; you'll fill that in shortly. The server side of that call is an MVC controller, so you need to do the following:

1. Right-click on Controllers in your solution, and select Add > Controller.
2. Name it GeoDataController.
3. When the controller opens, delete the `Index()` method; it won't be used.
4. In its place, add the `GetAddress` call as follows:

```
public JsonResult GetAddress(GeoPoint geoPoint)
{
    var ret = ReverseGeocode(geoPoint);
    return Json(ret, JsonRequestBehavior.AllowGet);
}
```

This code simply takes the `geoPoint` object passed in and reverse-geocodes it to get the nearest address to the coordinates. It then takes the output and converts it to a JSON object and sends it back to the client. The `JsonResult` object and corresponding `Json()` MVC function are helpers that allow you to quickly serialize objects into a format that's easily consumed by JavaScript.

REVERSE GEOCODING COORDINATES TO GET AN ADDRESS FOR A MAP POINT

The next code you need is the actual `ReverseGeocode` function, which you'll place right into the controller as a private method. Since the built-in MVC `Json` method doesn't give you everything you need to handle JSON data, you need to get another package:

1. In your solution, navigate the menus to Tools > Library Package Manager > Manage NuGet Packages for Solution.
2. Find the Online tab on the left, and then in the Search box at the top right type Json.NET.
3. Install that free package.

What about security?

Some might think that using the HTTP POST method in this Ajax call, rather than the default GET, would improve security, and to some extent they're correct. This would indeed solve the problem of another site calling your method to reverse-geocode a location.

We're using GET here for simplicity and to keep the focus on the Geolocation API and its most basic implementation. A typical production scenario would include securing your service endpoint both using the more secure POST method as well as using SSL (HTTPS) and adding security attributes to your controller call. Those improvements are out of scope for this book, but the MSDN library (http://msdn.microsoft.com) has plenty of security-related resources to get you rolling, depending on your application and deployment environments.

The ReverseGeocode function in listing 6.9 calls into the Bing Maps REST API with a point consisting of Latitude and Longitude properties. When provided with the point data, the REST service will return a JSON string that you can parse to find the address object it should contain. You serialize that object into your own GeoAddress object and return it.

The following code should be placed in the GeoDataController.cs file.

Listing 6.9 Using Bing Maps REST Services to reverse-geocode a coordinate

```
private GeoAddress ReverseGeocode(GeoPoint point)
{
    var key = "your bing maps key";
    var urlFmt =
        @"http://dev.virtualearth.net/REST/" +         Locations API is called to get address
        "v1/Locations/{0},{1}?o=json&key={2}";         though REST service has other features.
    var url = string.Format(urlFmt,
        point.Latitude.ToString(),
        point.Longitude.ToString(),                             Call web service
        key);                                                   by using
    var req = WebRequest.Create(url) as HttpWebRequest;   ◁──   HttpWebRequest.
    if (req != null)
    {
        using (var resp =                             HttpWebResonse will contain
            req.GetResponse() as HttpWebResponse)      address data in JSON format.
        {
            var rdr = new StreamReader(
                resp.GetResponseStream());
            var responseStr = rdr.ReadToEnd();
            JObject fullResponse =                        Use Json.NET JObject
                JObject.Parse(responseStr);              to parse response text.
            try
            {
                JToken addressResponse =               Parse data using Json.NET
                    fullResponse["resourceSets"]        into object with dynamically
                        .First()["resources"]           assigned properties.
                        .First()["address"];
```

```
            var settings = new JsonSerializerSettings();
            settings.ContractResolver =
               new CamelCasePropertyNamesContractResolver();
            var addr =
               JsonConvert.DeserializeObject<GeoAddress>(
                  addressResponse.ToString(),
                  settings
                  );
            return addr;
         }
         catch
         {
            return null;
         }
      }
   }
   else
   {
      return null;
   }
}
```

Serializer object allows for easy translation between incoming JSON and concrete object.

With new serializer perform operation to create new GeoAddress object.

If response is empty or throws exception return null to client.

That takes care of all the work required on the server side. Other than using the Bing Maps REST Services for reverse-geocoding, you can also perform other tasks, like getting real-time traffic data and performing routing calculations on the server. There's a lot of cross-pollination between the REST services and the Ajax control, so we decided to keep the work close to the client and use the Ajax routing features rather than the REST versions.

6.4.2   *Displaying routes between coordinates*

As you've probably noticed by now, the JavaScript we've had you write so far only allows two coordinates to be entered at a time. When the third point is added to the map, the first two are removed and the new point is added as the next starting point. But to call your freshly minted MVC controller, you need an Ajax call that passes in a data object.

First, you'll call GetAddress to find the normalized address for each location, and then you'll send two addresses to a Bind service to get turn-by-turn directions between them.

> TIP   Remember that while you're passing a JSON object with Latitude and Longitude properties to the controller, MVC's model binding feature will automatically convert that to a GeoPoint object because all the properties of the object match the property names in the JSON object (including capitalization). That means passing in a Latitude and Longitude results in a GeoPoint with no work on your part whatsoever!

Find the comment in the handleClick function in main.js where the Ajax call is supposed to go. In place of the comment, add the code shown in the next listing.

Listing 6.10   jQuery Ajax call to get an address from a controller action

```
$.ajax({
    url: "/GeoData/GetAddress",                          Call current application's
    dataType: "json",                                    GeoData/GetAddress
    data: {                                              controller method.
        Latitude: loc.latitude,
        Longitude: loc.longitude                         Pass named
    },                                                   parameters to service.
    success: function (data, textStatus, jqXHR) {
        if (!data || !data.FormattedAddress) {
            self.removePlace(place);
            return;
        }
        place.address = data;                            Assign returned address
        if (self.places.length == 2                      to current place object.
                && self.places[0].address
                && self.places[1].address)
                    self.getDirections(                  If two addresses exist build
                        self.places[0].address,          route between them.
                        self.places[1].address
                    );
    },
    error: function (jqXHR, textStatus, errorThrown) {   If error is returned
        alert("unable to get address: " + errorThrown);  remove place object
        self.removePlace(place);                         that caused error.
    }
});
```

In the preceding Ajax callback function, you call a number of other functions that don't yet exist.

The `removePlace` function goes into the `gis` object in main.js and takes a single place out of your local `places` array if there's an exception or if data doesn't have an address:

```
removePlace: function(place) {
    var index = $.inArray(place, this.places);
    if (index != -1) {
        this.places.splice(index, 1);
        this.map.entities.remove(place.pin);
    }
},
```

The `clearDirections` function removes displayed directions from the interface. This is done with the `directionsManager` object that we'll discuss soon. Remember that this function was part of a commented-out bit of code in the `clearPlaces` function, so you'll need to remove that comment:

```
clearDirections: function () {
    if (!this.directionsManager)
        return;
    this.directionsManager.resetDirections();
    this.$itinerary.fadeOut();
},
```

`clearDirections` also gets placed in the `gis` JavaScript object.

BUILDING AND DISPLAYING DIRECTIONS

Finally, you're at the last part of the application where you actually get turn-by-turn directions from the Bing Maps API and display them on the map. To do this, you'll create a function that has a private function inside it. It may look a little odd, but it helps to keep private logic out of the exposed API of the `gis` object.

The `directionsManager` object is a feature of the mapping API that must be loaded separately. This keeps the primary download smaller. This means that in order to get directions, you have to check for the existence of the object, and, if it doesn't exist, load it by calling its constructor. Once it's loaded, you can set up waypoints with it and then request directions between those waypoints.

The following listing shows how this works. This code should go at the end of the `gis` object code in main.js.

Listing 6.11　Building and displaying directions with the Bing Maps `directionsManager`

```
getDirections: function (addressA, addressB) {
   var self = this;

   function getRoute() {
      self.directionsManager.resetDirections();

      self.directionsManager.setRequestOptions({
         routeMode: Microsoft.Maps.Directions
            .RouteMode.driving
      });

      self.directionsManager.setRenderOptions({
         itineraryContainer: self.$itinerary[0]
      });

      self.directionsManager.addWaypoint(
         new Microsoft.Maps.Directions.Waypoint({
            address: addressA.FormattedAddress
      }));

      self.directionsManager.addWaypoint(
         new Microsoft.Maps.Directions.Waypoint({
            address: addressB.FormattedAddress
      }));

      self.$itinerary.fadeIn();
      self.directionsManager.calculateDirections();
   }

   if (this.directionsManager) {
      getRoute();
   }
   else {
      Microsoft.Maps.loadModule(
         "Microsoft.Maps.Directions", {
            callback: function () {
               self.directionsManager =
                  new Microsoft.Maps.Directions
                     .DirectionsManager(self.map);
```

> **getRoute function is private to direction-building function.**

> **setRequestOptions function can take number of parameters including map zoom level and current display type (aerial or road).**

> **RenderingOptions for route allow you to specify where or if turn-by-turn directions will appear.**

> **Add as many waypoint objects as needed for route and they'll be evaluated in order to build final directions list.**

> **Calling calculateDirections will perform actual routing work on server to return new route.**

> **directionsManager object is part of Microsoft.Maps.Directions module and must be explicitly loaded to be used.**

```
        Microsoft.Maps.Events.addHandler(          ◁─┐  If error occurs
            self.directionsManager,                   │  directionsError will fire.
            "directionsError",
            function (error) {
                alert("Directions error: " + error.message);
                self.clearPlaces();
            }
        );
        getRoute();
    }
  });
 }
}
```

TRY IT OUT!

When you run the application now, you should get the same HTML5 logo on each map click, but when the second icon appears, you should see a route built from point A to point B and directions displayed according to the style set for the itinerary <div>. Figure 6.10 shows the final product, complete with geolocation and Bing Maps integration.

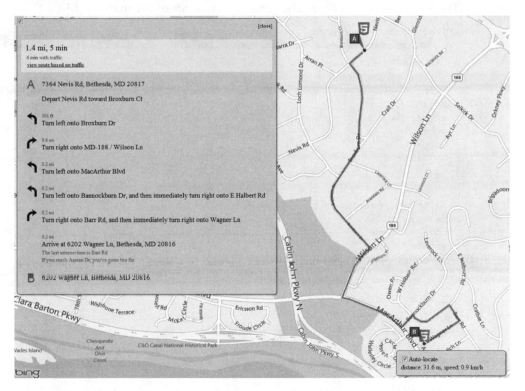

Figure 6.10   The completed application showing routing information and the user's current location

6.5 Summary

In this chapter you learned how to integrate the Geolocation API with an HTML or ASP.NET MVC application, as well as the basics of working with the Bing Maps Ajax Control and REST services. But beyond that, you saw how you can build location-awareness directly into your applications.

You've gained a reasonable understanding of how to get location data from a client machine and transmit it back and forth to the server to add value to your user experience. Geolocation is rapidly becoming a can't-live-without technology for application development, and this chapter was designed to give you a broad overview of what is possible right now for HTML applications.

Coming up next, we'll look at HTML5 Web Workers and the Drag-and-Drop APIs. These two features aren't related but complement one another effectively in a desktop environment that needs to perform a lot of processing without affecting the user experience.

6.6 Complete code listings

The following listing shows the complete contents of the maps.css file.

Listing 6.12 The maps.css stylesheet

```css
html, body, #main-map {
  position: absolute;
  left: 0;
  top: 0;
  right: 0;
  bottom: 0;
  margin: 0;
  padding: 0;
}

aside {
  position: absolute;
  right: 10px;
  bottom: 10px;
  width: 250px;
  padding: 10px;
  z-index: 1;
  background-color: #ddd;
  border: 1px solid #333;
}

#itinerary {
  display: none;
  position: absolute;
  left: 10px;
  top: 10px;
  padding: 10px;
  z-index: 2;
  background-color: #ddd;
  border: 1px solid #333;
```

```
      font-size: smaller;
}
#itinerary .close {
  float: right;
  cursor: pointer;
}

.box-round {
  -webkit-border-radius: 6px;
     -moz-border-radius: 6px;
          border-radius: 6px;
  -moz-background-clip: padding;
  -webkit-background-clip: padding-box;
  background-clip: padding-box;
}

.box-shadow {
  -webkit-box-shadow: 2px 2px 4px rgba(0, 0, 0, 0.3);
     -moz-box-shadow: 2px 2px 4px rgba(0, 0, 0, 0.3);
          box-shadow: 2px 2px 4px rgba(0, 0, 0, 0.3);
}
```

The complete JavaScript code for main.js is in the next listing.

Listing 6.13   The main.js JavaScript file

```
// ----------
$(document).ready(function () {
  gis.init();
});

// ----------
window.gis = {
  map: null,
  watchID: null,
  $autoCheckbox: null,
  $status: null,
  $itinerary: null,
  startTime: 0,
  distance: 0,
  previousLocation: null,
  places: [],
  directionsManager: null,

  // ----------
  init: function () {
    var self = this;

    this.$status = $("#status");

    this.$itinerary = $("#itinerary")
      .click(function() {
        self.$itinerary.fadeOut();
      });

    // ____ map
    this.map = new Microsoft.Maps.Map($("#main-map")[0],
      {credentials: config.mapKey});
```

```
    Microsoft.Maps.Events.addHandler(this.map, "click", function(event) {
      self.handleClick(event);
    });

    // ___ button
    this.$autoCheckbox = $("#auto").change(function() {
      self.setAutoLocate(self.$autoCheckbox[0].checked);
    });

    // ___ get started
    if (Modernizr.geolocation)
      this.setAutoLocate(true);
  },

  // ----------
  handleClick: function(event) {
    var self = this;

    if (event.targetType != "map")
      return;

    if (this.places.length >= 2)
      this.clearPlaces();

    var point = new Microsoft.Maps.Point(event.getX(), event.getY());
    var loc = event.target.tryPixelToLocation(point);
    var pin = new Microsoft.Maps.Pushpin(loc, {
      icon: "/Content/html5.png",
      width: 32,
      height: 32
    });

    var place = {
      pin: pin,
      address: null
    };

    this.map.entities.push(pin);
    this.places.push(place);

    $.ajax({
      url: "/GeoData/GetAddress",
      data: {
        latitude: loc.latitude,
        longitude: loc.longitude
      },
      success: function(data, textStatus, jqXHR) {
        if (!data || !data.FormattedAddress) {
          self.removePlace(place);
          return;
        }

        place.address = data;
        if (self.places.length == 2
          && self.places[0].address && self.places[1].address)
            self.getDirections(
              self.places[0].address, self.places[1].address);
      },
      error: function(jqXHR, textStatus, errorThrown) {
```

```javascript
        alert("unable to get address: " + errorThrown);
        self.removePlace(place);
      }
    });
  },

  // ----------
  removePlace: function(place) {
    var index = $.inArray(place, this.places);
    if (index != -1) {
      this.places.splice(index, 1);
      this.map.entities.remove(place.pin);
    }
  },

  // ----------
  clearPlaces: function() {
    var self = this;

    $.each(this.places, function(index, place) {
      self.map.entities.remove(place.pin);
    });

    this.places = [];
    this.clearDirections();
  },

  // ----------
  getDirections: function(addressA, addressB) {
    var self = this;

    function getRoute() {
      self.directionsManager.resetDirections();

      self.directionsManager.setRequestOptions({
        routeMode: Microsoft.Maps.Directions.RouteMode.driving
      });

      self.directionsManager.setRenderOptions({
        itineraryContainer: self.$itinerary[0]
      });

      self.directionsManager.addWaypoint(
        new Microsoft.Maps.Directions.Waypoint({
          address: addressA.FormattedAddress
      }));

      self.directionsManager.addWaypoint(
        new Microsoft.Maps.Directions.Waypoint({
          address: addressB.FormattedAddress
      }));

      self.$itinerary.fadeIn();
      self.directionsManager.calculateDirections();
    }

    if (this.directionsManager) {
      getRoute();
    } else {
      Microsoft.Maps.loadModule("Microsoft.Maps.Directions", {
        callback: function () {
```

```
            self.directionsManager = new Microsoft.Maps.Directions
              .DirectionsManager(self.map);

            Microsoft.Maps.Events.addHandler(
              self.directionsManager, "directionsError", function(error) {
                alert("Unable to get directions: " + error.message);
                self.clearPlaces();
              });

            getRoute();
          }
        });
      }
    },

    // ----------
    clearDirections: function() {
      if (!this.directionsManager)
        return;

      this.directionsManager.resetDirections();
      this.$itinerary.fadeOut();
    },

    // ----------
    setAutoLocate: function(value) {
      var self = this;

      if (this.auto == value)
        return;

      if (value && !Modernizr.geolocation) {
        this.$status.text("This browser does not support geolocation.");
        return;
      }

      this.auto = value;
      this.$autoCheckbox[0].checked = this.auto;

      if (this.auto) {
        this.$status.text("locating...");
        this.watchID = navigator.geolocation.watchPosition(
          function(position) {
            self.updateForPosition(position);
          },
          function(error) {
            if (error.code == error.PERMISSION_DENIED)
              self.$status.text("Please enable geolocation!");
            else if (error.code == error.POSITION_UNAVAILABLE)
              self.$status.text("Unable to get location.");
            else if (error.code == error.TIMEOUT)
              self.$status.text("Timeout while getting location.");
            else
              self.$status.text("Unknown error while getting location.");
            self.setAutoLocate(false);
          }, {
            enableHighAccuracy: true,
            maximumAge: 30000
          });
```

```
    } else {
      navigator.geolocation.clearWatch(this.watchID);
      this.watchID = null;
    }
  },

  // ----------
  updateForPosition: function(position) {
    var loc = new Microsoft.Maps.Location(
        position.coords.latitude, position.coords.longitude);
    var a = Math.min(25000, position.coords.accuracy) / 5000;
    var zoom = 16 - Math.round(a);
    this.map.setView({
      zoom: zoom,
      center: loc,
    });

    if (this.previousLocation) {
      var distance = this.computeDistance(this.previousLocation, loc);
      if (distance > position.coords.accuracy / 2) {
        // threshold to filter out noise
        var line = new Microsoft.Maps.Polyline(
            [this.previousLocation, loc], null);
        this.map.entities.push(line);

        this.distance += distance;
        this.previousLocation = loc;
      }

      var millisecondsPerHour = 1000 * 60 * 60;
      var hours = ($.now() - this.startTime) / millisecondsPerHour;
      var kilometerDistance = this.distance / 1000;
      var speed = kilometerDistance / hours;
      this.$status.html("distance: "
        + (Math.round(this.distance * 10) / 10)
        + " m, speed: "
        + (Math.round(speed * 10) / 10)
        + " km/h");
    } else {
      this.previousLocation = loc;
      this.startTime = $.now();
      this.$status.text("located");
    }
  },

  // ----------
  computeDistance: function (locationA, locationB) {
    var latA = locationA.latitude;
    var lonA = locationA.longitude;
    var latB = locationB.latitude;
    var lonB = locationB.longitude;
    var earthRadiusInKilometers = 6371;

    var dLat = (latB - latA) * Math.PI / 180;
    var dLon = (lonB - lonA) * Math.PI / 180;
    var a = Math.sin(dLat / 2) * Math.sin(dLat / 2) +
      Math.cos(latA * Math.PI / 180) * Math.cos(latB * Math.PI / 180) *
```

```
      Math.sin(dLon / 2) * Math.sin(dLon / 2);
    var c = 2 * Math.atan2(Math.sqrt(a), Math.sqrt(1 - a));
    var meters = c * earthRadiusInKilometers * 1000;

    return meters;
  }
};
```

Web workers
and drag and drop

This chapter covers

- Implementing drag and drop in a desktop browser
- Marshaling data while dragging user interface elements
- Building a multithreaded web application
- Transferring high-cost CPU operations to background threads

This chapter is all about making difficult things simple. In any HTML application with a significant amount of user interaction, you'll encounter requirements that conflict with one another, such as the need to upload a file or edit an image while maintaining a responsive interface. In this chapter, we'll show you how to balance the need for a responsive user interface (UI) with the requirement to perform complex, processor-intensive tasks with two new HTML5 APIs: Web Workers and Drag and Drop.

Depending on the host system's memory and processor, doing any heavy processing can often cause the screen to hang for a few moments. You may even encounter a browser message stating that it thinks you have a runaway process. The

185

Browser support

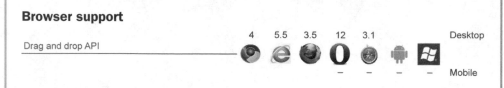

| | 4 | 5.5 | 3.5 | 12 | 3.1 | | Desktop |

Drag and drop API

— — — — Mobile

Chapter 7 map

Drag and drop is the ability to add functionality to any rendered element on a page to be picked up and dragged, along with additional data, across the page and dropped in another location. Drag and drop can be initiated via touch or mouse events. Each stage of a drag-and-drop sequence triggers JavaScript events that a developer can use to execute work.

We'll cover drag-and-drop topics in the following sections:

The drag-and-drop event model	page 191
Implementing drag-and-drop event handlers	page 191
The `dataTransfer` object	page 193
Using the drop event with data	page 194

Web workers are objects in JavaScript that are loaded from a separate JavaScript file and that execute work in a background thread. Web workers can receive messages from the hosting thread and can send messages back to the thread that created them.

We'll look at web workers in the following sections:

The web workers processing model	page 198
Sending work to another thread	page 199
Responding to updates from another thread	page 203

Web Worker API provides a good solution to this problem, allowing you to create background workers that can do work in different threads, thus freeing up the UI thread to redraw the page or perform other interactive logic.

On the UI side, we'll discuss the user's ability to pick up a piece of the interface and place it somewhere else. You could do this in earlier versions of HTML, but not without a lot of effort, and the resulting applications were incompatible across browser platforms. The HTML5 Drag-and-Drop API solves this problem with a simple set of features that are easy to understand and integrate. Drag and drop has traditionally been a resource-intensive operation for the browser to perform, so the ability to do it smoothly while executing a heavy-duty JavaScript task in the background should be a good test of processor capabilities.

In this chapter, we'll show you how to use both of these new APIs in a single example—a graphics processing application. We'll first take a quick look at the final app and lay the groundwork for building it. Then you'll work on these two main tasks:

- Implement drag and drop in JavaScript, including using the `dataTransfer` object and building a unit-of-work object
- Implement web workers, including sending work to another thread and integrating web workers into a JavaScript library

Let's dive right in with a high-level tour of the application, and then you'll start building.

7.1 Getting started: building an app that integrates Drag and Drop and Web Workers

The sample application consists of a single page in an ASP.NET MVC project. At the top of the page, it will present three images that the user can drag from their original locations and drop onto a set of `<canvas>` elements. When the drop occurs, your JavaScript library will take the image data from the dropped image and shuttle it off to a web worker.

The web worker, in turn, will change the image data and send it back to the main library to update the `<canvas>`. The process the web worker executes will make incremental changes to the image sent to it, sending those changes back to the main application library. This will allow the user to drag images onto the `<canvas>` elements very quickly without the processor needing to wait for available cycles.

The completed DragWorker project is shown in figure 7.1.

LAYING THE FOUNDATION FOR A DRAG-AND-DROP/WEB-WORKERS APPLICATION

Now that you know where we're headed, you'll create the solution, add the new page and images, set the styles, and create the view:

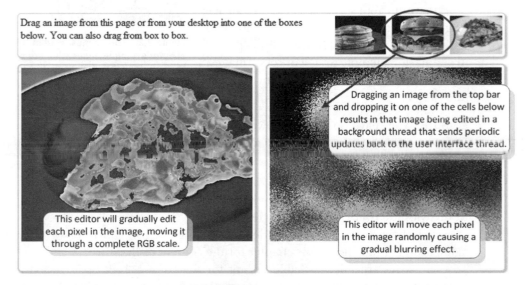

Figure 7.1   When complete, the DragWorker application will allow the user to drag images from the top bar and drop them onto one of the boxes for processing. Processing of the image data is done on a background thread using HTML5 web workers.

1 Create a new ASP.NET MVC web application and call it DragWorker.

2 Make it an internet application and, when it's loaded in Visual Studio, update all the NuGet packages by navigating to Tools > Library Package Manager > Manage NuGet Packages for Solution.

3 Find the Updates tab on the left, and when the center content loads, click the Update button on each of the packages.

4 Open _Layout.cshtml in the Views\Shared folder, and update the script tags to the versions that now exist in your Scripts folder.

CREATING THE PAGE

Now create the new page that will contain your HTML5 application:

1 Open the HomeController.cs file in the Controllers folder, and add the code that follows to the bottom of the class. This code creates the endpoint for your website to respond with an MVC view when /DragWorker is entered in the site URL.

```
public ActionResult DragWorker()
{
    return View();
}
```

2 Go back to the _Layout.cshtml master page and add this line item to the menus that appear at the top of the site:

```
<li>@Html.ActionLink("Drag Worker", "DragWorker", "Home")</li>
```

ADDING THE IMAGES

Next, you need to add the images that you'll be working with. Your example uses three images (figure 7.2) that you can find on GitHub at github.com/axshon/HTML-5-Ellipse-Tours/ tree/master/demos/drag-workers/Images. Place these images in the Content folder of the project.

Figure 7.2   **The images used in this chapter's sample application are available in the downloadable project files that accompany this book.**

> **NOTE** You may also use your own images. If you do, you'll need to find the areas where we reference the images in the solution and change them to refer to your own image filenames.

CREATING THE STYLESHEET

You'll be using a separate stylesheet instead of the default site.css because some of your styles will overwrite those in the ASP.NET MVC templates. So you need to create a new stylesheet in the Content folder called drag.css. You can refer to the complete code listing at the end of this chapter for the content of that file.

The styles are unremarkable except for the user-select style property, which, when set to none, won't allow the <img> element to appear selected when the user begins to drag it. This helps with consistent element styling during drag-and-drop operations but doesn't affect function at all. The rest of the layout helps with the placement of the images along the top bar on the DragWorker page.

BUILDING THE VIEW

It's now time to build the view for DragWorker:

1 Navigate back to the DragWorker endpoint in the HomeController, and right-click on it.

2 From the pop-up menu select Add View.

3 In the MVC view that's created, add the markup in the following listing. This is the UI that contains all the HTML elements in the screenshot in figure 7.3.

Listing 7.1 The complete markup for the DragWorker MVC view

```
@{ Layout = null; }                                    ◁── Set layout to null to keep master
<!DOCTYPE html>                                            page from being pulled in.
<html>
<head>
   <title>Drag & Drop and Web Workers</title>
   <meta name="viewport" content="user-scalable=no,
      initial-scale=1.0, minimum-scale=1.0,
      maximum-scale=1.0" />
   <script src="@Url.Content("~/Scripts/jquery-1.7.2.js")"
      type="text/javascript"></script>
   <script src="@Url.Content("~/Scripts/modernizr-2.5.3.js")"
      type="text/javascript"></script>
   <link href="@Url.Content("~/Content/drag.css")"
      rel="stylesheet" type="text/css" />
</head>
<body>
   <header class="box-round box-shadow">
      <img src="@Url.Content("~/Content/taco.jpg")" >          <img> elements by default
      <img src="@Url.Content("~/Content/burger.jpg")" >        are draggable so they don't
      <img src="@Url.Content("~/Content/pancakes.jpg")" >      need additional attributes.
      Drag an image from this page or from your
      desktop into one of the boxes below. You
      can also drag from box to box.
   </header>
   <section id="content">                                      <div> elements aren't
      <div id="unit1" class="unit box-round box-shadow"        draggable so they get
         draggable="true">                              ▷  draggable attribute applied.
            <canvas />
      </div>
      <div id="unit2" class="unit box-round box-shadow"   ◁── Each <div>
         draggable="true">                                    contains canvas
            <canvas />                                         where you'll
      </div>                                            ◁──   present image.
   </section>
   <script src="@Url.Content("~/Scripts/main.js")"
      type="text/javascript"></script>
</body>
</html>
```

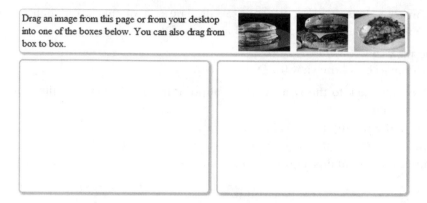

Figure 7.3   The page structure for DragWorker is ready, but no UI elements are enabled because the source drag-and-drop library isn't yet working.

The draggable attribute in listing 7.1 is new in HTML5, and it allows the page designer to assign specific elements as being draggable or not. Most browsers will allow images to be draggable by default, and a basic implementation is already in place. For other elements you'll need to set the attribute to true and then implement whatever logic you want to execute the drag-and-drop operations.

If you pulled in all the styles in drag.css listed at the end of this chapter, you should be able to run your application now and see the basic layout with the images in the top-right corner, as shown in figure 7.3.

Although it looks nice, nothing will work until you build out your main.js file. That's the next step.

7.2   *Implementing drag and drop in JavaScript*

The client libraries for the DragWorker application exist in two files. The first is main.js, which contains all the logic for detecting support, implementing drag-and-drop operations, and handling messaging back and forth between the web worker background process and the hosting page. The second file, worker.js, is where you'll build out the background web-worker tasks in section 7.3.

The basic structure of main.js is as shown in the following listing.

Listing 7.2   The outline of the main.js file

```
$(document).ready(function () {
    DragMain.init();                          ◁─┐  When page loads initialize
});                                                  DragMain object.

window.DragMain = {
    init: function () {
        var self = this;
        if (!Modernizr.draganddrop) {          ◁─┐  Check for
            alert("Drag and drop not supported.");   drag-and-drop
            return;                                   support.
```

```
        }
        if (!Modernizr.webworkers) {
            alert("Web workers not supported. ");
            return;
        }

        new Unit($("#unit1"), "cycle");
        new Unit($("#unit2"), "diffuse");
    }
};

window.Unit = function ($container, type) {
};

Unit.prototype = {
    useImage: function (url) {
    }
};
```

◁— **Check for web worker support.**

| **Create two Unit objects that correspond to <div> containers on page.**

◁— | **Unit objects are created with container object and flag value and will handle drag-and-drop and web worker messages.**

◁— | **Unit prototype's useImage function handles drawing image onto canvas.**

The code for the DragMain object is complete, but the main.js library still has a lot of work to be done. DragMain's only function is to create two Unit objects, sending each the jQuery selector necessary for the Unit to

- Find a page element
- Wire up drag-and-drop events

A Unit in this application is simply the container that you'll use to wrap the functionality for drag and drop as well as what you'll pass in to the web worker. The next step is digging into this object to make it implement HTML5 drag and drop.

First, though, you need some background on exactly what this API looks like and how it works.

7.2.1 *The HTML5 Drag-and-Drop API*

The drag-and-drop implementation in HTML5 is all about the event model. There are seven events that fire at various times during a drag-and-drop operation. The events fire either on the item that's being dragged or on the item that the dragged item is intercepting. These events, after the dragStart, can occur in just about any order.

Figure 7.4 shows a simple view of the entire drag-and-drop event model.

The overall model for drag and drop is quite simple and removes any requirement to track the drag operation in code. By using the various events and the object that's firing each event, you can give your users a very clear idea of exactly what's going to happen and when.

WARNING When we discuss drag and drop, we're usually talking about a desktop browser. The ability to drag elements in a touch interface, while possible, can lead to unmanageable event chains and interactions that are hard for the user to predict or cancel. It's better to use the touch and gesture programming models, rather than their low-level events, on devices like the iPad, iPhone, and tablets. You can search for iOS gesture events to find reference material for iPhone and iPad devices and search for pointer events for the

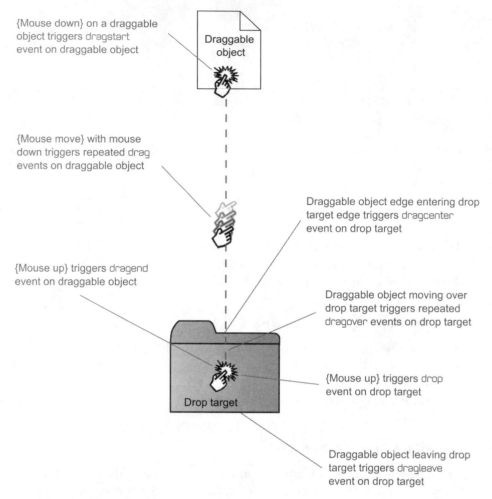

Figure 7.4   The drag-and-drop event model is executed between a draggable object and a drop target object. Various events fire on both objects when the mouse button is depressed, the mouse is moved, and the mouse button is released.

Windows 8 compatible event models. Deep integration with touch is beyond the scope of this book.

In addition to the events and the objects that fire them, certain events bring with them properties that you can use to provide even more functionality. The most important of these is the dataTransfer object that's attached to the dragStart and drop events. Let's take a closer look at that object.

7.2.2   *Using the dataTransfer object to pass data with drag-and-drop events*

Core API

When a `drag` operation occurs, you can easily target both the source of the action and its eventual target object. This is done simply by tracking the element firing each event. But what happens when the elements represent business objects and you need to perform some kind of operation with the underlying data?

For instance, what if you're attempting to drag a contact from a list into a screen element used for chat? It's helpful to bring all the contact information with you while you drag. Also, what happens when you want the drag operation to signify some specific action, like throwing an image in the trash? You could track identifiers and look them up when the operation fires, but the native drag-and-drop specification gives you a better option: the `dataTransfer` object, a property of both the `drag` and `drop` events, provides some interesting capabilities. This object is writable in the case of `dragStart`, the point in the process where you want to assign the data to drag, and it's read-only in the case of `drop`, where you'll read the data back.

In order to assign data to the `dataTransfer` object, you can use the `setData` function, passing in the content type and the actual data object as parameters. This function can only be called during the `dragStart` event because it's read-only at every other time. The `getData` function operates on the `drop` event and takes as its parameter the content type. When called, it returns the object assigned in `setData`.

For instance, the following code snippet shows the relevant parts of code from the drag-and-drop implementation you'll write shortly. This code assigns the data from a canvas element to the `drag` event and then gets it back on the `drop` event:

```
// Assign dataTransfer on dragStart
this.$container.bind("dragStart", function (e) {
    var url = self.$canvas[0].toDataURL();
    e.originalEvent.dataTransfer.setData("text/uri-list", url);
});

// Retrieve data from dataTransfer on drop
this.$container.bind("drop", function(e) {
    var url - e.originalEvent.dataTransfer.getData("URL");
});
```

Note that when you start the drag operation, you pick up the URL of the image that's being dragged and save it to the `dataTransfer` object. Then, when the drop operation occurs, you grab that URL and send it to the `useImage` function in the `Unit` object for processing. The image data isn't transferred, just the URL.

The `dataTransfer` object also has the ability to affect the UI by changing the drag icon when an element fires the `dragenter` or `dragover` events. This is most commonly used for changing the drag icon to a drop icon or to change the mouse cursor to a dragging fist.

The `dropEffect` property is set to `copy`, `move`, `link`, or `none` and allows you to specify that a particular kind of operation will be performed when `drop` fires.

Closely associated with dropEffect is effectAllowed. This property can be assigned for the source object only on dragStart, and for dragenter and dragover for the target object. It allows you to specify which effects are possible during these operations.

7.2.3   Building the object to transfer data during drag and drop

With that basic understanding of drag and drop under your hat, let's get back to the Unit object. Listing 7.3 shows its skeleton.

You first need to set up some local jQuery wrapped sets for the outer container, which, in this case, has a <div> and <canvas> element inside it. Then you build out some structural code for web workers. You'll enhance and fill in that code shortly. Finally, the important code for this discussion is the drag-and-drop event binders that you attach to the previously mentioned wrapped sets (the <div> container elements).

CREATING THE UNIT OBJECT TO CONTROL THE KIND OF WORK TO SEND TO THE WEB WORKER

The code in the following listing should be placed in main.js after the closing brace of the window.DragMain object. You should already have the stubbed-out function there from the earlier code listing.

Listing 7.3   The basic structure of the Unit object

```
window.Unit = function ($container, type) {
   if (!(this instanceof arguments.callee))
      throw new Error("Don't forget to use 'new'!");

   var self = this;
   this.$container = $container;
   this.$canvas = $container.find("canvas");
   this.context = this.$canvas[0].getContext("2d");

   //this.worker = new Worker("/Scripts/worker.js");
   //this.worker.onmessage = function (event) { };
   //this.worker.postMessage({ });

   // Draggable
   this.$container
      .bind("dragStart", function (event) {
      });

   // Drop target
   this.$container
      .bind("dragover", function(event) {
      })
      .bind("dragleave", function(event) {
      })
      .bind("drop", function(event) {
      });
};
```

Check to be sure that object was called with new keyword to ensure you get prototype.

Set up container element references and get reference to canvas drawing context.

Set up web worker implementation for later.

Bind dragStart so that element from one canvas can be dropped onto another canvas.

Bind rest of drag events to container to implement drop operations.

IMPLEMENTING DRAG-AND-DROP EVENT HANDLERS IN THE UNIT OBJECT

Core API

A few lines of code in the previous listing are commented out. Those are related to web workers and the background processing that we'll discuss in the next section. Our focus in listing 7.3 is on the drag-and-drop events you're binding to.

The <img> elements in HTML implement the dragStart function automatically, but if you want the user to be able to drag the image from one canvas onto another canvas, you need to manually wire up that event. In addition, when the dragover and dragleave events fire, you'll simply add and remove CSS class attributes to give the user the appropriate feedback without performing any actual work. dragend is where the real magic happens. That's where you take the dataTransfer object and paint the image onto the canvas when drop occurs.

The following listing shows how all this works inside the Unit object code. This code fills out the functions in the window.Unit object in main.js.

Listing 7.4 Implementing drag-and-drop event handlers in the Unit object

```
// Draggable
this.$container
    .bind("dragStart", function (event) {
        var url = self.$canvas[0].toDataURL();
        event.originalEvent
            .dataTransfer.setData("text/uri-list", url);
    });
// Drop target
this.$container
    .bind("dragover", function(event) {          )
        self.$container.addClass("drag-over");
        event.preventDefault();
        event.stopPropagation();
    })
    .bind("dragleave", function(event) {
        self.$container.removeClass("drag-over");
    })
    .bind("drop", function(event) {
        self.$container.removeClass("drag-over");

        var data =
            event.originalEvent.dataTransfer;
        if (!data)
            return;

        event.preventDefault();
        event.stopPropagation();

        var url = data.getData("URL");
        if (url && url.indexOf("file://") != 0) {
            self.useImage(url);
        }
        else {
            alert("Cannot drag that image into here");
        }
    });
```

When dragStart occurs use toDataURL function to get base64-encoded string of current pixels in canvas element.

Assign image string data as content of drag event.

When target element is notified that another element has entered its boundaries change styles of box.

Reverse the styling when element is dragged out of container.

When drop event fires get dataTransfer object reference.

Retrieve image data string from transfer object.

Draw image onto canvas element.

The stylesheet indicates that when the style class of drag-over is applied, the border should be set to 2 pixels: border: 2px solid #99f. As a result, when an element being dragged enters the boundary of the <div>, it should appear as shown in figure 7.5 and

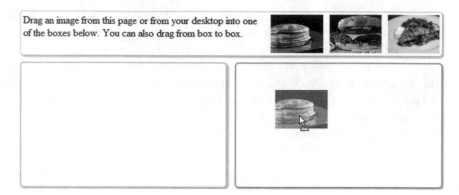

Figure 7.5   When an element is dragged over one of the two divs, the border should be highlighted to give the user feedback about what is about to happen.

will return to normal when the element is either dropped or exits the boundary of the target element.

THE DROP EVENT: DRAWING AN IMAGE TO SCALE ON THE CANVAS ELEMENT

Core API

When an image is dropped onto the `<div>`, the code you have so far will get the image contents of the `drop` event and call `useImage` on the current `Unit` object, tracking the events. Here's the core of the logic:

```
.bind("drop", function(event) {
   self.$container.removeClass("drag-over");

   var data = event.originalEvent.dataTransfer;

   var url = data.getData("URL");
   self.useImage(url);
});
```

This function is part of `Unit`'s prototype and allows you to improve code reuse. Using this method, any object that's dropped that can be converted to image data can call this function to paint that image onto the `<canvas>`.

The next listing accomplishes this; place it at the end of the main.js file.

Listing 7.5   The `useImage` function draws an image to scale on the canvas element

```
Unit.prototype = {
   useImage: function (url) {
      var self = this;
      var $image = $("<img>")
         .load(function () {
            var img = $image[0];
            var w = img.width;
            var h = img.height;
            var cw = self.$container.width();
            var ch = self.$container.height();
```

Create new image wrapped set in memory.

Attach event handler to load event.

Assign height and width properties based on parent container's size.

```
        var scale = cw / w;
        if (h * scale > ch)                        Find height and width
            scale = ch / h;                        scale properties so
        w *= scale;                                aspect is maintained.
        h *= scale;
        self.$canvas                               Set canvas object's height
            .attr("width", w)                      and width properties based
            .attr("height", h)                     on new adjusted size.
            .width(w)
            .height(h);
        self.context                               Draw image onto canvas from
            .drawImage($image[0], 0, 0, w, h);     previously assigned variable.
        try {
            var imageData =
                self.context
                    .getImageData(0, 0, w, h);
            //self.worker.postMessage({             Post new message with
            //   method: "setImageData",           image data to web worker
            //   imageData: imageData              to tell it to begin working.
            //});
        }
        catch (e) {
            alert("Cannot use images from other sites");
        }
    })
    .error(function () {
        alert("Unable to load " + url);            Assign src attribute to
    })                                             image which will fire load
    .attr("src", url);          ◄───────────      event when data is set up.
    }
};
```

We'll come back to the web worker part of the previous code listing soon. For now, the important parts of this useImage function are that you're creating an <img> element in memory, attaching a handler to its load event, and then setting the source value.

> **NOTE** Order of operations is important when building <img> elements from scratch. Assigning the src attribute before binding to the load event might work for larger images that load more slowly, but it would almost certainly fail for smaller images that load very quickly. In this situation, a smaller image could be loaded into the DOM before the event handler wire-up is completed, leaving the event uncaptured. In the previous listing there were a few lines of code that call self.worker.postMessage. These are specific to web workers and the code is commented to allow you to run a quick test on your application.

TRY IT OUT!

With drag and drop enabled, you should be able to start your application and drag an image from the top bar onto the boxes at the bottom of the screen. You should also be able to drag images from one bottom box over to the other and see it be painted there. Figure 7.6 shows how your page should look.

Drag an image from this page or from your desktop into one of the boxes below. You can also drag from box to box.

Figure 7.6   The application working with only HTML5 drag and drop implemented. Dragging an image from the top bar and dropping it onto either box at the bottom of the screen will draw the full-sized version of that image in the box. In addition, dragover icons will appear when the cursor is over a suitable box element.

At this point, you have a solution with a custom single-page application inside an ASP.NET MVC site. This page allows a user to drag images from their original locations onto a target and drop them there. The dropped image is then displayed.

The next step is to have the drop target (or in this case, the Unit object) implement logic sending the image data to a background thread for processing, where you'll manipulate individual pixels in a loop, simulating a processor-heavy task. You must also get that background thread to communicate back to the Unit when updates are complete. Enter the world of the web worker.

7.3   HTML5 Web Workers

Suppose you're writing an image editing tool that will do red-eye detection on uploaded photographs in the browser. In most cases, you'd create a function to detect the conditions related to red-eye in an image and then call it whenever a photo is received. This presents a problem, though, when a user wants to upload many images at once or wants to edit metadata about an image while the photo is being processed. Web workers solve this problem by allowing you to send the byte data that makes up the photo to a background thread for processing. When the work is done, the background thread calls back to the hosting thread, and the interface is updated.

Core API   Web workers are a very simple set of interfaces that allow you to start work in a thread owned by the browser but that's different from the thread used to update the interface. This means true asynchronous programming for JavaScript developers. Modern browsers' JavaScript engines perform asynchronous tasks blazingly quickly, but they don't provide truly concurrent processing, where two tasks are working simultaneously.

Conventional asynchronous tasks usually take the form of callbacks and are fine for simple applications. As the speed of JavaScript engines increases, it even works for many complex applications—a tremendous amount of research and development has been done to get every last ounce of performance out of traditional JavaScript applications. But web workers go a step further and allow you to offload an entire task to another thread, only responding when that thread has an update for the caller.

> **TIP** Refer to Nicholas Zakas's *High Performance JavaScript* (O'Reilly, 2010) for insights into how to get the most from a single thread in JavaScript.

The problem with the single thread, as you've probably realized, is that if you're using <canvas> to build an image or calling a server to round-trip a large data packet, there's really nothing you can do that won't slow down your UI, your complex task, or both. As the client side of web applications gets more complex, you'll find that a single thread is just not enough anymore. Figure 7.7 contrasts the current synchronous UI threading model with the new world of HTML5 web workers.

A web worker's lifetime can last only as long as your current page exists in the browser. If you refresh the page or navigate to a different page, that worker object will be lost and will need to be restarted from scratch if you want to have access to it again.

7.3.1 *The basics: sending work to another thread*

 Core API

A web worker isn't a static object that's always available, like the Geolocation API. Rather, it's an object that you create and reference with a variable.

You do that by calling new on the Worker object and passing it a script file. The file should be referenced by a complete URL or by a location relative to the current page location in your website:

```
var myWorker = new Worker('WorkerProceses.js');
```

Also worth noting is that a web worker doesn't necessarily have to be hosted by the UI thread. A web worker can spawn another web worker just as easily as the UI thread can. The terminology we'll use for the most part will be *host* and *worker*, where *host* is the thread that spawns a new web worker and *worker* is the thread executing the spawned script.

Once created, the worker won't timeout or stop its work unless told to do so via the worker.terminate function. Because the JavaScript is immediately executed into memory when the script file is loaded, the worker can immediately begin performing work such as making calls to Geolocation or making Ajax calls for data. It can also start sending messages back to its parent thread immediately.

The host's worker object has a postMessage(string) method that the host uses to pass in strings or JSON data. The worker also throws a message event that can be

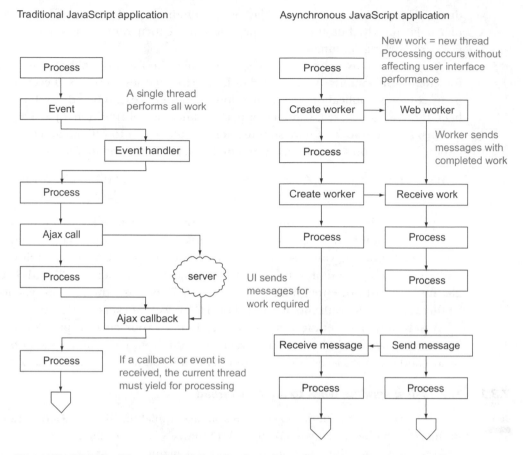

Figure 7.7   While traditional JavaScript applications allow only one thread to perform application tasks, web workers can spawn a new background thread and perform work there, communicating with the UI thread as needed without affecting UI performance.

wired up using either the addEventListener function in the host or by wiring a function to the onmessage event. Likewise, inside the worker object, you can call postMessage and attach a function to the message event. The worker also has a worker.terminate function callable by the host, which stops all work being performed inside the worker. Once terminate is called, no additional messages will be sent or received by the worker object. Figure 7.8 should give you a better idea of the basic methodology.

HOW DO HOST SCRIPTS WORK WITH WEB WORKER SCRIPTS?

An example is in order here. The next two code listings aren't part of this chapter's project, but they're simple examples of the way a host script and web-worker script operate together.

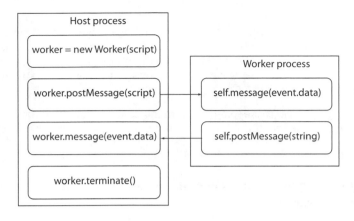

Figure 7.8 The hosting process (usually the UI thread) can post and receive messages using the same methods as the client (worker), except that the host calls these methods on the worker object, whereas the client process uses the `self` keyword to execute these functions.

Rules for web workers

Because web workers are isolated from the host browser's thread, there are certain rules that you need to understand before using them in your website:

- *A web worker will execute inside its own thread in the browser.* It has access to server resources and any data passed to it from the host thread. It also has the ability to start its own workers (called subworkers) and will then become the host thread for those workers. A web worker can also access the `navigator` object, which means it can communicate with the geolocation API. It can make its own Ajax calls and access the `location` object.
- *A web worker can't access any part of the UI.* This means that anything inside the `window` object is off-limits, as is the `document` object. In a JavaScript application, any variables declared are automatically in the global scope, meaning they're attached to `window`, so your web worker won't be able to access any application variables or functions or respond to any events or callbacks from the rest of your application.
- *A web worker uses a single JavaScript file to execute and, within that script, can pull in other files when it starts up.* This opens the possibility of having your entire application logic reside on a thread separate from the UI thread, but that's well outside the scope of this chapter. In the example application, you're offloading only the image processing and leaving drag and drop to the UI thread.

The specification states that web workers, by design, aren't intended for short-term execution and shouldn't be counted upon to be available after starting up. This means that the results of work you send to a web worker shouldn't have UI dependencies. Web workers are useful but heavy, so try not to use a big hammer on a small nail.

What is a host and what is a worker?

In the world of web workers, as in most multithreading scenarios, the terminology can be a little confusing. Why not just call the host the *UI thread* and the new thread the *background*? The answer is that a host process may very well be a worker itself.

Consider a large-scale business application that's managing business logic in a worker thread and communicating rules to the UI thread. If at some point it needs to do some graphics or intense calculations, the worker thread can spin up a worker of its own. The worker becomes the host while simultaneously maintaining its status as the worker for the UI-hosting thread.

Because of this capability, we're keeping the terminology consistent as *host* and *worker*, where the *host* is the creator of the new thread and *worker* is the thread that was created.

Read through the following listing. It assumes there's a button with an ID of test-Workers on an otherwise blank web page.

Listing 7.6 Creating a worker and sending messages to it

```
$(document).ready(function () {
    workerTest.init();                          Initialize object using regular
});                                             jQuery ready function.
window.workerTest = {
    myWorker: null,
    init: function () {
        self = this;                            Current page library
        self.myWorker = new Worker("/Scripts/myWorker.js");   creates new worker
        $("#testWorkers").click(                object and assigns it
            function () {                       as local variable.
                self.myWorker.postMessage("Test");     Same code then sends worker
            }                                   message whenever
        );                                      testWorkers button is clicked.
        self.myWorker.addEventListener("message",
            function (event) {
                alert(event.data);             When worker you created
            },                                 sends message back to page
        false);                                (host), notify user of page.
    }
};
```

The overall interface between a host application and a web worker is very simple, as you can see. The primary difference is that the host calls functions on its worker variable, whereas the client calls the same functions on self.

The next listing shows the code in the myWorker.js file.

Listing 7.7 A simple web worker script example

```
count = 0;                      You don't have access to window so you      Update count value
init = function () {            can't assign variables to it by default.    to show that work
    self.count++;              Variables here are scoped to script file.    has been done.
    self.postMessage("start count: " + count);
}                                                   Upon initialization you can call
self.addEventListener("message", function (event) {  postMessage event, proving
                                                     that messages can be sent not
                                                     in response to any host request.
```

Update
count
variable
whenever
message is
received.

```
    self.count++;
    setTimeout(function () {
        self.postMessage("Last Msg: " + event.data +
            ", count: " + count);
    }, 1000);
}, false);
init();
```

When message is received
wait one second and
respond with message sent
and current count value.

At end of script call
init function to start
performing work.

With this basic example out of the way, it's time to get back to your sample project and see how you can make web workers perform a task for your application.

7.3.2 *Integrating web workers into a JavaScript library*

In this section, you'll finish the main.js file by building in the integration with web workers and then building the worker.js file, which is the code that will execute in a background thread. The sample application has two locations in main.js where you placed code that was intentionally commented out: in the Unit object and in the Unit object's prototype useImage function.

You'll build the client's core Unit object first; it places image data on the current drawing context whenever a message is received from the web worker. Open the main.js file and find the code that starts with this.worker. Update that section with the code in the following listing.

Listing 7.8   Creating a web worker object and sending it a job to perform

Create
new web
worker by
supplying
relative
URL to
worker
script file.

```
this.worker = new Worker("/Scripts/worker.js");
this.worker.onmessage = function (event) {
    self.context.putImageData(event.data, 0, 0);
    setTimeout(function () {
        self.worker.postMessage({
            method: "nextFrame"
        });
    }, 30);
};

this.worker.postMessage({
    method: "setType",
    type: type
});
```

onmessage event
will fire whenever
worker calls
postmessage.

On a timer tell web
worker to fire next
frame of image
processing.

Locally take data
from postmessage
and draw it onto
canvas.

Once worker is created tell it to start working.
Type parameter is string value used to
instantiate Unit object (either cycle or diffuse).

You're not testing to see if the data received from the worker is actually an image because you're in control of the worker object. Because workers can't be started with scripts from another domain, such checks are unnecessary in a small project.

When an image is dropped, the following happens:

- A new Unit is created.
- The worker object is instantiated with a set of initialization variables.
- The Unit is prepared to respond to an updated image from the worker by immediately drawing it onto the drawing context.

With the message posted from the host to the worker, we now need to switch over and look at how the worker will respond.

RESPONDING TO MESSAGES FROM THE HOST PROCESS

Core API

The only thing left to do in the host process is to send the initial data to the web worker. This is handled in the prototype, but you need to flesh out the web worker first.

The operation of the `DragWorker` is simple:

1 Determine what kind of image processing to perform when `setType` is called. This is done when the `Unit` object is first instantiated; it will either perform a pixelation effect or a gradual changing of the colors in an image.

2 Get the `imageData` array from the drawing context on the UI thread.

3 Perform the first frame operation immediately on `imageData`.

4 Use `postMessage` to send a message back to the host thread with the updated data.

5 Wait for the next frame call for updated `imageData`, and execute the image modifications.

6 Use `postMessage` to send a message back to the host thread with the updated data.

If you haven't done so already, create the worker.js object in the Scripts folder and open it up. Add the code in the following listing to this file.

Listing 7.9   The worker.js file responds to messages from the hosting process

Check the method to be sure it's string and that method exists.

```
addEventListener("message", function (event) {
    var method = event.data.method;
    if (typeof method == "string" && method in DragWorker)
        DragWorker[method].call(DragWorker, event.data);
}, false);
```

Data using postMessage is available in event.data property.

Call function requested, passing in entire event.data object as parameter.

The most notable part of the previous code is the ability to `call` a function on an object using just a string and passing in two arguments. Using the built-in `call` and `apply` functions that are attached to the JavaScript function prototype, you can execute functions using arbitrary names.

Both `call` and `apply` perform the same task, with the primary difference being in their signatures. Whereas `call` takes only an object and a list of parameters, `apply` takes the object and an array of argument parameters. It's not enough of a difference to matter in this scenario, where you only want to execute a function with a single parameter, the `event.data` property.

CREATING THE IMAGE EDITING LOGIC

You referenced the `DragWorker` object in the event listener, so in worker.js you need to create it. The following listing provides the function signatures you need to modify individual pixels in an image and to transfer them back out to the hosting thread.

Listing 7.10   `DragWorker` contains the image editing logic

```
var DragWorker = {
    type: null,
    imageData: null,
```

imageData will contain image data originally taken from UI drawing context.

```
    directions: [
        [-1, -1],
        [0, -1],
        [1, -1],
        [1, 0],
        [1, 1],
        [0, 1],
        [-1, 1],
        [-1, 0]
    ],
```

Directions property is a map of coordinates for our diffusion method.

```
    setType: function (data) {
        this.type = data.type;
    },
```

Type property, assigned when you call setType, will describe the flavor of image processing.

```
    setImageData: function (data) {
        this.imageData = data.imageData;
        this.nextFrame();
    },
```

setImageData function assigns data to imageData but will also execute first frame.

```
    nextFrame: function () {
    },
```

nextFrame function performs image manipulation and is only code that posts messages back to host thread.

```
    getPixelIndex: function (x, y) {
    },
```

```
    getPixel: function (x, y) {
    },
```

These functions help us manipulate individual pixels in the image data.

```
    setPixel: function (x, y, pixel) {
    }
};
```

In your application, `setImageData` looks like this:

```
setImageData: function (data) {
    this.imageData = data.imageData;
    this.nextFrame();
},
```

In that snippet, you're assigning a local property from the data object and calling the `nextFrame` function, which executes the edits described in listing 7.11 pixel by pixel. We're listing them without explanation, because graphics algorithms aren't the core logic we want to show you here. Suffice it to say that the pixel data in an image consists of sets of four values strung together, arranged as

```
Red,Green,Blue,Alpha;
Red,Green,Blue,Alpha;
Red,Green,Blue,Alpha;
etc.
```

This RGBA combination of values is exactly the same as the CSS RGBA color values discussed in chapter 2.

The following listing shows the pixel editing functions that go into worker.js.

Listing 7.11 Pixel functions allow you to operate on a pixel rather than an array of data

```
getPixelIndex: function (x, y) {
    if (x < 0 || x >= this.imageData.width ||
      y < 0 || y >= this.imageData.height)
        return -1;

    return (y * this.imageData.width * 4) + (x * 4);
},
getPixel: function (x, y) {
    var index = this.getPixelIndex(x, y);
    if (index == -1)
        return null;
    return {
        r: this.imageData.data[index],
        g: this.imageData.data[index + 1],
        b: this.imageData.data[index + 2],
        a: this.imageData.data[index + 3]
    };
},
setPixel: function (x, y, pixel) {
    var index = this.getPixelIndex(x, y);
    if (index == -1)
        return null;
    this.imageData.data[index] = pixel.r;
    this.imageData.data[index + 1] = pixel.g;
    this.imageData.data[index + 2] = pixel.b;
    this.imageData.data[index + 3] = pixel.a;
}
```

EDITING AN IMAGE IN THE WEB WORKER AND POSTING IT BACK TO THE HOST THREAD

Finally, you've arrived at the crux of the web worker: the editing of an image in a background thread and the subsequent posting of that image back to the host thread.

The `nextFrame` function in worker.js is displayed in the next listing and includes a `switch` statement to determine the type of operation to execute. You could easily add more processing or more types of operations, like alpha fades or image rotation, to this function.

Listing 7.12 `nextFrame` will edit the image and send it back to the host

```
nextFrame: function () {
    switch (this.type) {
        case "cycle":
            var a;
            for (i = 0; i < this.imageData.data.length; i++) {
                if (i % 4 != 3) {
                    var value = this.imageData.data[i] + 1;
                    if (value > 255)
                        value = 0;
                    this.imageData.data[i] = value;
                }
            }
            break;
```

Cycle functionality gets every non-alpha color element in each pixel.

Increment value of pixel by 1 until it reaches 255; then return to 0.

Put new data back into original array.

```
case "diffuse":
  var x;
  var y;
  for (y = 0; y < this.imageData.height; y++) {
    for (x = 0; x < this.imageData.width; x++) {
      var direction =
        this.directions[
          Math.floor(Math.random() *
          this.directions.length)];
      var x1 = x + direction[0];
      var y1 = y + direction[1];
      var pixel = this.getPixel(x, y);
      var pixel1 = this.getPixel(x1, y1);
      if (pixel1) {
        this.setPixel(x, y, pixel1);
        this.setPixel(x1, y1, pixel);
      }
    }
  }
  break;
}
postMessage(this.imageData);
},
```

Diffuse functionality executes for loop on both height and width.

Pick random direction.

Get pixels in current location and new location.

Swap two pixels.

Send newly edited image back to host thread.

TRY IT OUT!

Run your application now, and you should be able to drag images onto the left and right panes of the screen to see the web workers doing their job and modifying the images, as in figure 7.9.

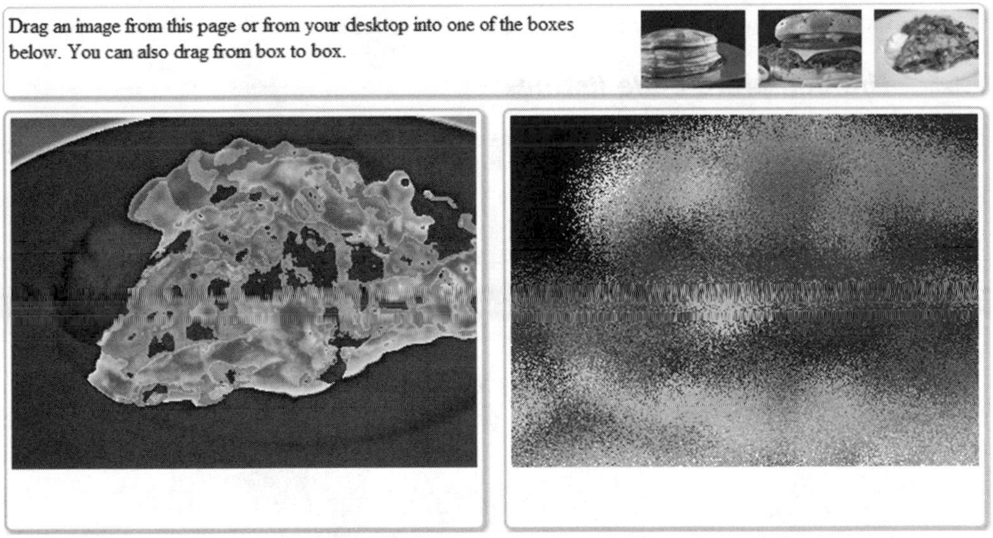

Figure 7.9 The completed application. Drag and drop events still fire, allowing a user to drop any image onto either box. Once the drop occurs, the web worker will take over and edit the image data, sending updates back to the hosting thread where the image is repainted on the page.

The strong contrasts on the updated image appear when the 255 value of any RGB value is hit and it reverts back to 0 to start again. If you wait long enough, that image should return to its original state for about 30 milliseconds.

On the right side, the image will always maintain the same number of pixels, and those pixels will never change color. They will, however, change positions and start to blur and pixelate the screen until the original image is no longer distinguishable.

7.4   Summary

In this chapter, you worked your way through the development of a drag-and-drop interface that modified images from a `<canvas>` element using web workers. Along the way, you looked at a means of moving data along with UI elements during a drag operation and at how to marshal data and objects back and forth between the host thread and the worker thread.

Drag and drop is a feature of desktop interfaces that has, in the past, been difficult to replicate without major branches in code to accommodate different browsers. The HTML5 API brings everyone onto a level playing field to reduce code and improve reliability. While the Drag-and-Drop API is limited to desktop browsers, there are far fewer limits to what you can do with web workers. As mobile devices get more processors and desktops become faster, it will be more important to use the Web Worker API to speed your application processing by taking work away from the main UI thread and giving it to background threads.

We'll continue this theme of improving performance with web applications in the next chapter, as we dig into the world of real-time communications between a web page and a server, otherwise known as Websockets.

7.5   The complete code listings

Listing 7.13   The complete code for main.js

```javascript
$(document).ready(function () {
  DragMain.init();
});

window.DragMain = {
  init: function () {
    var self = this;

    if (!Modernizr.draganddrop) {
      alert("This browser does not support drag and drop");
      return;
    }

    if (!Modernizr.webworkers) {
      alert("This browser does not support web workers");
      return;
    }

    new Unit($("#unit1"), "cycle");
    new Unit($("#unit2"), "diffuse");
```

```
    }
};

window.Unit = function ($container, type) {
  if (!(this instanceof arguments.callee))
    throw new Error("Don't forget to use 'new'!");

  var self = this;
  this.$container = $container;
  this.$canvas = $container.find("canvas");
  this.context = this.$canvas[0].getContext("2d");

  this.worker = new Worker("/Scripts/worker.js");
  this.worker.onmessage = function (event) {
    self.context.putImageData(event.data, 0, 0);
    setTimeout(function () {
      self.worker.postMessage({
        method: "nextFrame"
      });
    }, 30);
  };

  this.worker.postMessage({
    method: "setType",
    type: type
  });

  // Draggable
  this.$container
    .bind("dragStart", function (event) {
      var url = self.$canvas[0].toDataURL();
      event.originalEvent.dataTransfer.setData("text/uri-list", url);
    });

  // Drop target
  this.$container
    .bind("dragover", function(event) {
      self.$container.addClass("drag-over");
      event.preventDefault();
      event.stopPropagation();
    })
    .bind("dragleave", function(event) {
      self.$container.removeClass("drag-over");
    })
    .bind("drop", function(event) {
      self.$container.removeClass("drag-over");

      var data = event.originalEvent.dataTransfer;
      if (!data)
        return;

      event.preventDefault();
      event.stopPropagation();

      var url = data.getData("URL");
      if (url && url.indexOf("file://") != 0) {
        self.useImage(url);
      } else if ("FileReader" in window) {
        var files = data.files;
```

```
          var found = false;
          var a;
          for (i = 0; i < files.length; i++) {
            var file = files[i];
            if (!file.type.match("image.*"))
              continue;
            var reader = new FileReader();
            reader.onload = function(loadEvent) {
              self.useImage(loadEvent.target.result);
            };
            reader.readAsDataURL(file);
            found = true;
            break;
          }
          if (!found)
            alert("no image files dropped");
        } else {
          alert("This browser does not support dragging from desktop");
        }
      });
    };

Unit.prototype = {
  useImage: function (url) {
    var self = this;
    var $image = $("<img>")
      .load(function () {
        var img = $image[0];
        var w = img.width;
        var h = img.height;
        var cw = self.$container.width();
        var ch = self.$container.height();
        var scale = cw / w;
        if (h * scale > ch)
          scale = ch / h;
        w *= scale;
        h *= scale;
        self.$canvas
          .attr("width", w)
          .attr("height", h)
          .width(w)
          .height(h);
        self.context.drawImage($image[0], 0, 0, w, h);
        try {
          var imageData =
            self.context.getImageData(0, 0, w, h);
          self.worker.postMessage({
            method: "setImageData",
            imageData: imageData
          });
        }
        catch (e) {
          alert("Cannot use images from other sites");
        }
      })
```

```
        .error(function () {
          alert("Unable to load " + url);
        })
        .attr("src", url);
    }
};
```

Listing 7.14 The complete code for worker.js

```
addEventListener("message", function (event) {
  var method = event.data.method;
  if (typeof method == "string" && method in DragWorker)
    DragWorker[method].call(DragWorker, event.data);
}, false);

var DragWorker = {
  type: null,
  imageData: null,
  directions: [
    [-1, -1],
    [0, -1],
    [1, -1],
    [1, 0],
    [1, 1],
    [0, 1],
    [-1, 1],
    [-1, 0]
  ],

  setType: function (data) {
    this.type = data.type;
  },

  setImageData: function (data) {
    this.imageData = data.imageData;
    this.nextFrame();
  },

  nextFrame: function () {
    switch (this.type) {
      case "cycle":
        var a;
        for (i = 0; i < this.imageData.data.length; i++) {
          if (i % 4 != 3) {
            var value = this.imageData.data[i] + 1;
            if (value > 255)
              value = 0;
            this.imageData.data[i] = value;
          }
        }
        break;

      case "diffuse":
        var x;
        var y;
        for (y = 0; y < this.imageData.height; y++) {
          for (x = 0; x < this.imageData.width; x++) {
```

```
            var direction =
              this.directions[
                Math.floor(Math.random() *
                this.directions.length)];
            var x1 = x + direction[0];
            var y1 = y + direction[1];
            var pixel = this.getPixel(x, y);
            var pixel1 = this.getPixel(x1, y1);
            if (pixel1) {
              this.setPixel(x, y, pixel1);
              this.setPixel(x1, y1, pixel);
            }
          }
        }
      }
      break;
    }
    postMessage(this.imageData);
  },

  getPixelIndex: function (x, y) {
    if (x < 0 || x >= this.imageData.width ||
      y < 0 || y >= this.imageData.height)
        return -1;

    return (y * this.imageData.width * 4) + (x * 4);
  },

  getPixel: function (x, y) {
    var index = this.getPixelIndex(x, y);
    if (index == -1)
      return null;
    return {
      r: this.imageData.data[index],
      g: this.imageData.data[index + 1],
      b: this.imageData.data[index + 2],
      a: this.imageData.data[index + 3]
    };
  },

  setPixel: function (x, y, pixel) {
    var index = this.getPixelIndex(x, y);
    if (index == -1)
      return null;
    this.imageData.data[index] = pixel.r;
    this.imageData.data[index + 1] = pixel.g;
    this.imageData.data[index + 2] = pixel.b;
    this.imageData.data[index + 3] = pixel.a;
  }
};
```

Listing 7.15 The complete code for drag.css

```
* { margin: 0; padding: 0; }

html, body {
  position: absolute;
```

```
    left: 0; top: 0; right: 0; bottom: 0;
}

header {
  position: absolute;
  left: 10px; top: 10px; right: 10px; height: 60px;
  padding: 4px; border: 1px solid #ccc;
}

header span { float: left; }

header img {
  float: right; height: 100%;
  padding-left: 10px;
  -webkit-user-select: none;
  -khtml-user-select: none;
  -moz-user-select: none;
  -o-user-select: none;
  user-select: none;
}

#content {
  position: absolute;
  left: 10px; top: 90px; right: 10px; bottom: 10px;
}

.unit {
  position: absolute;
  padding: 4px; border: 2px solid #ccc;
}

.unit.drag-over {
  border: 2px solid #99f;
}

#unit1 {
    left: 0; top: 0; right: 51%; bottom: 0;
}

#unit2 {
    left: 51%; top: 0; right: 0; bottom: 0;
}

.box-round {
    -webkit-border-radius: 6px;
    -moz-border-radius: 6px;
    border-radius: 6px;
    -moz-background-clip: padding
    -webkit-background-clip: padding-box;
    background-clip: padding-box;
}

.box-shadow {
  -webkit-box-shadow: 2px 2px 4px rgba(0, 0, 0, 0.3);
  -moz-box-shadow: 2px 2px 4px rgba(0, 0, 0, 0.3);
  box-shadow: 2px 2px 4px rgba(0, 0, 0, 0.3);
}
```

Websockets 8

This chapter covers

- Understanding the basic difference between HTTP and TCP traffic
- Using Websockets and JavaScript to communicate in real time over the web
- Installing Node.js and building a simple TCP server

The Websockets specification is one of the most interesting and paradigm-shifting APIs in the HTML5 stack. When implemented in a web platform, your applications can go from sending a request and waiting for a response to talking to a server or other clients in real time.

With Websockets, you can build, for instance, a web application on a tablet device that can play a game with thousands of players in real time. MMOG (massively multiplayer online games) are already popular, and the versions based on HTML5 are getting more common all the time. How about a website that lets you fire it up, go for a run, and race with someone on the other side of the planet? Integrate Websockets with Geolocation, and you're literally on your way in every sense. Or consider the live streaming of a concert where you get to interact with people in

Browser support

Websockets API ——————————— 14   10   6   N/A   N/A   Desktop

N/A   N/A   N/A   N/A   Mobile

Chapter 8 map

Websockets allow a browser to communicate with a server via TCP. TCP communications are lighter and faster than normal HTTP communications, they're persistent, and they're bidirectional. Persistent connections allow the server to *push* data to a client without the browser requesting it, a feature not possible in HTTP. Bidirectional communications allow the client and server to be sending and receiving messages at the same time.

The `WebSocket` object	section 8.2.2
The `send` function	section 8.2.2
The `onmessage` event	section 8.2.2
The `readyState` property	section 8.2.2
Other connection events	section 8.2.2
The `close` function	section 8.2.2
Opening a server connection with Websockets	section 8.2.3

the audience or even the band. This is perfectly possible and may perhaps be commonplace very soon.

Using Websockets, your HTML application gains the ability to communicate in real time with a server and other users. You become a live node on a much larger network, able to push and pull data simultaneously without the formatting constraints of HTTP traffic.

In this chapter, you'll build a simple chat application that uses a single page inside an ASP.NET MVC application to communicate with a server built using Node.js. It will be easier than you think and faster than you might expect. You can look forward to these highlights as you move through the chapter:

- Building the chat web page
- Creating a library to bind to Websockets API events
- Installing Node.js and building a simple TCP chat server
- Connecting the client library to the server and discriminating between custom event types

First though, as a .NET developer, you may not be familiar with the ins and outs of HTTP and TCP, so we'll start with a little background on what they are and how they perform their respective tasks.

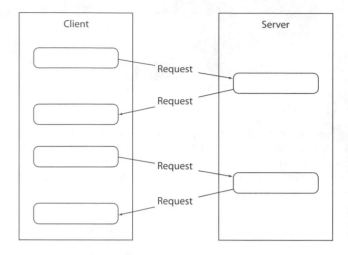

Figure 8.1 The HTTP specification is one of client-initiated requests and server responses. This provides for very good scalability and multiple kinds of caching, but it doesn't allow for bidirectional communication.

8.1   *HTTP and TCP—a quick primer*

Nearly all traffic to and from web browsers throughout the world flows by means of Hypertext Transfer Protocol (HTTP). This isn't the fastest means of text, data, or image transmission, but it's reliable. The Transmission Control Protocol (TCP) is a layer below HTTP, and it has fewer rules about how it can operate in the wild. Due to the lack of constraints, TCP is usually faster than HTTP.

Up until recently, TCP was not available to a native browser window and could only be implemented via a plugin like Silverlight or Flash or as a native desktop application. The introduction of the Websockets protocol into the HTML5 specification is changing that, though rather slowly.

In this section, we're going to walk through the basics of HTTP traffic and its limitations and then contrast it with TCP traffic. Neither technology is perfect for all scenarios, so this section will help you to understand where each fits, absent the current hype surrounding Websockets.

8.1.1   *An HTTP overview*

HTTP is designed around a request/response pattern. The client makes a request to the server. When the server receives that request, it checks to see if the resource requested is available and responds with a status code, a collection of text called the header, and, if available, the actual content that was requested. The content can be anything from a simple HTML page to a script to an image. Figure 8.1 shows the nature of HTTP communications.

While the client waits patiently for the response, many things happen that have kept HTTP at the top of the internet food chain:

- The hosting server can respond with the requested content from the original content source.
- The origin server can respond with a cached version of the content.

- The origin server can respond with an exception message and content.
- An intermediate server can respond on behalf of the origin server with a cached version of the content.
- An intermediate proxy server can reroute the request to a different server or through a secure firewall.

The hosting server is the network point that responds to a specific IP address and has access to the original version of the content requested. The hosting endpoint may be a façade that internally redirects traffic to a bunch of internet servers to further enhance scalability but, even then, the single IP address, from the client's perspective, is returning the requested content.

Servers like IIS can handle many thousands of concurrent connections and can respond to requests over those connections in any order they see fit. A web server can dynamically compress the content before sending it and will usually try to obtain cached content before trying to get at the original version.

While the request is in transit to its final IP address, intermediate servers will get it and forward it on as appropriate. These servers also have the option, depending upon the kind of request, to respond with their own cached version of the content. That means a request from Asia to a server in the United States may not have to travel all the way around the globe to fulfill its mission.

All of this makes for an extremely scalable, stable platform upon which to build applications and deliver content. It doesn't, however, provide the answer to every kind of communication problem. Communication using HTTP is always one way (request from client/response from server), and at its fastest it's still never real-time. In addition, the resource the client is interested in may not be on that server but in fact may be located on another client. The hosting server has no means of initiating a request to any client, let alone a specific one, to retrieve that content to fulfill the original client's request. It's just not possible using HTTP. Inasmuch as this is a problem, the solution is TCP.

8.1.2   *TCP communications in a nutshell*

The Transmission Control Protocol (TCP) is part of the foundation that makes HTTP work. Consider HTTP to be a very specific format of communicating via TCP. TCP is much "closer to the metal" on a server, handling many different kinds of communications between servers and between networked clients and servers. It uses a simple message for communications, unlike HTTP, which mandates a lot of header information that must travel with every request and response. This makes TCP capable of sending nearly any kind of data.

The characteristic that gives it its reliability is called *ordered delivery*. Ordered delivery is a means whereby a message passed from one server to another will be delivered in the same order as it was sent, or it will be rejected and retried by the requestor until a confirmation of receipt is returned. For example, a large image sent via TCP will be transferred in smaller packets, and if a packet is received out of order, it will be rejected and retried. This mechanism is well suited to duplex messaging capabilities because it's light and fast and can "talk" in both directions at the same time.

Anyone who has ever used a CB radio or a walkie-talkie understands the nature of half duplex and full duplex communications, even if they don't know the terms. Duplex, in this context, refers to having two parties in a communications chain. Half duplex, as shown in figure 8.2, means that only one party can talk at a time; the other party can only respond when the original party is finished. HTTP is a half-duplex mode of communications. Even though a client can send multiple requests very quickly, the server can't respond to a single request until that request is completely received.

TCP, on the other hand, is a full-duplex mode of communication, similar to a cell phone conversation, where two parties can be talking and listening at the same time. Teenagers seem to be exceptionally good at this kind of communication. One party is perfectly capable of responding to a request even if the request is incomplete or still in progress. Figure 8.3 shows two parties communicating simultaneously with each other.

TCP in a web-based scenario opens the door to interesting new areas, but it has a significant downside in that a connection can be consumed for every client in the system. Each connection, in turn, requires server processor time to create, use, and destroy it, even if it's only used for a tiny amount of time. An instant-messaging server,

Figure 8.2   In HTTP (half-duplex communications) when one party talks, the only thing the other party can do is listen. When the client sends a request, the server must listen before it can respond. While the server is responding, the client can only listen. Modern browsers try to mitigate this by allowing many connections at one time, but each single request can only be issued a single response.

Figure 8.3 In TCP (full-duplex communication) all parties on a call can communicate simultaneously. A request can be responded to before it's even completely received.

for instance, can experience many spikes during the course of a regular day. Still, the concept of a web application whose server side can actively push unrequested data to one or many clients is well worth the time to learn. Real-time gaming, real-time geolocation, and any kind of competitive sports could be great new areas for this technology.

This is where the Websockets HTML5 API comes in. It's a means of opening a TCP-based communication link to a server and then sending and receiving messages in the form of strings (or JSON objects) over that connection.

With that in mind, it's time for you to start learning about Websockets as you build a chat application.

8.2 *Building a Websockets chat application*

The sample application for this chapter will be, as mentioned, a chat service. You'll build both a client and server using JavaScript. We've got a lot of ground to cover here, so we'll only discuss the code that's pertinent to the overall function of the application. If you find yourself unsure about some of the JavaScript syntax, we recommend you take a look at appendix A, which provides a JavaScript overview.

The client you build will be able to

- Connect from inside an ASP.NET MVC application
- See all other users connected
- Be notified in real time when any other user sends a message
- Push messages immediately to all other users

You'll build the server using Node.js. Node.js is an open source server technology that runs the V8 JavaScript engine to handle requests and responses using JavaScript as its native language. Your solution will consist of a free, third-party JavaScript library that wraps all the TCP communication functions and a custom library that you'll write and execute locally. The server will be able to

- Keep track of users as they enter and exit the application
- Transfer any message from a user to all other users in the application

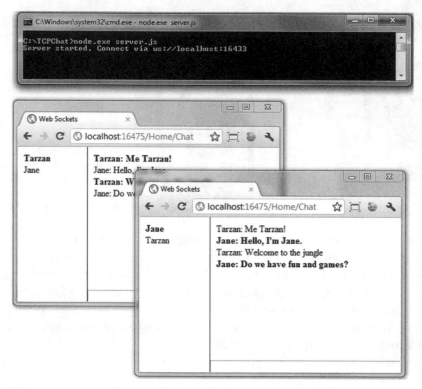

Figure 8.4   The working chat application will require the installation of Node.js and the use of its command-line interface to simulate a TCP server. When the server is running, any number of clients can be connected and chat in real time.

Figure 8.4 shows what the application will look like when it's complete. You'll run the chat server from a command window and open as many browser windows as you like to connect to it.

SETTING UP THE CLIENT PAGE'S BASIC STRUCTURE

To get started, follow these steps:

1 Open Visual Studio and create a new ASP.NET MVC application. Name it SocketChat.

2 When the new solution opens, go through the normal routine of updating the NuGet packages with the latest versions of all the default packages. (Navigate the menus to Tools > Library Package Manager > Manage NuGet Packages for Solution. Click the Updates tab on the left, and when the center content loads, click the Update button on each of the packages.)

3 Navigate to the Controllers folder, open the HomeController, and add a new method, as follows:

```
public ActionResult Chat()
{
```

```
            return View();
    }
```

You now have an endpoint, so running your application with /Home/Chat will result in that code being processed, but no view will be returned. By default, this view's name is Chat.cshtml, but it doesn't exist yet. You can create it now:

1 Right-click on the word View in your controller.
2 Select Add View.
3 Deselect the check box for Use a Layout or Master Page.
4 Click the Add button.

Your view won't be based on the normal master page, so the code in the following listing sets Layout = null when placed in the Chat.cshtml page.

Listing 8.1 The Chat.cshtml page

```
@{ Layout = null; }
<!DOCTYPE html>
<html>
<head>
    <title>Websockets</title>
    <script
        src="@Url.Content("~/Scripts/jquery-1.7.2.js")"          Scripts should be
        type="text/javascript"></script>                        updated to latest
    <script                                                      versions from
        src="@Url.Content("~/Scripts/modernizr-2.5.3.js")"       NuGet updates.
        type="text/javascript"></script>
    <link href="@Url.Content("~/Content/chat.css")"             Chat.css will be
        rel="stylesheet" type="text/css" />                     chat-specific
</head>                                                          stylesheet.
<body>
    <form id="login" class="box-round box-shadow">
        <p>Choose a name and hit return:</p>                    Login form will hide all
        <input id="name" type="text" />                        other content until
        <div id="login-status"></div>                          user logs in with name.
    </form>
    <section id="chat">
        <aside id="members"></section>                         Log area will show all messages
        <div id="log"></div>                                   as they're sent or received.
        <div id="input">
            <input id="entry" type="text" />                   Bottom of screen will
        </div>                                                 have text box for sending
    </section>                                                 messages to room.
    <script
        src="@Url.Content("~/Scripts/socketserver.js")"        Socketserver.js fill will
        type="text/javascript"></script>                      contain Websockets-
    <script                                                    specific code.
        src="@Url.Content("~/Scripts/main.js")"
        type="text/javascript"></script>                      Main.js will contain UI
</body>                                                        logic to update screen
</html>                                                        and send messages.
```

Members area will show all users currently in chat room.

WIRING UP THE MENU SYSTEM

The only part of the basic HTML structure left is to wire up /Chat to the menu system. To add a new Chat menu item to your application, open the file at Views\Shared_Layout.cshtml and place the following line in the menu structure:

```
<li>@Html.ActionLink("Chat", "Chat", "Home")</li>
```

ADDING STYLES

That takes care of the user interface (UI) except for the stylesheet, the contents of which need not be covered here in any detail. The complete CSS is listed at the end of this chapter if you're building the application as you read.

The primary thing you should know about the styles is how the current user's messages are differentiated from those of everyone else in the chat room. In your application, you'll do this with the following style declaration, which makes the text bold if the element has the local-member style class applied to it:

```
.local-member {
  font-weight: bold;
}
```

So now, when you see this line of jQuery, you'll know what it does:

```
$("element").toggleClass("local-member", userIsLocal || false);
```

This JavaScript uses the jQuery toggleClass function, which takes the class setting and turns it on or off using an optional switch value that should return true or false. If the value userIsLocal is true, the class assignment will be removed; otherwise it will be added to the wrapped set being acted upon.

> **NOTE** When you add the chat.css file to the project, be sure to place it in the Content folder.

With the styles out of the way, the basic structure is in place for your chat page. Let's turn our attention to the JavaScript logic. You'll build the chat client in two parts so that you can separate the Websockets API calls from the UI manipulation and data logic. Read on to find out why.

8.2.1 *Separating interface logic from Websockets communications*

The current level of support for Websockets is rather low in two ways. First, many browsers don't support the specification. Second, there are few server solutions available to traditional web programmers that can effectively handle TCP traffic. The second reason probably impacts the first, but that's speculation on our part.

The fact is that if you build a chat application, you'll likely have to implement both a TCP solution and an HTTP solution. HTTP chat would probably mean building a long-polling server that's described in a sidebar further on in this chapter, but the more direct impact on this sample application is that the server communication library needs to be loosely coupled to the UI logic. You'll do this by building two separate JavaScript libraries: one for interacting with the user and the page, and a second

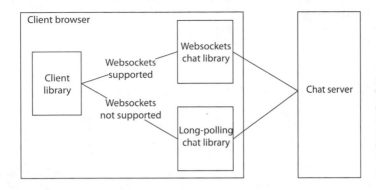

Figure 8.5 Because Websockets support is somewhat limited in modern browsers, most web applications still need a fallback capability to handle "live" communications with a server.

for communicating with the server via Websockets. This will allow you to determine if the Websockets API is available in the current browser and to fall back to a different solution if it isn't. You won't be implementing that logic here, because it's beyond the scope of this chapter, but we'll show you where that logic should go.

Figure 8.5 shows the basic premise of an application that detects Websockets support and falls back to a long-polling communication library if Websockets isn't supported. This approach is simpler but similar to the way Microsoft SignalR handles communications.

CREATING THE KEY JAVASCRIPT FILES

Start by creating two JavaScript files in the Scripts folder of your project: main.js and socketserver.js. The first file will hold the UI logic and call into the second to make calls to the server. This is a common pattern in JavaScript applications and isn't as rigid as a normal .NET application, where objects must be strongly typed or use specific inheritance chains. In JavaScript, the only limitation is that a JavaScript file must be loaded on the page before any methods are called on it. It seems pretty obvious, but when you begin loading files asynchronously, this limitation becomes very important.

The code in listing 8.2 is the outline of your main.js file. It has a jQuery `ready` handler and a `Main` object with an `init` function and a couple of other utility functions. No Websockets work is done here, other than to check Modernizr for compatibility. Note also that your `init` function contains a few other event handlers and a local `receive` function.

Listing 8.2 Code in the main.js file to set up the application function

```
$(document).ready(function() {
    Main.init();
});

window.Main = {
    user: null,                          ← Store local user.
    members: [],                         ← Store current list of
                                           all users in room.
    init: function () {
        var self = this;
```

```
      if (!Modernizr.websockets) {
          alert("Websockets not supported.");
          return;
      }

      if (!window.JSON) {
          alert("JSON not supported.");
          return;
      }
      function receive(method, data) {
      }

      this.$output = $("#log");
      this.$members = $("#members");
      this.$name = $("#name").focus();

      $("#login").submit(function (event) {
      });

      this.$entry = $("#entry").keypress(function(event) {
      });
    },

    addMember: function (data) {
    },

    removeMember: function (data) {
    },

    addMessage: function (data) {
    }
};
```

Local function responds when data is received from server.

Store local variables for page elements so that DOM doesn't have to be requeried.

Login button will add current user to chat room.

Keypress event will send message to room.

Adding and removing members from UI and local property is done with separate functions.

Add message to screen when anyone in room sends message.

8.2.2 *Implementing Websockets in JavaScript*

At this point in your application, you have the basic outline of your UI layer. Next, turn your attention to the communications layer: socketserver.js. This library will respond to all communications to and from both the server and the client layer. The basic layout of this file is to create a new SocketServer object and then append to its prototype the functionality you need. Take a look at the next listing, the base code for socketserver.js, and then we'll discuss the details.

Listing 8.3 The setup code for socketserver.js

```
window.SocketServer = function(callback) {
    this.callback = callback;
    this.connection = null;
};

SocketServer.prototype = {
    send: function (method, data, complete) {
        var self = this;
        if (method == "connect") {
            var Socket =
```

Set new SocketServer object passing in callback function.

Assign callback function to new property of SocketServer object.

Create null property that will later contain connection object.

Send function responds to all communications with method, data packet, and callback.

```
                window.WebSocket || window.MozWebSocket;
        if (Socket) {
            var url = "";
            this.connection = new Socket(url);

            this.connection.onopen = function () {
            };

            this.connection.onmessage =
                function (event) {
            };

            this.connection.onclose = function (event) {
            };
        }
        else {
            data.code = "failure";
            complete(data);
        }
    }
    else if (method == "message") {
    }
    }
};
```

> Assign connection property to new HTML5 WebSocket object or Mozilla WebSocket object if HTML5 version doesn't exist.

> When connection object initially opens this function will be executed.

> When message is received on connection this function is executed.

> When connection closes execute function.

> When message is sent from local client this code will execute.

In your Websockets library, the `connection` property corresponds to a `WebSocket` object. This API contains the following characteristics:

- The `WebSocket` object
- The `send` function
- The `onmessage` event
- The `readyState` property
- Non-message connection events
- The `close` function

These are all defined in the specification at http://www.w3.org/TR/websockets, and we'll discuss them each briefly in the following subsections.

THE WEBSOCKET OBJECT

 Core API

The `WebSocket` object handles all communications. It's instanced using the `new` keyword and it must have a connection string `url` parameter at a minimum. You can also use a `protocols` optional parameter to specify the kind of security to use and the port to communicate over. You can also provide these values as part of the URL:

```
var mySocket = new WebSocket('connection string');
```

Once you have an instance of a `WebSocket` object, you can bind to its various events and monitor its state.

THE SEND FUNCTION

 Core API

The only available method for pushing information from the client to the server is `send`. This function takes a single `data` parameter that can be one of three types:

```
mySocket.send(DOMString);
mySocket.send(Blob);
mySocket.send(ArrayBuffer);
```

> ## Websockets, WebSocket, or Web Socket?
>
> You may have noticed that we're referring in the text to "Websockets" while in code we use "WebSocket". A quick search on the internet will also reveal plenty of discussion around this technology using the two words "web sockets".
>
> The reason for this disparity is that although the current specification uses "Websockets" as both its title and in the normative text, browser vendors have created objects in their implementation using WebSocket. As a result, the correct name of the specification is Websockets but the correct name of the implemented object is WebSocket. Placing a space between the two words is never correct.

The DOMString parameter is just that; an escaped string value (meaning no special characters) that can be a serialized JSON object or any other bit of stringified data. The blob parameter is used to represent non-native JavaScript objects—usually files, though you're not limited to that. Finally, the ArrayBuffer is an array of byte data used to transmit information not easily convertible to strings. A classic example of this is the ImageData array from a <canvas> 2d context object. Using these three method signatures, you can send just about anything over the wire to the server.

THE ONMESSAGE EVENT

 The onmessage JavaScript function is called when the server sends a message to the client WebSocket. The event object passed contains a data property that's the actual message object sent from the server:

```
mySocket.onmessage = function (event) {
    var message = event.data;
    console.log('The server said: ' + message);
};
```

> **TIP**   This is a good time to mention that with the current WebSocket implementation, a browser can only communicate with a server. Communication directly between browsers on different machines isn't possible in this version of the specification. Using Node.js, you can pass data directly through to any specific client, but that's the extent of current client-to-client capabilities.

THE READYSTATE PROPERTY

 When a new WebSocket object is created, it will have a readyState property that's read-only to the calling JavaScript but will change to editable based on changes to the state of the connection.

Although the specification says this will be set to an empty value when created, the reality is that it will immediately start trying to connect to the server passed into the constructor. Therefore, it will always have a value that corresponds to one of the following constants:

- CONNECTING (value: 0)—Assigned as soon as the WebSocket tries to connect to its assigned server
- OPEN (value: 1)—Assigned when the connection to the server is established

- CLOSING (value: 2)—Assigned when the close() function is called but the connection is still open
- CLOSED—(value: 3) Assigned when the connection has been closed.

During normal operations, this property will be checked to ensure that a message can be sent or received, and often to change the status value displayed to the user. You can check this value in one of two ways: by using the numeric value or with the constant implemented in the WebSocket object itself:

```
if (mySocket.readyState === 1) {
.. open connection ..
}
if (mySocket.readyState === WebSocket.CLOSED) {
.. closed connection ..
}
```

NON-MESSAGE CONNECTION EVENTS

Core API

There are three more events you can tap to open and close connections or when an error occurs.

The onopen event fires after the connection is established whereas onclose fires after the connection is completely closed. These events are helpful for setup and teardown operations.

The onerror event occurs when anything unexpected happens, like a failed connection or a security exception. The error object returned is a standard JavaScript exception.

THE CLOSE FUNCTION

Core API

The close() function allows up to two optional parameters to be passed: a number and a string. The number is a status code, and the string is a human-readable value. Usually close is called with no parameters:

```
mySocket.close();
```

Your application now has the various chunks of code in place to respond to events and operations related to Websockets, but these operations have no actual implementations yet. Next, you'll fill in the code, both in main.js and in socketserver.js, to log into the chat room, send and receive messages, and log out.

8.2.3 Opening a Websockets server connection

This phase of development will get the current user logged into the chat server and thus into the chat room. Listing 8.4 shows how this is implemented in main.js.

First, you need to create a new SocketServer object and then immediately send a message with it. The SocketServer is defined in the socketserver.js file and is the single place in your application where you implement Websockets. In a production scenario, this would allow you to alternatively implement some other kind of communications if Websockets isn't available in the current browser.

You should already have a stub for the login button's submit event in the main.js file. Fill in the following code in that area.

Listing 8.4   Logging the user in via the `login submit` function

```
$("#login").submit(function (event) {
  event.preventDefault();
  var name = self.$name.val();                          ◁─────  Get name user is
  if (name) {                                                   attempting to log in as.
    var $status = $("#login-status").text("Connecting...");
    self.server = new SocketServer(receive);            ◁─────  Create new SocketServer
    self.server.send(                                           object as defined in
                                                                socketserver.js file.
      "connect",
      { From: name },                                   ◁─────  Pass in user's name
      function (result) {                                       as JSON object.
        if (result && result.code == "success") {       ◁─────
          result.local = true;
          self.user = self.addMember(result);                   Callback you send to
          $("#login").hide();                                   SocketServer will be executed
          $("#chat").show();                                    when login is complete. It will
          self.$entry.focus();                                  update UI by adding name to
        }                                                       list of chat members.
        else {
          $status.text("Failed to connect.");
        }
      }
    );
  }
});
```

Pass connect
string to
object to state
what kind of
action to take.

Core API
Remember that sending the message `"connect"` to the object defined in socket-
server.js will create a new instance of the HTML5 `WebSocket` object and wire up its various events. This more complete code is in listing 8.3 if you missed it, but here's the
critical part:

```
send: function (method, data, complete) {
   var self = this;
   if (method == "connect") {
      var Socket = window.WebSocket || window.MozWebSocket;
      if (Socket) {
         var url = "";
         this.connection = new Socket(url);

         this.connection.onopen = function () {
         };
      ...
```

Next, you'll finish the login experience by notifying the server that the current user
has successfully opened a connection to the server. This is done by the `SocketServer`
custom object first sending a message to the server and then executing the callback
you passed in with the user data object (containing the user's name).

The `method` name sent to the server is `"memberEnter"`. This is described in the following listing, which you should use to update the `connection.onopen` code area of
socketserver.js.

> **Listing 8.5   Responding to a newly opened Websockets connection in socketserver.js**

```
this.connection.onopen = function () {        ◁———  connection.onopen event fires when
    self.connection.send(JSON.stringify({     ◁         new connection is opened to server.
        method: "memberEnter",                         When opened send message to server
        data: data                                     stating that current user has entered room.
    }));
    data.code = "success";                             Now that user has notified server that
    complete(data);                          ◁———      it's online execute original callback.
};
```

Because you only send text back and forth but work with objects in the coded logic, you're formatting it into JSON objects and setting a `method` property with every call. This allows the server to parse the message and switch on the `method` to perform different tasks, which is the most transparent way of doing so because the string that you're sending can be easily read and debugged, but this isn't the only way. You could alternatively have passed in the name of a function to execute, or even a complete function body. These are less safe approaches and expose more functionality on the server side than we, and likely you, would prefer, so we decided to stick to the `method` name methodology.

Next, you'll spend some time getting messages to and from the server.

Long polling for pseudo-real-time web

We've been discussing TCP as the only means of real-time communication, but the functionality we're after has been available, albeit in a somewhat less attractive form, for a while. The solution is called *long polling*.

In an ASP.NET MVC application, long polling consists of a controller action requested by the client but held on the server until data is actually available to send. The client waits for a response, or abandons the request and sends a new request when new data is available to send to the server or when a specific timeout has expired.

Here's an example chat scenario:

Client:
Send chat request (with message) to server.

Wait for response.

Server:
Receive message from client.

Send message to all other clients.

Hold client request until a message is ready to send.

Client:

Abandon original request.

Send new chat request (with new message) to server.

Wait for response.

Server:

Receive message from client.

Send to all other clients.

Hold request until a message is ready to send to original client.

Server:

Receive message from a different client.

Send response to first client with message.

Client:

Receive response from server.

Update application with new message.

Immediately send request to server with no message.

Wait for response.

Using long polling, you can simulate real-time web applications but you don't have truly bidirectional communications. Everything is initiated by the client in true HTTP fashion. As a fallback position, though, this is a great way to allow Websockets-compatible clients to play in the same space as non-compliant browsers.

The main.js file in this chapter's solution provides a loosely coupled example that allows you to build in a long-polling library that's hot-swappable with the Websockets communications library.

8.2.4   *Sending messages*

Sending a message consists of taking data entered by the user in the `entry` text box element and sending it to the `SocketServer` object. That object, which is already maintaining an open TCP connection to the server (via Websockets), will add a method property and forward it on to the server. The server will only send messages to everyone else; it won't send the message it just received back to the original sender. Therefore, on the client that sent the original message, you just add the message to the screen by calling `addMessage`.

The following listing shows how the client (main.js) will respond when the `enter` key is pressed on the input text box. This code goes inside the `init` function.

Listing 8.6   Sending a message from page in main.js

```
this.$entry = $("#entry").keypress(function (event) {
    if (event.which == 13) {
```
Only execute if enter key was pressed.

```
var message = self.$entry.val();          ◁──┐  Get message that should
if (message) {                                │  be sent to server.
   self.$entry.val("");
   var data = {                               Build data object to contain current
      From: self.user.name,                   user and message to be sent.
      Message: message
   };
   self.server.send("message", data);      ◁────┐  Send message to
   self.addMessage(data);        ◁──────┐        │  SocketServer object.
}                                 Add message to
                                  current user's page.
}
});
```

The message has been sent to the SocketServer object, and that object must now forward it to the chat server. Listing 8.7 shows how this happens. First a method name is added to the object, and it's packaged up as JSON and fired off using the WebSocket object (the connection variable). This code goes at the end of the send function in SocketServer.prototype.

Listing 8.7   Sending a message to the server inside socketserver.js

```
else if (method == "message") {             Check readyState to ensure
   if (this.connection.readyState != 1)     connection is still open.
      return;                          ◁──┘
   this.connection.send(JSON.stringify({
      method: method,                       Build stringified JSON object
      data: data                            and send it to server.
   }));
}
```

This is a pretty simple solution so far. You have a connection opened to the server, and the first message sent will be one that logs the current user into the chat room. When a user sends a message, it's pushed from the UI to the main object, which passes it on to SocketServer. SocketServer then uses its WebSocket connection to send the message to the server, which passes it on to all the other users currently in the room.

Figure 8.6 shows the two phases of outbound message operations: logging in and sending a message.

Notice how little code you're using to execute all of this functionality. When complete, your entire node server code file will consume less than 90 lines of JavaScript. This makes for a very targeted system with only the functions that you really need. It stays fast and light, as JavaScript is meant to be!

8.2.5   Receiving messages

The next operation that you need to handle is receiving messages from the server. When any message is received, it will have a method property and a data object property. The method will tell the application whether a user has entered the chat room, or left, or posted a message.

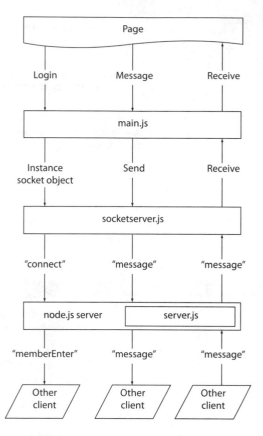

Figure 8.6 Each message sent will contain a `method` **string parameter that tells the** `SocketServer` **object how to handle that message. Login passes the** `"connect"` **method, whereas messages sent and received get the** `"message"` **method that the** `Main` **object knows should be used to add the message to the chat room.**

The Websockets implementation doesn't need to know anything about this, other than the property names, so the code in socketserver.js for handling message receipt is very simple:

```
this.connection.onmessage = function (event) {
   var envelope = JSON.parse(event.data);
   self.callback(envelope.method, envelope.data);
};
```

This bit of code simply parses the object received from the server and forwards it on using the original callback you wired up at the beginning.

The logic that does something with the message is in the `receive` function that goes inside of the `init` function of main.js. The following listing shows the full text of that function.

Listing 8.8 Receiving a message from the server in main.js

```
function receive(method, data) {
   if (method == "memberEnter") {
      self.addMember(data);
   }
```

Respond to new member entering chat room.

```
    else if (method == "memberExit") {
        self.removeMember(data);
    }
    else if (method == "message") {
        self.addMessage(data);
    }
}
```

> Respond to member exiting.

> Respond to new message from chat room member.

This part of the application takes whatever kind of message was received from the server and forwards it to one of three local functions in the `main` object. The only thing that's left in the `SocketServer` object is the code that responds when the local connection is closed. This is the `onclose` event mentioned earlier.

RESPONDING TO A CLOSED CONNECTION

In the socketserver.js file, find the `onclose` function call and add the following code:

```
this.connection.onclose = function (event) {
    data.code = "failure";
    complete(data);
};
```

This will execute the callback with a failure message and stop processing. It won't attempt to reopen the connection or determine what the problem is. In a live communication mechanism, this isn't uncommon, because the normal operation would be to purge and restart the connection process from scratch and not duplicate the connection testing logic.

UPDATING THE UI

You're nearly finished with the chat client. In the earlier code, you responded to a member entering, leaving, and sending a message to the chat room. Listing 8.9 shows the functions that update the UI when these events occur.

Note here that the local variables assigned in the `init` function prefixed with a dollar sign (`$`) are now being used. This methodology allows you to update the page without requerying the DOM—a good trick to have up your sleeve when you need every millisecond of performance out of the browser. This code fills out the functions you added earlier to main.js.

Listing 8.9 Responding to the addition and removal of members in main.js

```
addMember: function (data) {
    var member = { name: data.From };
    member.$element = $("<p>" + member.name + "</p>")
        .toggleClass("local-member", data.local || false)
        .appendTo(this.$members);
    this.members.push(member);
    return member;
},

removeMember: function (data) {
    var i;
    for (i = 0; i < this.members.length; i++) {
        var member = this.members[i];
```

> When members enter chat room add them to member list and assign CSS class based on whether it's local user or not.

> Push new member into local array of users.

```
        if (member.name == data.From) {
            member.$element.remove();
            this.members.splice(i, 1);
            break;
        }
    }
},

addMessage: function (data) {
    $("<p>" + data.From + ": " + data.Message + "</p>")
        .toggleClass("local-member",
            data.From == this.user.name)
        .appendTo(this.$output);
}
```

> When members leave remove them from interface and local array.

> Messages are posted to interface and same CSS logic is applied to messages.

Congratulations! You've just implemented a Websockets-based chat client that does exactly nothing. Nothing, that is, until you build the chat server capable of transmitting data via TCP. That's where Node.js comes in.

8.3   *Using Node.js as a TCP server*

Unless you've been living under a rock for the last two years, you've probably heard of Node.js. Many of the superstars in the software development universe have been trumpeting it for its speed and versatility. It hasn't been used much in production environments so far, but the foundation is being laid for a major jump forward in web server technology just over the horizon. But what exactly is Node.js?

The home page for Node.js (nodejs.org) describes it this way:

> Node.js is a platform built on Chrome's JavaScript runtime for easily building fast, scalable network applications. Node.js uses an event-driven, non-blocking I/O model that makes it lightweight and efficient, perfect for data-intensive real-time applications that run across distributed devices.

Did you get that? It's a web server that runs on JavaScript! How cool is that? If by this time in our book you aren't falling in love (or at least serious like) with JavaScript, then you may want to look into some of the Microsoft solutions available for handling TCP connections using WCF (Windows Communication Foundation) and possibly in the Windows 8 platform. For our part, we couldn't resist the urge to test Node.js's chops against a Windows computer and an HTML5 chat client.

INSTALLING NODE.JS

To get started, you need to download and install Node.js. Do this by clicking on the Download link at http://nodejs.org and running the installer. You should get a simple wizard-style setup screen similar to what you see in figure 8.7.

Follow the onscreen instructions until the wizard is finished. Once it's installed, you can run Node.js from any command line simply by entering the text node at the prompt. This will enter you into a JavaScript working environment where you can use any valid JavaScript language construct to execute code.

Why Node.js for TCP chat?

You might be wondering why we aren't using a .NET server technology to implement our server-side TCP socket code. The reason is that no production-ready implementation of a TCP service exists on the .NET stack that fulfilled our need for clarity and our desire to bring as few ancillary topics as possible into the mix.

We looked into SignalR, native WCF, and some others, but they all had one of two problems: they involved the inclusion of a large amount of code and settings that made the chapter too long and complex; or they abstracted the core Websockets functionality and focused the code too much on polyfills and patches for Flash and long polling. *Polyfills*, at a high level, are JavaScript shims that allow code to function as if the particular browser feature were a native part of the platform.

In the end, the buzz around Node.js and the fact that we could perform a few simple steps and have just a few lines of JavaScript code implement the entire server solution made it an easy choice.

For instance, figure 8.8 declares a variable, adds numbers, and prints the values out. Then it prints the words "hello world" to the screen. A simple start.

You can do much more than this, though. Using Node.js you can build libraries, include third-party utilities, and execute the entire thing as an operational server.

The chat server you're building will be a single JavaScript file in a folder of your solution. It will use a free third-party web service utility to send and receive TCP traffic to and from your web client. Let's get started.

PREPARING TO BUILD THE CHAT SERVER

The first thing you need to do is to create a new folder and install the Node Package Manager (npm):

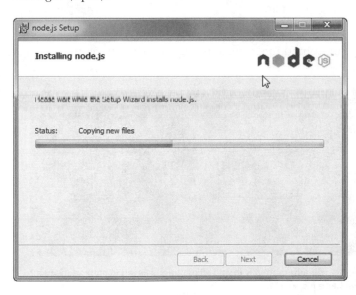

Figure 8.7 The Node.js installation wizard for Windows platforms

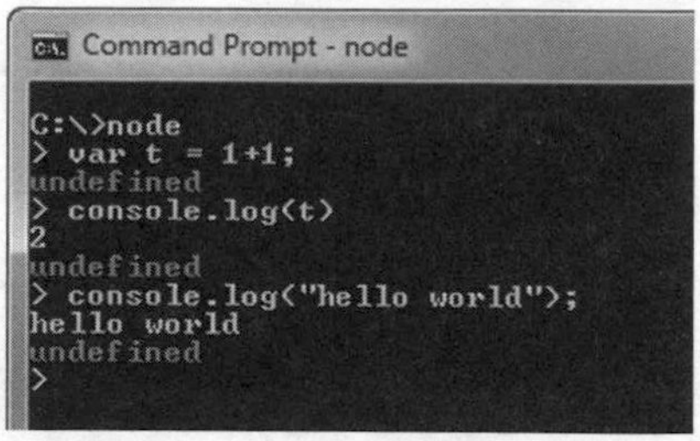

1　Create a new folder called NodeServer off the main project in your Visual Studio solution. This folder doesn't need to be inside your solution, but putting it inside it makes the example a bit easier and it gives you the ability to use the JavaScript IntelliSense built into Visual Studio.

2　Once the folder is created, add a new text file called package.json. This is a standard name for Node.js applications that will allow npm, a utility program that installs with Node.js, to find and install third-party libraries.

Figure 8.8 Entering node **at the command line enters you into the JavaScript environment where normal JavaScript code can execute.**

3　Place this text inside package.json:

```
{
    "name": "manning-socket-demo",
    "author": "iangilman",
    "version": "0.0.1",
    "dependencies": ["ws"]    // The unique name of the ws socket library
}
```

Name corresponds to the name of your application, and author is you. Version is your own application's version number, and dependencies is an array of libraries that should be downloaded and installed locally in a special location off the current folder.

4　When you have saved this file, open a command prompt and change the directory to NodeServer.

5　Run the following command:

```
npm install
```

That should result in something similar to figure 8.9, where the npm utility has installed the ws library.

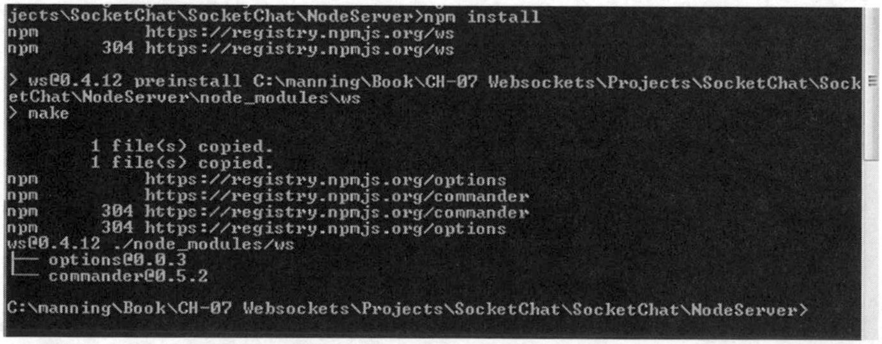

Figure 8.9 The npm utility will automatically install all packages listed in package.json into the folder where the package file exists.

When you look in this folder, you'll see a new subfolder called node_modules. This folder was automatically created and populated by the installation. Any external module you install on this node server will go, by default, into this folder.

BUILDING THE CHAT SERVER

Now you're ready to start building the actual chat server. Back in Visual Studio, create a new JavaScript file called server.js in your application's NodeServer folder and add the code in the next listing to that file.

Listing 8.10 Getting started building the Node.js chat server with the server.js file

```
var ws = require("ws");                              require is standard Node.js command that
var port = 16433;                                    includes other libraries into current application.
var socketServer = new ws.Server({ port: port });    Create new ws.Server
                                                     object to handle TCP traffic.
socketServer.on("connection", function (socket) {
   chatServer.addUser(socket);                       When new connection is
});                                                  made add new user to
                                                     chatServer.users array.
var chatServer = {
   users: [],                                        Define chatServer
                                                     object here.
   addUser: function (socket) {
   },                                                Remove user that
                                                     has disconnected.
   removeUser: function (user) {
   },
   sendToAllBut: function (userException, message) {  Send message to all users
   },                                                 except original sender.
   sendMembersTo: function (recipient) {
   }
};                                                   Post messages to new users for
console.log("Server started. " +                     each other user in system. This
"Connect via ws://localhost:" + port);               keeps all users synchronized
                                                     with people in chat room.
                                                     For developer explain what connection
                                                     URL should be for server.
```

Add user that has connected to users array.

The code in listing 8.10 performs a number of operations that should be explained a little further. First is the require keyword:

```
var ws = require("ws");
```

This is a Node.js-specific keyword that should be at the beginning of each library that has external dependencies. Calling require will tell the Node.js engine to load that library into memory so that its structure and content is available in the current scope. It's similar to adding a script tag to a web page.

Next you create a ws.Server object, passing in a port number:

```
var socketServer = new ws.Server({ port: port });
```

ws in this context is the ws library that you installed earlier, and you're expected as the developer to know what it does, because you required Node.js to load it earlier. No IntelliSense here, you're on your own!

The rest of the code in this library is just plain old JavaScript—nothing special to understand or load.

The basic structure is now complete; you just need to fill everything in and run your application. The `addUser` function in listing 8.11 will add a user to the local array and then wire up `message` and `close` events. This code goes into the main `chatServer` object defined in server.js. Keep in mind that a `user` object in the context of the server library is an open socket connected to a unique user at the other end.

Listing 8.11   Adding a user to the chat room and starting to listen for messages

```
addUser: function (socket) {
   var self = this;

   var user = { socket: socket };                           Add user to
                                                            users array.
   this.users.push(user);

   socket.on("message", function (message) {                Respond to new message
      var envelope = JSON.parse(message);                   coming from client.
      if (envelope.method == "memberEnter") {
         user.name = envelope.data.From;
         self.sendMembersTo(user);
      }
      self.sendToAllBut(user, message);
   });

   socket.on("close", function () {                          Respond to
      self.sendToAllBut(user, JSON.stringify({              new socket.
         method: "memberExit",
         data: {
            From: user.name
         }
      }));
      self.removeUser(user);
   });
},
```

NOTE   The `socket.on(string, callback)` event you're using is *not* part of the Websockets specification. It's defined and executed strictly inside the `ws` library. We decided to use this library because it's simple to use and small; it doesn't try to provide any polyfills for solutions other than TCP communications. Other utilities like Sockets.IO and SignalR provide end-to-end solutions with fallbacks and polyfills, but defining and building solutions around them would take up too much space in a single chapter.

Next, fill in the `removeUser` function, which simply finds a user leaving the chat room and deletes the user from the local users array:

```
removeUser: function (user) {
   for (var i = 0; i < this.users.length; i++) {
      if (this.users[i] == user) {
         this.users.splice(i, 1);
```

```
        break;
      }
    }
},
```

By now, you should be familiar enough with JavaScript array manipulation that this code requires no further explanation. The next listing, on the other hand, which calls the `user.socket.send` function for each user except the original sender of the message, does need a little bit of explanation. Take a look.

Listing 8.12   Distributing a message to users

```
sendToAllBut: function (userException, message) {
    for (var i = 0; i < this.users.length; i++) {
        var user = this.users[i];
        if (user != userException)
            user.socket.send(message);
    }
},
```
If current user in array isn't same as user sending message send message.

The code in listing 8.12 goes into the `chatServer` object in server.js. Recall that when you wired up the original `connection` event earlier, you passed in a `socket` object as a parameter to the `addUser` function. This `socket` is an open connection to the client that's created in the ws library and then passed as the connection parameter. It isn't a reference to a single, application-level connection.

The final step in your application is to send to each newly connected user a message with a data object representing each member currently connected. The `sendMembersTo` function is shown in the following listing and also goes into server.js.

Listing 8.13   Telling a user about the other users in the chat room

```
sendMembersTo: function (recipient) {
    for (var i = 0; i < this.users.length; i++) {
        var user = this.users[i];
        if (user != recipient) {
            recipient.socket.send(
                JSON.stringify({
                    method: "memberEnter",
                    data: {
                        From: user.name
                    }
                }));
        }
    }
}
```
Grab each user in current users list and filter out current user.

Execute message using each user's own connection.

Most commands available in browser that aren't DOM-related are also available in Node.js, including JSON.stringify. This is why you only check for JSON compatibility in browser.

Now you need to save the server.js file, open a command window, and navigate to the NodeServer folder. Type in the following command:

```
node server.js
```

That should give you a window with a message similar to figure 8.10.

```
node server.js
Server started. Connect via ws://localhost:16433
```

Figure 8.10   Node.js server is running and waiting for connections.

The last thing you need to do before you can try the chat application is edit the socket-server.js file so that the URL it uses to connect matches the URL that your server is presenting:

```
if (Socket) {
   var url = "ws://localhost:16433";
   ...
```

Once you've made this change, you can execute your MVC application.

TRY IT OUT!

Navigate to the Chat page and open another window using the same URL. You should be able to chat between the windows, connecting via the Node.js server. You should see something like figure 8.11—a working chat application that executes real-time updates using Websockets and TCP!

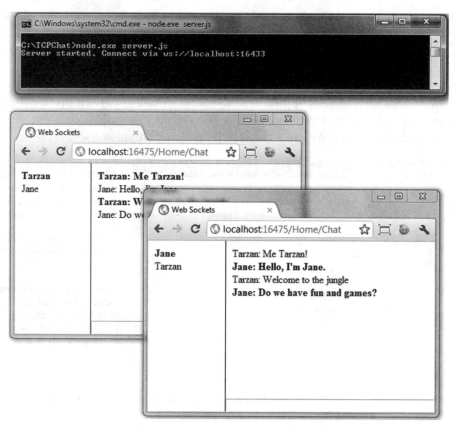

Figure 8.11   The working chat application will only be available locally, but the client URL is editable, so deploying a Node.js server should be a simple matter of purchasing the server and deploying your server.js file.

8.4   *Summary*

Direct TCP communications between applications was a very difficult proposition until just recently, but with the increasing acceptance of both Node.js and Websockets in the browser, expect it to get more popular and even more refined.

Building TCP communications into an existing ASP.NET MVC application is straightforward due to the lack of MVC interactivity required. As a foundation for real-time communications, the code in this chapter should suit you well. We hope that the creative minds reading this will already be thinking of ways to integrate geolocation, collaborative drawing, or any of the other HTML5 APIs into a real-time web scenario.

In the next chapter, we'll take a look at the LocalStorage API in HTML5. This feature is reasonably well supported in modern browsers and gives you the ability to download or build content on the client and then save it for use in a later session.

8.5   *The complete code listings*

The following listings provide the complete code for this chapter's sample application.

Listing 8.14   The complete chat.css stylesheet

```css
* {
  margin: 0;
  padding: 0;
}

html,
body {
  position: absolute;
  left: 0;
  top: 0;
  right: 0;
  bottom: 0;
  overflow: hidden;
}

#login {
  position: absolute;
  width: 200px;
  height: 74px;
  left: 50%;
  top: 50%;
  margin-left: -100px;
  margin-top: -37px;
  border: 1px solid #999;
  padding: 10px;
}

#login p {
  margin-bottom: 0.5em;
}

#login-status {
  margin-top: 0.4em;
}
```

```css
#chat {
  display: none;
}

#members {
  position: absolute;
  left: 0;
  top: 0;
  width: 100px;
  bottom: 0;
  border-right: 1px solid black;
  padding: 10px;
}

.local-member {
  font-weight: bold;
}

#log {
  position: absolute;
  left: 121px;
  top: 0;
  right: 0;
  bottom: 21px;
  padding: 10px;
}

#input {
  position: absolute;
  left: 121px;
  height: 20px;
  right: 0;
  bottom: 0;
}

#entry {
  width: 100%;
}

.box-round {
  -webkit-border-radius: 6px;
     -moz-border-radius: 6px;
          border-radius: 6px;

  -moz-background-clip: padding;
  -webkit-background-clip: padding-box;
  background-clip: padding-box;
}

.box-shadow {
  -webkit-box-shadow: 2px 2px 4px rgba(0, 0, 0, 0.3);
     -moz-box-shadow: 2px 2px 4px rgba(0, 0, 0, 0.3);
          box-shadow: 2px 2px 4px rgba(0, 0, 0, 0.3);
}
```

Listing 8.15   The complete main.js file

```javascript
// ----------
$(document).ready(function () {
```

```javascript
    Main.init();
});

// ----------
window.Main = {
  user: null,
  members: [],

  // ----------
  init: function() {
    var self = this;

    if (!Modernizr.websockets) {
      alert("Your browser doesn't support WebSockets.");
      return;
    }

    function receive(method, data) {
      if (method == "memberEnter")
        self.addMember(data);
      else if (method == "memberExit")
        self.removeMember(data);
      else if (method == "message")
        self.addMessage(data);
    }

    this.$output = $("#log");
    this.$members = $("#members");

    this.$name = $("#name")
      .focus();

    $("#login")
      .submit(function(event) {
        event.preventDefault();
        var name = self.$name.val();
        if (name) {
          var $status = $("#login-status")
            .text("Connecting…");

          self.server = new SocketServer(receive);
          self.server.send("connect", {
            From: name
          }, function(result) {
            if (result && result.code == "success") {
              result.local = true;
              self.user = self.addMember(result);
              $("#login").hide();
              $("#chat").show();
              self.$entry.focus();
            } else {
              $status.text("Failed to connect.");
            }
          });
        }
      });

    this.$entry = $("#entry")
      .keypress(function(event) {
```

```
          if (event.which == 13) { // return key
            var message = self.$entry.val();
            if (message) {
              self.$entry.val("");

              var data = {
                From: self.user.name,
                Message: message
              };

              self.server.send("message", data);
              self.addMessage(data);
            }
          }
        });
    },

    // ----------
    addMember: function(data) {
      var member = {
        name: data.From
      };

      member.$element = $("<p>" + member.name + "</p>")
        .toggleClass("local-member", data.local || false)
        .appendTo(this.$members);

      this.members.push(member);
      return member;
    },

    // ----------
    removeMember: function(data) {
      var i;
      for (i = 0; i < this.members.length; i++) {
        var member = this.members[i];
        if (member.name == data.From) {
          member.$element.remove();
          this.members.splice(i, 1);
          break;
        }
      }
    },

    // ----------
    addMessage: function(data) {
      $("<p>" + data.From + ": " + data.Message + "</p>")
        .toggleClass("local-member", data.From == this.user.name)
        .appendTo(this.$output);
    }
};
```

Listing 8.16   The complete socketserver.js file

```
// ----------
window.SocketServer = function(callback) {
  this.callback = callback;
  this.connection = null;
};
```

```javascript
// ----------
SocketServer.prototype = {
  // ----------
  send: function(method, data, complete) {
    var self = this;
    if (method == "connect") {
      var Socket = window.WebSocket || window.MozWebSocket;
      if (Socket) {
        var url = "ws://manning-socket-demo.nodester.com";
        this.connection = new Socket(url);

        this.connection.onopen = function() {
          self.connection.send(JSON.stringify({
            method: "memberEnter",
            data: data
          }));

          data.code = "success";
          complete(data);
        };

        this.connection.onmessage = function(event) {
          var envelope = JSON.parse(event.data);
          self.callback(envelope.method, envelope.data);
        };

        this.connection.onclose = function(event) {
          data.code = "failure";
          complete(data);
        };
      } else {
        data.code = "failure";
        complete(data);
      }
    } else if (method == "message") {
      if (this.connection.readyState != 1)
        return;

      this.connection.send(JSON.stringify({
        method: method,
        data: data
      }));
    }
  }
};
```

Listing 8.17 The complete server.js (node)

```javascript
// ==========
// socket server
var ws = require("ws");
var port = 16433; // or whatever port your server is set up for
var socketServer = new ws.Server({port: port});

socketServer.on("connection", function(socket) {
  chatServer.addUser(socket);
});
```

```
// ==========
// chat server
var chatServer = {
  users: [],

  // ----------
  addUser: function(socket) {
    var self = this;

    var user = {
      socket: socket
    };

    this.users.push(user);

    socket.on("message", function(message) {
      var envelope = JSON.parse(message);
      if (envelope.method == "memberEnter") {
        user.name = envelope.data.From;
        self.sendMembersTo(user);
      }

      self.sendToAllBut(user, message);
    });

    socket.on("close", function() {
      self.sendToAllBut(user, JSON.stringify({
        method: "memberExit",
        data: {
          From: user.name
        }
      }));

      self.removeUser(user);
    });
  },

  // ----------
  removeUser: function(user) {
    for (var i = 0; i < this.users.length; i++) {
      if (this.users[i] == user) {
        this.users.splice(i, 1);
        break;
      }
    }
  },

  // ----------
  sendToAllBut: function(userException, message) {
    for (var i = 0; i < this.users.length; i++) {
      var user = this.users[i];
      if (user != userException)
        user.socket.send(message);
    }
  },

  // ----------
  sendMembersTo: function(recipient) {
    for (var i = 0; i < this.users.length; i++) {
```

```
      var user = this.users[i];
      if (user != recipient) {
        recipient.socket.send(JSON.stringify({
          method: "memberEnter",
          data: {
            From: user.name
          }
        }));
      }
    }
  }
};

// ==========
console.log("Server started. Connect via ws://localhost:" + port);
```

Local storage
and state management

This chapter covers

- Storing data locally in the browser
- Retrieving stored data and restoring application state
- Managing objects and properties using LocalStorage

Any application that handles a lot of user interaction and customization will benefit from the ability to store stateful information without the fuss and transactional support of sending it to the server and retrieving it when the user returns to the site. Consider a game site where the user wants to keep the last five highest scores. Only the highest score goes to the server for display; the rest are stored locally on the client for as long as the user wants. This reduces traffic and storage loads on the server while keeping the data accessible to the user.

Previous versions of HTML have a couple of options for storing this kind of data, but HTML5 goes a few steps further to give you a reasonably simple and stable means of keeping track of the information that your server solution doesn't care about.

Typical kinds of values that might be stored locally are user preferences for sorting lists or previous search terms, but that certainly isn't the end of the story.

Browser support

Localstorage API	4	8	3.5	10.5	4		Desktop
				11	3.2	2.1	7.5	Mobile

Chapter 9 map

The LocalStorage API allows a browser to store persistent data inside the browser cache without using hidden HTML fields or cookies. Data can be created, stored, and retrieved locally with no server communications at all.

You can also use local storage to reduce bandwidth requirements and speed application initialization time. This is done by requesting static data only once and then placing it in the local store for reuse the next time the site is visited.

In this chapter, you'll learn how to use LocalStorage as you build a simple interface with draggable boxes that can have their background colors edited. The locations and colors of these boxes are saved locally and are restored when the page is revisited later. As this chapter progresses, you'll

- Get a preview of the example application and lay the foundations for it
- Structure a JavaScript library to maintain state
- Use the LocalStorage API to create, read, update, and delete (CRUD) data
- Use data saved in local storage to manipulate the user interface
- Learn about other uses for LocalStorage

Let's begin with a closer look at this chapter's sample application.

9.1 A LocalStorage example application

This chapter's example is simple, but it illustrates how you can save data in Local-Storage and then use it the next time you return to the site or reset values back to their initial settings. In the process, you'll take a couple of sideways looks at bits of jQuery syntax that might be new to you as you integrate jQuery UI and touch. jQuery UI is a JavaScript UI library designed to help you build beautiful interfaces more quickly. Touch integration happens by means of a very simple jQuery plugin, and the core LocalStorage application page is built into an ASP.NET MVC application.

> **TIP** You'll be using the LocalStorage API in this chapter, but it isn't the only means of managing data locally on the client. Cookies, IndexedDB, client-side databases like SQLite, and HTML-only methods like hidden `<input>` fields are all useful and work well. LocalStorage, however, has the best combination of compatibility in modern browsers, a low barrier to entry in terms of code, and low traffic volume during normal HTTP request/response operations.

Figure 9.1   When complete, this chapter's sample application will allow elements on the page to be repositioned and their background colors changed. Edits to the screen will be stored in LocalStorage for retrieval the next time the page is loaded.

As the application operates, the user will be able to create multiple boxes, reposition them on the screen, and change their background color. Once the color has changed or an object has been moved, other tabs in the same browser viewing the same page will reflect those changes through LocalStorage event listeners. Additionally, if you close the page and reopen it, the elements will be colored and placed exactly where they were previously until the screen is reset or the browser cache is manually cleared by the user. Figure 9.1 gives you a preview of what the running page will look like.

BUILDING THE STRUCTURE OF YOUR PAGE

To get started, follow these steps:

1 Open Visual Studio and create a new ASP.NET MVC application called LocalStorageApp.

2 When it has loaded, go through the normal routine of updating the NuGet packages with the latest versions of all the default packages. (Navigate the menus to Tools > Library Package Manager > Manage NuGet Packages for Solution. Click the Updates tab on the left, and when the center content loads, click the Update button on each of the packages.)

3 Open the _Layout.cshtml file in the Views\Shared folder of your solution and update the links to the versions of Modernizr and jQuery listed in your Scripts folder.

4 In your application, open the HomeController.cs file and add a new controller action:

```
public ActionResult Storage()
{
    return View();
}
```

5 Now go back to the _Layout.cshtml file and update the menu unordered list
   with the following item:

```
<li>@Html.ActionLink("Local Storage", "Storage", "Home")</li>
```

This will add a new menu for the Local Storage application page to the top of
the website.

6 Back in the Home controller, right-click on the word View.

7 In the pop-up menu, select Add View.

8 Uncheck the Use a Layout or Master Page check box and click Add to get the
   basic outline of a page.

Now, replace the entire contents of this view with the markup in the following listing,
which gives you all the structural elements you need. Play close attention to the style
classes listed for the various tags. These are important for the jQuery UI implementation you'll be using.

> **Listing 9.1 The complete markup for the Storage.cshtml page**

```
<!DOCTYPE html>
<html>
<head>
    <title>Local Storage</title>
    <script src="@Url.Content("~/Scripts/jquery-1.7.2.js")"
        type="text/javascript"></script>
    <script
       src="@Url.Content("~/Scripts/
           jquery-ui-1.8.19.js")"                          jQuery UI is required
           type="text/javascript"></script>               for application.
    <script
    src="@Url.Content("~/Scripts/
           jquery.ui.touch-punch.js")"                     Touch-punch plugin is
           type="text/javascript"></script>                free utility that adds
    <script src="@Url.Content("~/Scripts/modernizr-2.5.3.js")"    touch to existing
        type="text/javascript"></script>                   jQuery UI widgets.
    <link href="http://ajax.aspnetcdn.com/ajax/
           jquery.ui/1.8.16/                                When using jQuery UI
           themes/smoothness/jquery-ui.css"                widgets include theme to
        rel="stylesheet"                                   style elements on page.
        type="text/css" />
    <link href="@Url.Content("~/Content/storage.css")"
        rel="stylesheet" type="text/css" />
</head>
<body>

    <div id="dialog" title="Choose Hue">                   Choose Hue dialog box
        <div id="hue"></div>                               will be displayed over
    </div>                                                  elements to be edited.

    <button id="new">New</button>                          New and Reset buttons will create new
    <button id="clear">Clear</button>                      box on page or clear existing boxes.

    <script src="@Url.Content("~/Scripts/main.js")"        main.js file is primary library
        type="text/javascript"></script>                  for this application.
```

```
</body>
</html>
```

GITing an open source JavaScript library

You've updated all the existing JavaScript libraries in your application by means of NuGet, but you don't have the jquery.ui.touch-punch JavaScript file listed in the HTML `<script>` tag. This is a freely downloadable library written by David Furfero. The project for this library is located on GitHub at https://github.com/furf/jquery-ui-touch-punch/.

You could pull this library down by copying and pasting the JavaScript, but we wanted to give you a little insight into how you can do this with Git, one of the most popular source-control and source-sharing tools available today:

1 Download and run the latest executable installer of Git for Windows from http://code.google.com/p/msysgit/downloads/list.

2 Create a folder on your local drive called MyGitProjects with a subfolder called Touch-Punch.

3 Find and execute the Git Bash program that installed as part of Git. Enter the following commands, as shown in figure 9.2:

```
cd C:\MyGitProjects
cd Touch-Punch
git init
git pull https://github.com/furf/jquery-ui-touch-punch
```

Your Git Bash window should look something like figure 9.2. Assuming you placed your MyGitProjects folder on the C: drive, you should be able to navigate to C:\MyGit-Projects\Touch-Punch and copy the jquery.ui.touch-punch.js file into your solution

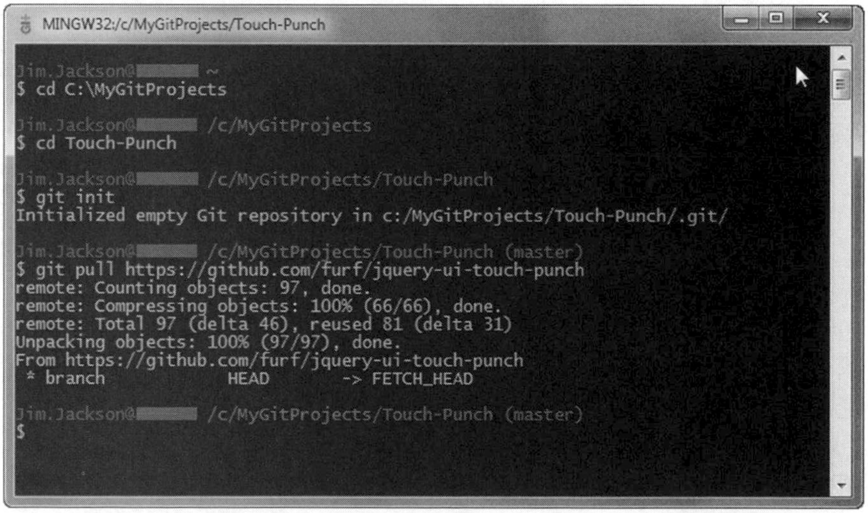

Figure 9.2 Pulling a library from GitHub requires that you initialize a folder as a repository and then pull from the original source into that folder by means of the project URL.

folder. The touch-punch library must be loaded into your page after jQuery UI, but once that's done, any jQuery UI widget will be touch-enabled.

> **WARNING**   Using open source libraries from a public repository can save you time, money, and headaches, but you *must* read through the licensing for each library you intend to use to be sure you're in compliance with the wishes or demands of the original authors. This is part of being a good citizen of the open source community.

Our primary purpose in including jQuery UI in this application is to give you the polished horizontal slider in a way that doesn't take the focus away from the core purpose of this chapter. The theme we included is also arbitrary—you could use any of the themes available or a custom theme you create yourself. We'll also be using the jQuery `draggable` interaction to show an alternative to wiring up your own HTML5 drag-and-drop implementation.

The styles that you'll use (outside of the jQuery theme styles) are important in this application only in that the box is absolutely positioned in the primary object. That means its style is set to `position:absolute`. This allows you to place it anywhere on the page.

Other than that, you're providing just enough styling to give the page a clean and pleasant look. The real work in this chapter is, once again, a JavaScript library. Let's take a look at its structure and function.

9.2   *Structuring a JavaScript library to maintain state*

You'll be spending your remaining time in this chapter down in the weeds of the JavaScript code. The application you're building must create, discriminate, display, store, and reset multiple objects that share many of the same characteristics with only minor differences between them. The object-creation logic must also try to make each element slightly different from all the others, so the user can tell which is which.

First, you'll build the basic structure of the main.js file, and then you'll see how a single element is created in code. Both of these involve taking a closer look at the LocalStorage API.

9.2.1   *Creating an application outline that supports local storage of objects*

Your JavaScript application structure must support all the operations necessary to position and style elements on the screen and provide for their persistence in Local-Storage. You do this in six steps:

1   Create an object with properties and events.
2   Add the object to the page and to LocalStorage.
3   Allow the user to change the position and other properties of the object.
4   When any change is made, update the object in LocalStorage.

5   When the user comes back to the page, load all previous objects from Local-
     Storage and display them on the page.

6   Allow the user to remove all objects from LocalStorage.

To enable your application to take those steps, create a new JavaScript file named
main.js and place it in the Scripts folder in your solution. This is the primary application library for the chapter; it's listed at the bottom of the <body> element in your
main MVC view.

The following listing shows the basic outline of this library.

Listing 9.2   Wiring up `document.ready` and building the `Main` object

```
$(document).ready(function () {
    Main.init();
});

window.Main = {
    nextBoxIndex: 0,
    offset: 0,
    $slider: null,
    $selectedBox: null,

    init: function () {
        var self = this;

        if (!Modernizr.localstorage) {
            alert("Local storage not supported.");
            return;
        }

        if (!Modernizr.hsla) {
            alert("hsl colors not supported.");
            return;
        }

        if (!window.JSON) {
            alert("JSON not supported.");
            return;
        }
    },

    createBox: function (key) { },

    saveBox: function ($box) { },

    clearAll: function () { },

    loadAll: function () { },

    removeBox: function ($box) { },

    startDialogFor: function ($box) { },

    setHue: function ($box, hue) { },

    initDialog: function () { }
};
```

Local properties are used to give boxes unique ID and position them on page.

Properties will be assigned as wrapped sets to perform operations.

Check for support for LocalStorage, CSS HSLA, and JSON.

Create box object and return it to caller.

Save box object to LocalStorage.

Clear LocalStorage of all saved boxes.

Remove single box from LocalStorage.

Load all boxes from storage.

Open jQuery UI dialog box for changing box color.

Assign color to box.

Create in-memory slider control for use in dialog box.

Reading through the code, you should get a decent idea of the scope of the problem you're solving with this application. You initialize your `Main` object in the document ready function and then check for compatibility with all the APIs you'll be using. You have functions that create objects (`createBox`) and some that manipulate page elements like dialog boxes and slider controls. Along the way, pay close attention to the `saveBox` and `loadAll` functions, because they're the keys to working with LocalStorage.

As you progress, you'll update the `init` function when necessary to respond to a page event and then fill in the function call that executes the unit of work.

9.2.2 *Building UI elements that can be stored locally*

The first bit of functional code you need to write is against the button that creates a new box object. You'll wire up this button so that it responds by creating the new box object and saves it to LocalStorage.

Place the following snippet in the `init` function:

```
$("#new")
    .button()
    .click(function () {
        var $box = self.createBox();
        self.saveBox($box);
    });
```

Make button object into jQuery UI button.

Use chaining to bind click event to button.

Create new box object.

Immediately save box object.

You create the box and immediately save it, which is a simple pattern that's perfectly acceptable in a single-user environment like a browser. A single box object in your application is actually a jQuery wrapped set that has a reproducible interface, a unique identifier, and a few events attached to it to allow it to be dragged and its background color to be changed.

The following lsiting shows what the `createBox` function in main.js should look like. This will create a box, give it an `id` value, style it, and then place it on the page.

Listing 9.3 The `createBox` function can create an object with a specific `id` or a fresh box

```
createBox: function (key) {
    var self = this;

    var index;
    if (key) {
        var parts = key.split("-");
        index = parseInt(parts[1], 10);
        this.nextBoxIndex =
            Math.max(index, this.nextBoxIndex) + 1;
    }
    else {
        index = this.nextBoxIndex;
        key = "box-" + index;
        this.nextBoxIndex++;
        this.offset += 20;
    }
```

If key value is passed in use it to create unique id for box.

If no key value is passed use next counter value available. Keys can be any string value so long as they're unique.

```
var html = "<div class='box box-shadow box-round'>"
    + "Drag Me<br>"
    + "or <button class='change-color'>"
    + "Change color</button><br>"
    + "or <button class='remove'>"
    + "remove</button>"
    + "</div>";
```

Build box markup on the fly by concatenating strings.

```
var $box = $(html)
    .attr("id", key)
    .css({
        left: this.offset,
        top: this.offset,
        "z-index": index
    })
```

Take string and build wrapped set out of it.

```
    .appendTo("body")
    .draggable({
        stop: function (event, ui) {
            self.saveBox($box);
        }
    });
```

After box has been created add it to current page.

```
this.setHue($box, this.offset);

$box.find(".change-color")
    .button()
    .click(function () {
        self.startDialogFor($box);
    });
```

From new wrapped set find change color button and wire it up.

```
$box.find(".remove")
    .button()
    .click(function () {
        self.removeBox($box);
    });
```

Find the remove button and wire its click event up as well.

```
    return $box;
},
```

Return completed box to caller.

The `box` object you created is ready to roll when `createBox` is complete. You added it to the interface, styled it, and bound the appropriate event handlers to its various subelements.

Note also that you called a function called `draggable` on your box. This is a jQuery UI function that will inject the appropriate behaviors into the box to make it respond to drag events without a lot of unnecessary flags and *x,y* coordinate math.

Because you're also including the touch-punch plugin, touch events will also be automatically wired up to respond to drag events.

Figure 9.3 shows what the box and its hue selector dialog box will look like at runtime.

Figure 9.3   The box object you build in `createBox` has all events prewired and dialog boxes ready for operation.

9.3 Using the LocalStorage API

Here we arrive at the meat of the chapter, where you'll dig into the LocalStorage API and see how data is stored, read, and removed on the client. In this section, you'll specifically learn how to do the following:

- Add and remove items from the localStorage object the not-so-easy way
- Add and remove items the easy way
- Move data from localStorage to the page
- Delete items from localStorage
- Clear all items from localStorage
- Use the localStorage event

First up, we'll show you how to add items to and remove them from the localStorage object the not-so-easy way, just so that you know how to do it. This is helpful in JavaScript when you need to build a function call in code and execute it using either the call or apply JavaScript keywords. We won't cover these implementations in detail since they wouldn't significantly add to the LocalStorage discussion.

9.3.1 Adding and removing items to and from LocalStorage the not-so-easy way

 Core API

Suppose you're writing the game application we mentioned briefly at the opening of this chapter. You want to store the last five high scores for the current user, updating the list as new games are finished, and then retrieve them for display on the user's home screen.

The localStorage.getItem(key) function could be used to retrieve a single score as a string from storage based on a unique user-defined key string (in this case, the date and time string when the user completed the game). If the string returned is actually a JSON object, it will have to be parsed back into that object. Numeric values that are retrieved will be coerced using normal JavaScript parsing methods, or they can be forced into their legitimate types by casting them directly. If the key passed into getItem doesn't exist, the item won't be created and no exception will be thrown, but null will be returned:

```
var t = localStorage.getItem("lastKey");
```

localStorage.setItem(key, value) will create or overwrite a single item in storage based on the key provided. If the key doesn't exist, the item will be created in Local-Storage. If the key does exist, the value of the item in LocalStorage will be completely overwritten with the new value. If an exception is thrown from calls to either storage object when setting a value, it will almost always be a QuotaExceededError that should be specifically tracked. This exception means that the current storage object can't write the data because the value, when added to the currently consumed storage, will exceed what's allotted by the browser. The setItem function doesn't return a value:

```
localStorage.setItem("lastKey", 2);
```

These methods of getting and setting data items in LocalStorage are perfect for situations where the key of the element you're working with is a generated or concatenated value. The second way of getting and setting values, described next, will work in the same scenarios, but `getItem` and `setItem` give your code a bit more specificity. In the end, it's a personal choice which way you decide to set and retrieve LocalStorage items.

9.3.2 *Adding and removing items the easy way*

Core API

Now that you know the API calls to get and set items in LocalStorage, let's look at the easy way to add and remove items. The process is exactly the same as using `getItem` and `setItem`, but it's quicker to write and easier to read.

The LocalStorage API allows you to assign values as properties directly by using standard setters and getters. This means that as long as the key value you want to use is a valid string with no special characters, you can just use this code to set and get values:

```
localStorage.box = "myBox"; // set value
var t = localStorage.box;   // get value
```

This creates and then reads an entry in LocalStorage with a key of `box` and a value of `"myBox"`.

If your value contains characters like dashes (interpreted as minus) or other special characters, you can use the following code to force the key to be exactly what you need:

```
localStorage["box-0"] = "myBox"; // set value
var t = localStorage["box-0"];   // get value
```

Those two snippets of code are functionally equivalent.

Because this chapter's application allows a user to create as many boxes as they want, you need to assign an ID value that includes an incrementing number. For this, you can use the second syntax to add a `box` object to LocalStorage, as shown in the following listing.

The `saveBox` function should already be stubbed out in main.js. This code completes it.

Listing 9.4 Saving an item to LocalStorage using a property setter

```
saveBox: function ($box) {
    var position = $box.position();
    localStorage[$box.attr("id")] =
        JSON.stringify({
            left: position.left,
            top: position.top,
            hue: $box.data("hue")
        });
},
```

Pass in id value to localStorage object to create or update LocalStorage entry in browser.

LocalStorage items can contain anything but simplest method is to assign values you want to JSON object and stringify it.

Transactional data in LocalStorage

The save operation in listing 9.4 brings up an important feature of LocalStorage. Browsers by their very nature operate in a single-user environment, so local data operations seldom need total transactional support. But even the simplest operations must have some features that larger database engines take for granted.

LocalStorage ensures that data written to and read from storage is atomic, consistent, and isolated. *Atomicity* means that data is guaranteed to be completely written or not written at all. If an exception is thrown while writing to LocalStorage, you don't need to clean up after yourself and go look for the data. Failure means complete failure, and success means complete success. *Consistency* ensures that the data you read is in exactly the state that it was in when you wrote it to storage, and that nothing written will be changed by the browser engine. *Isolation* requires that nothing half-written can be read. Data records are locked until writing is complete.

The final feature of normal database transactions is *durability*, which isn't really within the scope of LocalStorage.

9.3.3 *Moving data from LocalStorage to the page*

Core API

Now that the box or boxes have been saved to LocalStorage, you can read them back out. Because any change to a box will be updated to LocalStorage right away, you don't need to worry about adding a single item when the new button is clicked. Instead, wait for an event that tells the code that something happened in LocalStorage, and then just read everything out that you've saved and drop it on the screen.

That's the purpose of the loadAll function in main.js, shown in the following listing. You do this with the help of the length property of LocalStorage, which returns an integer corresponding to the number of separate items currently saved.

Listing 9.5 loadAll takes everything from LocalStorage and dumps it to the page

```
loadAll: function () {
    var ids = [];
    for (var i = 0; i < localStorage.length; i++) {
        var key = localStorage.key(i);            // Get key from
        if (key.indexOf("box-") !== 0)            // LocalStorage based
            continue;                             // on its index.

        var data = localStorage[key];             // Get value based on key name
        var box = JSON.parse(data);               // and create box object from data.
        var id = "#" + key;
        ids.push(id);
                                                  // Assign box object's id based
        var $box = $(id);                         // on LocalStorage key name.
        if (!$box.length)
            $box = this.createBox(key);           // Create box if it
                                                  // doesn't already exist.
        $box
            .css({                                // Move box to position
                left: box.left,                   // where it was last saved.
                top: box.top
```

```
        });

      this.setHue($box, box.hue);
    }

  var found = ids.join(", ");
  $(".box").not(found).remove();
},
```

| | Set box color to its last saved value. |

| | Take all ids found and remove box objects no longer in storage. |

You should keep in mind an assumption from the `loadAll` function; namely, that the number of `box` objects stored is small enough that read and write operations will be fast. JavaScript engines even in today's mobile browsers are blazingly fast, so this is a pretty reasonable assumption.

9.3.4 *Deleting items from LocalStorage*

Core API

Your library can now successfully load a new `box` object or all `box` objects that have been saved to LocalStorage. The next step is to fill in the remove functionality that you wired up in the `createBox` function. This fires whenever the `remove` button is clicked for any `box`. The following snippet shows the simple code you need to execute this operation:

```
removeBox: function ($box) {
  $box.remove();
  localStorage.removeItem($box.attr("id"));
},
```

First remove object from user interface.

Second remove entry from LocalStorage.

As you can see, you can add and update LocalStorage properties directly using setters and getters, but complete removal of a stored record requires that you use the `removeItem` API function. This function will search through all items in the current storage object and remove the item whose key matches the input parameter. If the key doesn't exist, no exception will be thrown and no work will be performed. The `removeItem` function doesn't return a value.

9.3.5 *Clearing all items from LocalStorage*

Core API

The next functional element in the LocalStorage API that you need to look at is the ability to clear everything from the current browser's LocalStorage data. You do this with the `clear` function, which removes all items currently in storage without regard for their contents or how many exist. Use this function wisely (and sparingly).

You already have a `clear` button on the page, so you just need to wire up its `click` event. Do this in the `init` function as follows:

```
$("#clear")
  .button()
  .click(function () {
    self.clearAll();
  });
```

Then implement the `clearAll` function in your `Main` object, like so:

```
clearAll: function () {
    $(".box").remove();
    localStorage.clear();
},
```

With that code, you take everything with the .box class, remove it from the page, and clear the storage object completely. There's no going back and no confirmation when clearing items, so if you saved anything else to LocalStorage in another part of the application, it's gone for good.

9.3.6 *Using the LocalStorage storage event to detect changes*

 The last part of the LocalStorage story is making sure that whenever a change is made to the localStorage object, all other code in the current application updates appropriately. The storage event fires whenever anything is saved, updated, or removed from localStorage.

Place the following snippet inside the init function (at the end) to start listening for the storage event. When the event fires, you reload every box currently stored:

```
$(window)
    .bind("storage", function () {
        self.loadAll();
    });

this.initDialog();
this.loadAll();
```

Note that only changes to stored data will fire the storage event, not reads. Updating a value to an identical value will also fire the storage event, because it's technically an update.

> ### LocalStorage and SessionStorage
>
> There are two kinds of storage available in the HTML5 specification: LocalStorage and SessionStorage. SessionStorage isn't as durable as LocalStorage and won't persist between page refreshes. It will also not be available to the other tabs or browser windows on the same client machine open to the same domain.
>
> A good use for SessionStorage might be a single page survey site, where the user is asked questions but the answers don't need to be saved between page loads. In that kind of scenario, the ability for the site to automatically "clean" itself could be helpful.
>
> Note that although the storage event specification document indicates that the storage object (Session or Local) is passed along as part of the storage event, tests indicate that this has not yet been implemented in any browser.

9.4   *Adding UI elements to complete the application*

The sample application is nearly complete. You're reading, editing, and removing data from LocalStorage, and now you must get your code to implement the user interface behaviors that will do the actual data edits. We're going to walk you through creating a jQuery UI slider object that lets the user drag a slider to the left or right to change the background color of the box. Just like the draggable and dialog functions, the slider function will take over an assigned element (in this case the #hue element) and set it up as a slider.

CREATING A JQUERY UI SLIDER

slider takes as parameters the minimum value (farthest to the left), the maximum value (farthest to the right), and a set of events. In this case, you'll use only the slide and change events. The slide event will fire as the slider element moves, and the change event will fire when the slide movement stops.

This may seem redundant, but it's important, because if changes are made to the slider value programmatically, those changes won't be bubbled in the slide event, only change. On the other hand, if a user is dragging the slider around, they'd probably like to see the result of the changes immediately in the UI element. For that, change isn't responsive enough. Wiring up to both events allows you the best of both worlds.

The following listing shows the details. This code should fill in the initDialog function in main.js.

> **Listing 9.6   Initializing a jQuery UI slider with event managers attached**

```
initDialog: function () {
   var self = this;

   this.$slider = $("#hue")              Calling .slider on UI element will
      .slider({                          create jQuery UI slider control.
         min: 0,
         max: 360,                       Min and max values correspond
         slide: function (event, ui) {   to degrees on color wheel.
            self.setHue(self.$selectedBox, ui.value);
            self.saveBox(self.$selectedBox);
         },
         change: function (event, ui) {
            self.setHue(self.$selectedBox, ui.value);
            self.saveBox(self.$selectedBox);        When each event fires
         }                                          assign background color
      });                                           of box and save it.
}
```

USING SETHUE

This brings us to the setHue function, which needs a little more explaining. First, take a look at the function in the following snippet:

```
setHue: function ($box, hue) {
   $box.data("hue", hue);
   $box.css({
```

```
        "background-color": "hsl(" + hue + ", 100%, 75%)"
    });
},
```

This function calls the jQuery css function, passing in a concatenated string as the value for background-color. The complete hsl value will look something like hsl(80, 100%, 75%) after concatenation. The function takes the box object and a hue value as parameters.

This simple function is called from various places in the code to assign the background color of each box element. Remember from chapter 2 that HSL is assigned using three values and a color wheel. The color wheel (shown in figure 9.4) shows red at the top (0 degrees), green at 4 o'clock (120 degrees), and blue at 8 o'clock (240 degrees).

The first parameter to hsl is the number of degrees to use to select the base color. The second value describes, as a percentage, how far out from the center of the circle (between 0 and 100 percent) the color should be assigned, and the final value describes how light or dark the value is.

With that in mind, the setHue function concatenates a string for the appropriate hsl function and assigns it to the background color.

DISPLAYING A SLIDER IN A JQUERY UI DIALOG BOX

The last function left to complete is startDialogFor. This function takes a box object as its input parameter and finds the change-color button. With that button's position, it draws a dialog box over it and inserts the slider object you created earlier. This lets you reuse one slider for the entire application, saving memory and speeding the application a bit.

The following listing shows how startDialogFor works. You should have a stubbed function for startDialogFor in main.js. This code completes it.

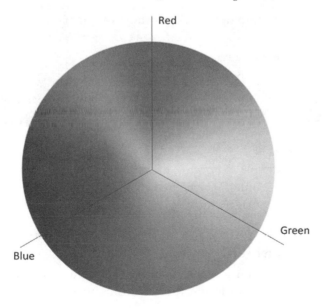

Figure 9.4 An HSL color wheel can describe any color by the angle of the color from 0 (straight up), the distance from the center as a percentage, and how light or dark the value is.

Listing 9.7 The `startDialogFor` function displays a slider in a jQuery UI dialog box

```
startDialogFor: function ($box) {
    var $dialog = $("#dialog")                    Create fixed-size jQuery
        .dialog({                                 UI dialog object.
            resizable: false
        });

    var $colorButton = $box.find(".change-color");   Find change-color button
    var buttonPosition = $colorButton.offset();      and get its position.
    $dialog.dialog(
        "option",                                    Update dialog with
        "position",                                  position value calculated
        [                                            from color-change button.
            buttonPosition.left +
                (($colorButton.outerWidth() - $dialog.outerWidth())
                    / 2),
            buttonPosition.top +
                ($colorButton.outerHeight() * 1.5)
        ]);

    this.$selectedBox = $box;
    this.$slider.slider("value",                     Add slider to dialog.
        this.$selectedBox.data("hue"));
},
```

At this point, you should be able to run the application, drag the boxes around the interface, change the colors of boxes, and the entire page should reload in another tab to the exact same values as the current page. If you close your browser and reopen it, you should get a page that looks exactly like it did before you closed it.

You should also be able to inspect the values in LocalStorage. The easiest way to do this currently is in the Chrome browser:

1 Open your page in Chrome and right-click anywhere on the page.
2 Select Inspect Element.
3 In the Inspector, select the Resources tab.
4 Expand the Local Storage tree node.

You should see something like figure 9.5, with a JSON-text entry for each box displayed on the page.

9.5   *Other uses for LocalStorage*

What you've seen so far is an example of how to work with local storage in an HTML5 application—but it's only the beginning. You might also want to use LocalStorage as a proxy for server data, or to save images, to bring additional features and enhancements to your websites.

9.5.1   *Using LocalStorage as a proxy for server data*

Suppose you're writing a weather application. You want your program to be as responsive as possible for your users, so you decide to use LocalStorage to store the last

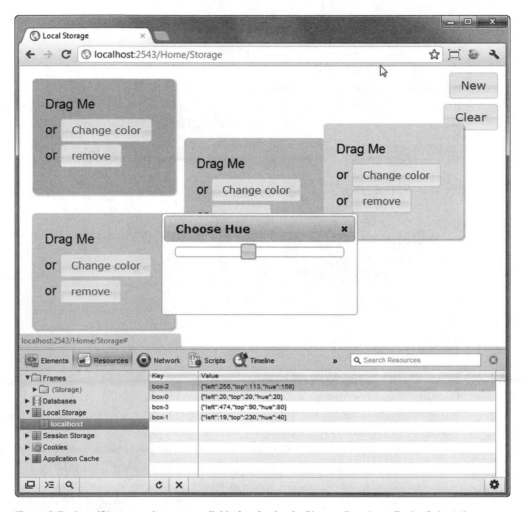

Figure 9.5 LocalStorage values are available for viewing in Chrome Developer Tools. Select the Resources tab and the Local Storage tree node. What's more, these value are editable for testing purposes! All other browser developer toolkits contain similar functionality.

weather reading for the user's current location. When the application starts, you immediately read the value from LocalStorage and display it while requesting updates from the server. The user sees a very responsive (if somewhat out-of-date) application that updates a few moments later with the current reading.

This way of using LocalStorage is part of the `data.Store` feature of the Ext JS framework, but you can build your own with very little effort. The core of the solution is a custom JavaScript layer over LocalStorage that will request the data you need from the server only if it hasn't been previously saved locally. The data might be static, used across multiple pages, or it might be large enough that you would prefer not to download it each time your page is loaded. Using LocalStorage as a proxy, you pull down the data only once and it's available seamlessly whenever you need it for the life of the cache or the life of the page.

The primary danger with this solution is that you ought to have a mechanism to expire the local data if it isn't completely static. You'll also need to name the key for your data so that it won't be overwritten by any other part of the application. If you can get a grip on these two issues, though, you can significantly increase the speed and reduce the server traffic in your application. The following listing shows an example of this.

Listing 9.8 A simple proxy over LocalStorage

```
function getMyData() {
   if (localStorage.myData) {
      return localStorage.myData;           ◁──┐  Function checks for locally stored
   }                                             data first and returns it if it exists.
   else {
      $.ajax({
         url: 'http://mysite.com/getData',  ◁──┐  If data doesn't exist browser
         success: function(data) {               retrieves it from server,
            localStorage.myData = data;          stores it, and returns it.
            return localStorage.myData;
         }
      });
   }
}
```

9.5.2 Using LocalStorage to save images

Looking at images on a mobile platform can be very painful. iOS, in particular, has a notoriously low limit for the total size of images cached for a site, after which no additional images will be requested.

One solution to this problem is to convert your images on the server to base64-encoded strings, which lets you pass the string down to the client on any GET call and save the data to LocalStorage. Then you set the source value of your selected image to the string value, and your image will appear in the page. LocalStorage in this instance allows you to reduce traffic on your site. Even though base64-encoded images are slightly larger than their normal image counterparts, you only need to request these images once. They will consume part of your LocalStorage quota, but not your image size quota on an iOS device.

The next listing shows how you can build a base64 string from an image using C# code.

Listing 9.9 Using LocalStorage to save base64 images

```
// Server C#                                    Using C# you get image
var img = Image.FromFile(filePath);       ◁──  object from file path.
using (var mem = new MemoryStream())
{
                                                Load base64 string for image
                                                and return it to client. Prefix of
   img.Save(mem, ImageFormat.Jpeg);             base64 string tells image element
   return "data:image/jpeg;base64," +           how to present string data.
      Convert.ToBase64String(mem.ToArray());  ◁──┘
}
```

```
// Client JavaScript
localStorage.myImage = stringFromServer;
$("#image").attr("src", localStorage.myImage);
```

Client stores string locally so it doesn't have to call server each time.

Client assigns image object src attribute to base64 image string.

9.6 Summary

LocalStorage is one of those simple tools, like a hammer or a screwdriver. You'll want to keep it handy in all of your applications as a first-line solution to reducing server traffic or maintaining local data across sessions that doesn't need to reside on the server. With its wide support and speed of access, you'll find more uses for it the more you look.

The downsides are the lack of support for automatically clearing items based on age, and the inability to prevent a user from clearing cached items manually. Still, as a local data store, it would be difficult to imagine a simpler or more usable solution than LocalStorage.

In the next chapter, we'll look at another HTML5 API that's useful on its own but that's also very complementary to the LocalStorage API: the Offline API. This API lets your users work with your application even if their devices are disconnected from the internet!

9.7 The complete code listings

The following listings are provided to help you check your work or to build the solution from scratch if you haven't been building the solution while you read.

Listing 9.10 The complete contents of main.js

```javascript
$(document).ready(function () {
  Main.init();
});

window.Main = {
  nextBoxIndex: 0,
  offset: 0,
  $slider: null,
  $selectedBox: null,

  //
  init: function () {
    var self = this;

    if (!Modernizr.localstorage) {
      alert("Local storage not supported.");
      return;
    }

    if (!Modernizr.hsla) {
      alert("hsl colors not supported.");
      return;
    }

    if (!window.JSON) {
      alert("JSON not supported.");
```

```
      return;
    }

  $("#new")
    .button()
    .click(function () {
      var $box = self.createBox();
      self.saveBox($box);
    });

  $("#clear")
    .button()
    .click(function () {
      self.clearAll();
    });

  $(window)
    .bind("storage", function () {
      self.loadAll();
    });

  this.initDialog();
  this.loadAll();
},

// ----------
createBox: function (key) {
  var self = this;
  var index;

  if (key) {
    var parts = key.split("-");
    index = parseInt(parts[1], 10);
    this.nextBoxIndex = Math.max(index, this.nextBoxIndex) + 1;
  } else {
    index = this.nextBoxIndex;
    key = "box-" + index;
    this.nextBoxIndex++;
    this.offset += 20;
  }

  var html = "<div class='box box-shadow box-round'>"
    + "Drag Me<br>"
    + "or <button class='change-color'>Change color</button><br>"
    + "or <button class='remove'>remove</button>"
    + "</div>";

  var $box = $(html)
    .attr("id", key)
    .css({
      left: this.offset,
      top: this.offset,
      "z-index": index
    })
    .appendTo("body")
    .draggable({
      stop: function (event, ui) {
        self.saveBox($box);
```

```
        }
      });

    this.setHue($box, this.offset);

    $box.find(".change-color")
      .button()
      .click(function () {
        self.startDialogFor($box);
      });

    $box.find(".remove")
      .button()
      .click(function () {
        self.removeBox($box);
      });

    return $box;
  },

  // ----------
  saveBox: function ($box) {
    var position = $box.position();
    localStorage[$box.attr("id")] = JSON.stringify({
      left: position.left,
      top: position.top,
      hue: $box.data("hue")
    });
  },

  // ----------
  clearAll: function () {
    $(".box").remove();
    localStorage.clear();
  },

  // ----------
  loadAll: function () {
    var ids = [];
    for (var a = 0; a < localStorage.length; a++) {
      var key = localStorage.key(a);
      if (key.indexOf("box-") !== 0)
        continue;

      var data = localStorage[key];
      var box = JSON.parse(data);
      var id = "#" + key;
      ids.push(id);

      var $box = $(id);
      if (!$box.length)
        $box = this.createBox(key);

      $box
        .css({
          left: box.left,
          top: box.top
        });
```

```
          this.setHue($box, box.hue);
      }
    var found = ids.join(", ");
    $(".box").not(found).remove();
  },

  // ----------
  removeBox: function ($box) {
    $box.remove();
    localStorage.removeItem($box.attr("id"));
  },

  // ----------
  startDialogFor: function ($box) {
    var $dialog = $("#dialog")
      .dialog({
        resizable: false
      });

    var $colorButton = $box.find(".change-color");
    var buttonPosition = $colorButton.offset();
    $dialog.dialog("option", "position", [
      buttonPosition.left + (($colorButton.outerWidth() -
          $dialog.outerWidth()) / 2),
      buttonPosition.top + ($colorButton.outerHeight() * 1.5)
    ]);

    this.$selectedBox = $box;
    this.$slider.slider("value", this.$selectedBox.data("hue"));
  },

  // ----------
  setHue: function ($box, hue) {
    $box.data("hue", hue);
    $box.css({
      "background-color": "hsl(" + hue + ", 100%, 75%)"
    });
  },

  // ----------
  initDialog: function () {
    var self = this;

    this.$slider = $("#hue")
      .slider({
        min: 0,
        max: 360,
        slide: function (event, ui) {
          self.setHue(self.$selectedBox, ui.value);
          self.saveBox(self.$selectedBox);
        },
        change: function (event, ui) {
          self.setHue(self.$selectedBox, ui.value);
          self.saveBox(self.$selectedBox);
        }
      });
  }
};
```

Listing 9.11 The complete contents of storage.css

```css
* {
  margin: 0;
  padding: 0;
}

html,
body {
  position: absolute;
  left: 0;
  top: 0;
  right: 0;
  bottom: 0;
  overflow: hidden;
  font-family: sans-serif;
}

.box {
  position: absolute;
  left: 10px;
  top: 10px;
  width: 180px;
  height: 140px;
  padding: 20px;
  font-size: 20px;
  line-height: 2em;
}

.box button {
  font-size: 16px;
}

#dialog {
  display: none;
}

#new {
  position: absolute;
  right: 10px;
  top: 10px;
}

#clear {
  position: absolute;
  right: 10px;
  top: 60px;
}

#info {
  position: absolute;
  right: 10px;
  bottom: 10px;
  max-width: 500px;
  color: #999;
  font-size: 14px;
}
```

```css
p {
  margin-bottom: 1em;
}

a,
a:hover,
a:active,
a:visited {
  color: #666;
}

a,
a:visited {
  text-decoration: none;
}

.box-round {
  -webkit-border-radius: 6px;
     -moz-border-radius: 6px;
          border-radius: 6px;

  /* useful if you don't want a bg color
  from leaking outside the border: */
  -moz-background-clip: padding;
  -webkit-background-clip: padding-box;
  background-clip: padding-box;
}

.box-shadow {
  -webkit-box-shadow: 2px 2px 4px rgba(0, 0, 0, 0.3);
     -moz-box-shadow: 2px 2px 4px rgba(0, 0, 0, 0.3);
          box-shadow: 2px 2px 4px rgba(0, 0, 0, 0.3);
}
```

Offline web applications

Offline web applications

10

This chapter covers

- Building a stable offline web application
- Synchronizing to a server in occasionally connected applications
- Understanding the constraints of building offline web applications

On a recent trip to visit family, I, Jim Jackson, had an opportunity to watch my nephew playing games and surfing the web on his iPod. I talked to him a little about modern web design and showed him a few sites with some interesting new features. Later, while in the car, I asked him to go back to one of the sites we had visited together. To his amazement, the site still worked!

Not having a background in software development, his was a pretty typical reaction to an HTML5 offline application. The idea that you can browse to an application while online, and then go back to it when you're offline to continue reading or working, goes against everything most people have learned about how the internet works. But this offline-capable concept is gaining momentum and familiarity with users.

In this chapter, you'll learn to build offline applications in the context of a simple shopping list application that can be edited online and offline. The build will be done in the following steps, with each step building on previous work:

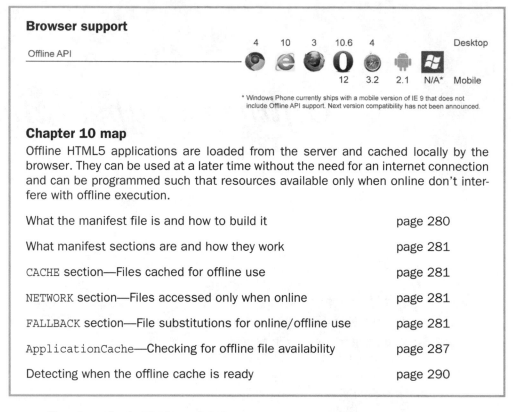

Browser support

Offline API

	4	10	3	10.6	4				Desktop
				12	3.2	2.1	N/A*		Mobile

* Windows Phone currently ships with a mobile version of IE 9 that does not
include Offline API support. Next version compatibility has not been announced.

Chapter 10 map

Offline HTML5 applications are loaded from the server and cached locally by the browser. They can be used at a later time without the need for an internet connection and can be programmed such that resources available only when online don't interfere with offline execution.

What the manifest file is and how to build it	page 280
What manifest sections are and how they work	page 281
`CACHE` section—Files cached for offline use	page 281
`NETWORK` section—Files accessed only when online	page 281
`FALLBACK` section—File substitutions for online/offline use	page 281
`ApplicationCache`—Checking for offline file availability	page 287
Detecting when the offline cache is ready	page 290

1 Creating a basic HTML and CSS structure.
2 Developing a JavaScript interface using jQuery.
3 Using an application manifest to tell the browser how to handle content when offline.
4 Writing offline JavaScript logic to effectively manipulate the offline HTML5 API.
5 Building server components to receive and send data to the client when online.

In addition to all the JavaScript and jQuery goodness, we'll cover all the facets of the current Offline API specification detailed in figure 10.1.

As in previous chapters, we'll build the markup and stylesheet and then dig into the application library in stages to highlight the HTML5 API and various jQuery functions. Complete listings for the build are provided at the end of the chapter, as are the complete JavaScript file contents. Put on your coding hat and let's get to work!

10.1 Building an offline HTML5 application

Suppose your partner is upset because you never seem to remember to buy needed supplies at the grocery store. You know that the criticism is deserved, and you've committed to never forgetting again. To that end, you're going to design and build a simple shopping list application that can be edited either online or offline. This

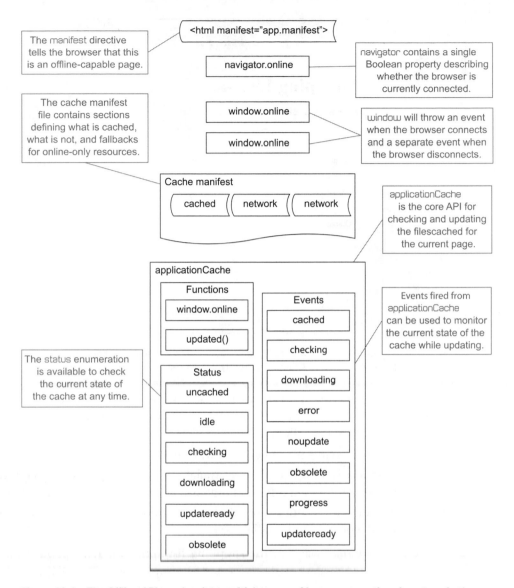

Figure 10.1 The Offline API reaches into multiple areas of browser operation, from tags in the markup to `window` and `applicationCache` events to new file types.

way, your partner can add stuff to the list, and you can access it even when you're at the grocery store.

Figure 10.2 shows the simple, usable interface you'll be creating.

The basic premise of an offline web application is that, with specific directives in the markup and careful site preparation, you can take your application with you even when you aren't connected to a network. With this feature, though, come some unique challenges and important design decisions.

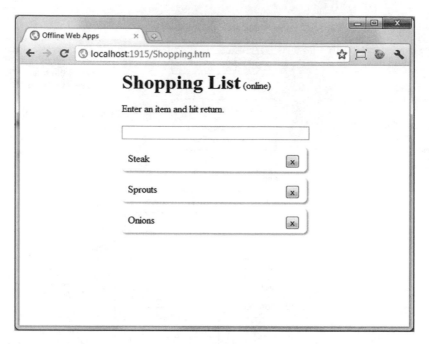

Figure 10.2   The complete application will allow a user to add and remove shopping items regardless of whether or not they're currently connected.

To make your current site or HTML application available offline, you must first inventory the resources that you currently use. Every file you include in your site will need to be evaluated against the following criteria:

- Is the resource static or is it dynamically called?
- If the resource is static, should it be available when the application is offline?
- If it's not available when offline, should a substitute resource be provided?
- If the resource is dynamic, how will the application handle requests for it when no network connection is available?

Let's first consider the design of the shopping list app. The application must show when the user is connected or disconnected. A simple cue on the screen will help there. Then you must decide how to store the data generated locally, so that it can be synchronized back and forth with the server. This chapter's sample application will use LocalStorage and an MVC controller to handle the storage and synchronization. Finally, the client-side logic must work the same way from the user's perspective whether they're connected or disconnected, and it should gracefully handle changing connectivity states internally. This is where the Offline HTML5 API and some smooth jQuery operations come in.

With those design considerations "considered," you'll now create the basic site structure and then the offline JavaScript library.

Going offline versus being offline

There are two scenarios that you'll have to consider when building your offline website.

The first occurs when a user is online and then loses connectivity. This could be because they're using a portable Wi-Fi device and walked out of range or because an "airplane mode" was switched on. Whatever the reason, the important part is that the page was not reloaded, and the browser was not closed and reopened, but the network connection was suddenly unavailable. In this scenario, you need to track the current connection status from within the page. This chapter's sample application will show you one way to do just that.

The second scenario is when the user visits an offline-accessible page and then closes the browser. When the user reopens the browser and navigates back to the page, there is no connection, so nothing can be loaded from the server. At that stage, all content previously saved to the cache is loaded.

Both of these scenarios imply the ability for the page to suddenly come back online. When that happens, the page should be notified and any connection-related functions should fire. That brings us to the problem of data synchronization, a topic that's out of scope for this book.

Using ASP.NET MVC with offline HTML5 applications

This application will be built on an MVC (Model View Controller) platform using a simple JSON controller for the data synchronization and a singleton object to emulate a data storage server, but the page we'll be visiting won't be an MVC view. Instead we'll use a simple HTML page.

We must do it this way because offline web applications require a physical page to reference as the starting point for the offline cache. The standard MVC application, by comparison, only presents a URL endpoint, not a physical file.

So, to be clear, you must have a physical HTML file in place for ASP.NET MVC to support an offline scenario.

10.1.1 Creating the basic site structure

Start by opening Visual Studio and creating a new ASP.NET MVC web application, and call it ShoppingList. Be sure to make it an internet application that uses the Razor engine and HTML5 semantic markup when you come to the New Project dialog box. Using MVC allows you to create a controller to feed data to and from the client via Ajax, but remember that it doesn't allow you to use a Razor view for your offline application.

Inside the new solution, you first need to create your offline page. Follow these steps:

1. Right-click on the solution node and select Add > New Item > HTML Page.
2. Name the new page Shopping.htm, after which your page should appear in the application's root folder.

3 Inside the new page, add the complete markup (provided in the code listing section at the end of this chapter).

The next listing shows the entire HTML markup for the Shopping.html page. One thing we do want you to note about the initial markup is the attribute in the opening `<html>` tag that points to a file named app.manifest.

Listing 10.1   The Shopping.htm page

```
<!DOCTYPE html>
<html manifest="app.manifest">
<head>
  <title>Offline Web Apps</title>
  <meta name="apple-mobile-web-app-capable" content="yes" />
  <meta name="viewport"
    content="user-scalable=no, initial-scale=1.0,
    minimum-scale=1.0, maximum-scale=1.0" />
  <script
    src="http://ajax.aspnetcdn.com/ajax/
      jquery/jquery-1.7.2.js"
    type="text/javascript"></script>
  <script
    src="http://ajax.aspnetcdn.com/ajax/
      modernizr/modernizr-2.0.6-development-only.js"
    type="text/javascript"></script>
  <link href="Content/offline.css"
    rel="stylesheet" type="text/css" />
</head>
<body>
  <section id="content">
    <h1>Shopping List</h1>
    <span id="status"></span>
    <p>Enter an item and hit return.</p>
    <input id="input" type="text" />
    <div id="items"></div>
  </section>
  <script src="Scripts/main.js"
    type="text/javascript"></script>
</body>
</html>
```

App.manifest is the file that, by its presence, tells the browser that this page should be available offline. More on the contents of that file shortly.

Next is the styling for the application. In Solution Explorer, do the following:

1 Right-click on the Content folder and select Add > New Item > Style Sheet.
2 Name the new stylesheet offline.css.
3 Grab the markup from listing 10.10 at the end of this chapter, and add it to the stylesheet.

You'll be creating a brand new set of styles for this offline application because it isn't necessary to duplicate the normal tabbed interface in the rest of the application. This will give the user a cue that this page is different and allow you to keep things as streamlined as possible. And because most of that content is unremarkable, and isn't related to the API featured in this chapter, we won't discuss it here.

Telling the user that a site is available offline

Building the CSS file provides a good opportunity to think about how to let your users know that the site they're visiting is available offline. Each application is different, so at this point it's more important to understand the scope and nature of the problem rather than to focus on specific suggestions for resolving it.

The first part of the problem is letting your users know in a fluent fashion that the site they're visiting will be available to them later, even if they aren't connected. It's unnatural for users to consider opening a browser on a device when they know that there's no connection, so what kinds of indicators on the site could provide that cue? Additionally, you'll probably only be building a subset of the site's functionality for offline consumption, so how can this be indicated to the user?

Next, while a user is working with the site, it's reasonable to expect an occasional loss of connectivity. How can your application tell the user what has happened, and indicate that there's no cause for concern because their work is being saved locally?

Offline web pages are still very new, so little or no research has been done to standardize on a method of identifying these conditions to your users. This leaves the door open to practically any solution, with your creativity being the only limitation. Chrome, for instance, changes its home page to monochrome icons if the system isn't currently online. This is a very intuitive indicator, but you might choose to include an icon or glyph in the corner of the browser window that shows the currently connected status. Even a banner that appears temporarily in your site isn't unheard of, though some might consider it heavy handed.

Your final solution should make it very clear to anyone visiting the site what is possible and what the current connectivity status is. Anything less that this is a recipe for confusion, or worse, an unused website.

10.1.2 Creating the offline JavaScript library

Now that the CSS is loaded, it's time to work on the JavaScript interface to help sort through which functions are responsible for which tasks during execution. The offline HTML application will use local storage to contain two kinds of data:

- The current list of shopping items
- A listing of required actions to update the server to reflect the client state

You'll also add functions to manage state on the page and reduce duplication of code.

You haven't yet created the main.js file in the Scripts folder of the site, so do that now. Open it and add the code in listing 10.2 to stub out the entire API. This code creates the outline that you'll fill in as we dig deeper into offline applications. (Remember, if you have any questions about where specific pieces of code fit in the main.js file, the complete listing is at the end of this chapter.)

Listing 10.2   The JavaScript API for the offline web application

```
$(document).ready(function () {
  Main.init();
});

window.Main = {
  $status: null,
  $input: null,

  shoppingItems: [],

  itemActions: [],

  init: function () {
  },

  updateForNetStatus: function (connected) {
  },

  newItem: function (title) {
  },

  loadState: function () {
  },

  saveState: function () {
  },

  syncWithServer: function () {
  }
};
```

ShoppingList object will contain placeholder for status and input elements to prevent from having to requery DOM every time.

◁—— **Keep list of current shopping items.**

◁ **Keep list of all items that must be synchronized to server.**

◁ **Initialize object.**

◁ **Start listening for current online status.**

◁ **newItem function updates UI with new element and assigns element's delete key to anonymous function.**

◁ **loadState function is called when initializing screen and pulls data from LocalStorage calling newItem on each value.**

◁ **saveState takes all items in local shoppingItems array and updates LocalStorage with same.**

◁ **syncWithServer takes all items cached for server updates and sends them off.**

This JavaScript file is the last client-side file you need before starting the process of making the site available offline. We'll fill in the logic soon, but for now it's time to turn your attention to the file unique to an offline HTML5 application: the application manifest.

10.2 *The manifest file*

The manifest is a simple text file located somewhere on your website and linked to an attribute of the <html> element of your page. When the browser encounters the manifest, it will immediately read it and start processing it line-by-line to determine which parts of the current page should be saved. Every page that you want available offline should have a manifest directive linked like so:

```
<html manifest="app.manifest">
```

A manifest attribute can be relative to the current page URL or it can be an absolute location, as long as that location is on the same domain as the current page. Elements inside the manifest with relative URLs will be loaded relative to the manifest location, not the current page location.

For instance, to load a script file from the scripts subfolder, you could use this as a relative path:

```
/scripts/jquery.js
```

This is an absolute path:

```
http://mysite.com/scripts/jquery.js
```

Additionally, when the browser requests the manifest file, it will use the content type of text/cache-manifest. You'll need to ensure your web server supports this content type and the .manifest file extension.

> **TIP** The .manifest file extension is provided by convention, but you can choose to use any extension you like, as long as your server will serve it with the appropriate content type.

In this section, you'll add a cache manifest to the sample application, and then dive in to learn the various parts of the manifest and how you can use those parts.

10.2.1 Adding the application manifest to the sample project

There is no built-in template in Visual Studio for the manifest, so you'll just format a simple text file:

1. Right-click on the ShoppingList project node and select Add > New Item.
2. From the dialog box, select Text File and name the file app.manifest. This should put the file in the root folder of your application where it will be available to the rest of the application.
3. Open the new app.manifest file and add the following code, which tells the browser to download and keep copies of the CDN (Content Delivery Network) versions of jQuery and Modernizr as well as the main.js and site.css files:

```
CACHE MANIFEST
# v11
http://ajax.aspnetcdn.com/ajax/jquery/jquery-1.7.2.min.js
http://ajax.aspnetcdn.com/ajax/modernizr/modernizr-2.5.3.js
Scripts/main.js
Content/offline.css
```

Note that you don't need to list the current page; it contains the manifest directive, so it will automatically be cached. Note also that the file must always start with CACHE MANIFEST or an exception will be thrown in the browser.

> **TIP** The # v11 comment line denotes an arbitrary version for the file. This isn't part of the specification, but it's handy because it will act as a cache buster to tell the browser whenever a change has been made or to force all clients to update.

10.2.2 Exploring manifest sections

 Core API The manifest for this project is very simple, listing only a set of static resources that should be available offline, but the HTML5 specification allows for far more complex organization if you need it. White space is ignored during parsing, so feel free to use it to help organize the file content.

The manifest can also be divided into sections by placing special single-line directives in the text to define specific offline behaviors. A directive defines a section in the file, and each type of section can be defined multiple times and be placed in any order. As the browser reads in the file, it will handle each section as a unit when it encounters these directives. A complete cache manifest file could look something like the following snippet:

```
CACHE MANIFEST
```
Top line of manifest file is always same.

```
CACHE:
site.css
/scripts/header.jpg
appcode.js
```
CACHE section tells browser which elements to store locally for use later.

```
NETWORK:
signup.html
signup.js
```
NETWORK section is list of files that will only be accessed when connected.

```
FALLBACK:
twitterfeed.js hidetwitter.js
```
FALLBACK section specifies which files to substitute when disconnected.

THE CACHE SECTION

Core API

The CACHE directive is optional if no other directives precede it in the manifest. If the order of entries must be maintained such that multiple CACHE sections are used, this directive will signal the beginning of a list of files that will be downloaded and cached by the browser for offline use.

Remember that the *exact* directive specified in the manifest must be what your application references. Any change in capitalization or relative location will cause the retrieval from the cache to fail.

We aren't using the CACHE directive in this sample application because there are no other sections in the manifest file, so the browser will default to handling the manifest file content as a CACHE section.

THE NETWORK SECTION

Core API

This section of the manifest describes files that must always be requested from the network. If the application isn't online and a request is encountered for these resources, the request won't be honored, no request will be executed, and no exception will be thrown.

Note that this list of resources to use only when connected doesn't generally include Ajax calls. Those calls would normally be wrapped inside a navigator.onLine check. Rather, the NETWORK section is used for pages that are built dynamically by the server or server processing resources, such as .cgi URLs.

The following manifest says that the update.cgi resource will only be called when online, and it specifies that the stylesheet should be cached:

```
CACHE MANIFEST
NETWORK:
/update.cgi
CACHE:
```

```
/styles.css
/main.js
/logo.png
```

Notice the order of elements in the preceding code. Manifest files are read from top-to-bottom, and, as the section headers are encountered, the browser will change the mode of operation to account for the listings in that section.

In a simple scenario, this doesn't make much difference, but as an offline application gets more complex, it can become more important to declare items as network-only before other items are accounted for. For instance, in an MVC application, it isn't unheard of to have the manifest file created dynamically from a Razor view. When you build in this way, it's possible to list a resource in the application multiple times. The last-in rule applies here, so only the last listing of the resource in the manifest file will be honored.

THE FALLBACK SECTION

Core API

The FALLBACK section is used to tell the browser that whenever a particular resource is requested, something else needs to be substituted for that resource. This can be very simple:

```
FALLBACK:
/login.htm /offline.htm
```

This FALLBACK section states that when the login.htm file is requested in the offline page, the offline.htm file should be returned instead.

While the other sections just list the resources by URL, a FALLBACK entry has two parts: the requested resource and the replacement resource. It gets a little more complicated because the requested resource can be either specific or something called a *fallback namespace*. Fallback namespaces are really just simplified pattern matches specific to URLs. They can start with complete or relative URLs, and they don't require a specific filename. Consider the following example:

```
FALLBACK:
/Images/OnlineOnly /Images/ImageNotFound.jpg
```

The following listing states that any image requested from the relative path /Images/ OnlineOnly/... should instead be replaced with the ImageNotFound.jpg file when browsing offline. As with the other sections, though, the requested resource must match exactly the fallback namespace in terms of capitalization and relative URLs.

> **Listing 10.3 A complex cache manifest with multiple sections**

```
CACHE MANIFEST
# v4.34.5

CACHE:
style.css
require.js
myApp.js
main.js
```

◁ **CACHE MANIFEST must always be first line of manifest file.**

◁ **CACHE section tells browser that everything that follows should be downloaded and saved.**

```
FALLBACK:
online.json offline.json
```

offline.json file will be used when offline and online.json file will be used when connected.

FALLBACK section specifies replacement resources to use when offline.

This manifest file listing will cache the stylesheet and a few JavaScript files, and then, whenever a call is made to load data from online.json, the offline.json file will be substituted and no exceptions will be thrown.

Manifest file breadcrumbs

Every page that needs to be available offline should be listed in the manifest file, but browsers don't, at this time, follow a trail of pages that contain listings of different manifest files. So if PageA references ManifestA, and ManifestA says PageB is available offline, the browser will download and cache PageB. But if PageB contains a reference to ManifestB, that manifest file won't be downloaded or its listings cached.

The more appropriate solution is to create a single manifest file for your entire site that lists all the elements that should be included for the desired offline functionality to work.

SPACE CONSTRAINTS FOR OFFLINE APPLICATIONS

As you build your manifest file, remember that every browser will have some kind of space constraint placed upon it for offline applications. This limitation may be due to the browser's application cache being limited to a specific size, like the current iOS Mobile Safari limit of 5 MB. It may also be a natural limit imposed by the amount of disk or storage space available to the browser, or by you as the developer based on the amount of time it would take to download the full contents listed in the manifest.

A best practice is to limit your offline application to about 5 MB per domain (including subdomains), but you should do your own research because devices are getting more powerful daily, and browser vendors are wising up to the possibilities offered by offline web applications.

Duplicating downloads with offline applications

Older implementations of the HTML5 offline APIs would download all the regular content for a site and request the offline content separately, thus incurring a lot of extra bandwidth. Testing indicates that the current crop of modern browsers for desktops and mobile devices will download content only once, so if a particular resource is required for both online and offline operation, it will only be downloaded once.

Additional content listed in the manifest but that's not necessary for the current page will also be downloaded when the page loads.

This information isn't published by browser vendors; it was determined by loading various applications into all available browsers and watching traffic.

The overall layout of your manifest file should be logical and read like a story. The elements that you want available offline could logically go at the beginning if your application is primarily used offline. But if you're building a mortgage calculation website, the services and server data points that should only be available when connected (in the NETWORK section) could logically be placed first. In that instance, the CACHE directive would be further down in the file.

Having the ability to repeat section headings also allows you to describe entire areas of functionality in your application as a unit, with comments surrounding them. The application manifest file can be as simple or as complex as necessary to suit your needs.

10.3 *Offline feature detection and event binding*

Back in the shopping list application, you now have a manifest file and you're prepared to handle the automated download of content whenever a browser hits the website.

Let's now turn our attention to the initialization function for the JavaScript object, presented in listing 10.4. This function, placed in the init function of main.js, provides the following functionality:

- Detects features
- Handles the addition of new items to the shopping list by capturing the Enter key
- Captures the state change from connected to disconnected and back within the page
- Loads the application from saved state when the page is reopened

Listing 10.4 The `init` function to assign local variables and wire up events

```
init: function () {
    var self = this;
    var msg = "This browser does not support ";
    if (!Modernizr.applicationcache) {
        alert( msg + "offline apps");
        return;
    }
    if (!Modernizr.localstorage) {
        alert(msg + "local storage");
        return;
    }
    if (!window.JSON) {
        alert(msg + "JSON");
        return;
    }

    this.$status = $("#status");

    this.$input = $("#input")
        .keypress(function (event) {
            if (event.which == 13) {
```

Use Modernizr and window object to validate offline, local storage, and JSON capabilities

Describes online/offline status of application

Listens for Enter key to start UI update logic

```
            var value = self.$input.val();
            if (value) {
                var item = self.newItem(value);
                self.itemActions.push({
                    type: "add",
                    title: item.title
                });
                self.saveState();
                self.$input.val("");
                if (navigator.onLine)
                    self.syncWithServer();
            }
        }
    })
    .focus();

$(window)
    .bind("online", function () {
        self.updateForNetStatus(true);
    })
    .bind("offline", function () {
        self.updateForNetStatus(false);
    });
this.loadState();
this.updateForNetStatus(navigator.onLine);
}
```

Uses itemActions array to synchronize with server

When Enter key is pressed calls newItem to add item typed by user to interface and to array property of shopping items

Whenever Enter key is pressed attempts to synchronize with server if you're connected

Throws both online and offline events whenever connectivity status changes

Once events are bound and local variables assigned loads interface from previously saved state and updates connected status in UI

The init() function provides your first hints at the ways JavaScript deals with occasionally connected web applications. You have to call Modernizr to check for the applicationcache feature, and you also need to perform some work based on the navigator object's online Boolean property. Then you wire up two events thrown from the window object to respond when connectivity is lost and when a connection is regained. Both of these events have no parameters.

jQuery chaining and the use of the self keyword

As a short tangent into jQuery, note that you're using chaining on the $input variable to find the element with a selector, bind the keypress event handler, and set the focus all in one statement. We've broken these kinds of chains up into multiple lines for readability, but the execution is still much faster than executing the same selector multiple times against the DOM to perform different tasks.

Consider also that although you're declaring a self variable at the top of the init function, you're only using it inside the event handlers. In all other places in this code, you're using the this keyword to assign and read values. This is to distinguish between the parts of the code that are wrapped in a closure and those parts that aren't. This isn't necessarily an industry best practice, but it does provide a good opportunity for training and self awareness when writing JavaScript. (Did you see what we did there?)

10.4 *The ApplicationCache object*

Core API

Now that your application can handle input from the user, knows whether or not you're connected, and will automatically download the offline content, the next item that needs an introduction is the ApplicationCache object. This JavaScript object is provided by the browser; it has a very limited set of functions and a few properties, and it publishes a short stack of events. All of these ApplicationCache components are used to explain to your library how the browser is currently handling the download and storage of offline-accessible content.

ApplicationCache doesn't give you a means of directly accessing or modifying cached content. Instead, the browser handles everything internally and performs some sleight-of-hand whenever content is requested. You can think of it as an internal proxy to the network: when connected, resources will be loaded from the list of resources in the manifest; when not connected, resources will be pulled from the locally cached versions that were loaded and saved the last time the page was online.

The need to integrate with the ApplicationCache object in an application grows as the application grows in size and complexity. By allowing you to tap into changes to the cache status, the ApplicationCache object ensures your code can wait until all necessary resources are downloaded before attempting to use an offline-only piece of content.

> **NOTE** Although the sample application you're building in this chapter isn't complex or large enough to warrant the integration of the ApplicationCache object, we thought it was important to walk through a few snippets of code to show you the details of its operation.

The basic question that the ApplicationCache answers for each offline resource in the application is, "Is it available to me right now?" The answer will be based on whether or not the application is online, whether the resource was assigned in the manifest as being available offline, and whether the browser is currently in the process of downloading the resource.

The first time the browser arrives at a page that's listed as being offline-accessible (containing a manifest directive in the opening <html> tag), it will load the manifest file and then attempt to cache all elements listed.

The next time the browser navigates to the same page, a number of checks will be performed:

- Is the browser currently offline?
- If offline, is there a manifest listed?
- If there is a manifest, do files listed for offline access exist in the cache?

The answers to these questions will determine how the browser responds to the page. Note that the page may be cached and contain a manifest attribute but still not have all the elements required by the markup. In this case, requests for resources will generally throw an INVALID_STATE_ERR exception from the window object.

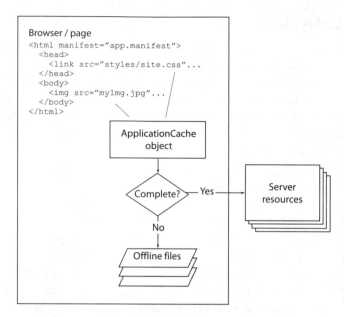

Figure 10.3 The proxy cycle occurs after the cache has completed loading. If the page is offline, each request for a resource that's assigned in the manifest is redirected to the cache. If the page is online, resources are pulled from the server as necessary.

As long as the cache is up to date, no exceptions will be thrown, and the browser will respond normally to requests while it's connected and redirect requests to the application cache when disconnected. Figure 10.3 shows how the ApplicationCache determines where to find resources based on the connected state.

APPLICATIONCACHE EVENTS

Core API

The ApplicationCache events outlined in figure 10.4 come from the W3C documentation. Figure 10.4 also shows you how those events correspond to one another during normal operations. The checking, downloading, progress, cached, updateready, and noupdate events will all be fired at various times based on the condition of the current cache in the browser and on the hosting server.

When your code receives the updateready event from the ApplicationCache object, you should respond by calling the ApplicationCache.swapCache() function. This function will remove the currently cached elements and replace them with the newly downloaded items.

During the normal caching process, you can also check the ApplicationCache.status property. This is an enumeration that exists inside the ApplicationCache object and can be referred to in that way or by the numeric value for each status. Here are the various status values:

- applicationCache.UNCACHED = 0
- applicationCache.IDLE = 1
- applicationCache.CHECKING = 2
- applicationCache.DOWNLOADING = 3
- applicationCache.UPDATEREADY = 4
- applicationCache.OBSOLETE = 5

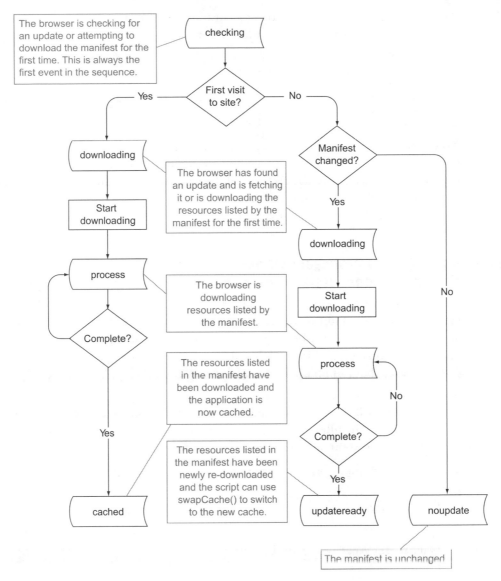

Figure 10.4 The ApplicationCache event model. Note that the checks for whether or not the manifest has changed and the current download status are at the discretion of the browser-vendor and not defined in detail in the specification.

You can bind to any of the events listed and check the status of the application cache at any time in your code by using a simple addEventListener call. A loading bar might be helpful for the progress event, and a confirmation that everything is ready would work well with the cached event.

The only event that requires you to react beyond just notifying the user is the updateready event. As noted in the diagram, this event will fire when an update to the cache has completed downloading. At that time, your code will need to swap the current cache with the fresh version, as shown here:

```
window.applicationCache.addEventListener("updateready", function() {
    // The new cache has been downloaded
    appCache.swapCache();
    if (confirm("A new version of this site is available. Load it?"))
        window.location.reload();
}, false);
```

Note that you have to call `window.location.reload` after calling `swapCache`. This is because, although the fresh content has downloaded and been placed in the cache, the user can't access this new cache until the window is refreshed. The reason, according to the HTML5 specification, is that the new cache is stored but not associated with the current cache document until after a refresh. While annoying, this is easily handled in your code.

10.5 Adding state management and displaying connected status

With that important aside on the application cache out of the way, you're now very close to a functional offline HTML5 application. Your site can download the appropriate content and check for features. It can also respond to `online` and `offline` events and to new entries typed into the input box. The remaining logic will fill in the various functions that plumb up the JavaScript library.

ADDING ONLINE OR OFFLINE STATUS TEXT

Your first stop will be to update the interface with the status text of either "online" or "offline". Do this by filling in the `updateForNetStatus` function. This function simply takes the current status and updates the UI appropriately:

```
updateForNetStatus: function (connected) {
    if (connected) {
        this.$status.text("(online)");
        this.syncWithServer();
    }
    else {
        this.$status.text("(offline)");
    }
}
```

> **TIP** When running this project using the web server built into Visual Studio (called Cassini), your site will probably not throw the `online` and `offline` events, nor will the manifest file be sent with the correct content type. To remedy this, you can use IIS Express to get a complete experience without delving too deeply into the normal setup procedures for a deployed internet application. This setup is described in appendix C.

ACCEPTING NEW ITEMS FROM USERS

The next step in completing the client logic is the `newItem` function. You called this function earlier from an anonymous handler inside `init` that responds when the Enter key is pressed.

`newItem` will take a line of text entered by the user and add it inside a `<div>` element on the page with a close button next to it. The same item will also be added to the local array of items to be synchronized to the server when connected. You'll assign style classes to the new element, add it to the DOM (Document Object Model), and then wire up the Close button's event handler.

Fill out the stub for the `newItem` function based on the following listing.

Listing 10.5 The `newItem` function updates the page and binds to the remove button

```
newItem: function (title) {
    var self = this;
    var item = {                                      Create new object to contain text plus
        title: title                                  element you'll be adding to page.
    };

    var html =                                        Create new <div> and
        "<div class='item box-round box-shadow'>"     <button> elements by
        + title                                       concatenating strings.
        + "<button class='close'>x</button></div>";

    item.$element = $(html);
        .prependTo("#items"),

    item.$element.find(".close")                      With new element reference
        .click(function () {                          find close button by class.
            var index =                               Check to see if new item is in current
                $.inArray(item, self.shoppingItems);  shoppingList array property.
            if (index != -1)
                self.shoppingItems.splice(index, 1);  If item exists remove it
                                                      from array property and UI.
            item.$element.remove();

            self.itemActions.push({                   You still have reference to the item
                type: "delete",                       object, so add it to itemActions
                title: item.title                     array for server removal.
            });

            self.saveState();                         Save all items back to LocalStorage.

            if (navigator.online)                     If online synchronize with server. If not
                self.syncWithServer();                online synchronization will happen later.
        });

    this.shoppingItems.push(item);
    return item;                                      Return new item to caller (in this
}                                                     case, Enter key from input element)
```

Annotations (left margin):
- **Create new element, assign it to your property, and add it to top of items list.**
- **Bind anonymous handler to new button's click event.**
- **Add new item to local list of shopping items.**

A lot of things are happening in this function, but it shows some interesting facets of development with jQuery. For instance, the concatenation of a string and subsequent

---

Working with arrays

JavaScript arrays are quite straightforward. You can create an empty one just by putting two square brackets together: []. You also use the square brackets to get and set values at specific indexes, just like with most programming languages. You push elements (numbers, objects, even other arrays) onto the end with the array's push() method, and pop them back off with pop(). To push and pop things onto and off of the front, use unshift() and shift() respectively. For adding or removing in the middle of an array, use splice().

In addition, jQuery provides some nice helper functions, such as $.inArray(), which returns the index at which a specified value appears. One of the most powerful is $.map(), which allows you to create a new array based on a transformation function. For instance, if you had an array of book objects, you could use $.map() to return an array of just the authors whose names begin with *A*.

---

creation of a wrapped set is the fundamental logic inside most of the client-side templating engines around today.

The prependTo function is used to insert an item at the beginning of the item's <div> and is different from the prepend jQuery function only in that one is an inverted version of the other. If you wanted to accomplish the same result with prepend you would use this code:

```
item.$element = $(html);
$("#items").prepend(item.$element);
```

The jQuery inArray utility function is one of a few that are helpers around basic JavaScript functionality and have no direct correlation to wrapped sets of DOM elements. Using this function, you can quickly test to see if an object or property exists in an array, and get its index if it does.

LOADING THE CURRENT OBJECT FROM SAVED VALUES

Loading the current object from saved values in LocalStorage is straightforward, as is saving state back into LocalStorage. (For a complete discussion of LocalStorage, refer to chapter 9.)

Find the loadState and saveState functions stubs in your library, and fill in the code from the following listing.

Listing 10.6 Loading and saving state using LocalStorage and JSON

```
loadState: function () {
    if (localStorage.itemActions)
        this.itemActions =
            JSON.parse(localStorage.itemActions);
    var data = localStorage.shoppingItems;
    if (!data)
        return false;
    var items = JSON.parse(data);
    var i;
```

> Parse itemActions from LocalStorage if any exist.

> Shopping items must exist before you can load any state values.

```
    for (i = 0; i < items.length; i++)
        this.newItem(items[i]);
    return true;
},
saveState: function () {
    localStorage.itemActions =
        JSON.stringify(this.itemActions);

    var items = [];
    var i;
    for (i = 0; i < this.shoppingItems.length; i++)
        items.push(this.shoppingItems[i].title);

    localStorage.shoppingItems = JSON.stringify(items);
}
```

> **When saving state stringify current itemActions and save to LocalStorage.**

> **Push each item from shoppingItems list into new array.**

> **New array is stringified and assigned to LocalStorage.**

Using the JSON object, you can serialize JavaScript objects into strings for storage and reverse the process as often as necessary. The current crop of browser JavaScript engines performs these tasks very quickly, but string manipulations are inherently one of the slower parts of any language, so keep this in mind while designing your application libraries.

Synchronizing data generated offline

The ability to create a page that shows your users static content when offline is fine and helpful in some situations, but much more is possible in the world of HTML5. By determining that the current connection status is offline, an HTML application can store data in LocalStorage or IndexedDB, or by using cookies. Then, when the connection is reestablished, the data can be synchronized back to the server automatically.

The exact nature of the offline storage and synchronization processes will be up to you as the site developer, because nothing is written in the HTML5 specification on the subject. This isn't a new problem, however, so finding a solid solution should not be difficult. This chapter's sample application describes a rudimentary solution for data synchronization that purges local data and calls the server using an ASP.NET MVC controller.

The client-side code is nearly complete. When the user types texts and hits the Enter key, the new item will be saved and made ready for server synchronization. The interface will clearly indicate when the application is connected, and content that must be available offline is specified in the manifest.

CONNECTING TO THE SERVER

The final step you need to handle is the connection to the server. The `syncWith-Server` function in listing 10.7 is the last bit of untouched code in the client library, and it does just what its name says. Once this step is complete, you'll begin work on the MVC controller and singleton storage object, but having this call in place will help you understand what you're trying to accomplish on the server.

This code will fill in the synchWithServer function in main.js that you stubbed out earlier.

Listing 10.7   Synchronizing with the server using Ajax and jQuery

```
syncWithServer: function () {
    var self = this;

    $.ajax({
        url: "/ShoppingList/SyncShoppingList",
        type: "POST",
        dataType: "json",
        contentType: "application/json; charset=utf-8",     With current item actions list
        data: JSON.stringify({                              create new JavaScript object
            itemActions: this.itemActions                   that includes name.
        }),
        success: function (data, textStatus, jqXHR) {
            if (!data || !("length" in data)) {
                alert("Unable to synch with server");
                return;
            }
                                                            Once controller has returned
            var i;                                          list as it exists on server
            for (i = 0; i < self.shoppingItems.length; i++)  remove all interface elements
                self.shoppingItems[i].$element.remove();    related to shoppingItems
                                                            array and clear out array.
            self.shoppingItems = [];

            for (i = 0; i < data.length; i++)               For each item in returned array
                self.newItem(data[i]);                      call newItem to reinitialize item
                                                            (including UI element).
            self.itemActions = [];
            self.saveState();
        },
        error: function (jqXHR, textStatus, errorThrown) {
            alert("Unable to sync with server: " + errorThrown);
        }
    });
}
```

The MVC framework controller you'll build will automatically coerce the itemActions object you send it into a generic list of strongly typed objects, as long as the name of your data payload corresponds to the inbound parameter name on the controller. This is called MVC model binding, and it prevents you from having to pass in an array of parameters.

We've discussed the need to reduce interface repaints (called *reflows*) a number of times in this book, but in this instance we decided to remove and recreate all the list items when the controller action returns data. We did this to simplify the code and to prevent item identifier conflicts. Synchronization with a server can be rather chaotic, because both client and server could theoretically be adding, editing, or deleting individual items simultaneously. To simplify things, we assigned the server version as the data of record and let the chips fall where they may on the client. This allows you to maintain a list without a unique identifier for each shopping item, and it removes the necessity for deconfliction code. Because your shopping items have no unique identifier, you have no value to assign as the id for the HTML element on the screen, and that means you need to drop and create all your items with each screen refresh.

The client side of the application is now complete, but the application won't run because there's no server-side functionality yet. Your next step is to build the components necessary to maintain the shopping list on the server.

10.6 Building the server side of an offline application

Recall that the basic structure for this chapter's sample application is an HTML page that lives inside an MVC application and calls a custom controller with two actions: one to get all current shopping list items, and one to synchronize the client list with what's on the server. You'll also be creating two objects: a simple POCO (Plain Old CLR Object) and a singleton to act as your server. The singleton will contain a generic list of shopping items, and when items are added or removed, it will lock the thread to execute the activity. This will keep things simple but reasonably scalable.

Both the POCO and singleton objects should be placed in the Models folder of your MVC solution. The POCO object, transmitted in JSON format back and forth between client and server, should look like this:

```
public class ShoppingItemAction {
    public string type { get; set; }
    public string title { get; set; }
}
```

This POCO object has a type property that describes whether the item should be added or removed from the list, and it has a title property that will be stored in the list inside your singleton.

THE SINGLETON SERVER

Your singleton object will serve as the data server. It contains a generic list of strings that make up your shopping list and an object called a ReaderWriterLockSlim. This object is designed to give you a very lightweight yet scalable means of locking the current thread. It has the ability to perform a read, write, or upgradeable lock that can transition from read to write. It adds a bit to the line count in your code, but it makes the thread-locking logic easy to read and track. This is an updated method of handling thread locking, as compared to the object-locking method common in older .NET programs.[1]

The next listing shows what your completed ShoppingServer object should look like.

---

[1] For a more complete discussion of object locking, see the "Implementing the Singleton Pattern in C#" article on the *C# in Depth* website: http://csharpindepth.com/Articles/General/Singleton.aspx.

Listing 10.8   The `ShoppingServer` singleton object

```
public class ShoppingServer {

  private static ReaderWriterLockSlim locker =
    new ReaderWriterLockSlim();

  private static List<string> CurrentShoppingList =
    new List<string>();

  static ShoppingServer() { }

  public static List<string>
    Update(List<ShoppingItemAction> itemActions) {
    foreach (var item in itemActions)
    {
      switch (item.type)
      {
        case "add":
          Add(item.title);
          break;
        case "delete":
          Delete(item.title);
          break;
      }
    }
    if (ItemCount() > 100)
    {
      Clear();
      Add("Too many items. List cleared.");
    }
    return GetAll();
  }

  public static void Add(string item) {
    try {
      locker.EnterUpgradeableReadLock();
      if (!CurrentShoppingList.Contains(item))
      {
        try {
          locker.EnterWriteLock();
          CurrentShoppingList.Add(item);
        }
        finally {
          locker.ExitWriteLock();
        }
      }
    }
    finally {
      locker.ExitUpgradeableReadLock();
    }
  }

  ...

  public static List<string> GetAll() {
    try {
```

ReaderWriterLockSlim will be used to lock current thread for reads and writes.

CurrentShoppingList is internal data store. Whenever it's touched thread must be locked to avoid conflicts.

Static constructor ensures that your object will only be instanced once in your application.

Update function will evaluate each inbound item and call Add or Delete based on itemAction object's type property.

As safety mechanism kill entire list if it reaches more than 100 shopping items.

ReaderWriterLockSlim object uses bookend style format. Each call to execute lock must be accompanied by associated call to release lock.

GetAll function returns everything in current list without making any changes.

```
          locker.EnterReadLock();
          return CurrentShoppingList;
        }
        finally {
          locker.ExitReadLock();
        }
      }
    }
```

The ShoppingServer object isn't robust enough for a production environment, but as a pattern it shows off a simple, scalable, thread-safe singleton. Because it has a static constructor, it will only ever be instanced once on the server, regardless of how many requests come in to modify shopping list items.

THE MVC CONTROLLER

Next, you need to create the ShoppingList controller. In your Visual Studio solution, do the following:

1 Right-click on the Controllers folder.
2 Select Add > Controller.
3 Name the new controller ShoppingListController.
4 Leave the controller template assigned as Empty Controller.
5 Once your controller is open, remove the Index ActionResult method.

The controller should now be virtually empty. In place of the original Index Action-Result, add the code from the following listing.

Listing 10.9 The ShoppingList controller

```
public class ShoppingListController : Controller
{
  [HttpPost]
  public ActionResult SyncShoppingList(
    List<ShoppingItemAction> itemActions) {
    var ret = new List<string>();
    if (itemActions != null)
      ret - ShoppingServer.Update(itemActions);
    else
      ret = ShoppingServer.GetAll();
    return Json(ret);
  }
}
```

> **HttpPost attribute allows SyncShoppingList to respond to POST method and make changes to ShoppingServer singleton.**

Note that this controller uses a single POST method to both update the existing list and return all items, even if no actions are required. This allows the code in your JavaScript client to reduce its footprint and operate in a more traditionally functional manner.

ADDING THE MANIFEST CONTENT TYPE TO THE SERVER

The last thing you need to do before you can run your application is to add the manifest content type to your server. You can do this using IIS Express (as illustrated in figure 10.5):

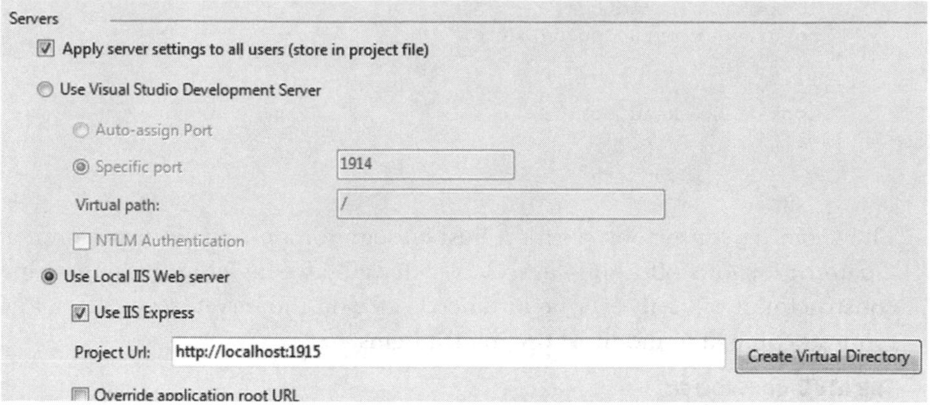

Figure 10.5   Setting up the manifest as a valid content type requires running the solution inside either IIS or IIS Express.

1 Right-click the project node of your solution and select Properties.
2 Select the Web tab.
3 Find the Servers node and select it.
4 Turn on the Use Local IIS Web Server radio button.
5 Check the Use IIS Express check box.
6 Leave the default project URL as is.
7 Click the Create Virtual Directory button.

If you don't have IIS Express installed, you can find instructions on how to download and install it in appendix C. Now when you run your solution, you'll be using the local IIS Express instance instead of the Cassini server that Visual Studio defaults to.

The application will run now, but it won't work when disconnected because the server doesn't recognize the application manifest content type. The next step is to add this content type to the local server.

Open a command prompt running as a local administrator, and navigate to the IIS Express folder. This will be named IIS Express and will be either inside Program Files or Program Files (x86). Once in that folder, execute the following commands:

```
appcmd set config /section:staticContent
/-[fileExtension='.manifest',mimeType='application/x-ms-manifest']

appcmd set config /section:staticContent /
    +[fileExtension='.manifest',mimeType='text/cacheManifest']
```

It should complete and look something like figure 10.6.

You can now safely run your application! After you start it, you can navigate to / Shopping.htm and see your offline application page. You'll see an online or offline indicator in the heading area, depending upon whether your computer is connected to a network or not. If you're not connected, you'll be able to continue working and synchronize to the server whenever a connection is reestablished. Note the indicator at the top of the page in figure 10.7.

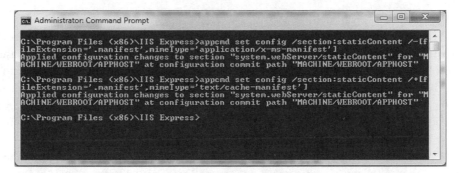

Figure 10.6   Setting up the manifest file as a valid content type requires you to reset a Microsoft default and add the new type using appcmd.exe located in your IIS Express folder.

Try adding a few items to your shopping list and then disconnect from your network. Add a few more and delete one or two, then reconnect. Set breakpoints both in the client JavaScript and on the server to see when calls are made and what the contents of each call are. Now close the browser entirely and reopen it, navigating to the shopping list page. You should see all your items still there, even if you disconnected before you reopened the browser. This is the beauty and power of an offline web application!

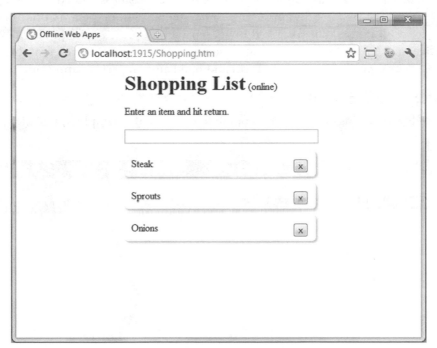

Figure 10.7   The completed application should work both online and offline.

10.7   *Summary*

Offline web applications can be robust and responsive in most modern browsers, and the proliferation of tablet-based devices with only Wi-Fi support should increase their popularity. The biggest drawback is still the fact that users are unaccustomed to using a website while not connected. Once this barrier is overcome, though, proper design and attention to details in an offline application will yield a rich experience and a website that's usable in many more circumstances than has been traditionally possible in web development.

In this chapter, you learned how to bind to the browser events that tell an application whether or not it's connected and some interesting ways to use jQuery to show the user that the connection state has changed. We looked at the application manifest file, the core of an offline application that describes which resources to make available offline, which to ignore, and which to provide replacements for when disconnected. We also took a close look at the ApplicationCache object and saw how it lets you monitor the cached state of the current application. Finally, we tied everything together by using more jQuery, JavaScript, and an ASP.NET MVC server project to store and return the user's shopping list items. You now have a complete HTML5 application that will work both online and offline in a variety of browsers.

We hope you enjoyed this book, especially all the fantastic ways that you, as a .NET developer, can impact the future of the web, both for business and consumer applications. This book was not designed to be a complete reference manual but rather to provide you with the tools you need to get started with professional JavaScript coding practices and up to the level of knowledge necessary to leverage the great things that HTML5 is bringing to the web. Go forth and build amazing HTML applications!

10.8   *The complete code listings*

The following listings provide the complete code for the sample application in this chapter.

Listing 10.10   CSS required to align and style the shopping list items

```css
#content {
  width: 100%;
  max-width: 300px;
  margin: 10px auto;
}

h1 {
  display: inline;
}

#input {
  width: 100%;
}

#items {
}
```

```
.item {
  margin: 10px 0px;
  padding: 10px;
}

.item .close {
  float: right;
}

.box-round {
  -webkit-border-radius: 6px;
  -moz-border-radius: 6px;
  border-radius: 6px;
  -moz-background-clip: padding;
  -webkit-background-clip: padding-box;
  background-clip: padding-box;
}

.box-shadow {
  -webkit-box-shadow: 2px 2px 4px rgba(0, 0, 0, 0.3);
  -moz-box-shadow: 2px 2px 4px rgba(0, 0, 0, 0.3);
  box-shadow: 2px 2px 4px rgba(0, 0, 0, 0.3);
}
```

Safari 3 and 4, iOS 3.0 and earlier, Android 1.6 and earlier

Opera 10.0, IE 9, Safari 5, Firefox 4, iOS 4, Android 2.1 and greater, and all versions of Chrome

Firefox 3.6 and earlier

Used to mask background color on rounded corners

Safari 3 and 4, iOS 4.0.2 through 4.2, and Android 2.3 and greater

Firefox 3.5 and 3.6

Opera 10.5, IE 9, Firefox 4 and greater, Chrome 6 and greater, and iOS 5

Listing 10.11   The complete main.js JavaScript file

```javascript
/// <reference path="http://ajax.aspnetcdn.com/ajax/
    jquery/jquery-1.7.1.js" />
/// <reference path="http://ajax.aspnetcdn.com/ajax/
    jquery/jquery-1.7.1-vsdoc.js" />

$(document).ready(function () {
  Main.init();
});

window.Main = {
  $status: null,
  $input: null,
  shoppingItems: [],
  itemActions: [],

  init: function () {
    var self = this,
    var msg = "This browser does not support ";
    if (!Modernizr.applicationcache) {
      alert(msg + "offline apps");
      return;
    }
    if (!Modernizr.localstorage) {
      alert(msg + "local storage");
      return;
    }
    if (!window.JSON) {
      alert(msg + "JSON");
      return;
    }
```

```
    this.$status = $("#status");

    this.$input = $("#input")
      .keypress(function (event) {
        if (event.which == 13) {
          var value = self.$input.val();
          if (value) {
            var item = self.newItem(value);
            self.itemActions.push({
              type: "add",
              title: item.title
            });
            self.saveState();
            self.$input.val("");
            if (navigator.onLine)
              self.syncWithServer();
          }
        }
      })
    .focus();

    $(window)
      .bind("online", function () {
        self.updateForNetStatus(true);
      })
      .bind("offline", function () {
        self.updateForNetStatus(false);
      });

    this.loadState();
    this.updateForNetStatus(navigator.onLine);
  },

  updateForNetStatus: function (connected) {
    if (connected) {
      this.$status.text("(online)");
      this.syncWithServer();
    }
    else {
      this.$status.text("(offline)");
    }
  },

  newItem: function (title) {
    var self = this;
    var item = {
      title: title
    };

    var html = "<div class='item box-round box-shadow'>"
      + title
      + "<button class='close'>x</button></div>";

    item.$element = $(html)
      .prependTo("#items");

    item.$element.find(".close")
      .click(function () {
```

```javascript
        var index =
          $.inArray(item, self.shoppingItems);
        if (index != -1)
          self.shoppingItems.splice(index, 1);

        item.$element.remove();

        self.itemActions.push({
          type: "delete",
          title: item.title
        });

        self.saveState();

        if (navigator.online)
          self.syncWithServer();
      });

    this.shoppingItems.push(item);
    return item;
  },

  loadState: function () {
    if (localStorage.itemActions)
      this.itemActions =
        JSON.parse(localStorage.itemActions);
    var data = localStorage.shoppingItems;
    if (!data)
      return false;

    var items = JSON.parse(data);
    var a;
    for (a = 0; a < items.length; a++)
      this.newItem(items[a]);

    return true;
  },

  saveState: function () {
    localStorage.itemActions =
      JSON.stringify(this.itemActions);

    var items = [];
    var a;
    for (a = 0; a < this.shoppingItems.length; a++)
      items.push(
        this.shoppingItems[a].title);

    localStorage.shoppingItems = JSON.stringify(items);
  },

  syncWithServer: function () {
    var self = this;

    if (this.itemActions.length) {
      $.ajax({
        url: "/ShoppingList/SyncShoppingList",
        type: "POST",
        dataType: "json",
        contentType: "application/json; charset=utf-8",
```

```
          data: JSON.stringify({
            itemActions: this.itemActions
          }),
          success: function (data, textStatus, jqXHR) {
            if (!data || !("length" in data)) {
              alert("Unable to synch with server");
              return;
            }

            var a;
            for (a = 0; a < self.shoppingItems.length; a++)
              self.shoppingItems[a].$element.remove();

            self.shoppingItems = [];

            for (a = 0; a < data.length; a++)
              self.newItem(data[a]);

            self.itemActions = [];
            self.saveState();
          },
          error: function (jqXHR, textStatus, errorThrown) {
            alert("Unable to sync with server: " + errorThrown);
          }
        });
      }
      else {
        $.getJSON(
          "/ShoppingList/GetShoppingList",
          function (data) {
            alert(data);
          });
      }
    }
  }
};
```

Listing 10.12   The `ShoppingServer` **singleton object**

```
public class ShoppingServer {

  private static ReaderWriterLockSlim locker = new ReaderWriterLockSlim();

  private static List<string> CurrentShoppingList = new List<string>();

  static ShoppingServer() { }

  public static List<string> Update(List<ShoppingItemAction> itemActions)
  {
    foreach (var item in itemActions)
    {
      switch (item.type)
      {
        case "add":
          Add(item.title);
          break;
        case "delete":
          Delete(item.title);
          break;
```

```
    }
  }
  if (ItemCount() > 100)
  {
    Clear();
    Add("Too many items. List cleared.");
  }
  return GetAll();
}
public static void Add(string item) {
  try {
    locker.EnterUpgradeableReadLock();
    if (!CurrentShoppingList.Contains(item))
    {
      try {
        locker.EnterWriteLock();
        CurrentShoppingList.Add(item);
      }
      finally {
        locker.ExitWriteLock();
      }
    }
  }
  finally {
    locker.ExitUpgradeableReadLock();
  }
}
public static void Delete(string item) {
  try {
    locker.EnterUpgradeableReadLock();
    if (CurrentShoppingList.Contains(item))
    {
      try {
        locker.EnterWriteLock();
        CurrentShoppingList.Remove(item);
      }
      finally {
        locker.ExitWriteLock();
      }
    }
  }
  finally {
    locker.ExitUpgradeableReadLock();
  }
}
public static void Clear() {
  try {
    locker.EnterWriteLock();
    CurrentShoppingList.Clear();
  }
  finally {
    locker.ExitWriteLock();
  }
}
```

```
public static int ItemCount() {
  try {
    locker.EnterReadLock();
    return CurrentShoppingList.Count();
  }
  finally {
    locker.ExitReadLock();
  }
}

public static List<string> GetAll() {
  try {
    locker.EnterReadLock();
    return CurrentShoppingList;
  }
  finally {
    locker.ExitReadLock();
  }
}
```

appendix A
A JavaScript overview

JavaScript is the primary client-side programming language you'll be using when writing HTML5 applications. Using JavaScript, you can select anything on a rendered page, save and work with data in memory, and communicate asynchronously with the server. Using additional frameworks such as jQuery, you can speed up your development tasks while reducing the volume of delivered code.

You may be somewhat familiar with the basics of JavaScript, but this appendix may still help you iron out some of the details that aren't very apparent during normal operations. Things like unobtrusive JavaScript and method chaining can be a real challenge without a solid foundation in the language.

A.1 The JavaScript core language

JavaScript is a functional language that's deployed uncompiled in text files. It's possible to use JavaScript as an object-oriented language, but you would be mistaken to try and use it the way you use C#. JavaScript looks very similar in construction to C#, but they're completely different languages providing very different development experiences.

First, we'll look at the various pieces of construction syntax that make up JavaScript code:

- Variables
- Operators
- Flow control
- Strings and dates
- Declaring and using functions
- Timers
- Arrays
- Checking for null, undefined, and NaN
- Comments in JavaScript

A.1.1   Variables

A variable in JavaScript is untyped and declared using the `var` keyword. When we say untyped, we mean that it can either be a simple value type, an object, or a function:

```
var myName = "Jim Jackson II";
```

A variable is accessible anywhere within the function it's defined in. If the variable is defined outside of any function, or if the `var` keyword is left off, the variable will reside at global scope, accessible everywhere. You should keep your global variables to a minimum, however, as they can easily cause confusion, and they could collide with the existing global variables the browser defines (such as `window`, `document`, `navigator`, and so on). Even though JavaScript allows you to leave the `var` keyword off, it's a best practice to always include it.

If you were writing a function to perform work and needed a geolocation object that you wanted to call `navigator`, you could be dropping a serious bomb on the rest of your application. This code,

```
navigator = "Current location is North of Main Street";
```

would create a `navigator` variable that explicitly overwrites the browser's `navigator` object. The following code, however, when placed inside a function, will hide the `navigator` object locally but won't overwrite the global object:

```
var navigator = "Current location is North of Main Street";
```

> **The userAgent**
>
> The `navigator.userAgent` variable is used in all browsers to tell the hosting server who exactly it is in terms of browser vendor, version, and several other elements. When feature detection doesn't work, the `userAgent` is a good fallback to determine compatibility levels in your application. It should be regarded as read-only, but as you can see from the `var` discussion, anything in JavaScript can be overwritten.

A.1.2   Operators

Operators in JavaScript are generally the same as in any other language—just a slightly different flavor, in some cases. When shifting back and forth between JavaScript and C#, there are some minor things to keep in mind, but these are pretty easy to figure out. Visual Basic developers will have a little steeper learning curve.

In this section, we'll cover five types of operators:

- Mathematical operators
- Comparison operators
- Assignment operators
- Logical operators
- Conditional operators

First are the mathematical operators.

MATHEMATICAL OPERATORS

Table A.1 lists the mathematical operators in JavaScript. They're used to perform simple math operations between variables.

Table A.1   Mathematical operators in JavaScript

Operator	Description	Usage	Result
+	Addition	var t = 5 + 5;	10
	Concatenation	var t = "a" + 5;	a5
-	Subtraction	var t = 13 - 4;	9
*	Multiplication	var t = 4 * 4;	16
/	Division	var t = 16 / 4;	4
%	Modulus	var t = 15 % 4;	3

COMPARISON OPERATORS

The next set of operators is used for comparing one value against another. When executed, the comparison operators in Table A.2 will return `true` or `false`.

Table A.2   Comparison operators in JavaScript

Operator	Description	Usage	Result
==	Equality	5 == 6	false
===	Exact equality	5 === "6"	false
!=	Not equal	5 != 10	true
>	Greater than	100 > 50	true
<	Less than	100 < 50	false
>=	Greater than or equal to	100 >= 100	true
<=	Less than or equal to	100 <= 120	true

In the examples in table A.2, the `===` comparison operator deserves further discussion. The exact equality operator is used to avoid scenarios where a value is assigned as a string but checked as a number, and vice versa. Although you can't specifically assign a type for any variable you use, JavaScript will infer the type of every variable.

We'll discuss more of the various types as we move forward in this appendix, but suffice it to say that there is *equal* and there is *really, really equal*. Use the exact comparison operator as often as you can to avoid unintended consequences in checking values.

Truthy and falsy

The double-equals operator (==) is one of the ways that an expression in JavaScript can return a *truthy* or *falsy* result. These terms refer to any expression that can be evaluated as Boolean but isn't inherently Boolean. So a 0 value is falsy even though it isn't technically false, and any nonzero value is truthy. Likewise, an empty string is falsy, and a string containing any value is truthy. This also helps when evaluating for the presence of a value because you can simply ask "is it?" and return a Boolean value.

ASSIGNMENT OPERATORS

Assignment operators are used to set the value of one variable to another. They're listed in table A.3.

Table A.3   Assignment operators in JavaScript

Operator	Description	Usage	Result
=	Assignment	t = 5	t is 5
++	Increment	var t = 5; t++;	t is 6
--	Decrement	var t = 5; t++;	t is 4
+=	Add second part to the first	var t = 5; t += 6;	t is 11
-=	Subtract second part from the first	var t = 5; t -= 3;	t is 2
/=	Divide second part by the first	var t = 15; t /= 5;	t is 3
*=	Multiply the second part by the first part	var t = 5; t *= 3;	t is 15
%=	Assign first variable to modulus of first parameter divided by second parameter	var t = 15; t %= 4;	t is 3

LOGICAL OPERATORS

The fourth set of operators is smaller but no less important. The logical operators listed in table A.4 provide a means of comparing multiple true or false statements.

Notice the parentheses surrounding the logical operators. Depending upon the nature of your code, these may not be completely required, but they provide scope to the operators so they're recommended.

Table A.4　Logical operators in JavaScript

Operator	Description	Usage	Result
&&	AND operation	(5 > 10 && 6 < 20)	true—5 is greater than 10 and 6 is less than 20
||	OR	(4 > 5 || 6 < 20)	false—4 isn't greater than 5 even though 6 is less than 20
!	NOT operation	! (5 > 5)	true—5 isn't greater than 5

CONDITIONAL OPERATORS

The final operator is the conditional, and it's more of an expression than an operator. It's used to provide what you may have called an "Immediate If" statement in Visual Basic or Excel. It states that if the comparison operator is true, return the first argument to the expression; otherwise return the second.

It uses a question mark (?) to delimit the test condition and a colon (:) to delimit the true and false values:

```
var rpm = 6850;
var minutes = 5;
var engine = (rpm >= 6000 && minutes > 3) ? "Boom" : "Vroom Vroom";
```

Now that the operators are out of the way, let's look at how program flow is controlled inside your code. This is done with a variety of flow-control structures.

A.1.3　Flow control

In order for any program to respond to varying conditions, it must be able to branch and loop its logic based on evolving conditions. Flow-control constructs in the JavaScript language are minimal, but they provide everything you need for just about any scenario in a normal application.

In this section, we'll cover five flow-control constructs:

- if
- switch
- for
- while
- do..while

The first is the if statement.

THE IF STATEMENT

The if construct in JavaScript has a few different options to make it more or less terse as conditions permit. if is called on a true/false condition placed in parentheses, and if the condition returns true, the next code block will execute. If the condition returns false, the next code will be ignored and if an else block exists, it will be executed instead. The code block to be executed can be multiple lines of code inside curly brackets { ... } or it can be a single line of code.

The following listing shows the options for an if block.

Listing A.1   Variations of the `if` statement in JavaScript

```
var x, y;
if (1 == 1) {
    x = "condition returned true";
}
y = "this code always executes";

if (1 == 1)
    x = "condition returned true";
y = "this code always executes";

if (1 == 0) {
    x = "condition returned true";
}
else {
    x = "condition returned false";
}
var = "this code always executes";

if (1 == 0)
    x = "condition returned true";
else
    x = "condition returned false";
y = "this code always executes";
```

Evaluate for true/false and execute content of block if true.

If no curly braces are used only one statement executed before returning to normal flow.

Execute else block if evaluation returns false.

Same curly brace rules apply to else blocks.

THE SWITCH STATEMENT

The `switch` statement is executed in the same way as `switch` statements in C#. An initial expression is evaluated inside parentheses, and then a progressive set of `switch` statements is compared from top to bottom.

For example, when the condition following a `case` is met, the code in the following listing, up to the `break` keyword, is executed.

Listing A.2   `switch` statements evaluate from top to bottom based on the expression

```
var t;
switch (favoriteAuthor) {
    case "Beck":
        t = "Politics is so in";
        break;
    case "Rand":
        t = "Distopian future";
        break;
    case "Alinsky":
        t = "Community organization";
        break;
    default:
        t = "Author not found";
}
```

Switched expression always in parentheses.

Each switch statement evaluated in order.

Default statement should always provide fallback for "not found" situations.

THE FOR STATEMENT

The `for` statement is a means of evaluating a number of values in a list or for evaluating a condition a specific number of times. Like the `if` statement, it can be used with or without curly braces, but if none are provided, only one line of code immediately following the for statement line will be executed:

```
var max = 10;
var myValue = 1;
for (var count = 1; count <= max; count++) {
    myValue *= count;
}
return myValue;
```

Add one to count variable while it's less than or equal to max variable. Execute on each iteration.

In body of block. Result here would be 3,628,800.

WHILE AND WHILE...IN STATEMENTS

The next structures that allow you to control the flow of code are the while and while...in statements. These are used to evaluate a condition and to continue to execute while it's true. The difference between while and for is that the while loop won't change the iterator's value, so the possibility of an infinite loop is opened up. Most current JavaScript engines will detect this and warn the user that they should stop executing, but good software should never introduce this possibility:

```
var now = new Date();
var i = now.getSeconds();
var count = 0;
while (i < 20) {
    now = new Date();
    i = now.getSeconds();
    count++;
};
```

Get current seconds value.

Check value iteratively.

Add to count value until seconds are greater than 20. Expect value in the millions.

THE DO...WHILE LOOPING CONSTRUCT

The do...while looping construct is a modification of the while loop, where the conditional statement is placed at the end. Whereas the previous listing may not execute at all and leave the counter at 0, the do...while in the following listing will always execute at least one time. Therefore, the exact same sequence can be guaranteed to have a count value greater than 0 regardless of other conditions.

> **Listing A.3 The do...while construct guarantees at least one iteration**

```
var now = new Date();
var i = now.getSeconds();
var count = 0;
do {
    now = new Date();
    i = now.getSeconds();
    count++;
} while ( i < 20);
```

A.1.4 *Strings*

In this section, we'll cover basic string manipulation, parsing and dividing strings, and finding a string inside of another string.

String manipulation in JavaScript is very easy on the surface, but as in many other programming languages, looks can be deceiving. Handling strings in JavaScript should be done as efficiently as possible to reduce code speed bumps. Doing things right the first time will also make your code easier to read and maintain later.

There are a number of JavaScript string manipulation functions built in that are also worth learning.

BASIC STRING MANIPULATION

Basic string concatenation can be done in two major ways.

You can use the + operator to append one string to another:

```
var nm = "Statue" + " of " + "Liberty";
```

You can also use the += operator to perform an additive append:

```
var nm = "Statue";
nm += " of ";
nm += "Liberty";
```

When performing larger or more cumulative tasks, you can use some of the built-in string manipulation functions of JavaScript. These functions give you more control over where text is inserted in the target string as well as the ability to break apart a string into specific bits and pieces.

The length property can be evaluated against any string to determine the number of characters in the string or against an array to determine the number of elements it contains. If the string that length is called against is undefined, the function will throw an exception:

```
var t = "alphanumeric";
var tlen = t.length;            // 12
var nlen = "AnotherString".length;     // 13
```

DIVIDING STRINGS

Next is the split function. This will break apart a string based on a separator character you pass in. An optional parameter will also split the inbound string only a specific number of times and then stop processing. The result will be an array of string values. Note that the separator you pass in will be removed from the output array. This search is also case sensitive:

```
var t = "Peter Piper Picked a Peck of Pickled Peppers";
var outPut = str.split("P");
```

The outPut from the preceding code will be as follows:

```
["eter ","iper ","icked a ","eck of ","ickled ","eppers"]
```

The next two string functions are substr() and substring(), which allow you to find and return a specific part of another string. The difference between the two is that substr() takes as a parameter the zero-based starting index and the length of the string to return, whereas substring() takes the zero-based starting index and the zero-based ending index of where to stop:

```
var t = "Peter Piper Picked a Peck of Pickled Peppers";
var u = t.substr(29, 7);       // Pickled
var v = t.substring(29, 36);    // Pickled
```

The values of the variables u and v in the preceding code are exactly the same.

FINDING ONE STRING INSIDE ANOTHER STRING

The next functions provide the ability to get a single character or the location of a string inside another string.

The indexOf() function performs a case-sensitive search of a string for the existence of another string, and it returns the zero-based index of the beginning of the found value. indexOf() will return -1 if the value was not found.

The charAt() function will return the single character in the index location specified, or an empty string if there is no character at the specified index:

```
var t = "Peter Piper Picked a Peck of Pickled Peppers";
var chr = t.charAt(29);      // P
var iof = t.indexOf("Pepper"); // 37
```

In the preceding code, chr is "P" while iof is 37. The replace() function will take the regular expression or a substring and replace it with the new string value parameter doing a case-sensitive search. The original string value isn't changed during a replace() operation:

```
var t = "Crossbows were used by the Romans";
var rep = t.replace("Crossbows", "Longbows");
```

In the preceding code, t is unchanged whereas rep has the value "Crossbows" replaced with "Longbows".

The final two functions are toLowerCase() and toUpperCase(). They take no parameters and are used primarily to get around the case sensitivity of the other functions. They're called as "myString".toLowerCase() or myVar.toUpperCase().

Regular expressions and pattern matching

JavaScript comes natively with the ability to pattern match using regular expressions. The RegExp object is used to handle regular expression matching.

Regular expressions are their own micro-language, and they can be very powerful when used correctly, but they're also terribly difficult to debug. I recommend starting out by looking at the w3schools site (http://www.w3schools.com/jsref/jsref_obj_regexp.asp) for a very brief introduction to the subject and then moving on to something more substantial, like the *Regular Expressions Cookbook* by Jan Goyvaerts and Steven Levithan (O'Reilly, 2009).

A.1.5   *Dates*

Date handling in JavaScript can be a bit of a problem, especially for .NET developers. Although there are plenty of ways to get the current date or to create a date from scratch in JavaScript, the dates that come down from your server-side code or that go back up will often require some massaging due to differences in the way dates are formatted by the different languages.

Getting the current date and time is fairly simple:

```
var dt = new Date();
```

Printing off `dt` would result in something like: "Mon Sep 1 06:38:18 EDT 2014", which is certainly readable but won't format directly into a `DateTime` data type in .NET.

What you need to do is reformat this date into a string that can be accepted by the server as well as translate the value from the server into a valid JavaScript `Date` value. You need to do three things with the target date in this example:

1 Take a .NET date and convert it to a JavaScript-readable date string.
2 Take a JavaScript-readable date string and create a date object from it.
3 Take a JavaScript date object and convert it to a .NET readable date string.

Using the following simple technique, you'll still have to convert to and from dates in your work, but the data that's passed should be easily readable and translatable in either direction. Here's the relevant code:

```
// JavaScript
var dtInput = new Date("Fri Nov 02 2012 21:23:58");
var dtOut = dtIn.toDateString() +
    " " + dtIn.toLocaleTimeString();
//
var dt = DateTime.Parse("Nov 2 2011 21:23:58");
var dtOut = dt.ToShortDateString() +
    " " + dt.ToLongTimeString();
```

Convert JavaScript date/time string to .NET DateTime

Convert .NET DateTime to JavaScript-readable date/time string

Convert .NET-produced date/time string to JavaScript Date object

Convert JavaScript Date object to .NET-readable date/time string

While not as robust as some date/time handling JavaScript libraries, this code has the advantage of the date being perfectly readable in both frameworks and while it's being transferred back and forth. The disadvantage is that the user's local time settings are removed by default, so time zone information is lost.

Once you have your date value in JavaScript, you can work with it as an actual date, making comparisons and editing its value.

A.1.6 *Basic function declarations*

We've covered so far how to work with various types of data in JavaScript. Now it's time to look deeper at how to create reusable pieces of functionality. In JavaScript, this is done using functions. Functions are objects declared using the `function` keyword, and they come in a variety of flavors.

We'll discuss three here:

- Anonymous functions
- Named functions
- Self-invoking functions

We'll start with anonymous functions.

Type coercion and conversion

Type coercion in JavaScript is one of Douglas Crockford's bad parts in his book *JavaScript: The Good Parts* (O'Reilly, 2008).

Coercion of values in JavaScript occurs when a comparison is made between two values that aren't of the same type using the operators == or !=. JavaScript will attempt to coerce the values into the same type and then compare them. This is bad because a string value of "1" isn't the same as a numeric value of 1. If you disagree, then try this simple piece of code:

```
var numA = "1";
var numB = 1;
var test1 = numA == numB;
var test2 = numA === numB;
var result = numA + numB;
```

If the result you're looking for is 11, then ignore this and move to the next section. If, in your world, 1+1=2, then you should have a clear understanding of what type coercion is.

The value of test1 in the preceding code is true, and the value of test2 is false. False is the correct answer, because if you wanted to add two numbers but one is a string, JavaScript will automatically convert all values in the formula to strings and concatenate them, not operate on them mathematically.

The appropriate way to perform a conversion in the preceding code would be to convert numA to an integer using the parseInt(numA, 10) function. The second value (radix) in parseInt assigns the result as a decimal number.

Also of note is that the plus (+) operator will try to automatically convert a value to a number when placed in front of a variable. The following code will convert the variable b to the number 1 from the string "1".

```
var a = "1";
var b = +a;
```

ANONYMOUS FUNCTIONS

Anonymous functions don't have names, but they're full-fledged functions and can return values using the return statement. They're generally used inline as the callback argument for another function. The format is as follows:

```
function() { ... }
```

When an Ajax call is made to a server, it usually has a success callback function. If it makes sense in the context of the application, and if the success handler won't be used anywhere else, you can use the anonymous function directly inside the Ajax function call to handle the results returned. The following snippet shows how to do this in a jQuery call. (The longer form of using XMLHttpRequest would distract from the point here.)

```
$.ajax({
    url: "myRequest.html",
    success: function(data){
```

Anonymous function assigned to success parameter of Ajax request.

```
   ...                              ◁────── Execute function body when success returns.
   }
});                                  ◁─┐  Close anonymous function before
                                       │  any other code is executed.
```

NAMED FUNCTIONS

Named functions have the same wrapping curly braces, but they also get a name that can be used to refer to them. They can also return values using the `return` statement.

Here's a named function:

```
function execAddValues(firstNum, secondNum) {
   ...
   return (firstNum + secondNum);
}
```

SELF-INVOKING FUNCTIONS

A function is self-invoking when its entire declaration is wrapped in parentheses and it's followed by another set of parentheses. The wrapping parentheses are used to encapsulate the entire function as an immediately executable block. The empty parentheses at the end then immediately execute the entire block.

This snippet shows how this kind of function is written:

Once function is complete another set of parentheses is used to invoke it.

```
(function helloWorld() {                        Function is declared
   alert("I am here!");           ◁─────        normally but inside
})();                                           parenthetic block.
        ◁─┐  Body of self-invoking function is
          │  same as any other function.
```

Self-invoking functions can also take parameters and, as you'll see when we discuss object-oriented JavaScript, they have public and private properties.

Self-invoking functions are critical to the plugin model of the jQuery and jQuery UI frameworks, so you should become familiar with their structure. Once invoked, they're available in memory and from any other piece of code in your application.

The following are all valid function wrappers:

```
function() {}
function foo() {}
var bar = function() {};
var bar = function foo() {};
```

A.1.7   *Functions as parameters*

We mentioned earlier that a callback inside an Ajax call can be an anonymous function or it can be a named function. The following code shows how this can be done in just a few lines of code. This is helpful because if the `successCallback` function (in this case, assigned to `dataReturned`) is useful to other Ajax calls, it no longer has to be repeated in every instance:

```
var dataReturned = function(data) {              ◁─┐  Declare named
   alert("found " + data.length + " items");        │  function.
};

$.getJSON(                                       ◁─┐  Function has same
   "http://www.mySite.com/getData",                 │  signature as callback.
```

```
        dataReturned
)
```
◄——┐ **When data is returned**
        execute named function.

This code barely scratches the surface of what's possible using callbacks. We won't be discussing deferred functions and promises in jQuery, but you can pick up the latest edition of Bear Bibeault and Yehuda Katz's *jQuery in Action* (Manning, 2008) to get a good handle on these enormously powerful features.

A.1.8 Timers

In JavaScript, there are two built-in functions that allow you to perform work based on a timed interval and two additional methods to clear out those timed events.

THE SETTIMEOUT FUNCTION

The first function is setTimeout(), and it's used to execute a callback function when a specific number of milliseconds has expired (1,000 milliseconds is equal to 1 second). It returns an integer that's unique to that timer. The timer ID value can be passed into the clearTimeout() function to stop it from processing at any time.

setTimeout() executes only one time unless it's placed inside some other loop. Like every other callback in JavaScript, the function that's called can be either named or anonymous.

The following listing shows a very basic timed event.

Listing A.4 Using the setTimeout() and clearTimeout() methods

```
var timerID = null;
var timerID = null;
function toggleTimeout() {
    if (timerID) {
        clearTimeout(timerID);
        console.log("cancelled");
        timerID = null;
    } else {
        timerID = setTimeout(function() {
            console.log("expired");
            timerID - null;
        }, 3000);
        console.log("started");
    }
}
toggleTimeout();
toggleTimeout();
toggleTimeout();
```

Does timer exist?

Cancel, log, and destroy it.

Make new timer that logs message and resets.

◄——— **Timer will execute every 3 seconds.**

Log that time has started.

Log shows "started".

Log shows "cancelled".

◄——┐ **Log shows "started", and**
        3 seconds later "expired".

THE SETINTERVAL FUNCTION

The next timed event function is setInterval(). This operates in almost the same way as setTimeout() except that it executes continuously until stopped, firing its callback whenever the interval is hit. The following listing shows a simple interval timer.

Listing A.5   `setInterval()` performs like `setTimeout()` but continues to execute

```
var intervalCount = 0;
var intervalID = setInterval(function() {           Make new interface that
    intervalCount++;                                increments count when fired.
    console.log("Count: " + intervalCount);         ◁——— Log count.
    if(intervalCount == 10) {                        If this is l0th interval,
        clearInterval(intervalID);                   clear variable.
        intervalID = null;
    }
}, 2000);                          ◁——— Iterate every 2000 milliseconds (or 2 seconds).
```

The `setInterval()` function isn't used very often in JavaScript for user interface operations because it's very easy to get into a looping condition where a stack of interval methods are all waiting for some user interaction. It's also impossible to determine how quickly a user will interact with the interface to prevent the stacking of timed messages. `setInterval()` is much more appropriate for background operations that should continue to process while other work is occurring.

Timers as `DoEvents()`

There are some things to note regarding timers and intervals in JavaScript. According to Nicholas Zakas in his book *High Performance JavaScript* (O'Reilly, 2010), `setTimeout()` can be used very effectively to allow the browser to finish other tasks while your JavaScript code is executing. This is done by executing code inside very short timers (250 milliseconds or less). Be sure not to make the timer interval any smaller than 25 milliseconds, though, because the operating system may not be granular enough to detect the timeout, and it may just execute the callback instantly.

A.1.9   *Array*

The next element of the JavaScript language that we should explore is the array. Arrays are just lists of elements, and they're automatically coerced into the type each value in the array represents. This means that a single array can contain strings and integers and they can both be acted upon as their base value types.

To create an array, you simply declare a variable as an array and start adding elements to it based on index position:

```
var myStuff = [];
myStuff[0] = "toy truck";
myStuff[1] = "book";
```

You can also instance an array inline by providing the data directly to the variable:

```
var otherStuff = ["uniform", "bicycle", "hat"];
```

Once elements are in an array, you can loop through them using a simple `for` loop and the array's `length` property:

```
for(var i = 0; i < arr.length; i++) {
    var item = arr[i];
}
```

Arrays can also be sorted and inverted. In the preceding code, `otherStuff.sort()` would yield an array containing "bicycle", "hat", "uniform". Likewise, calling `otherStuff.reverse()` on the updated array would give you "uniform", "hat", "bicycle". You can also put two arrays together using either the `join()` or `concat()` functions. The `join()` function will output a string (separated by commas, by default) that contains all elements in the array, whereas `concat()` will return a new array based on the contents of two arrays.

To use an array as a queue to hold items for processing, you can choose to either remove them in a first-in-first-out (FIFO) or first-in-last-out (FILO) methodology. The `shift()` function will remove the first element in an array and return it to the caller, whereas the `pop()` function removes the last element from an array and returns it.

To get elements into an array, you can use the `push()` function to add elements to the end of an array or the `unshift()` function to add elements to the beginning.

A.1.10 null, undefined, and NaN

While you're building your software, you'll occasionally come across instances where a variable is `undefined`. Alternatively, there are instances where a variable is `null`. It's important to understand the difference between these two.

A variable that's `undefined` has been declared but not given a value:

```
var myVariable;
```

`myVariable` in this code is equal to `undefined` because it wasn't given a value. In addition to an unassigned variable, any reference to a variable that hasn't been declared at all will return `undefined`.

On the other hand, a `null` value in a variable indicates a positive action taken by the code and not by the JavaScript engine. `null` is an object that indicates "no value" in the variable that contains it.

`null` can be used to clear the contents of a variable so that it can be reused, but a `null` value can't be concatenated or coerced into a string. When calculated upon, `null` takes the value of 0:

```
var a = null;
var b = null;
var c = 10;
var d = a + b;
var e = a + c;
var f = a.toString()
```

(null + null) always equals 0.

(null + 10) equals 10.

Attempting to coerce null into string will throw exception.

Not-a-number (aka `NaN`) is another value built into JavaScript, and it's used to state that something went wrong somewhere along the way. It can be assigned in your code to indicate things like an out-of-bounds value, or it can be assigned automatically when attempting to parse a value into a number that isn't numeric, or when a calculation is invalid.

To check a value to see if it's NaN, use the isNaN() built-in JavaScript function.

```
var car = "Corvette";
var year = parseInt(car);          ◄──────    Try to assign number to non-numeric value.
var yearIsNaN = isNaN(year);       ◄─────      Check value for NaN
var month = 13;                                using built-in function.
if (month > 12) {                   Assign NaN
    month = NaN;                    specifically.   ◄──    isNaN returns true or
}                                 ◄─────                   false regardless of
var monthIsNaN = isNaN(month);    ◄─────                   parameter passed.
```

A.1.11   Commenting JavaScript

Comments in JavaScript can be marked by either a double-hack (or double-slash)

```
// This is a comment
```

which will tell JavaScript that the rest of the line is a comment, or by enclosing multiple lines between hack/star (or slash/star) tags:

```
/*  This is a comment on multiple
lines of JavaScript code. */
```

Everything inside a comment is ignored by the JavaScript runtime compiler, but comments are used by the Visual Studio IDE when formatted and placed properly. Listing A.6 shows how a function can be commented so that IntelliSense will appear as you build out your project. The parameter tags are the same as those available in C#, but there's no type checking of parameter types, and the number of available tags is somewhat more limited.

> **Listing A.6   Code comments in JavaScript using Visual Studio**

Paragraph tags can be used and you can use spaces to indent text in summary and parameter tags.

```
///<summary>First paragraph of the function summary      ◄──   Summary element
///<para>   Second paragraph of function summary</para>B        appears when you type
///</summary>                                                   opening parenthesis
///<param name="start" type="integer">Starting year</param>  ◄─ on function.
///<param name="showall" type="boolean">
///Show all timelines (true) or just highlights (false)         Parameter type
///</param>   ◄─────                                            value is optional but
                     To make Visual Studio aware of these for   name and content
                     IntelliSense purposes special triple-hack is used.   description are
                                                                required.
```

The other comment helper that Visual Studio provides is the ability to dynamically import and background compile other scripts into the current file so that IntelliSense is also available on those objects and functions. Here's how it's done:

```
///<reference path="/Scripts/MyLibrary.js" />
```

This comment will import the MyLibrary.js file from a location relative to the current file, compile it in the development environment, and provide IntelliSense as you work.

A.2 The DOM

The Document Object Model (DOM) is the API through which JavaScript can gain access to your pages. The browser will build up this DOM tree of elements and objects and keep it synchronized with the actual graphical representation in the browser window.

Your goal is to write great software using HTML and JavaScript, so with the basics of the language out of the way, it's time to dig into exactly how you get references to parts of the DOM using JavaScript.

In this section, we'll cover basic rendered HTML element references and events.

> **WARNING** When building a JavaScript application, it's important to understand that everything you do in your code must execute in the same thread that your browser is using to perform updates and receive callbacks from Ajax. This means that any looping you do should be minimized, and any edits to layout properties should be batched as much as possible. We'll cover batching of UI updates in detail later. The only alternative is to use background threads with the HTML5 Web Workers API, discussed in chapter 7.

A.2.1 Elements

First, you need to understand how JavaScript can get access to elements in the DOM, and then you can start working with them. This can be handled in a number of ways using built-in functions.

There are three primary functions that are available in all browsers, and they're all attached to the `document` object:

- `document.getElementById("searchId")` will take the `searchId` passed in and return a single element from the current document, if it exists. Remember that an element's ID should be unique to the page, so this function returns a single value: either the element in question, or `null` if the ID isn't found.
- `document.getElementsByName("searchName")` takes the `searchName` value and returns an array of all elements in the document with that name applied.
- `document.getElementsByTagName("searchTag")` takes the `searchTag` value and returns an array of all elements on the page of that type.

Once you have a reference to an element or an array of elements, there are properties on each object that you might want to track or edit. Some of these are read-only, but many can be edited while your application is running. A few that might be important are the `innerHTML` and `innerText` properties. These give you the entire HTML markup inside an element and the plain text inside that element respectively. The `children` property will return a collection of child elements of the current element, if any exist.

You can also read attributes using the `attribute` property of the HTML element and set each one's `value` based on the ordinal position of the attribute in the element or by its `name`. This is a little difficult to grasp without an example, so the following listing starts at the top-level `body` element in an existing page and then walks the entire

DOM tree, collecting a few properties from each element along the way. This will also give you a chance to exercise your newly minted knowledge of functions.

Listing A.7   Walking the DOM tree and storing properties

```
function walkDOMTree() {
    var elements = document.getElementsByTagName("body");     ← Get element reference.
    var properties = [];                                         Declare
    iterateProps(elements, properties);         Iterate through   iterateProps
    console.dir(properties);                    each property.    function.
}
function iterateProps(elements, properties) {            ←        Walk each
    for (var i = 0; i < elements.length; i++) {         ←         element
        var element = elements[i];                               inside current
        properties.push({                                        element.
            id: element.id,
            height: element.clientHeight,       Collect data about each
            tag: element.tagName                nested element.
        });
        if (element.children.length)
            iterateProps(elements.children, properties);    ⋈  When all children
    }                                                           are evaluated
}                                                               properties array will
walkDomTree();                                                  contain references.
```

A.2.2   DOM events

While your users are executing your application, there are many events that can be captured or fired. Your JavaScript code can assign functions to these events and respond to them whenever they occur. These events can also trigger other events, and so on. Events also propagate themselves, meaning that they travel into and out of the DOM tree when fired, depending upon how they're registered. This warrants a little further explanation.

There are two phases in every event in the browser: capturing and bubbling. The capturing phase starts out at the highest level in the document and passes the event through to the eventual target. The bubbling phase occurs after the event has been processed at the target and bubbles the event back up from child to parent element, all the way to the top. While most browsers handle these operations in the background, you'll find that sometimes your code behaves unexpectedly when one event triggers the next, which in turn triggers the first.

The way to avoid this problem, aside from good coding practices and well-documented requirements, is to be sure to stay consistent in the way you wire up your event handlers. The JavaScript addEventListener function, available in all modern browsers, is used to attach functions to DOM events (though it isn't available in Internet Explorer before version 9). addEventListener has the following signature:

```
element.addEventListener(eventName, callbackHandler, useCapture);
```

The first parameter is the name of the event, like click or blur. The second parameter is the function to execute when the event fires, and the final parameter is optional and states whether to fire the function on the capturing phase or bubbling phase of the event.

TIP jQuery generally uses the bubbling phase for event binding, so you're generally safer setting `useCapture` to `false` if you need to add an event listener outside of jQuery. This isn't a hard and fast rule, though, so do what makes the most sense in your scenario.

A.3 JavaScript environment

The environment that your code operates in gives you certain advantages in modern browsers. Not only do you have the full JavaScript language at your disposal, you also have numerous other tools that can be used to help debug and control the work being performed.

In this section, we'll discuss some of the higher-level pieces of the JavaScript language as well as some built-in tooling to help keep your project rolling. Specifically, this section covers

- Browser JavaScript engines
- The JavaScript environment global scope
- Built-in JavaScript objects
- JavaScript debugging tools

A.3.1 Browser JavaScript engines

Browser JavaScript engines were not exactly the life of the party just a few years ago. Performance profiles and benchmarks were available, but they were generally ignored by most developers. Such is not the case in the current browser market. The game is on, and all the major players are achieving levels of performance that rival compiled Java and .NET libraries.

The reasons for this center around a few vendors deciding that just because your free email account is entirely browser-based doesn't mean that it has to be slow and clunky. Google's Gmail software broke open new areas of the market and showed that effective use of JavaScript in the browser can produce a rich, motivational, and intuitive experience. Over the last few years, the other browsers on the market got the message, refining and replacing JavaScript engines regularly.

Table A.5 lists the major engines available today.

Table A.5 Browsers and their JavaScript engines

Browser	JavaScript engine
Microsoft Internet Explorer	Chakra (introduced in IE9)
Google Chrome	V8
Apple Safari	Nitro
Mozilla Firefox	TraceMonkey and most recently JaegarMonkey
Opera	Karakan (or Carakan)

These are names to remember, because along with layout engines, these will be the most likely causes of browser incompatibilities in your projects. In addition to these desktop browser engines, each mobile browser you encounter will also have a JavaScript engine. Unfortunately, the market for web devices is moving so quickly right now that any information we wrote down would be almost guaranteed to be outdated by the time you read it. The easiest place to find information about the latest browsers is www.caniuse.com.

A.3.2   *Global scope*

All variables and functions in JavaScript have a specific scope. This scope can and should be limited to a namespace or a function, but it doesn't necessarily have to be. The global scope in JavaScript is where the document object and all of the built-in JavaScript engine features live.

Recall the test we did earlier, where we overwrote the `navigator` object in the browser. You could just as easily assign a variable in your application to any other object. Even inside your functions, if you declare a variable incorrectly, it can be placed into global scope.

Best practices indicate that you should place all your variables into your own namespace rather than into the global scope, but how exactly do you do that? The following listing shows the right and wrong ways to make declarations and to declare variables and functions.

Listing A.8   Assigning variables in a namespace instead of the global scope

```
window._app = {                          ◁──── Create object named _app.
    mode: "clean",
    setupInfo: {                                              Add mode
        startUpTasks: {},           Add function              property.
        cacheInfo: {}               property.
    }
};

_app.theme = {                           ◁──── Create new object
    color: "blue"                              inside _app object.
};

currentUser = {                          Current user has been mistakenly
    userName: "Earnest"                  placed in global namespace.
};
```

An entire JavaScript application working inside a single namespace can be broken up into as many sub-areas as are appropriate to the application. This results in an architecture that's navigable like most .NET applications and performs the same logic-division function.

A.3.3 *Built-in objects*

There are a few objects that come packaged in your browser's JavaScript engine. Some are user interface containers and others are helper objects that can be trusted to work the same way across platforms.

NAVIGATOR OBJECT

The `navigator` object is most often used for either its `userAgent` string or, in HTML5, for the `geolocation` object. There are other important bits to it though, like the `mimeTypes` which gives you an array of acceptable media types that can be processed by the current browser. You can also look at the `language` variable and check for `cookieEnabled`. In addition, there are specific vendor and version properties, but these are usually retrieved from the `userAgent` string.

> **More on the** `navigator.userAgent`
>
> The `userAgent` string is the basis for browser detection and the opposite side of the coin from direct feature detection for your application. Both methods are used to determine which browser is currently serving up your application and, by extension, which features should be enabled or disabled.
>
> Browser detection using the `userAgent` string should be your second choice when deciding what features to enable in your application, due to the sheer volume of possible variations. The `userAgent` string is different for every version of every browser on the market. While you can parse out individual values, there's no guarantee that the flag you looked for in the last version will be remotely similar in the new version. This leads to a lot of branching logic. Still, there are certain features and known bugs that can't be feature-detected and must be found by searching the `userAgent` string for a known value.

MATH OBJECT

The `Math` object gives you all the features you've come to expect in other software development languages. Using `Math` you can round numbers, compute geometries, and find square roots. If you do any work with geolocation, among other things, you'll find the `Math` object invaluable.

WINDOW OBJECT

The `window` variable refers to a `DOMWindow` object, and it's the top-level browser window. This is the main area that you have to work with when rendering your application. You can measure both the available real estate for your application as well as the entire space the browser window consumes. `window` also refers to the global namespace, so `window.myApp` and `myApp` both refer to the same object.

SCREEN OBJECT

The `screen` object refers to the operating system screen where the browser resides. If the browser occupies more than one monitor, `screen` will generally use the largest screen size available, but this isn't guaranteed.

DOCUMENT OBJECT

The document object is the HTML markup that was loaded from a URL location to the browser. It's the object representation of your entire HTML document with an API wrapped around it. It has properties for head, body, scripts, and stylesheets, along with event handlers that you can wire up in your application.

The difference between the window object and the document object is that the window object is provided by the JavaScript environment, whereas document is the DOM representation of your rendered page, including any changes that you make in your application. document is a property of window.

As you saw in the earlier examples, the document object is the starting point for finding elements in the current page. It's also the place where you can look at the body element and determine the overall dimensions of the current page, regardless of the browser window size. Using the window and body sizes, you can make adjustments for hiding elements offscreen and bringing them into view smoothly. You can also tell quickly how much of the page isn't currently visible.

LOCATION OBJECT

The location object contains properties and methods to manipulate the URL of the current window. This is pretty straightforward but merits a short example because you'll be using location so frequently. The following is a simple URL to play a video:

```
http://www.youtube.com/watch?v=h9ThvOyrPCw
```

From this URL, you can get the following information from the location object:

```
location.protocol = http:
location.host = www.youtube.com
location.pathname = /watch
location.href = http://www.youtube.com/watch?v=h9ThvOyrPCw
location.search = ?v=h9ThvOyrPCw
```

A.3.4   *Debugging tools*

Debugging a JavaScript application while it's running was once very difficult, but the last few years have added numerous tools to help you investigate systems on the fly. The developer toolkits that are delivered with modern browsers offer an array of inspectors and debuggers that can help you understand nearly any facet of your application in almost any scenario. The two lowest-level debugging tools, though, are alert and console.

The alert() function provided by JavaScript is something that all JavaScript developers have used, right up to the point where they accidentally put it inside an iterator that loops one thousand times. A JavaScript alert is just a message box posted by the browser that must be responded to by the user. Generally, background processes will stop while the alert appears, but there are circumstances where timers and CSS transitions will continue if they were already started before the alert was triggered.

The syntax is very simple:

```
alert("hello world");
```

The problem with alerts is that you have to definitively respond to them; they can't just queue up for you to investigate later. That's where `console` helps you out.

The `console` object in the JavaScript environment is now a part of every modern browser. You use it by placing one of a series of function calls directly into your code. When the code is executed, the result will appear in the developer tools that come with the browser.

The most common statement is `console.log("message");`, and it can be used in any executable place within your JavaScript code. Other methods available in the console are `warn` and `error`. These will display different icons in the console area to help you more quickly find problems in your executing code.

> **WARNING** Some browsers don't support `console`, so use it sparingly or not at all in production code. There are polyfills for `console` and many JavaScript libraries that you can add to your application to provide logging while maintaining backward compatibility. One that's particularly helpful and stable is Ben Alman's debug library: http://benalman.com/projects/javascript-debug-console-log.

One other feature worth noting is the `console.assert()` method. This is used as a sort of inline unit tester. When provided with an expression as its first argument, it will either do nothing when the value evaluates to `true`, or it will print the string contents of the second argument. For instance, this statement,

```
console.assert((Math.PI === 3.15), "No, that is not PI")
```

will print the message

```
"No, that is not PI"
```

whenever your application passes this section of code. While it's not a real unit-testing framework, this should certainly help you in a development environment.

> **WARNING** `console` is only available to you while you're in development. Console calls that are still in your code when it goes into production will throw exceptions. This means that if your users don't have development tools installed in their browser of choice (and why would they?) they'll hit these exceptions.

A.4 Object orientation

JavaScript is a loosely typed functional language that contains a lot of object-oriented features. The objects you use in JavaScript aren't like those you build in .NET. They're classless, meaning they don't have specific object definitions or a predefined inheritance hierarchy. As a prototype-based language, it instead achieves its object-oriented features by means of a collection of properties and a prototype. Some examples of how to build out objects should make these concepts very clear.

In this section, we'll cover the following:

- Object declarations and namespaces
- Dynamic properties and property iteration

- Functions
- Prototype
- this and scope
- A simple object pattern
- Closures
- Exception handling

A.4.1   *Object declarations and namespaces*

We've described the idea of namespaces for segregating your application logic from the global namespace. What you're actually doing when you instantiate a new namespace is creating a new object where all of your code can operate, safe from other namespaces that may have been created by plugins or other libraries like jQuery.

Normally, you instantiate a namespace by means of an empty object declaration:

```
var myApp = {};
```

Once the browser reads past this line of code, the myApp object is available for use. Although the way you declare additional features on this namespace is different from .NET code, its use is very similar, as you'll see shortly.

To add new properties to this namespace that are themselves other objects you can reuse the previous technique, separating objects in the hierarchy using dot notation:

```
myApp.Initializer = {};
```

A.4.2   *Dynamic properties and iteration*

Properties on JavaScript objects can be instantiated and assigned when they're first used or when the object is instantiated, and they're always case sensitive.

The notation for assigning a property and then immediately using it is simple; it can be done either using braces ([]) or using the dot notation and providing the assigned value. You can also define the property without assigning a value, in which case the property will exist but its value will be undefined. This is shown in the following listing.

Listing A.9   Instantiating properties on JavaScript objects

Properties instantiated without value are assigned value undefined.

```
var myObj = {};
myObj["firstName"] = "Rick";
myObj.age = 31;
myObj.weight;
alert(myObject.firstName + " is " + myObject.age +
    " and weighs " + myObject.weight);
```

Declaring property on object using bracketed names.

Properties can also use dot notation if property names aren't JavaScript keywords.

Result should be "Rick is 31 and weighs undefined".

The next method of declaring properties is executed when the object is instantiated. Rather than using the empty curly braces to instantiate a new object, you fill in the body of the object with the properties you'll be using. Naming conventions still apply, and unset properties will still be set to undefined.

Inside the object declaration, a colon delimits the property name from its value, and both must be wrapped in quotes if they contain keywords, special characters, or spaces. A comma separates each property declaration.

Individual properties can also be declared as objects using the curly brace notation:

```
var roadster = {
    year: 1965,
    make: "Ford",
    model: "Shelby 427 SC",
    "top speed": "186 mph",
    engine: {
        displacement: "427 ci",
        horsepower: "500+"
        "red line rpm": 6800
    }
};
```

A.4.3 Functions

Functions are instantiated similarly to properties except that they get the keyword `function` in their declaration and they contain an executable definition. Functions are very interesting in that they can also be passed around as properties and be assigned and reassigned as variables. This makes for a very powerful construct that can do a lot of work with very little code:

```
var bike = {
    chainRing: 32,
    cog: 12,
    gearRatio: function() {
        return (this.chainRing / this.cog);
    }
};
alert("Gear ratio: " + bike.gearRatio());
```

Function declarations are similar to properties except for use of function keyword.

When executing function inside object the this keyword refers to containing object.

A.4.4 Prototype

Every object in JavaScript has a prototype from which it inherits properties and functions. New objects created from an object with a custom prototype will automatically receive changes to methods and properties, as long as those values aren't overwritten in the new object.

This is difficult to understand without an example, so the following listing should help to clarify this concept.

Listing A.10 Understanding prototypes in JavaScript

```
function Truck() {
}
Truck.prototype.wheels = 4;

var ford = new Truck();
console.log(ford.wheels);    // 4
```

Declare truck function.

Give truck's prototype wheels property with value of 4.

Create new truck instance.

```
var chevy = new Truck();
chevy.wheels = 6;
console.log(chevy.wheels);      // 6
console.log(ford.wheels);       // 4

Truck.prototype.wheels = 8;
console.log(ford.wheels);       // 8
console.log(chevy.wheels);      // 6
```

Create another instance but assign wheels value as 6.

Ford still has 4 wheels.

Change prototype to 8 wheels.

← **Ford has 8 wheels.**

Chevy has 6 wheels.

A.4.5   'this' and scope

If you have children or siblings, the question "who started it?" is probably familiar to you. In JavaScript, the use of the this keyword is completely dependent upon the answer to that question.

this is always available in JavaScript, but what exactly this refers to will be a matter of scope. this is primarily a means of dealing with objects, be it a JavaScript object or an HTML element. If an HTML element directly executes a piece of code, that element started the execution, and this will be a reference to that originating element. If the function that's called then turns around and fires a second function, this will revert to the default ownership, the window or global namespace:

```
var el = document.getElementById("myElement");
el.addEventListener("click", elementClicked, false);
function elementClicked() {
    alert(this);
    secondLevelFunction();
}
function secondLevelFunction() {
    alert(this);
}
```

Assign event handler to HTML element using JavaScript.

When executed this refers to element with ID of "myElement".

Because no references were passed or assigned this in second function refers to window or global namespace.

A second feature of the language, and a significant reason for using unobtrusive JavaScript, is made apparent when attempting to directly wire up an event to an element on the page:

```
<div id="myDiv" onclick="elementClicked()">Click Here</div>
```

In the preceding code, this will refer to the global namespace, not to the myDiv element. Why? The reason has to do with the way assignments are made.

When an assignment is made using the onclick="elementClicked()" method, the assignment is only a reference to the original function. On the other hand, when the assignment is made using JavaScript, as in el.addEventListener("click", elementClicked), the click event handler is assigned to an actual object, the element-Clicked function. The handler now has an in-memory *copy* of the original function, not a reference to it. By extension, if changes are made to the original function, they won't be available in the copied function.

It seems obvious that you'd want to use the second method of event assignment where this actually has a usable value, and the current trend in the JavaScript community provides exactly that solution. Unobtrusive JavaScript is a means of developing applications where binding of events and data is performed apart from the actual markup. While it can often mean developers new to the paradigm get an instant headache, the result of assigning functions to elements outside of the markup is that this will always refer to the originating element. So you'll always know who started it!

A.4.6   *A simple object pattern*

There are plenty of patterns for building objects in JavaScript. The book *JavaScript Patterns* by Stoyan Stefanov (O'Reilly, 2010) is comprehensive in its coverage of various object patterns.

It's important to understand all of them to some degree, but an example of a simple object will help you understand how the object is instantiated, as well as some other features of the language, like closure. Notice also, in the next listing, the use of the this keyword.

Listing A.11   A simple JavaScript object

```
function Counter() {                    ⟵── Define counter function.
   this.count = 0;
   var self = this;                         Assign variables to
   setInterval(function() {                 store reference to self.
      self.increment();
   }, 1000);                                When created start timer
}                                           that increments every second.
Counter.prototype = {
   increment: function() {                  Prototype contains the
      this.count++;                         increment function.
   }
};                                          When new counter object is
var counter = new Counter();                instantiated timer will start.
```

A.4.7   *Closures*

Closure in JavaScript is both maligned by those new to the language and much loved once those same developers begin to understand its power. Closure is one of those concepts that's very difficult to explain but that gets easier as you see and use examples of it.

It starts with the concept that in JavaScript you can declare functions inside of other functions. This is often handy for event handlers and callbacks. One interesting feature of these nested functions is that the inner function has direct access to all of the variables declared in the enclosing function, even if the enclosing function is no longer running. This feature is called 'closure', and it can be very handy.

Here's an example:

```
function outer() {
   var count = 1;
```

```
function inner() {
    count++;
}

console.log(count);

inner();
console.log(count);

setTimeout(inner, 5000);
console.log(count);
}
```

Still equal to l; we haven't run inner() yet.

Now equal to 2.

Still equal to 2, setTimeout won't fire for another 5 seconds.

When it fires in 5 seconds count will be 3 even though outer() is no longer running.

What does this really mean? Basically, it comes down to a question of scope and where a particular variable or object is or isn't available.

When an anonymous function is created to handle the callback event of an Ajax request, that function is called separately from the original wrapper, but the variables declared inside that wrapper are still available due to closure. In the previous object example, notice the line inside the setInterval callback function that refers to the self variable. Even though this is executing inside a separate function, the Counter object provides the closure mechanism, so self is still available and contains a value.

We won't go into any additional detail, but we do reference the concept when we encounter it and explain in context throughout the rest of the book. In the end, if you understand closure and selectors in JavaScript and jQuery respectively, you're well ahead of the game.

A.4.8 Exception handling

Exception handling in JavaScript uses the same structure as C#, and it's not very different from Visual Basic.NET, so this section should be a quick review for you.

There are three parts to an exception-handling block: try, catch, and finally. They work almost exactly as you would expect, except for the fact that both the catch and finally blocks are optional in JavaScript, whereas only the finally block can be omitted in C#.

The following listing shows some basic options.

Listing A.12   Various optional `try/catch/finally` exception management blocks

```
try {
    // do work and ignore all exceptions
}
```

`try` block with no exception management will ignore all errors.

```
try {
    // do work
}
catch (ex) {
    alert(ex.name + " " + ex.message);
}
```

Normal `try/catch` block where no additional processing is necessary after an exception.

```
try {
    // do work
}
```

Full `try/catch/finally` block where all optional areas are used.

```
catch (ex) {
    alert(ex.name + " " + ex.message);
}
finally {
    // finish up
}
```

**Full `try/catch/`
`finally` block where all
optional areas are used.**

Your JavaScript application also has the ability to throw a new exception simply by using the `throw` keyword:

```
throw new Error("An error was thrown.");
```

All exceptions have at least the name and message properties, but you can add more, and some browsers also add more information, like the line number where the exception was thrown. Be careful of relying on these extended exception features, though, because they vary between browser vendors.

Selective catch

It's also possible to catch multiple different kinds of exceptions, but in this case you'll need to check the type of each error using the `instanceof` operator:

```
catch (ex) {
    if (ex instanceof TypeError) {
        // Handle TypeError exception
    }
    else {
        // Handle other exceptions
    }
}
```

The following specific error types can be used in `catch` blocks: `Error`, `RangeError`, `ReferenceError`, `SyntaxError`, `TypeError`, and `URIError`.

A.5 *Communications*

JavaScript can make asynchronous requests back to a server using Ajax, and it can also load data and files directly from a URL. These capabilities allow you to build extremely smooth yet lightweight interfaces.

In this section, we'll cover the following topics:

- `XmlHttpRequest` object
- Sending data to a server
- JSON and JSONP
- Basic JSON syntax
- Complex JSON syntax

A.5.1   XmlHttpRequest

The first thing that you need to understand about asynchronous communications with JavaScript is the XmlHttpRequest object. This is otherwise known as Ajax.

This object requires four operations to make it work:

1 Declare an XMLHttpRequest object.
2 Assign an OnReadyStateChange handler function.
3 Open the request object.
4 Send the request.

The following listing shows the minimal requirements to make a request for a file in the same location as the current HTML page. This assumes a server is available to handle the requests and responses, of course.

> **Listing A.13 XmlHttpRequest used to GET data from the server**

```
var req = new XMLHttpRequest();
req.onreadystatechange = function() {
    if (this.status === 200 && this.readyState === 4) {
        alert("Response: " + this.response);
    }
}
req.open("GET", "test2.html");
req.send();
```

Status code is a standard HTTP value, and readyState varies from 0 to 4 where 4 is ready.

Response value of request will contain all data from server.

When opening request standard HTTP methods are always used.

A.5.2   Sending data

It's also possible to send data using the XMLHttpRequest object. To do this, you pass your data package in the send function call and assign a request header content type parameter.

The data you send should be formatted based on the content type you assign:

```
var req = new XMLHttpRequest();
var data = "fname=Abraham&lname=Lincoln";
req.open("POST", "postValues.html");
req.setRequestHeader("Content-Type", "application/x-www-form-urlencoded");
req.send(data);
```

A.5.3   JSON and JSONP

Other than HTML, the three kinds of data you'll generally use are XML, JSON, and JSONP. We'll be sticking with JSON and JSONP here because of their wide acceptance in the JavaScript community, their easy-to-follow syntax, and their relatively small payload size.

For instance, the following content shows the difference between the same person object represented in XML versus JSON. The XML data would have to be parsed, whereas the JSON data, in addition to being much smaller, can be used to directly hydrate a new JavaScript object:

```
<person>
    <firstname>John</firstname>
```

```
    <lastname>Hancock</lastname>
    <birthdate>Jan 23 1737</birthdate>
</person>

{
    "firstname":"John",
    "lastname":"Hancock",
    "birthdate":"Jan 23 1737"
}
```

JSON stands for JavaScript Object Notation, and it's used for transferring text-based data from one point to another over HTTP. It can and has been used for many other purposes, but its roots are in the web. JSON uses specific characters to wrap text into serialized fields with very little effort and overhead. It's fast, human readable, and broadly supported.

JSONP stands for "JSON with Padding," and it's used to get JSON data from a remote site. If the data were regular JSON, it would break the same-origin policy built into JavaScript, so instead, a function wrapper is placed around the data and the entire package is sent as a script. Because scripts can be loaded from any origin, the function returned by the script is evaluated and read into memory as data, even though it's technically a script and not a JSON data island.

A.5.4   *JSON syntax*

JSON syntax is extremely simple. Data types of values are implied, not specified, the objects need not conform to a specific schema, and arrays of objects can contain anything. When parsed, a JSON data island will contain an object or an array of objects containing only name/value pairs.

Here are the basic rules:

- Curly braces {} wrap each object instance.
- Each property in an object has a name and value separated by a colon.
- Each property in an object is separated from the next by a comma.
- Property names and property values that are strings are quoted.
- Square brackets [] wrap each array instance.
- Objects in arrays are separated by a comma.
- Object properties can be other objects or arrays.
- Whitespace is allowed between any elements.

Here is a simple JSON object:

```
{"fname":"George","lname":"Washington"}
```

This code will result in the direct creation of a JavaScript object with two properties, each with a value.

A.5.5   Complex JSON objects

Some projects will require sending large amounts of data to the client, and JSON is perfectly capable of doing this as well. This JSON code contains an array of two objects, each containing a timeline that can be immediately parsed and used in JavaScript.

```
[{
    "Timeline":"1800s",
    "StartYear":1800,
    "EndYear":1899,
    "Events": [
        {"Date":1803,  "Event":"Louisana Purchase"},
        {"Date":1808,  "Event":"Napoleon Occupies Spain"},
        {"Date":1821,  "Event":"Missouri Admitted"},
        {"Date":1828,  "Event":"Greece Wins Independence"},
        {"Date":1845,  "Event":"Texas Admitted"},
        {"Date":1848,  "Event":"California Gold Rush"},
        {"Date":1896,  "Event":"Utah Admitted"}
    ]
},
{
    "Timeline":"1900s",
    "StartYear":1900,
    "EndYear":1999,
    "Events": [
        {"Date":1917,  "Event":"US Declares War"},
        {"Date":1920,  "Event":"Prohibition"},
        {"Date":1933,  "Event":"TVA"},
        {"Date":1941,  "Event":"US Declares War"},
        {"Date":1959,  "Event":"Alaska Admitted"},
        {"Date":1963,  "Event":"Kennedy Assassinated"},
        {"Date":1983,  "Event":"Star Wars"},
        {"Date":1991,  "Event":"Desert Storm"}
    ]
}]
```

Throughout this book, we send most data using regular JSON calls. Both WCF web APIs and MVC 3 support JSON data natively, so you should consider it a core part of your data strategy.

A.6   Structured libraries

A library in JavaScript refers to a single file or a group of files that are deployed and operate together within an application. The term *structured library* generally refers to a library that operates autonomously, either as an independent functioning unit or as a foundation for a larger application. This is really not a technical term but rather a way to describe how a specific library should be deployed and used.

In this section, you'll find information on the following topics:

- Libraries
- Script locations
- Non-blocking scripts

- Immediate functions and object initialization
- JavaScript file operations

A.6.1 *Libraries*

A single library loaded using a `script` tag in an HTML page or loaded asynchronously will usually execute all of its code immediately. This isn't to say that it will fire all events and perform all work, but rather all structural elements and global elements will be immediately created and loaded into memory. This makes the order of the `script` tags in your pages very important.

Remember that when JavaScript encounters a variable that isn't already instantiated, it will try to create it. If a piece of code is expecting a default value and encounters `undefined`, it will usually throw an exception. Likewise, a property nested in an object that has not been instantiated will also throw an exception.

A.6.2 *Script locations*

A `script` tag can be in any location in your page, within either the `<head>` or `<body>` tags, but there are two primary locations where they're most effective.

The first location is in the `<head>` element, where you'd expect it. Place files here only if they have code that will dynamically change the layout of the page. Although most of your layout should come from CSS, it's possible that certain scenarios will require you to make tweaks based on conditions in the browser. Scripts in the `<head>` element will block execution of the page, so be sparing in their use and size.

The second location has been extensively performance tested by the Yahoo User Interface team (responsible for the YUI library) and should be your primary location for setting up script references. This is at the end of the `<body>` element, just before the closing tag. Placing scripts here allows them to load after the rendering of the page has completed and, in modern browsers, allows the browser to start downloading scripts before rendering is even complete. For a complete discussion, go to http://developer.yahoo.com/performance/.

A.6.3 *Non-blocking scripts*

When a JavaScript file loads, it will block rendering in the browser, regardless of where the script is loaded. While placing scripts at the end of the `<body>` tag helps, if you're loading many files or large libraries, there's still the possibility that some startup task in your application can be blocked by loading a library that won't be needed until later.

There's a `defer` attribute of a `<script>` tag that can help with Firefox and Internet Explorer, but it's hardly a workable solution for cross-browser software and it only causes the script to wait until the browser determines that the document is ready. What you really need is the ability to, in code, decide when a script needs to be loaded.

That's the purpose of the `addScript` function in the next listing. This bit of code will dynamically download a script any time it's required and give it an ID that will prevent it from being reloaded on the page.

Listing A.14   A script loader that doesn't block processing in the host application

```
function addScript(url) {
    var id = url.replace(/[^\w]/gi, "");
    var element = document.getElementById(id);
    if (!element) {
        element = document.createElement("script");
        element.type = "text/javascript";
        element.src = url;
        element.id = id;
        document.getElementsByTagName("head")[0]
            .appendChild(element);
    }
}
```

Generate new element id based on script file URL.

See if script already exists on current page.

If script is new create new element of type script.

Set source of new script element to input parameter.

Load element onto current page. This also executes code after loading is complete.

This code will load the script once and only once, and execute it after it has loaded the first time. If your program makes structural or data changes to the library, these won't be affected by any attempts to reload the script.

A.6.4   *Immediate functions and immediate object initialization*

One of the ways to keep the global namespace a little more clean is to use JavaScript's immediate execution syntax. When a script is wrapped and then immediately executed, it's operating inside its own functional space, isolated from other areas of the application. There are two flavors of immediate execution: immediate functions and immediate object initializations.

An immediate function is wrapped in parentheses and then has parentheses after it to provide the cue to "run this now."

```
(function () { ... })();
```

You can also return a value from inside an immediate function by returning and assigning a value to a variable:

```
var x = (function () { return 10; })();
```

And finally, you can pass variables to an immediate function:

```
var greet = (function (fname, lastname)
{
    return "Hello " + fname + " " + lname;
}("Ian", "Gilman");
```

Immediate object initialization uses similar syntax, except that it uses object notation rather than a functional wrapper. The following listing describes an object that sets up an operating environment upon initialization. The object is wrapped in parentheses and then a startup method of the object is immediately called. Once parsed and executed, this object is immediately available.

Listing A.15　Immediate object initialization

```
({
    start: function() {
        // Perform startup tasks here.
    }
}).start();
```

A.6.5　*JavaScript files*

So you're working furiously on your project, building out "the next big thing" in HTML applications, and you realize that your application is starting to slow down. Further investigation leads to the discovery that you're loading 23 JavaScript files with every page and have ten thousand lines of code. What to do?

Well, you have a number of options, all of which can work together to make a good solution. Visual Studio will perform the following tasks on your JavaScript files for you, but for now a good understanding of what they mean will be useful.

Each of these performance enhancements can be used with Visual Studio as either a predeployment script or as a post-build command in the development environment.

MINIFICATION

Minification of a JavaScript file refers to the removal of whitespace and comments in a file. If you open a minified file in a text editor with word wrapping off, it will generally appear as one long continuous line of text. Some minification tools also rename long variable and function names to shorter versions.

Minification can save a lot of space in your JavaScript files, and most of the development tools available for browsers can "prettify" JavaScript on the fly as you're debugging. This indented and carriage-returned version won't be as readable as the original if you have shortened names, but minification is the most common performance improvement a JavaScript application gets, and nearly all open source libraries ship with development and minified versions.

COMBINE

Because each JavaScript file downloaded will require a new connection to the server (if it hasn't been previously cached), it sometimes makes sense to combine multiple JavaScript files into a single file for deployment. This doesn't hurt execution and speeds application load time if there are a lot of files to process.

COMPRESS

File compression goes a step or two beyond normal minification procedures. It takes a little longer to execute and can sometimes introduce bugs into the resulting libraries as part of the compression process. A JavaScript compressor will take the existing JavaScript and use various algorithms to shrink it to the smallest functional piece of code and then minify that code. Most names inside the code are changed, and functions can be completely rewritten or relocated inside the code. Don't expect to have easily debuggable code after compression has been performed on it.

> **Understanding JavaScript licensing for production applications**
>
> Most open source projects come with some kind of license that allows you to use them in your projects. These licenses almost always require that the original author be attributed in the code via comments and that the licensing model also be included. Minification and combining of JavaScript in your application can result in the removal of these comments, thus breaking the licensing agreement that allowed you to use the code in the first place.
>
> If you need to do your own minification of an open source library and can't get the comments to be reinserted after the fact, your best option is to contact the original author and see about putting a global licensing text document in your project somewhere, and refer to it using a variable inside your code:
>
> ```
> var OpenSourceLicense = "http://ellipsetours.com/licenses.html";
> ```
>
> Just remember that the code belongs to the original author, and they have a right to attribution.

A.7   jQuery

Now that you have a foundation for understanding the JavaScript language, it's time to take our discussion to the next level. jQuery is John Resig's creation and has, in just a few short years, revolutionized web and JavaScript development. A number of Microsoft product managers and evangelists have a penchant for saying that many developers don't code JavaScript anymore, they code in jQuery.

The basic building block you'll need to start using jQuery is the library itself. You can get it from http://jquery.com for free. Include it in a script tag in your application either as a local file or as a CDN-based reference, and your application will immediately have the $ available for use. The $ sign is an alias similar to the _app alias you set up in an earlier example. Using $ you can find elements and execute jQuery functions.

We cover many examples of jQuery throughout this book. This basic understanding of the nomenclature and how to turn the key and start the engine of jQuery in your application will help you here and in your personal and professional projects.

In this section, you'll gain knowledge of the following:

- jQuery selectors
- Wrapped sets
- Chaining
- Event handling
- Animations and effects
- Ajax
- jQuery helper utilities
- Extending jQuery with plugins
- Including jQuery in a project

A.7.1 Selectors

Understanding CSS selectors is one of the most important skills in JavaScript development because most of jQuery's DOM manipulation is handled by means of selectors. Using selectors you can select one or many elements by ID, class name, tag type, position in the DOM, or by the existence of particular attributes. For instance, to find all <div> elements on a page, you'd use $("div"), and you could begin to work on these elements as a group or iterate through them to do work individually.

Proper use of selectors is key to the incredible amount of work you can do with just a tiny bit of code using jQuery.

A.7.2 Wrapped sets

A selector in jQuery returns a wrapped set. Wrapped sets can contain no objects, a single object, or a collection of objects. To determine how many objects have been returned by a selector, you can call the length property on the wrapped set:

```
$("div").length;
```

Remember that when you're executing a selector, you'll be returning a wrapped set, so be very careful. Applying a style to all <div> elements on a page is generally not a good idea, but the code to do it is deceptively simple.

A.7.3 Chaining

Once you have a wrapped set, you can start to execute functions on it. In jQuery, each function returns the result of the work performed, so if you want to remove all <div> elements on your page that have the class name of highlight, you could do this:

```
$("div.highlight").remove();
```

The result returned from the remove() function is a wrapped set of the elements just removed from the DOM. You could then reinsert those elements in another location on the page using the appendTo() function, and so on.

A.7.4 Event handling

jQuery allows you to bind functions directly to event handlers in the DOM simply by using the bind() function, the click() function, or any of various other built-in event-handling functions. In coordination with selectors, you can wire up event handlers on a form or page very quickly and reliably.

A.7.5 Animations and effects

jQuery has a number of animations that can be applied to the CSS properties of elements, like fading them in and out of view or sliding them around the page based on user interaction. You can apply various effects to these animations using delay timers to chain effects together and, as you'll see in the next section on jQuery UI, there's also a set of additional features that start where the basic jQuery library leaves off.

A.7.6   *Ajax*

jQuery has built-in support for Ajax requests to get JSON data, POST data to a server, and perform any other asynchronous task you like. The latest versions of jQuery have a completely new Ajax implementation that promises to provide even easier implementations.

A.7.7   *jQuery helper utilities*

The jQuery library also has a number of utility functions that will help you parse JSON, build and manipulate arrays, and create copies of existing objects. We'll deal with each as we encounter them in the various examples throughout the book.

A.7.8   *Extending jQuery with plugins*

One of the best features of jQuery is the ability to extend it with plugins. There are literally thousands of plugins available for free that will do practically any kind of work you like. Some are helpful just for learning specific features, and others provide support for things like URL manipulation. Whatever the repeatable task you want to perform, there's likely a plugin already out there to do it. The only question will be whether you want to add the plugin to your project or use what you learn from its code to build your own implementation.

A.7.9   *Including jQuery*

We mentioned briefly that you just need to include the jQuery library as a script tag in your page to start using it. This can take a number of forms. The simplest is to go to the jQuery site and download the latest debug and minified versions, and include them in your project. There are other options though.

The best way is to use a content delivery network (CDN) that will use edge-cached servers to provide files, often more quickly than your own server can. Using the Microsoft- or Google-hosted CDN versions of jQuery is also helpful, because your browser will cache that file from that location and be able to use it if another site makes the same request. The overall performance of all projects that use jQuery is improved when you use a CDN.

The Microsoft CDN has a page at http://www.asp.net/ajaxlibrary/cdn.ashx with links to all the latest libraries, including debug versions that have Visual Studio comments built in! This alone should make learning jQuery a much faster journey.

The Google CDN is located at http://code.google.com/apis/libraries/ and has links to various pages containing links to multiple versions of jQuery and jQuery UI, along with many other libraries.

A.8   *jQuery UI*

Although we use jQuery as the DOM manipulation and application framework throughout the book for application logic and page manipulation, there's another library that we'll be relying on for additional presentation help: jQuery UI.

Available from the same CDN locations as jQuery, jQuery UI provides three basic features to your application:

- Widgets
- Effects
- Themes

Here's the 15-second drill on each.

> **TIP** jQuery UI is a separate project and development team from jQuery proper. This means the release schedules are different and version numbers aren't coordinated. There is, however, plenty of communication between teams, so you can expect that any incompatibility between versions will be thoroughly documented.

A.8.1 Widgets

A widget is a user interface element that jQuery UI creates for you that encapsulates a specific functionality. By including jQuery UI in your project, you no longer have to build your own custom datepicker control or tabbed interface. Widgets can be declared in code that you would normally have to create yourself. Each widget comes with its own set of properties and events.

A.8.2 Effects

Effects in jQuery UI are extensions to the basic effects in jQuery. You can add custom or prebuilt Bezier functions to animations and animate colors, and there are more involved effects for showing and hiding content.

A.8.3 Themes

Themes in jQuery UI are usually built using ThemeRoller, a tool that works in Firefox to help you build out custom themes. The theme itself consists of stylesheets and JavaScript files that, when included in your project, will give it a very polished look and feel. Themes are sets of styles with very specific names that jQuery UI components will use to automatically change user interface properties and states when events are fired.

We'll discuss some of the operations and features available in jQuery UI in this book, but if you want a deeper understanding, you should consider the latest edition of *jQuery in Action* by Bear Bibeault and Yehuda Katz (Manning, 2008). This book has an entire section on jQuery UI that will help you gain a more complete understanding.

A.8.4 Component inclusion

Because jQuery UI has so many different components, the development team took a different approach from the default jQuery library CDN distribution model. When you navigate to http://jqueryui.com/download, you're presented with a set of options that allow you to decide which specific options you want in your application and to download only those. This makes for a much lighter library in your application. If you decide later that you want some other features, just rebuild your custom download and you're ready to go!

appendix B
Using ASP.NET MVC

As a .NET developer building an HTML application, you have a number of decisions to make, not the least of which is the server-side framework and toolset to use. There are plenty of options in the industry and quite a few even within the scope of .NET development.

We'll focus here on ASP.NET MVC, a web framework with rich templates for Visual Studio, ideal for building HTML5 applications. MVC is part of a larger web programming topology in the Microsoft stack that includes classic ASP.NET and ASP.NET Web APIs.

The approach to this family of tools lately has been to consider them all as "web applications" and not to differentiate too much between them. This is fine if you're a developer with a clear understanding of the advantages, disadvantages, and patterns in each of the tools, but it doesn't help you understand where each of the applications fits in if you're new to HTML applications. This appendix will teach you the basics of an ASP.NET MVC application so that you're comfortable enough with the templates to build the sample applications throughout the rest of this book.

B.1 Using MVC

MVC stands for Model-View-Controller, a development pattern that helps with the clear separation of concerns when developing a website (see figure B.1). The model in this pattern maintains business logic and the view provides the presentation. The controller responds to actions from the view and can react by redirecting the client to a different view, by manipulating model data in some way, or both.

The beauty of MVC for an HTML application developer is the clarity of the markup you can create, and the speed at which you can create it. Other frameworks are a bit more drag-and-drop, such as traditional ASP.NET Web Forms and non-Microsoft tools such as Dreamweaver; MVC, in contrast, requires you to understand

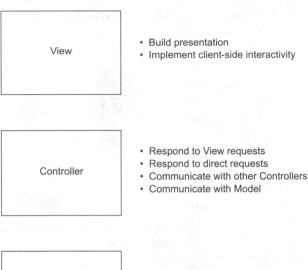

**Figure B.1   The MVC pattern
clearly separates a web
application into specific parts.**

the actual markup that will exist in your page when you build the user interface. This helps keep you, as a developer, more in touch with the possible semantic aspects of your pages, which should help in maintainability and readability.

MVC also has the concept of master pages, which allow you to leverage default layouts in your application so that you can focus on the actual content. The Razor view engine that's packaged with MVC makes for very productive application interface build cycles. It also doesn't hurt that the MVC pattern is quite common throughout the non-Microsoft web development industry, so your skills with this framework will give you a head start in learning and understanding other development frameworks.

B.2   Starting a new MVC application

The sample application in this appendix will be a set of simple signup pages for an email newsletter. It will be built using Visual Studio 2012, but where appropriate we'll add notes to show differences between this and the previous version of Visual Studio. The signup page will have field-level rules applied both on the client and on the server, and it will have the ability to check the server for a list of all current subscribers. Let's get started.

B.2.1   Getting (or updating) ASP.NET MVC

In order to use the MVC framework in Visual Studio 2012, you must have the appropriate templates and Visual Studio add-ins installed. These templates are installed by default in Visual Studio 2012 and will work with all web development versions of Visual Studio, including the free Express version.

If your version doesn't have the ASP.NET MVC templates installed, go to http://www .microsoft.com/web/downloads and you'll be presented with the option to download the Web Platform Installer (figure B.2).

The Web Platform Installer will review your system and present an interface that shows you what is and isn't installed in your system. If you don't already have ASP.NET MVC with any Tools Updates installed under the Products menu, click the Add button and then the Install button to get them (figure B.3).

Microsoft Web Platform Installer

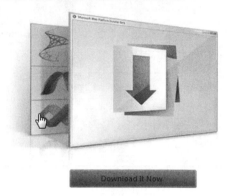

Figure B.2   The Web Platform Installer, free from Microsoft

TIP   Be sure to pick the latest version of ASP.NET MVC because it's released out-of-band from the normal Visual Studio and .NET Framework releases. This means it can be updated far more often than the core frameworks and developer tools. The version used in this appendix is ASP.NET MVC 4.

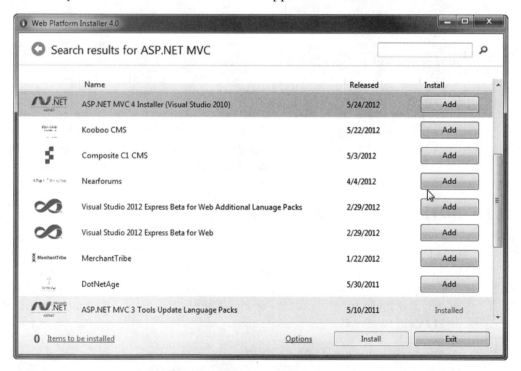

Figure B.3   Finding and starting the installation of ASP.NET MVC

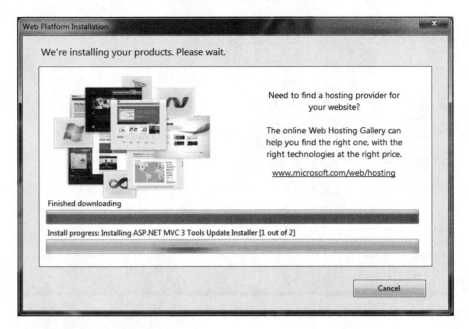

Figure B.4   Installing ASP.NET MVC

Accept the terms of use and begin the installation (figure B.4).

When the installation is complete, confirm the installation in the window that's presented and exit the Web Platform Installer. That's all there is to it! You're ready to start building an ASP.NET MVC web application.

B.2.2   Steps to building a new application

Now that you have the latest tools for your development environment, it's time to start building.

Open Visual Studio and select File > New > Project from the menu. In the dialog box that appears (figure B.5), find the latest version of the ASP.NET MVC Web Application template. Name it MVCNewsletter and click OK.

Once you select the template and give it a name, you're presented with another dialog box (figure B.6) that allows you to decide what kind of plumbing (if any) to build into your new application by default.

TIP Just because you select an empty application template doesn't mean that you won't be able to take advantage of the MVC add-ins to Visual Studio that enhance your development experience. On the contrary, all features will still be available to you, but you won't get any of the basic security structures or styling starters that come with the other templates.

For this example, you'll be building an Internet Application, using the Razor engine. This will, by default, give you HTML5 semantic markup in your pages. For now, leave

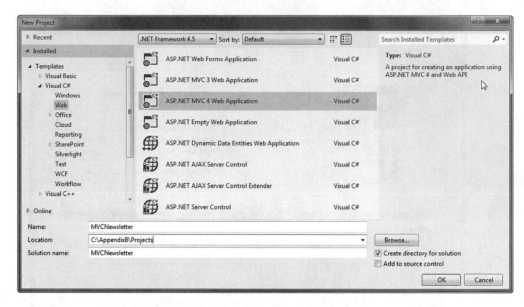

Figure B.5   The new ASP.NET MVC Web Application template

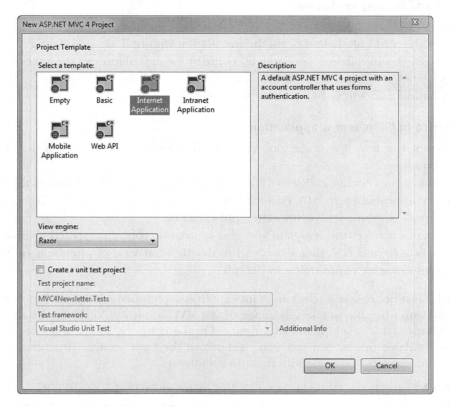

Figure B.6   The MVC site template selector

the Create a Unit Test Project check box unselected. This application won't include unit tests. Click OK to build your base project.

When it's complete, your solution structure should look something like figure B.7. Take note of the various folder names and where files are located throughout the structure. We'll be referring back to the folder structure throughout the rest of this appendix.

Believe it or not, you now have a working MVC web application! Press F5 to run your application, and you should see something similar to figure B.8.

You've built an MVC application, but you still don't know any more about how it works than when you started. A look through the code generated in the template will be a useful exercise, so that's what we'll do next.

Figure B.7 The starting solution structure of an MVC internet application

B.3 Walking through an MVC application

A look at how the various pieces in your basic application operate will help you understand MVC in general. More specifically, it'll show you how you can get your markup and data into the browser where the real fun begins!

> **NOTE** One thing worth mentioning about MVC is that the pattern is storage-agnostic. This means there's nothing in the pattern that prescribes how you should store or retrieve stateful data. This is good, because storage technologies and mechanisms can be vastly different, and they often depend on the deployment environment infrastructure and can't be chosen by a developer. When using MVC, the web application developer can focus more on the business rules and user experience than on data persistence.

B.3.1 Models

The model in the MVC pattern is the part that handles business rules and structured data. It could be referred to as the "business objects," but that would be too limiting. In fact, the model should mimic the way the data is used in the application, which may include somewhat more or less than would be required in a conventional business object.

Take listing B.1, for example; the `LogInModel` object (found in the Models\AccountModels.cs file) has only three properties: `UserName`, `Password`, and `RememberMe`. These properties are annotated using data attributes corresponding to business rules.

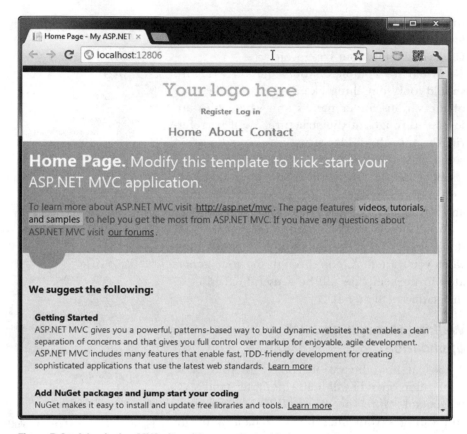

Figure B.8   A beginning MVC site with no content added

More complex models can have methods and custom rules applied, but those rules are usually limited to only what is required to perform model-specific tasks. There's no need to build an entire user object with a complete object graph when all you need are these three bits of information to log the user into the system.

Listing B.1   The `LogInModel` object in the default MVC template

```
public class LogInModel
{
    [Required]
    [Display(Name = "User name")]
    public string UserName { get; set; }

    [Required]
    [DataType(DataType.Password)]
    [Display(Name = "Password")]
    public string Password { get; set; }

    [Display(Name = "Remember me?")]
    public bool RememberMe { get; set; }
}
```

Data annotations used to efficiently implement some rules; others require use of coded logic directly in model.

Only UserName, Password, and RememberMe properties required for user to log in, so these are all that are used in this particular model.

Take a look at the other model objects in the AccountModels.cs file that's included by default in the template you used to build the project. The `RegisterModel` contains some information that's shared with the `LogInModel` and some additional properties, but it's missing the `RememberMe` field because it's not required for a user to register on the site. Efficiency and a view toward the final use of the data are key in developing your models.

Speaking of efficiency, there are times where, in simpler areas of an application, a model isn't required but is instead inferred. If your application needs to retrieve a bit of data from the server, the model doesn't exist as an independent set of objects, but rather as the result of a call to or from storage. The pattern still fits this situation, but the model is less tangible in the code.

This use of multiple objects with similar sets of properties all corresponding to the same real-world entity is called *domain modeling*. A domain model is one that tries to view the whole system at once, including all business problems it involves. A finished domain model will have objects, functions, and composites of these that solve all the business problems as efficiently as possible with no excess.

In looking at the model in MVC, you should look for the specific problem you're dealing with and use the object or base type that most closely solves it. For example, to check on whether a user's account has been suspended, you can make a service call to a server and return a Boolean value. In that case, the Boolean value would be the model.

B.3.2 Controllers

The next part of the pattern is the controller. Controllers handle user interaction and respond using model data and business rule validations. The controller is then responsible for determining which view to return to the client. We'll discuss views shortly.

In ASP.NET MVC, the controller responds to client requests by means of action methods, and MVC application routing is used to determine which action method of which controller should be used. Controllers may contain one or many action methods, each responding to a different signature combination of URL and parameters. Controllers should be considered your primary application organizing tool in an MVC application.

The following listing shows a good example of a controller that handles multiple action method calls.

Listing B.2 Sample `AccountController` methods in the MVC 3 template

1 Default call to the /Account/Register URL results in an empty model being passed to Register view object. This displays an empty form that's ready for user input.

2 POST method uses model binding to parse incoming values into a RegisterModel object. GET methods also use model binding.

```
public ActionResult Register()
{
    return View();                                   ◄──┘  1
}

[HttpPost]
public ActionResult Register(RegisterModel model)    ◄──   2
```

```
{
    if (ModelState.IsValid)                              ←      Properties of model are
    {                                                           validated and ModelState.IsValid
        // Attempt to register the user                        Boolean is checked.
        MembershipCreateStatus createStatus;
        Membership.CreateUser(                           ←      Once object is valid object's
            model.UserName,                                     properties are processed into data
            model.Password,                                     store to officially register user.
            model.Email,
            null, null, true, null,
            out createStatus);
        if (createStatus == MembershipCreateStatus.Success)
        {
            FormsAuthentication                                 If registration was handled
                .SetAuthCookie(model.UserName, false);          properly user is registered
            return RedirectToAction("Index", "Home");    ←      and you can call
        }                                                       RedirectToAction method
        else                                                    using Index method of
        {                                                       Home controller.
            ModelState.AddModelError(
                "", ErrorCodeToString(createStatus));
        }
    }
    // If we got this far, something failed, redisplay form     If there was an error
    return View(model);                                  ←      view is returned to
}                                                               user and ModelState
                                                                will include exceptions
                                                                encountered.
```

You'll notice that the call to Register() is practically empty ❶. It just returns View(). What does this mean? Well, in the convention-over-configuration methodology of MVC, this will cause the framework to go look for a View object named Register, preferably inside the Account folder of the application (because you're using the Account controller).

Convention-over-configuration means that the application will execute tasks based on the names of objects. When you call http://mysite.com/Account, MVC will look for an AccountController object with an Index method. No custom code needs to be written to make this happen; it's simply the convention that the name of the HTTP URL action corresponds to the name of the controller, and the default view will always be named Index.

Next, notice the second overloaded instance of Register() that has an HttpPost attribute assigned ❷. It takes a RegisterModel object as a parameter. This combination of attributes and properties means that when the view does a form POST to the /Account/Register URL, this method will try to parse the incoming parameters into a RegisterModel object and then work with that object to register the current user. When complete, the controller responds with the RegisterView containing updates made to the model by the user. This process of transforming the incoming parameters into a model object is called model binding, and listing B.2 shows these two methods.

There's certainly a lot happening inside the AccountController object. As the main organizing object in an MVC application, controllers are the hub around which everything else turns. As mentioned, which method of which controller responds to a specific URL call from the client is based on the routes assigned in the application. That's our next stop on the MVC line.

B.3.3 *Routing basics*

Routing is the process of handling incoming URL requests from a client and determining, by means of a table of possible route patterns, which controller in your application should respond to the request.

When an MVC application starts, it builds a list of routes called the `RouteTable`. When an incoming request is detected, the routes in the `RouteTable` are searched, in order, for the first route that matches the scheme. The controller listed in that route is then called and passed all the context information from the incoming request. Routing is one of the main stages in an MVC application, as shown in figure B.9.

You should have a default route already assigned in the sample application you're building. Open the Global.asax.cs file and find the `RegisterRoutes` method. This will include the code in the following listing, which creates a new route and maps it to a specific controller and a specific action on that controller.

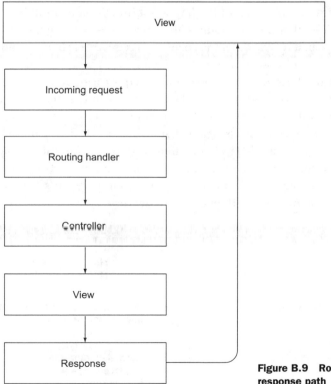

Figure B.9   Routing in the overall MVC request/response path

Listing B.3   Adding a default route to the MVC `RouteTable`

```
routes.MapRoute(
    "Default",                                    Name of        URL pattern to use when matching
    "{controller}/{action}/{id}",                 route          incoming requests; property names
    new {                                                        in next argument must match
        controller = "Home",                                     parameterized values in URL pattern
        action = "Index",                                Controller to use when
        id = UrlParameter.Optional                       route is matched
    }                                 Handling
);                                    specification for    Default method name
                                      id value in route    to use on controller
                                      if it exists         for route
```

In listing B.3 you should be able to see that routing is nothing more complicated than pattern-matching on incoming URLs. It can get a little bit confusing at times if routes are added in the wrong order or when one route mistakenly catches a request instead of it falling through to the next, but once you understand the basics, the rest will come with experience.

B.3.4   Views and Razor

The view is the final piece of the MVC puzzle, and it's responsible for presentation. It also includes script tags to include all of the JavaScript functionality built into MVC.

You might be thinking that the view sounds like a regular HTML page, and, from the perspective of the browser, it is. The difference between a regular HTML page and an MVC view is the amount of repetitive work required to build it. MVC Views use the Razor view engine to automate many of the tasks that would usually require a lot of typing and testing.

Just look at listing B.4. Notice all the @ symbols throughout the markup. These tell Razor that a bit of code will come next. Razor is smart enough to determine where the code stops and regular markup starts again. Using Razor you can intertwine your hand-coded HTML with generated HTML anywhere you like inside the view, perform looping operations to iterate over collections, and check other parts of the application for additional information to include in the final page. It's an integrated approach to building a semantic HTML page on the server.

Listing B.4   The templated Login view in MVC application

```
@model MVCNewsletter.Models.LoginModel              Model declaration often starts
                                                    MVC view but this isn't required.
@{
    ViewBag.Title = "Log in";                  ViewBag is dynamic object that can pass
}                                              information from controller to view.

<hgroup class="title">
    <h1>@ViewBag.Title.</h1>                 Normal markup can        BeginForm wraps
    <h2>Use this form to enter your          be placed anywhere       everything inside
    user name and password.</h2>             in view code.            using statement in
</hgroup>                                                              HTML form that will
                                                                      be posted back to
@using (Html.BeginForm(new { ReturnUrl = ViewBag.ReturnUrl })) {      controller.
```

```
@Html.ValidationSummary(true, "Log in was unsuccessful.
    Please correct the errors and try again.")

<fieldset>
    <legend>Log in Form</legend>
    <ol>
        <li>
            @Html.LabelFor(m => m.UserName)
            @Html.TextBoxFor(m => m.UserName)
        </li>
        <li>
            @Html.LabelFor(m => m.Password)
            @Html.PasswordFor(m => m.Password)
        </li>
        <li>
            @Html.CheckBoxFor(m => m.RememberMe)
            @Html.LabelFor(m => m.RememberMe,
                new { @class = "checkbox" })
        </li>
    </ol>
    <input type="submit" value="Log in" />
</fieldset>
<p>
    @Html.ActionLink("Register", "Register")
        if you don't have an account.
</p>
}
@section Scripts {
    @Scripts.Render("~/bundles/jqueryval")
}
```

Postback will use form name attributes for posted values.

Razor HTML helper methods can be used to build elements and bind directly to properties.

TextBoxFor supplies input of type "text".

PasswordFor creates input of type "password".

CheckBoxFor builds check box element and binds to Boolean value.

Closing using block tells Razor to insert closing form tag.

Client-side JavaScript can be included using regular HTML script tags or MVC script bundling.

B.3.5 Controlling views

We noted that the controller is the main organizational element in an MVC application and that a single controller can return different views based on the conditions it detects. There are a number of ways for a controller to do this. All are straightforward, but they deserve a little attention just to be sure that you can trace the views being presented in the browser to the code on the server sending them out.

To redirect output from a controller to a view, you can return the view itself or redirect to another controller that will then be responsible for returning a view:

```
return View();
return View(viewName);
return RedirectToAction(actionResult, controller);
```

Both the View and the RedirectToAction methods have multiple overloads, including versions that take model objects.

You can determine the result of a controller call by starting with the default values based on the controller name, and then get more specific as additional parameters are provided in the code. Figure B.10 shows a few examples of how calls from the HomeController might result in output from various elements in the application.

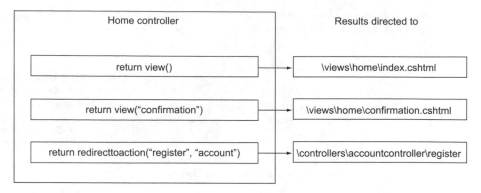

Figure B.10   Controllers can connect to multiple views and other controllers using naming conventions or by specifying the exact objects and methods to use. Each method also has overloads to pass along a model object.

Other ways of directing output from a controller to the browser involve overloading the View and RedirectToAction methods, but the approaches described here will be used most often.

B.3.6   *Combining views to build up the presentation*

You may have noticed in the earlier view code that there was no markup to describe the <html>, <head>, or <body> elements. If you ran the project and looked at the output, you'll have noticed that a lot of markup exists that didn't come from the view.

MVC didn't magically generate this markup; it came from the master layout page for your application. In fact, because a layout property was not explicitly defined in the view, MVC used the default view built into the template. This is pulled by convention from the _ViewStart.cshtml file in the top level of your Views folder. It contains only this line of code:

```
@{ Layout = "~/Views/Shared/_Layout.cshtml"; }
```

This says that the layout to use is in the /Views/Shared/_Layout.cshtml file.

The _ViewStart.cshtml file starts out simple, but it's a great foundation for more in terms of global logic or additional markup. This is the foundation, and you're free to create as much supporting content, script includes, and style directives here as you need for your particular application.

The _Layout.cshtml file, in turn, is used as a master page to provide semantic organization to any view that doesn't override it with a @{ Layout = "" } directive.

There are some interesting things to note about the _Layout.cshtml file, as illustrated in the following listing. Note that the markup is complete, including links to various resources, scripts, and Razor directives pointing to other elements from the project that should be rendered into the page.

Listing B.5 The `templated_Layout` **shared view**

```html
<!DOCTYPE html>
<html lang="en">
  <head>
    <meta charset="utf-8" />
    <title>@ViewBag.Title - My ASP.NET
      MVC Application</title>
    <link href="~/favicon.ico"
      rel="shortcut icon" type="image/x-icon" />
    <meta name="viewport"
      content="width=device-width" />
    @Styles.Render("~/Content/themes/base/css",
      "~/Content/css")
    @Scripts.Render("~/bundles/modernizr")
  </head>
  <body>
    <header>
      <div class="content-wrapper">
        <div class="float-left">
          <p class="site-title">
            @Html.ActionLink("Your logo here",
            "Index", "Home")</p>
        </div>
        <div class="float-right">
          <section id="login">
            @Html.Partial("_LoginPartial")
          </section>
          <nav>
            <ul id="menu">
              <li>@Html.ActionLink("Home",
                "Index", "Home")</li>
              <li>@Html.ActionLink("About",
                "About", "Home")</li>
              <li>@Html.ActionLink("Contact",
                "Contact", "Home")</li>
            </ul>
          </nav>
        </div>
      </div>
    </header>
    <div id="body">
      @RenderSection("featured", required: false)
      <section class="content-wrapper
        main-content clear-fix">
        @RenderBody()
      </section>
    </div>
    <footer>
      <div class="content-wrapper">
        <div class="float-left">
          <p>&copy; @DateTime.Now.Year -
            My ASP.NET MVC Application</p>
        </div>
```

Default doctype declares HTML5 page.

Razor syntax included to display data from ViewBag.

External resources like scripts and stylesheets can also be included.

Complete sections of HTML build out structure of the page.

Html.ActionLink will build link using controller name and action method name.

RenderBody fills in remaining content of final physical Razor view.

```
        <div class="float-right">
            <ul id="social">
                <li><a href=http://facebook.com
                    class="facebook">Facebook</a></li>
                <li><a href=http://twitter.com
                    class="twitter">Twitter</a></li>
            </ul>
        </div>
    </footer>

    @Scripts.Render("~/bundles/jquery")
    @RenderSection("scripts", required: false)
    </body>
</html>
```

You can include partial views or regular views. Once again, there's no magic here, only conventions and markup interspersed with Razor syntax to control what output will be sent to the browser. The following listing shows a partial view from the application that builds links based on whether a user is logged in or not.

Listing B.6 The `_LogOnPartial` partial view

```
@if (Request.IsAuthenticated) {                              Razor can detect
  <p>Hello, @Html.ActionLink(User.Identity.Name,       ◄──  what is and isn't
      "ChangePassword", "Account",                           code as it
      routeValues: null, htmlAttributes:                     processes view.
        new { @class = "username", title = "Change password" })!
      @Html.ActionLink("Log off", "LogOff", "Account")
  </p>
} else {                                                     Html.ActionLink is
  <ul>                                                       primary way to
    <li>@Html.ActionLink("Register", "Register", "Account", ◄── render MVC-ready
      routeValues: null, htmlAttributes:                     links inside view.
        new { id = "registerLink" })</li>
    <li>@Html.ActionLink("Log in", "Login", "Account",
      routeValues: null, htmlAttributes: new { id = "loginLink" })</li>
  </ul>
}
```

Now that you understand what happens where in an MVC application, let's dig a little deeper and build out a real application using the MVCNewsletter sample application.

B.4   An MVC application in action

The example newsletter application will show you some important features available in the MVC framework that are relevant to HTML application builders:

- Posting form data to a specific controller action
- Client and server business rule validation using MVC
- Redirecting a controller to a different view

To get started on this part of the project, you'll build the data entry page with an HTML form inside.

B.4.1 Building a data entry form

The simplest means of data entry in any web application is to post an HTML form to some location on a web server and use the posted data to enter data into storage. In the sample application, you'll post a user's name, email address, and agreement to fictitious terms and conditions. The page that hosts your form will include its business rules automatically from the server business object, and rules will be enforced in both locations.

The form that presents the appropriate screen to the user is shown in the following listing. Open the existing Index.cshtml page inside the Views\Home folder, and update it so it matches this code.

Listing B.7 The newsletter signup form in the Home\Index.cshtml view

```
@model MVCNewsletter.Models.Subscriber          ◄── Model for this view is
@{                                                   subscriber object, created
  ViewBag.Title = "Home Page";                       later in appendix.
}
@section featured {                             ◄── Directive is feature of MVC 4 that
  <section class="featured">                          allows named section of content
    <div class="content-wrapper">                     to be automatically filled when
      <hgroup class="title">                           placed in master page.
        <h1>@ViewBag.Title.</h1>
      </hgroup>
      @using (Html.BeginForm(                   Creates a form using Razor
        "SignupNow",                            syntax that directs posts
        "Home",                                 to SignupNow method of
        FormMethod.Post,                        Home controller.
        new { id = "signup" }))          ◄── You may also pass HTML attributes
      {                                      into form as anonymous object.
        <p class="myForm">
          @Html.LabelFor(m => m.FirstName)          Labels, text boxes, and
          @Html.TextBoxFor(m => m.FirstName)        error validation messages
          @Html.ValidationMessageFor(m => m.FirstName)  are created using Razor
          <br />                                    syntax based on model's
          @Html.LabelFor(m => m.LastName)           annotated field-level rules.
          @Html.TextBoxFor(m => m.LastName)
          @Html.ValidationMessageFor(m => m.LastName)
          <br />
          @Html.LabelFor(m => m.Email)
          @Html.TextBoxFor(m => m.Email)
          @Html.ValidationMessageFor(m => m.Email)
          <br />
          @Html.CheckBoxFor(m => m.TermsAccepted)
          @Html.LabelFor(m => m.TermsAccepted, new { id = "chkLabel" })
          @Html.ValidationMessageFor(m => m.TermsAccepted)

        </p>
        <input type="submit" value="Submit" id="submit" />   ◄── Post form using
      }                                                           normal HTML
    </div>                                                        Submit button.
  </section>
}
```

ELEMENT IDENTIFIERS AND FORM PROPERTIES

When your form is presented on the server, it will have an action attribute that points to /Home/SignupNow, an ID of signup, and a method of post.

Each input object has a name property that will be posted to the server along with the value in the text box. The check box added using CheckBoxFor will return a value that's automatically converted to a Boolean.

The names of elements are important because these names will be automatically parsed into the same parameter names as the controller method. If the names don't match, null values will automatically be used for parameter values and your data will be lost.

Because you're using a model object, though, this is all handled for you by MVC's model binding. You simply need to state that your controller will post a Subscriber object to the SignupNow method of the Home controller.

USING THE CONTROLLER TO HANDLE POSTED FORM DATA

A normal ActionResult method in an MVC controller will handle post operations without a specific attribute. If you have an overloaded method, though, you can use attributes to specify methods for get and post. You saw an example of this overloading in the Register methods earlier in the appendix. If the name of the controller method is unique, MVC will automatically route the posted data to it, and no additional attributes are necessary on the controller.

B.4.2 *Validating posted data on the server*

At this point you're going to use the normal MVC pattern by validating business rules inside a model object. You'll create both the business object and a custom attribute to validate the TermsAccepted rule.

To do so, right-click on the Models folder of the project and select Add > Class. Name the new class "Subscriber", and when the file opens, add the code in the next listing to the object.

> **Listing B.8   The UserModel object is used to store and validate user information**

```
public class Subscriber
{
  [Required(ErrorMessage = "*")]
  [StringLength(80, MinimumLength = 3,
    ErrorMessage = "First name must be 3 to 80 characters")]
  [DisplayName("First Name")]
  public string FirstName { get; set; }

  [Required(ErrorMessage = "*")]
  [StringLength(80, MinimumLength = 3,
    ErrorMessage = "Last name must be 3 to 80 characters")]
  [DisplayName("Last Name")]
  public string LastName { get; set; }

  [Required(ErrorMessage = "*")]
  [RegularExpression(@"^[a-zA-Z][\w\.-]*[a-zA-Z0-9]@[a-zA-Z0-9]
    [\w\.-]*[a-zA-Z0-9]\.[a-zA-Z][a-zA-Z\.]*[a-zA-Z]$",
```

Using .NET data annotations simple property validations can be added quickly.

DisplayName attribute will be displayed when LabelFor is called in Razor view.

Regular expressions can also be used; this one validates email pattern.

```
        ErrorMessage = "Invalid email address")]
    public string Email { get; set; }

    [IsTrue(ErrorMessage = "You must accept terms and
        conditions before proceeding.")]
    [DisplayName("I agree to all terms and conditions")]
    public bool TermsAccepted { get; set; }
}
```

> **IsTrue attribute isn't part of .NET but will be added in next section.**

With no procedural code at all, you're very close to completely validating your business object. The only thing you need to implement is the `IsTrue` attribute.

In the `IsValid` code you'll just check each property to verify that all rules are valid. So far, nothing is using this model, though, so that's your next step.

HOW TO GET MVC TO USE A DIFFERENT VIEW

Next, you'll build a new method in the `HomeController` called `SignupNow`. This uses what you've learned about redirecting to a different view after validating the business rules, adding the user to the repository, and then returning a view named `Confirmation`. This method takes as a parameter your `UserModel` object. Using MVC model binding, the named values coming from the posted form are automatically converted into a new object. After validating the business rules, you'll add the user to your cache (described soon) and then return a confirmation page with the Boolean result of the action. The code in the following listing goes directly into the HomeController.cs file.

In the Models folder, add another new class and call it `IsTrueAttribute`. The following listing shows the code you should use.

> **Listing B.9   `IsTrueAttribute` is applied to the Boolean property of the business object**

```
using System;
using System.ComponentModel.DataAnnotations;

namespace MVCNewsletter.Models
{
    [AttributeUsage(AttributeTargets.Property,
        AllowMultiple = false, Inherited = false)]
    public class IsTrueAttribute : ValidationAttribute
    {
        public override bool IsValid(object value)
        {
            return value != null && value is bool && (bool)value;
        }
    }
}
```

> **Assigning AttributeUsage ensures that you can only assign this attribute to property.**

> **ValidationAttribute is base class for IsTrueAttribute.**

> **Simple null/Boolean check will return whether attribute validates or not.**

That takes care of all the business rule validations that you'll implement in this example. More complex attributes and business rules could be added here, but the basic idea should be clear to you by now. Next, we'll turn our attention to the controller so that the form you implemented earlier in the Index.cshtml view will have somewhere to go when it posts.

The following listing shows the new method that needs to be added to the Controllers\HomeController.cs file. Note that you reference a `CacheRepo` object in this code. That code will come soon.

Listing B.10   The `ActionResult` for a posted form using convention-based routes

```
public ActionResult SignupNow(Subscriber sub)      ◁─┤
{
  if (this.ModelState.IsValid)                      ◁─┤
  {
    var msg = CacheRepo.AddUser(HttpContext.Cache, sub);
    if (msg == "Email already exists")
      return View("Index", sub);
    else
      return View("Confirmation", sub);             ◁─┐
  }
  else
  {
    return View("Index", sub);                      ◁─┐
  }
}
```

> Parameter passed in from form will automatically be parsed into object using model binding.

> ModelState property is set up by .NET Framework because of attributes applied earlier.

> If repository finds that email already exists Index view will be returned for updates.

> If email doesn't already exist and ModelState is valid confirmation screen is loaded.

> If ModelState isn't valid, original Index view is returned.

Note that in this scenario, you don't return any information about business rule failures. That's because while you expect your form to be the only thing to ever post to this controller, you can't guarantee it. If you wanted to handle business rules more gracefully on the server, you could respond with more information or a JSON object containing exception information. In the current approach, however, you get validation on the client and the server because of the integration between data annotations and the MVC `Html.ValidationMessageFor` method.

ADDING THE VIEW

The controller is performing all the business rule validations and sending necessary information on to the soon-to-be-built repository for storage, but the result of a successful submission, the Confirmation view, doesn't yet exist to respond to the `View` request from `SignupNow` in the `Home` controller. To build this view, right-click on the Views\Home folder and select Add > View. Set it up as shown in figure B.11 and your new view should be ready to go.

The resulting view will have almost nothing in it, so you can build it out a bit using HTML and Razor to provide different messages based on the model's value. You can also add a little script that will be useful later for calling your web service. The following listing shows the complete contents of the Confirmation.cshtml page.

Listing B.11   The `Confirmation` view based on a Boolean model

```
@model MVCNewsletter.Models.Subscriber
@{
    ViewBag.Title = "Confirmation";
}
```

> Model for this view is Subscriber.

```
<h2>Confirmation</h2>
Thanks for registering, @Model.FirstName!<br />
Your subscription will be sent to @Model.Email<br />

<button id="getAll">Get All Subscribers</button>
<div id="subList"></div>
@section scripts {
<script type="text/javascript">
</script>
}
```

Because you have valid model returned to view, you can use any property in it.

getAll button will be used shortly to make Ajax call back to server.

Before long, we'll come back to the Confirmation view to look at the contents of the <script> tag at the bottom, but for now you need to return to the server to add the CacheRepo repository object we've mentioned twice now.

B.4.3   Adding a repository to store data

The cache repository object in this example is a simple tool to store data in memory on the server. In general, though, a repository is an object or layer in an application that provides an abstraction between business data and data storage. It can be very simple or very sophisticated. You're using it here to ensure that no data-storage code needs to be duplicated between the form that saves posted data and the service that retrieves it.

The following listing shows a simple repository used to store a Subscriber object and retrieve a list of Subscribers from the ASP.NET memory cache available to web applications. Create a new class file called CacheRepo.cs in the Models folder to hold this object.

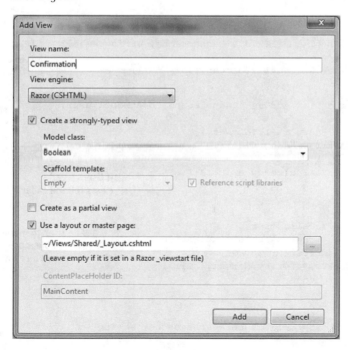

Figure B.11   Adding a confirmation view to the SignupNow controller action

Stylesheet edits to pretty up the page

It's worth a quick look at the styles we use to enhance the pages. These styles should be added to the end of the Content\Site.css file that already exists in your solution:

```css
div.showName {
    background-color: Gray;
    color: White;
    margin-left: 20px;
    padding: 5px;
}
p.myForm label {
    width: 100px;
    display: inline-block;
}
#chkLabel {
    width: 250px;
}
```

Listing B.12   A simple object to cache server data

```csharp
using System;
using System.Collections;
using System.Collections.Generic;
using System.Web.Caching;

namespace MVCNewsletter.Models
{
    public class CacheRepo
    {
        public static bool EmailExists(Cache cache, string email)
        {
            return (cache.Get(email.ToLower()) != null);
        }

        public static string AddUser(Cache cache, UserModel user)
        {
            var email = user.Email.ToLower();
            if (EmailExists(cache, email))
            {
                return "Email already exists";
            }
            else
            {
                cache.Add(email, user,
                    null, Cache.NoAbsoluteExpiration,
                    new TimeSpan(0, 10, 0),
                    CacheItemPriority.Normal, null);
                return "Added"
            }
        }

        public static UserModel GetUser(Cache cache, string email)
        {
```

Repository starts with Boolean check for particular email address in cache.

Method adds user to cache if it doesn't exist based on email address.

If User already exists tell the caller.

Add user to memory cache object passed in if it doesn't already exist.

```
        email = email.ToLower();
        if (EmailExists(cache, email))
            return cache[email] as UserModel;          ◄─── When getting single user,
        else                                                make sure to convert it
            return null;                               ◄─── back to UserModel object.
    }
                                                        ◄─── Return null if user
    public static List<UserModel> GetAllUsers(Cache cache)      wasn't found.
    {
        var ret = new List<UserModel>();
        foreach (var itm in cache)                    ◄─── Cycle all objects in
        {                                                   cache, check their
            if (itm is DictionaryEntry &&                   types, and return
                ((DictionaryEntry)itm).Value is UserModel)  them if they're of
                    ret.Add(GetUser(cache,                  type UserModel.
                        ((DictionaryEntry)itm).Key.ToString()));
        }
        return ret;
    }
  }
}
```

Now that you have the repository object completed, the client and server logic to register a subscriber for your fictitious newsletter is complete. Run the application by pressing F5 in Visual Studio, and you should see a data-entry screen similar to the one in figure B.12.

Try entering short names with only two characters or email addresses that are incorrectly formatted. You should see error messages and no data saved by the Cache-Repo object. Fix all the data entry errors and click the Submit button again. You should see the confirmation screen as in figure B.13.

You could stop there and have a decent application, but you'd miss half the MVC story. The other side of the story is client-initiated calls to the server that don't need

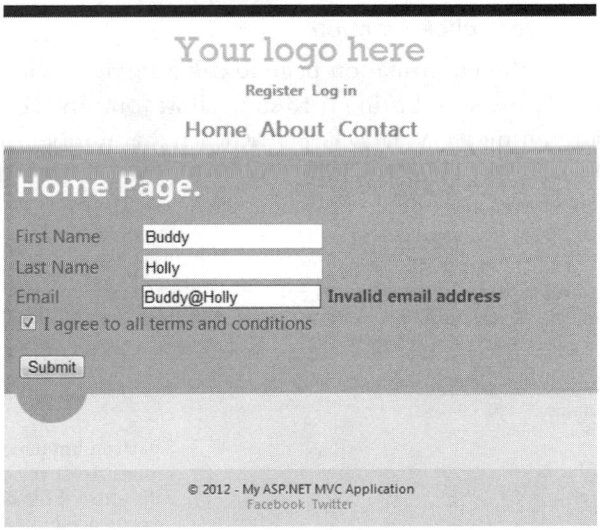

Figure B.12 The working data-entry screen for your MVC application will validate business rules in the form when the Submit button is clicked and will transfer to the confirmation page when a successful post is executed.

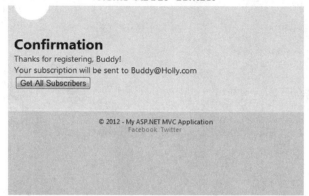

Figure B.13   The confirmation screen will display some information from the model so that you can see a successful post to the repository object.

a form to post. This is the function of Ajax, and it's the last step in building this sample application.

B.5   *Getting data asynchronously from the server*

So far you've implemented business rules on the client and the server and are storing `Subscribers` in an object called `CacheRepo` from inside the `SignupNow` method of the `HomeController`. Next, you'll fill in the functionality behind the Get All Subscribers button. This will call into the server to get all subscribers currently cached. In a real-world application, this kind of call could ask for filtered data or request a rollup of information about all subscribers.

B.5.1   *Wiring up events using the jQuery click function*

You'll use the `getAll` button in the confirmation page to call a service located at the relative location of /Home/GetAllUsers. Listing B.13 shows how you can call a jQuery Ajax function specifically for getting JSON data. `$.getJSON()` has a number of parameter variations, including overloads to catch failures, but this example uses the most basic version. This code goes right into the `<script>` tag you placed at the end of the Confirmation.cshtml file.

Listing B.13   Binding a button click and making an Ajax call with jQuery

```
$("#getAllUsers").click(function () {
   var url = location.protocol + "//" +
      location.host + "/Home/GetAllUsers";
   $.getJSON(
      url,
      function (data) {
      }
```

$.getJson implements GET request to specific URL and will return JSON-based data as return value.

```
    );
});
```

The anonymous function here doesn't do anything with the data, so you need to implement that next.

B.5.2 *Appending new data to the document using jQuery*

Another slick method available in jQuery is the $.each looping iterator. This function takes the input data object and a function that must have an indexer and a value object as parameters. On each iteration of the data object's collection (if a collection exists), the index is incremented with the appropriate array index, and the value object contains the actual item from the array.

Place the code in the following listing into the anonymous callback you just added to Confirmation.cshtml (in listing B.13).

Listing B.14   The jQuery $.each function to iterate JSON objects and build HTML

```
$.each(data, function (index, value) {
    var htm = "<div class='showName'>" +
        value.Email + ", Name: " +
        value.FirstName + " " + value.LastName +
        "</div>";
    $(htm).appendTo($("#subList"));
});
```

The code in listing B.14 takes the Email, FirstName, and LastName properties of each value and puts them into a string that's appended to the current HTML document. In a real application, this would be where you operate on each item and edit parts of the interface or populate some other array of variables in the application.

B.5.3 *Building a data-only controller method*

Next, you'll go back to the Home controller and add the new data endpoint. The next listing shows the method that the getJson jQuery function calls.

Listing B.15   GetAllUsers in HomeController gets data from the repository

```
public JsonResult GetAllUsers()
{
    var users = CacheRepo.GetAllUsers(HttpContext.Cache);
    return Json(users, JsonRequestBehavior.AllowGet);
}
```

That's all there is to it! You already built the functionality in the CacheRepo object, so all that's necessary is to call into it and return the data in JSON format. Run the application again and add a few subscribers. Then, in the confirmation screen, click the Get All Subscribers button and you should see results like figure B.14.

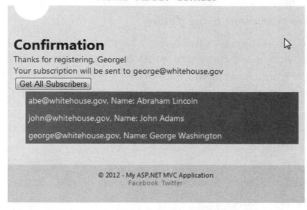

Figure B.14   The completed application will save users using a form post and then get them back from the server using an Ajax request returning JSON data.

B.6   Complete code listings

Listing B.16   The complete `HomeController` code

```
using System;
using System.Collections.Generic;
using System.Linq;
using System.Web;
using System.Web.Mvc;
using MVCNewsletter.Models;

namespace MVCNewsletter.Controllers
{
  public class HomeController : Controller
  {
    public ActionResult Index()
    {
      ViewBag.Message = "Modify this template to
        kick-start your ASP.NET MVC application.";

      return View();
    }

    public ActionResult About()
    {
      ViewBag.Message = "Your app description page.";

      return View();
    }

    public ActionResult Contact()
    {
      ViewBag.Message = "Your contact page.";

      return View();
    }
```

```
public ActionResult SignupNow(Subscriber sub)
{
  if (this.ModelState.IsValid)
  {
    var msg = CacheRepo.AddUser(HttpContext.Cache, sub);
    if (msg == "Email already exists")
      return View("Index", sub);
    else
      return View("Confirmation", sub);
  }
  else
  {
    return View("Index", sub);
  }
}

public JsonResult GetAllUsers()
{
  var users = CacheRepo.GetAllUsers(HttpContext.Cache);
  return Json(users, JsonRequestBehavior.AllowGet);
}
}
}
```

Listing B.17 The complete Home\Confirmation.cshtml code

```
@model MVCNewsletter.Models.Subscriber
@{
    ViewBag.Title = "Confirmation";
}
<h2>Confirmation</h2>
Thanks for registering, @Model.FirstName!<br />
Your subscription will be sent to @Model.Email<br />

<button id="getAll">Get All Subscribers</button>
<div id="subList"></div>
@section scripts {
<script type="text/javascript">
  $("#getAll").click(function () {
    var url = location.protocol + "//" +
      location.host + "/Home/GetAllUsers";
    $.getJSON(
      url,
      function (data) {
        $.each(data, function (index, value) {
          var htm = "<div class='showName'>" +
          value.Email + ", Name: " +
          value.FirstName + " " +
          value.LastName + "</div>";
          $(htm).appendTo($("#subList"));
        });
      }
    );
  });
</script>
}
```

appendix C
Installing IIS Express 7.5

In a number of places throughout this book, we use Internet Information Services (IIS) Express to run a project outside of the localhost environment. Many versions of Visual Studio come with IIS Express version 7.5 already installed. This server platform is also included with Microsoft WebMatrix. If, however, you're working with an installation of Visual Studio that doesn't have IIS Express, you didn't install it, or you're testing on a machine without Visual Studio, you'll need to follow these procedures to get it working and available.

C.1 Installing Web Platform Installer

The quickest way to get IIS Express installed is to use the Web Platform Installer. Open a browser, point it to http://www.microsoft.com/web/, and find the Microsoft Web Platform Installer section displayed in figure C.1.

Click the Download It Now button, and when the File Download window appears, click Run, as shown in figure C.2.

Once it's installed, navigate through your Windows menu to Microsoft Web Platform Installer, shown in figure C.3.

Microsoft Web Platform Installer

Design, develop and deliver Web-based applications

The Microsoft Web Platform Installer is a free tool that makes it simple to download, install and keep up-to-date with the latest components of the Microsoft Web Platform, including Internet Information Services (IIS), SQL Server Express, .NET Framework and Visual Web Developer. Download it now.

Figure C.1   The Web Platform Installer can be found on the Microsoft site.

372

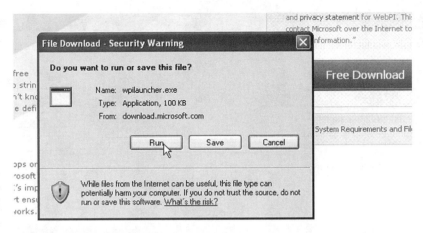

Figure C.2   Installing the Web Platform Installer

C.2   *Finding IIS Express 7.5*

Once the Web Platform Installer starts, look for the top-left search text box. Enter "IIS Express 7.5" and press Enter. You should see a screen similar to figure C.4.

Now click the Install button, and follow the various prompts and confirmations till you get to the installation stage shown in figure C.5. You may be asked to restart your computer during this installation process.

Once the installation has completed, you should get the confirmation screen shown in figure C.6.

Once installation is complete, you can assign a website to run using IIS Express from within Visual Studio 2010 SP1 or later.

Figure C.3   Run the Web Platform Installer.

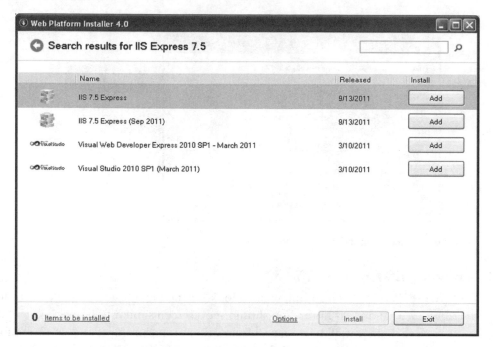

Figure C.4   Find IIS Express 7.5 and click the Add button.

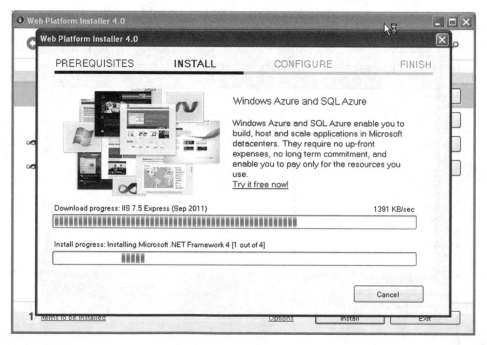

Figure C.5   Installing IIS Express 7.5

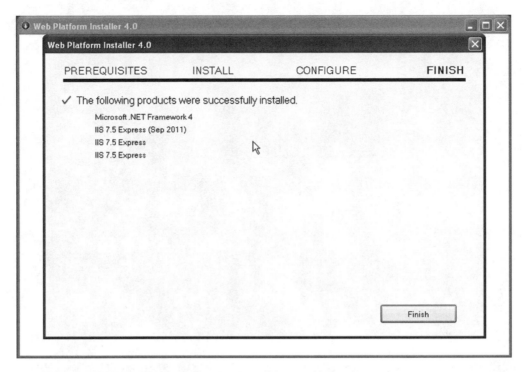

Figure C.6   Installation of IIS Express 7.5 is complete.

index

Silverlight 5 in Action
by Pete Brown

ISBN: 978-1-617290-31-2
1000 pages, $59.99
June 2012

Windows 8 XAML in Action
by Pete Brown

ISBN: 978-1-617290-94-7
600 pages, $49.99
February 2013

ASP.NET MVC 4 in Action
by Jeffrey Palermo, Jimmy Bogard, Eric Hexter,
Matthew Hinze, and Jeremy Skinner

ISBN: 978-1-617290-41-1
440 pages, $49.99
May 2012

ASP.NET 4.0 in Practice
by Daniele Bochicchio, Stefano Mostarda,
and Marco De Sanctis

ISBN: 978-1-935182-46-7
504 pages, $54.99
May 2011

For ordering information go to www.manning.com

YOU MAY ALSO BE INTERESTED IN

Secrets of the JavaScript Ninja
by John Resig and Bear Bibeault

ISBN: 978-1-933988-69-6
300 pages, $39.99
November 2012

jQuery in Action, Second Edition
by Bear Bibeault and Yehuda Katz

ISBN: 978-1-935182-32-0
488 pages, $44.99
June 2010

Third-Party JavaScript
by Ben Vinegar and Anton Kovalyov

ISBN: 978-1-617290-54-1
300 pages, $44.99
December 2012

Single Page Web Applications
by Michael S. Mikowski and Josh C. Powell

ISBN: 978-1-617290-75-6
325 pages, $44.99
May 2013